Edward Ellis Morris

**Cassell's Picturesque Australasia**

Edward Ellis Morris

**Cassell's Picturesque Australasia**

ISBN/EAN: 9783744756655

Printed in Europe, USA, Canada, Australia, Japan

Cover: Foto ©Andreas Hilbeck / pixelio.de

More available books at **www.hansebooks.com**

SYDNEY, FROM THE SOUTH HEAD.

# CONTENTS.

**SYDNEY: THE CITY.—E. P. FIELD.**
  The Approaches to the City—The Heads—The Harbour—The Gardens—Public Buildings—Hyde Park—Captain Cook's Statue—The Streets—Steam Trams—Pitt and George Streets—New Post Office—Chinese Quarter—Circular Quay—History of Sydney Cove—The Tank Stream—The Town Hall—Peel Market . . . 1

**SYDNEY: THE SUBURBS.—E. P. FIELD.**
  Coogee Bay—Maroubra Bay—The North Head—The South Head—Long Bay—Botany Bay—Little Bay—Hospital for Lepers—Point Sutherland—Illawarra—The University—Newtown—Parramatta—The Champion Course—Ryde—Old Government House—Watson's Bay—The Gap—Wreck of the *Dunbar*—Middle Harbour—Manly—Double Bay and Rose Bay . . . 14

**SYDNEY: ITS ORIGIN.—E. P. FIELD.**
  Discovery of Sydney Harbour—Botany Bay—Landing at Sydney Cove—Sickness—The Aborigines—Loss of the *Sirius*—Famine—Martial Law—Despair—Relief—Better Days—Past and Present . . 29

**MELBOURNE PROPER.—THE EDITOR.**
  General Features of the City and the Suburbs—Elizabeth Street—Australian Creeks—The Cathedrals—The Churches—Government House—Princes Bridge—The Town Hall—The Wards—The Hospital—The Public Library—The Working Man's College—The Old and the New Law Courts—The Royal Mint—Collins Street—Flinders Street—Little Collins Street—Bourke Street—The Post Office and the Eastern Market—Parliament House—Little Bourke Street . . . 38

**GREATER MELBOURNE.—THE EDITOR.**
  Distinctive Features—Richmond Park—The Yarra Yarra—Rowing Clubs and River Picnics—Suburban Municipalities—Means of Locomotion—Collingwood—Prahran—Hotham—Exhibition Building and the "Zoo"—The Colonial Colney Hatch—Toorak—South Yarra—St. Kilda—Brighton—Flemington—Public Holidays—The Ports of Melbourne; Sandridge and Williamstown—Origin of Local Names—Admiral Collingwood . . . 56

**LITTLE BOURKE STREET.—HUME NISBET.**
  Among the Chinese at Midnight—Lotteries—Chinese Shops—A Typical Cookshop—"The Grand Secret"—A Gambling Hell—A Barber at Work—"Nance" Going Home—Opium Dens—Taking a "Pull"—Vice in a Veil—Pandemonium—Philosophy under Difficulties—A Devoted Housebreaker 75

**LORD MELBOURNE.—THE EDITOR.**
  The First Lord Melbourne—His Early Days—First Successes—*The* Lord Melbourne—In the House of Commons—Home Secretary under Lord Grey—Prime Minister—"Kicked Out!"—A United Cabinet—Death of William IV. . . . 84

**A VANISHED WONDERLAND.—PROFESSOR T. G. TUCKER.**
  The Hot Lakes—A Terrible Catastrophe—Oxford and Cambridge—Rotorua—The Boiling Springs—Ohinemutu—Whakarewarewa—Wairoa—Lake Tarawera—Lake Rotomahana—The Wonderland—The White Terrace—The Steam Demon—The Pink Terrace—Vanished!—A New Wonderland . 89

## CONTENTS.

**BRISBANE.—G. WASHINGTON POWER.**

The Approach by River—North Brisbane—Victoria Bridge—Stanley Street—The Breweries—The Gaol—The Water Supply—City Charities—Grammar Schools—The Botanical Gardens—Government and Parliament Houses—The Churches—Exhibition Buildings and Places of Amusement—Newspapers—'Buses and Trams—The Ferries . . . . . 101

**UNTRODDEN TRACKS IN FIJI.—G. WHARTON MARRIOTT.**

Fiji—Its History—Suva—Government House—Cricket and Tinka—Armstrong's Point—The Botanical Gardens—Viti Levu—Sugar Plantations—Nandronga—A Fijian House—Fijian Comestibles—A Dance—Yangona—An Early Start—Refreshments—A Native Hut—Photographing—Mount Tomainivi—Hairdressing—Halts—The Summit—Na Matakula—Fijian Boats—A Moonlight Dance—A Fish Weir—Levuka . . . . . 116

**YASAWA-I-LAU.—G. WHARTON MARRIOTT.**

The Start—Fijian Hospitality—A Beautiful Cave—A Weird Scene—More Caves—Late Dinner—"Mekes" . . . . . 136

**HOBART.—R. D. POULETT-HARRIS.**

Situation—Cape Pillar and Tasman's Island—Port Arthur—Cape Raoul—Franklin Island—The Derwent—A General View—A Bird's-eye View—Main Road—Macquarie Street—The Royal Society's Museum—Franklin Square—The First Australian Brewery—The Queen's Domain—Domain Road—Government House—The Botanical Gardens—Distinguished Legislators—The High School—Liverpool and Elizabeth Streets—The Bank of Van Diemen's Land—Memorial Church—"Mr. Robinson's House"—The Roman Catholic Cathedral . . . . . 140

**THE ENVIRONS OF HOBART.—R. D. POULETT-HARRIS.**

Mount Wellington—Cook's Monument—A Magnificent Prospect—The Pinnacle—"The Organ Pipes"—Lost on the Mountain—The Wellington Falls—Brown's River—Kingston—Queenborough—The Bonnet Hill—Mount Nelson—Mount Direction—The Largest Man in the World—Risdon—A "Rupert of Debate"—Kangaroo Point and Bellerive—Mount Rumney—Newtown—Elwick Racecourse—A Landslip—Austin's Ferry—Bridgewater Causeway—Newtown and Cornelian Bays . . . 155

**GOLD.—M. GAUNT.**

The First Rush—Victoria Deserted—The Reflux—Life at the Diggings—A Primitive Post Office—Ingenuous Advertisements—Law and Order—The Composition of the Police—The Force of Nature—"Big Finds and Petty Squabbles"—Open Rebellion—"From the East and the West, and from the North and the South"—Murder and Rapine—The Murder at Indigo Creek—The Gold Escort Attacked and Defeated—A Raid on a Ship—Sailors' Luck—The Mongol and his Tribulations—Boisterous Extravagance—Pegging out a Claim—Mining Processes, Past and Present—Alluvial Mining—The "Jewellers' Shops"—"Shepherding"—Big Nuggets—Quartz Mining—A Novice's Impression of a Gold Mine—Mount Brown—Kimberley . . . . . 168

**NEW GUINEA: PORT MORESBY TO KEREPUNA.—HUME NISBET.**

An Island with a Future—Missionaries and Traders—Port Moresby—Elevara—Native Occupations—The Sources of Fever—Funeral Customs—An Unexecuted Sentence—The Ascent of Mount Pullen—The Laloki and Goldie Rivers—The Guilelessness of the Natives—Their Treatment of Women—Courtship and Marriage—Betel Chewing—Native Hunting—Kapa-Kapa—Hula—The Bau-bau—A Clever Trickster—Kerepuna—Nature and Civilisation—Work Days and Rest Days—Festivities—Spirit-seers—Canoe Makers—Fond Farewells—Rejoicings . . . . . 196

## CONTENTS.

**NEW GUINEA: KEREPUNA TO CAUTION POINT.—HUME NISBET.**
Cloudy Bay—South Cape—East Cape—Heath, Palm, and Dinner Islands—A High Sense of Honour—Milne Bay—Cliffy and Teste Islands—A Nocturne—Caution Point—German New Guinea—An Expedition up the Aird River . . . . . . . . 219

**NEW GUINEA: YULE ISLAND AND THE TORRES STRAITS.—HUME NISBET.**
Yule Island—Motu-Motu—Across the Papuan Gulf—Darnley Island—The Murray Group—York Island—Lotus-eaters . . . . . 227

**ADELAIDE.—THE EDITOR.**
"A Model City"—The Plan of the City—South Adelaide—Victoria Square—King William Street—The Post Office—The Town Hall—The Terraces—Hindley Street—North Adelaide—The Anglican Cathedral—A City of Churches—Religion and Morals—The River Torrens and its Bridges—Old Parliament House and New Parliament House—The Public Library, Museum, and Art Gallery—The University—The Park-lands—The Suburbs—The Mails—Port Adelaide—Semaphore—Largs Bay—Glenelg—Proclamation Tree—The First Government House—Brighton . . . 231

**BALLARAT.—M. GAUNT.**
Virgin Forest—The Gold Fever—Mounts Buninyong and Warrenheip—Black Hill—The City, The Town, and The Borough—Sturt Street—The Public Buildings—The "Corner"—The Town Hall—The Miners' City—"Our Lake"—The Botanical Gardens—Ballarat East—Bridge Street—The Chinese Quarter—"Hunting the Devil"—The Suburbs—Lal-Lal—Bakery Hill—Bungaree—An Irish Settlement—Bits of Old England . . 247

**THE EUREKA STOCKADE.—M. GAUNT.**
Bakery Hill—Desolation—Mutterings before the Storm—A Miscarriage of Justice—The Fate of the Eureka Hotel—The Reform League—The Meeting on Bakery Hill—Declaration of War—The Stockade—The Night Attack—An Awful Scene—The Sequel . . . 263

**THE DAILY LIFE OF THE BUSH.—O. SAWYER.**
Stations and Stations—Sheep or Cattle—General View of a Good Station—"Running In"—Bush Hospitality—An Ardent Dancer—Loafers—"Mustering"—Stock Whips—Catholicism—"Sprees"—A Thriving Drunkard—"You See" . . . 271

**DUNEDIN.—R. E. M. TWOPENNY.**
New Zealand Towns—First Appearances—View of Dunedin from the Bay—The Surveyor v. Nature—The People—Two Banks—The Public Buildings—The Town Hall—The Athenæum—The High Schools—The University—The Churches—First Church—Knox Church—The Lunatic Asylum—The Hotels—Business in Dunedin—The Harbour—The Town Belt—The Suburbs—"Ocean Beach"—The Refrigerating Company—Dairy Farming—General Prosperity . 283

**THE VALLEY OF THE HUNTER.—C. LIPPER.**
"Nobby's"—Newcastle Harbour—Newcastle—The Business End—The Coal Centre—The Cathedral—The Reserve—Lake Macquarie—The Shipping—The River—Raymond Terrace—Stroud—Miller's Forest—Morpeth—The Paterson—East and West Maitland—Wollombi—Singleton—Muswellbrook—Scone—Murrurundi . . . 296

# LIST OF ILLUSTRATIONS.

SYDNEY : THE CITY.                                    PAGE
The Heads, Sydney Harbour . . . . 1
Statue of Captain Cook . . . . 1
Plan of Harbour . . . . . 3
Government House . . . . . 4
Farm Cove . . . . . 5
Athletic Sports, Moore Park . . . . 7
Tram-car . . . . . 8
Public Buildings of Sydney . . . . 9
Plan of the City . . . . . 10
The Post Office . . . . . 11
Vestibule of the Town Hall . . . . 11
Arrival of the English Mail at the Post Office 12
The Circular Quay . . . . . 13

SYDNEY : THE SUBURBS.
A Regatta, Sydney Harbour . . . . 14
Coogee Bay . . . . . 16
At Coogee . . . . . 17
The University . . . . . 20
Clontarf, from Shell Cove . . . . 21
Mrs. Macquarie's Chair . . . . 21
Sydney Ferry Steamer . . . . 21
Parramatta, from the Park . . . . 21
The Champion Course . . . . 22
Old Government House, Parramatta . . 23
Lighthouse on South Head . . . . 24
The "Gap" . . . . . 25
Middle Harbour . . . . . 28

SYDNEY : ITS ORIGIN.
The Botanical Gardens . . . . 29
Double Bay . . . . . 32
The Observatory . . . . . 33
Rose Bay and Shark Island . . . . 36
Steam Ferry, Sydney Harbour . . . . 36
Garden Island by Moonlight . . . . 37

MELBOURNE PROPER.
Distant View of Melbourne from Doncaster
  Tower . . . . . 38
Plan of the City of Melbourne . . . 39
In the Botanical Gardens . . . . 40
A Melbourne Gutter in Earlier Days . . 41
Burke and Wills Monument . . . 43
The Scots and Independent Churches, Collins
  Street . . . . . 44
Government House, from Botanical Gardens . 45
The Town Hall . . . . . 46

MELBOURNE PROPER—(continued).                         PAGE
Interior of the Town Hall . . . . 47
Melbourne Public Library . . . . 49
Melbourne Hospital . . . . . 51
The New Law Courts . . . . 52
Melbourne University . . . . 53
The Old Law Courts . . . . . 54
The Mint . . . . . 54

GREATER MELBOURNE.
In the Fitzroy Gardens . . . . 57
Map of Greater Melbourne . . . . 59
Cricket Match, Melbourne . . . . 60
On the Yarra Yarra . . . . . 61
The "Eight Hours a Day" Procession passing
  the Town Hall . . . . . 64
The Drive, Albert Park . . . . 65
The Lake by Moonlight . . . . 65
The Pier and Esplanade, St. Kilda . . . 68
The Ports of Melbourne . . . . 69
Brighton Beach on a Public Holiday . . 73

LITTLE BOURKE STREET.
A Typical Scene . . . . . 77
At Play . . . . . 81
At Work : A Chinese Kitchen . . . 81
Chinese Opium Smokers . . . . 83

LORD MELBOURNE.
Castle Street, Melbourne, England . . . 84
Arms of Lord Melbourne . . . . 84
Lord Melbourne . . . . . 85
Melbourne Hall, Melbourne, Derbyshire . 88

A VANISHED WONDERLAND.
Ohinemutu . . . . . 89
Waterfall at Wairoa . . . . . 92
Fissure in Road near Tikitapu Bush, after
  the Eruption . . . . . 93
Lake Tarawera before the Eruption . . 96
Lake Tarawera after the Eruption . . 97
The White Terrace, Rotomahana, before the
  Eruption . . . . . 100

BRISBANE.
Brisbane, from Bowen Terrace . . . 101
Map of Brisbane . . . . . 103
Steamer leaving Brisbane with Miners . . 104
Public Buildings of Brisbane . . . 105

## LIST OF ILLUSTRATIONS.

vii

BRISBANE—(continued).
| | PAGE |
|---|---|
| Dry Dock | 107 |
| The City from One Tree Hill | 108 |
| The River from One Tree Hill | 108 |
| View from the Botanical Gardens | 109 |
| In the Botanical Gardens | 112 |
| A Bit of the Bush House, Acclimatisation Gardens | 113 |
| Fountains | 113 |
| The Aviary | 113 |
| Sandgate Pier | 115 |

UNTRODDEN TRACKS IN FIJI.
| | |
|---|---|
| Near Suva | 116 |
| View of the Rewa River | 117 |
| A Sugar-cane Plantation | 120 |
| Fijian Houses | 121 |
| A Fijian Village near Levuka | 125 |
| Head of a Fijian (Male) | 128 |
| A River Bathing-place | 129 |
| Levuka | 133 |

YASAWA-I-LAU.
| | |
|---|---|
| A Fijian Lagoon, Mango | 136 |
| A "Meke" | 137 |

HOBART.
| | |
|---|---|
| The City, from Kangaroo Point | 140 |
| Cape Pillar | 141 |
| The Franklin Monument, Franklin Square | 144 |
| The High School | 145 |
| Trinity Church | 148 |
| Port Arthur | 149 |
| Government House | 151 |
| Government House from Macquarie Point | 152 |
| Entrance to the Royal Society's Gardens | 153 |

ENVIRONS OF HOBART.
| | |
|---|---|
| Aborigines of Tasmania | 155 |
| Kangaroo Point, from Hobart | 157 |
| The Shot Tower, Brown's River Road | 160 |
| Mount Wellington, from the Huon Road | 161 |
| Newtown | 161 |
| The Grand Stand, Elwick Racecourse | 165 |

GOLD.
| | |
|---|---|
| The Whim | 168 |
| A Gold Rush | 169 |
| Prospecting | 172 |
| A Post-office at the Diggings | 173 |
| Breakfast on the Gold-fields | 176 |
| A Black Trooper | 177 |
| A Store at the Diggings | 180 |
| The Whip. "Hand up!" | 181 |
| "Fossicking" | 184 |
| Cradling and Panning | 185 |
| Quartz Crushing | 188 |
| Boring | 189 |
| Section of "Stope" | 191 |
| "Timbering" | 192 |
| Teetulpa Gold-field | 193 |

NEW GUINEA: PORT MORESBY TO KEREPUNA
| | PAGE |
|---|---|
| A New Guinea Temple | 196 |
| Port Moresby | 197 |
| Native Dwellings at Port Moresby | 200 |
| Elevara | 201 |
| Another Native House | 201 |
| Section of New Guinea (Plan) | 204 |
| A Tree House | 205 |
| A Heathen Temple | 205 |
| A Lime Calabash | 207 |
| The Owen-Stanley Ranges, from the Sea | 209 |
| The Bau-bau | 211 |
| Hula | 212 |
| Tupuselei | 213 |
| A Battle Axe | 215 |
| Wooden Sword and Drum | 215 |
| Kerepuna | 216 |
| Chiefs' Houses, Kerepuna | 217 |
| New Guinea War Shield | 218 |

NEW GUINEA: KEREPUNA TO CAUTION POINT.
| | |
|---|---|
| Cloudy Bay | 220 |
| Dinner Island | 221 |
| Trading Vessels | 224 |
| Palm Island | 224 |
| South Cape | 224 |
| Native House with Palms | 224 |
| Teste Island | 225 |

NEW GUINEA: YULE ISLAND AND THE TORRES STRAITS.
| | |
|---|---|
| Murray Island | 228 |
| Darnley Island | 228 |
| Motu-motu | 229 |
| Prow of a Canoe | 230 |

ADELAIDE.
| | |
|---|---|
| King William Street | 232 |
| Supreme Court | 233 |
| Botanical Gardens | 233 |
| Museum and Art Gallery | 233 |
| The Rosary, Botanical Gardens | 236 |
| Fountain in Botanical Gardens | 237 |
| City of Adelaide (Plan) | 240 |
| Torrens Lake | 241 |
| Port Adelaide Lighthouse | 242 |
| Proclamation Tree, Glenelg | 245 |

BALLARAT.
| | |
|---|---|
| The Cathedral | 247 |
| Mount Buninyong, from Lal-Lal | 248 |
| The "Corner" | 249 |
| Ballarat at Twilight | 249 |
| Lake Wendouree | 253 |
| The Lal-Lal Falls | 256 |
| The Post Office | 257 |
| Chinamen's Huts at Golden Point | 260 |
| The City, from Black Hill | 261 |
| Gold Miners' Tools | 262 |

## LIST OF ILLUSTRATIONS

THE EUREKA STOCKADE.

| | PAGE |
|---|---|
| The Eureka Stockade Monument (from the Designs) | 265 |
| Distant View of Ballarat, from Mount Warrenheip | 269 |
| Monument to Diggers who were Killed in the Rising | 272 |
| Monument to Soldiers who Fell at the Stockade | 273 |

THE DAILY LIFE OF THE BUSH.

| | PAGE |
|---|---|
| A Horse and Cattle Station | 276 |
| Milking | 276 |
| A Stockyard | 277 |
| A Two-storeyed House in the Bush | 280 |
| A Stockrider | 281 |

DUNEDIN.

| | PAGE |
|---|---|
| The Cargill Fountain | 283 |
| Princes Street | 284 |

DUNEDIN (continued).

| | PAGE |
|---|---|
| Knox Church | 285 |
| The High School, from Roslyn | 288 |
| The Town Hall, as designed | 289 |
| The Botanical Gardens | 292 |
| Nichol's Creek Falls | 293 |
| Looking Across the Harbour from the South-West | 295 |

THE VALLEY OF THE HUNTER.

| | PAGE |
|---|---|
| Colliers leaving Newcastle Harbour | 296 |
| "Nobby's" | 297 |
| The Bathing Place, Newcastle | 299 |
| Newcastle Harbour | 300 |
| The Reserve, Newcastle | 300 |
| Newcastle, from "Nobby's" | 301 |
| Watt Street, Newcastle | 304 |
| A Bush Track, Murrurundi | 305 |
| Maitland | 307 |
| Murrurundi | 309 |

## LIST OF PLATES.

| | | |
|---|---|---|
| Sydney, from the South Head | . | Frontispiece |
| Sydney Harbour, from Belle Vue Hill | . | To face p. 30 |
| The "Block," Collins Street, Melbourne | | „ 54 |
| The Pink Terrace, Rotomahana | . | „ 90 |
| A Cocoa-nut Plantation, Fiji | | „ 132 |
| Attack on the Gold Escort between McIvor and Melbourne | . | To face p. 182 |
| Sunrise at York Island, Torres Straits | . | „ 202 |
| The Band Stand and Rotunda, Adelaide | | „ 242 |
| A Mob of Cattle | . | „ 274 |
| The Town Belt, Dunedin | . | „ 294 |

We are indebted to the following photographers for the assistance our artists have derived from their photographs in preparing the illustrations on the pages mentioned below:—

To Mr. H. KING (Sydney), for those on pp. 1, 4, 9, 11, and 20; to Mr. LINDT (Melbourne), on pp. 44, 51, 52, 53, 55; to Messrs. LOMER & Co. (Brisbane), on p. 105; to Messrs. DUFTY BROS. (Levuka), on pp. 117, 133, 136; to Mr. H. H. BAILEY (Hobart), on pp. 152, 153; to Messrs. ANSON BROS. (Hobart), on pp. 157, 160, 161; to Mr. WINTER (Hobart), on p. 165; and also to Messrs. BURTON BROS. (Dunedin).

THE HEADS, SYDNEY HARBOUR.

# CASSELL'S
# PICTURESQUE AUSTRALASIA.

### SYDNEY: THE CITY.

The Approaches to the City—The Heads—The Harbour—The Gardens—Public Buildings—Hyde Park—Captain Cook's Statue—The Streets—Steam Trams—Pitt and George Streets—New Post Office—Chinese Quarter—Circular Quay—History of Sydney Cove—The Tank Stream—The Town Hall—Paul Market.

STATUE OF CAPTAIN COOK.

THERE are two principal approaches to Sydney, the one by sea, the other by land. The express from Melbourne runs through, by way of Albury, in less than twenty hours, and for those who suffer from sea-sickness the railway journey has its advantages. The entrance into Sydney by rail is, however, dull, flat, and unprofitable; whereas the approach by sea is full of interest, and creates a delight which can never be forgotten. The North and South Heads of Sydney Harbour stand separated by a mile of troubled waters. On the south the grey and yellow sandstone cliffs of the coast trend to a point of little altitude, while the North Head is a bold and almost perpendicular cliff, conspicuous at a great distance because of its height and its peculiarly uncompromising appearance. As the incoming vessel enters the Heads her bow points directly towards another bold rocky point only some three-quarters of a mile distant from the South Head. This is Middle Head, the southern point of the entrance to Middle Harbour. To anyone looking in from the outside ocean, this last-mentioned headland appears to mark the limit of the land-locked waters, and it was this fact, probably, that led Captain Cook to pass over the place as of small importance. Once inside the Heads, a wide and apparently endless expanse of waters is disclosed, and as the vessel steams along the channel to the south and west, innumerable wooded headlands, with their corresponding bays, are passed in quick succession.

No words can fitly describe the wonders of this magnificent scene; no pencil can adequately picture its beauty. Anthony Trollope, writing of it, says: "I despair of being able to convey to any reader my own idea of the beauty of Sydney Harbour. I have seen nothing equal to it in the way of land-locked scenery; nothing second to it. Dublin Bay, the Bay of Spezia, New York, and the Cove of Cork, are all picturesquely fine. Bantry Bay, with its nooks of sea running up to Glengariff, is very lovely. But they are not equal to Sydney, either in shape, in colour, or in variety . . . It is so inexpressibly lovely that it makes a man ask himself whether it would not be worth his while to move his household gods to the eastern coast of Australia, in order that he might look at it as long as he can look at anything."

The windings and turnings of this inland sea are virtually endless. The shore-line is said to have been calculated, and to amount to not less than several hundred miles. The map of Port Jackson also shows eighty-two well-marked bays and nine islands, and each bay is a delight to the eyes, each island a jewel set in silver. Shark Island is a beautiful spot, and of no inconsiderable size; but, as it is used for a quarantine ground for cattle, it is little visited and little known. Clark Island is a favourite picnicking and fishing ground; and a little nearer is the City Garden Island, which was once truly a natural garden, but is now being fitted for a naval depôt, and has lost much of its beauty. Tradition has it that this was a favourite duelling ground in the old days when the home regiments were stationed in Sydney, and it is said that certain skeletons have been dug up here, which gives colour to the story.

Not far from Garden Island is Fort Denison, a small stone fort and Martello tower, built on a low-lying reef; it is of no real value as a defence in these days of modern improvements, and is no longer seriously reckoned among the harbour defences. The best of these are stationed a little closer to the city, in Farm Cove, where the *Nelson*, the *Miranda*, and other men-of-war lie at anchor. Beyond the *Nelson* stretches the north shore, and a few hundred yards astern of her peeps out a charming point of land, which bears the curious name of Mrs. Macquarie's Chair, Mrs. Macquarie being the wife of one of our most popular early Governors.

The Botanical Gardens, of which a view is given on page 29, slope down gently to the very edge of the water. These Gardens take their horseshoe form from the Cove, and are among the most beautiful in the world, owing very much of their beauty to Nature herself. Here may be seen almost every variety of plants of tropical and semi-tropical growth, the magnificent Norfolk Island pine being specially prominent. Long, sloping, well-kept lawns of emerald-green invite repose, and, though the city is not far distant, its noise is heard only as a gentle murmur, mingling pleasantly with the wash of the sea on the low sea-wall which forms the northern border of the Gardens. Just topping this wall may be seen the white wings of yachts, and the masts and

## FARM COVE.

colours of the men-of-war beyond. Between us and them many a bright flower-bed and many a graceful shrub break the long stretch of sunlit green, and over the whole is felt the happy influence of the azure waters, sparkling and brimming over with delight.

Truly the people of Sydney are blessed in the possession of these Gardens. And the blessing appears to be well appreciated. On Saturdays and Sundays, when the working world is at rest, hundreds of men, women, and children may be seen enjoying themselves here, for the place, fortunately, is within easy access of almost every part of the city, and within fifteen minutes' walk of Wooloomooloo, where many of the poorer population live. The favourite walk is through the Domain, round Macquarie's Point, and back through the Gardens. This Domain is a very fine park, some eighty or more acres in extent, and as it lies higher than the Botanical Gardens, it presents many points from which distant views may be obtained. On its eastern face lie the quiet waters of Wooloomooloo Bay, in which are reflected the pleasant villas and gardens of Potts Point. Here also are the bathing grounds, fenced off from the hateful shark, the bête noire of Australian bathers, by secure palisadings. To the south of the Domain another public park, named after the Hyde Park of the mother country, stretches away, with its leafy avenues and flower-walks, over an area of some fifty acres. Again, on the north, the Domain

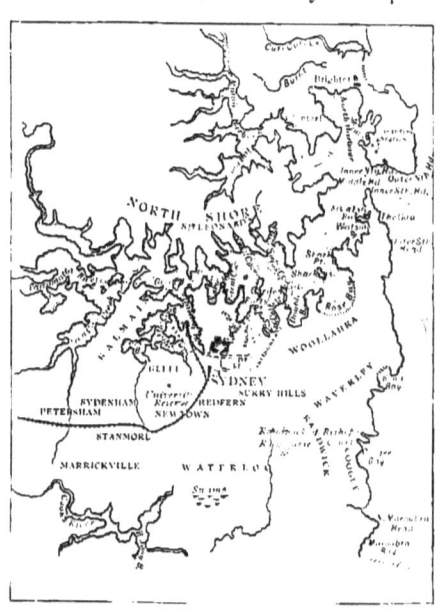

PLAN OF THE HARBOUR.

is bounded by the Inner Domain, which includes the well-kept grounds of Government House. Government House itself stands on the western point of Farm Cove, Mrs. Macquarie's Chair occupying the eastern point, while the Botanical Gardens lie extended between. From every part of these grounds the views obtained of the water are perfect in loveliness.

It is extremely difficult—and, in truth, well-nigh impossible—to convey to one who has not visited Sydney any adequate idea of the beauties of its scenery. The pencil of the artist has done what pencil can do, but the divine glories of the Sydney skies do not allow of reproduction. On a bright sunny morning, such as is enjoyed on at least six days out of every seven, the waters of the Harbour reflect the brilliancy and colour of the sky. Indeed, the colours are vivid to such a degree that if we might imagine it possible for the artist to depict the very same colours on his canvas, the ordinary untravelled Englishman would denounce his painting as unreal and such as cannot be seen in nature. But here they are repeated day after day in all their glory.

> "The sun is warm, the sky is clear.
> The waves are dancing fast and bright;
> Blue isles and bluer mountains wear
> The purple noon's transparent might;
> The breath of the moist earth is light
> Around its unexpanded buds;
> Like many a voice of one delight,
> The winds,' the birds,' the ocean floods,
> The city's voice itself is soft like Solitude's."

This sunny gladness, this joy of earth and sky, is the one great characteristic of life in Sydney. Nature here breathes this feeling of jubilancy into the hearts of men continually, and it is not too much to say that the influence of her inspiration can be discerned even amid the wear-and-tear of everyday life. How can it be otherwise when she bestows such cheery greeting morning after morning as we go to work, and blesses us as we return?

This trait of genial brightness is everywhere noticeable, and if the Gardens and parks are full of it, the famous Macquarie Street, which skirts them, is no less so. Macquarie Street runs north and south from the water's edge past the Government House Grounds and the Domain Gates, and contains several important buildings. The Free Public Library, the Colonial Secretary's Office, the House of Assembly, and the Legislative Council Chamber,

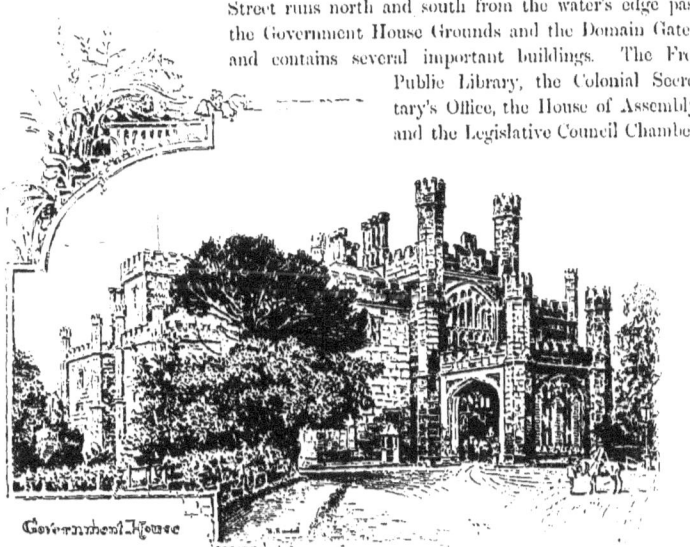
Government House.

FARM COVE.

the Sydney Hospital, and the Mint are all placed here, and formerly, within the Domain Gates, stood the large and costly Garden Palace. This famous building, which was used for the purposes of an exhibition, formed while it stood a very striking object, and could be seen from a great distance by vessels entering the harbour. But in 1880 it was accidentally burnt down, and rarely has Sydney witnessed a grander conflagration. It was in the early hours of the morning, and as a high westerly wind was blowing at the time, portions of the burning building were carried by the gale for more than a mile. Fortunately, the structure had by that time served the purposes for which it was principally intended, and by far the greater part of the exhibits had already been removed.

The other buildings which have been mentioned, if not remarkable for beauty, are all of a substantial character. The Colonial Secretary's Office is perhaps the finest. Another large stone building, intended as an addition to the old Hospital, is in course of erection. Composed of the Sydney sandstone, these buildings, apart from their other qualities, lend a pleasing touch of colour to the scene, and the warm yellows and reds form a happy contrast with the dark green of the avenue which runs down the centre of Hyde Park beyond. This avenue is composed chiefly of the broad-leaved Moreton Bay fig-trees, together with firs of various species. In the warm summer months the smooth asphalte path under the thick shade of these trees is a favourite promenade for all classes, and in the mornings and evenings especially there may be seen here one long continuous stream of persons of both sexes going to and returning from the business of the day. This walk at one point passes close by the statue of Captain Cook, the great explorer being represented at the moment when the glad sight of this glorious land first bursts upon him. Between this statue and the Museum runs College Street, which skirts Hyde Park along its entire length. The College, from which the street obtains its name, is the old Sydney Grammar School—an excellent school, in which many of the most eminent men in the colony received their education. Separated from the Grammar School by only a small garden stands the Sydney Museum, a severe and massive building, very well lighted, and admirably adapted for its purpose. Here may be seen specimens of all the birds, beasts, and fishes of Australia. Without a visit to some such collection it would be impossible to form any fair appreciation of the country itself, or the forms of life which it contains. A short distance from the Museum stands the Roman Catholic Cathedral, which promises to be, when finished, the finest building in Sydney, and will be larger than many of the famous Cathedrals of the mother country. It is being built slowly, but then it is being built for all time. Moreover, no debt is incurred, but little by little is added as the money is obtained.

From College Street it is only to step across Macquarie Street, and then we commence the easy decline of King Street, which, running east and west, and crossing Phillip, Elizabeth, Pitt, and George Streets, thus passes through the centre of the city till it reaches the waters of Darling Harbour. Near the eastern end of King Street stands St. James's Church and the Supreme Court House, both ugly buildings, but interesting because of their connection with the history of the town and colony. Unfortunately, while both are ugly and interesting, they differ from each other in one respect. The former, which we may describe as belonging to the "Early Australian" order of architecture, is at any rate well suited for the purposes for which it is intended. The Supreme Court House is altogether unsuitable—small, badly lighted, and bad for sound. It is, indeed, in every way inferior to many of the Court Houses in the small country towns of the colony.

Along one frontage of the Supreme Court, and at right angles to King Street, runs Elizabeth Street, with its tram-lines. The tram-cars, heavy and hideous, are drawn by steam motors. From the Bridge Street terminus they run to almost all the suburbs, even as far as to Botany and Coogee, and the system is still being constantly extended. When first introduced, these steam trams were the cause of many accidents, and from a section of the public there has from the first been a constant outcry against them; but the convenience of the majority is greatly served by their use, and now, when accidents do occur, they are in most cases due to the negligence of the sufferers. For any visitor to Sydney who has only a limited amount of time at his disposal, these trams afford an excellent means of seeing the different parts of the city. Mounted on the top of a Bondi, Waverley, Coogee, or Botany car, a stranger may during the trip see a very considerable portion of the city, and form some idea of its extent and of the nature of the surrounding country; and, should he choose any of the three first

named, he will obtain on the way most beautiful bird's-eye views of Sydney and the
blue mountains beyond, with the blue waters of Botany Bay and the dark foliage of
the National Park stretching far to the south. On his return, he should get off the
tram at the intersection of Elizabeth and King Streets, and walk down the latter to
see Pitt Street and George Street. These are the two principal thoroughfares of
the city, and contain many of the large business warehouses. Both, running more
or less parallel to each other, commence from Dawes Street and the waters of the
Sydney Cove, and extend through the city till they reach the suburbs of Redfern
and Darlington.

ATHLETIC SPORTS, MOORE PARK (p. 11).

Here, more than anywhere, the imagination is carried back over the past hundred
years, and the mind is struck with the contrast between the place as it is now and as it
was then. Then the ground had only been hurriedly cleared, and a few small huts
marked the lines now known as Pitt and George Streets. Between these a small stream
flowed quietly down into the waters of the Harbour. It was long known as the Tank
stream, from the numerous tanks which were placed there by the colonists for the
purpose of storing water as a supply in seasons of drought. Now this old stream has
vanished underground, and, bricked into the form of a tunnel, serves to carry off the
drainage.

Thousands of tons of sandstone, bricks, and mortar have been reared above it, and
on both sides, into public offices, warehouses, and shops. From early dawn till midnight
a ceaseless traffic passes, and during business hours the noise of omnibuses, hansom cabs,
and vehicles of every description, and the crush of foot-passengers on the pavements,

bear a close resemblance to the scenes characteristic of the capital of the mother country. Here is, indeed, a little London, differing from the old metropolis chiefly in the absence of smoke, and darkness, and fog. Sometimes, indeed, there may be, to some tastes, a little too much sun; but, if there be, the long lines of verandah afford an excellent protection. From end to end of all the principal streets, and not only in the principal streets but in many of the smaller lanes and byways, strong, substantial verandahs of considerable height extend across the entire width of the pavements, so that in the middle of summer, when the sun is highest, it is possible to walk for miles without exposing oneself to its rays. In rainy weather also these awnings are a great protection; and under the heavy tropical rains which are not infrequent in Sydney this is an important matter. These uses, however, are only incidental, for the chief

TRAM-CAR.

object of the verandahs is, doubtless, to protect the goods displayed in the windows of the tradespeople. The people themselves, of both sexes, conform closely to the English fashions of dress, and present in this point no marked peculiarities for observation. By the men, even in the summer months, tall black hats and black coats are commonly worn, and those items which in England are generally regarded as necessary parts of a Sydney outfit, viz., white ducks and helmet, are here seldom seen. In the country, helmets and slouch hats are frequently worn; but in Sydney such a head-dress would at present be regarded as *outré*. Perhaps before long the custom may change. At present, at any rate, the fact remains that in the general view of a Sydney street these reminders of a warm climate are not by any means conspicuous.

Probably, the best course for a visitor who wishes to understand the city of Sydney is to take a view of it from the top of one of the many towers of large buildings Of these the most remarkable is that belonging to the new Post Office, an immense

PUBLIC BUILDINGS OF SYDNEY.

structure of warm-tinted sandstone, with one face to George Street and one to Pitt Street. The tower is some two hundred and fifty feet in height, and from the top, which is easily reached, a most extensive view may be obtained both of the city and of the harbour. George Street is overlooked for the greater part of its length, and at its far extremity the extensive buildings of the Sydney University stand up boldly against the sky. Should the ascent of the Post Office tower be considered too

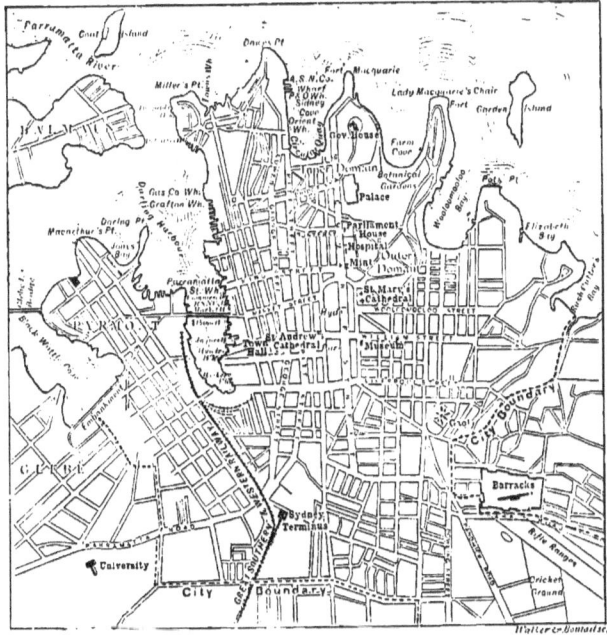

PLAN OF THE CITY.

arduous an undertaking, similar views may be obtained from the tops of some of the large furniture warehouses, where a comfortable lift carries the visitor to his lofty point of view.

At the northern end of George Street we come into what is known as Lower George Street. Here it is that the Chinese residents most do congregate, and the locality has thus come to bear the name of the Chinese Quarter. The roadway on both sides is bordered by Chinese stores, alternating with English public-houses; and scattered here and there, with entrances chiefly from the byways and alleys, are the opium dens. Over these the authorities keep a constant and salutary supervision, checking in great

THE POST OFFICE.

VESTIBULE OF THE TOWN HALL.

measure the habits for which the Chinese are noted. Still, gambling, opium-eating and smoking, and vices of every sort are continually carried on, in spite of all the vigilance and activity of the police, and, for those who are interested in such phenomena, constitute one of the sights of Sydney. The foul plague of leprosy—now, as in old time, perhaps the most fearful, certainly the most relentless, of diseases—has been introduced by this people here, as in America and in every other portion of the globe in which they have been allowed to settle. But the Government medical authorities are much on the alert, and on the first suspicion of the disease, and before the symptoms have had time to develop, the patient is removed to the Little Bay Hospital, and there secluded from all contact with the outside world.

The northern end of Lower George Street brings us to the Circular Quay, close to that part of it where the Peninsular and Oriental steamers are usually berthed. The sketch given on page 13 is taken from a part of Dawes Point which is still further north than this, and shows the long reach of the Quay. This is the bay known to the first colonists as Sydney Cove, and chosen by them on account of its depth and easy anchorage. Everywhere, close to the very shore-line, the chart marks not less than four fathoms. In the immediate foreground is a portion of the old and useless Dawes Point Battery. In the middle distance the Brisbane steamers lie alongside, and in the background on the left of the picture, and on the eastern bank of Sydney Cove, stand some of the wool stores; behind these rise the turrets of Government House and the leafy grounds of the Domain. The Circular Quay itself is always full of life. The large vessels of the Peninsular and Oriental Company and the Messageries steamers, and the hundreds of small steamboats carrying passengers from all parts of the Harbour, present a brilliant and pleasing scene.

ARRIVAL OF THE ENGLISH MAIL AT THE POST OFFICE.

After feasting the eye on all this movement and busy life, it is interesting to read the account of the same Bay given in the history published in 1798 by David Collins, a Judge Advocate and Secretary of the Colony. According to the description of this author, "the spot chosen for the landing-place was at the head of the Cove (Sydney Cove), near the run of fresh water, which stole silently along through a very thick wood, the stillness of which had then, for the first time since the Creation, been interrupted by the rude sound of the labourer's axe." The "run of fresh water" here referred to, afterwards called the Tank stream, is shown in the plan of Sydney Cove in Governor Phillip's narrative of his voyage to Botany Bay, published in 1789, nine years previous to the account of David Collins. This plan, which is dated July, 1788, shows the waters of the Harbour extending much farther inland than they do at present—as far almost as the spot on which the *Sydney Morning Herald* Office now stands. Here, too, the Tank is seen flowing into the Harbour waters, and forming a broad estuary, with sandy beaches. The whole of this, as we have already said, has long since been covered with buildings, and, as far as physical appearances go, no trace remains of what the place was in the past. Yet, after reading these descriptions of Sydney as it was, and examining the old pictures of the place, it is easy, by paying attention to the natural slope of the ground, to trace the course of the old

## FESTIVITIES.

Tank stream for at least a part of its distance. In Bridge Street the indications are quite clear, for on either side there is a slope down to where the Old Bridge stood.

Most of the buildings of Sydney have already been described, but two still remain, both of which deserve mention. The first is the Town Hall, the exterior of which has not secured universal admiration. The second is Peel Market, which presents a scene full of human interest. Here are not only buyers and sellers, but disinterested spectators who have no thought of buying, but go only to see and be seen. The climate of Sydney tempts every one out of doors, and in the long evenings hundreds and thousands turn out for a stroll. On summer evenings, and especially on Saturday, the crowds in the principal streets are a sight worth seeing. On such nights the pavements are far too narrow to hold the people, who swarm out into the roadway till omnibus and cab traffic is well-nigh stopped. At no time during the week are the streets so thronged, for people come from all the surrounding suburbs, and swarm to see the various street shows, and to listen to the music of the street bands, some of which are by no means to be despised. The scene is a gay one, and the hearts of the people are glad, and Sydney on these occasions, as on all others, maintains her character as the gay and joyous city of the South, whose pleasures cannot be understood until they are experienced, nor its beauties realised until they are seen.

THE CIRCULAR QUAY.

A REGATTA, SYDNEY HARBOUR.

## SYDNEY: THE SUBURBS.

Coogee Bay—Maroubra Bay—The North Head—The South Head—Long Bay—Botany Bay—Little Bay—Hospital for Lepers—Point Sutherland—Illawarra—The University—Newtown—Parramatta—The Champion Course—Ryde—Old Government House—Watson's Bay—The Gap—Wreck of the *Dunbar*—Middle Harbour—Manly—Double Bay and Rose Bay.

THE suburbs of Sydney are as varied as they are numerous and delightful. There are harbour suburbs and river suburbs, inland suburbs and coast suburbs, suburbs of wood and suburbs of brick and mortar. They are so numerous that it is no easy task to remember them, and so varied that it is impossible to give any idea of their beauties. It would, indeed, be difficult to find any town so gifted as Sydney is in its surroundings. London has its Brighton, fifty miles distant, and yet highly appreciated. But Sydney is surrounded with a number of miniature Brightons all within a distance of some five or six miles. A circle drawn from the Post Office as a centre with a six mile radius would take in Bondi and Waverley, Coogee, and all the coast between. Take Coogee Bay as an example. The tram runs down from the City terminus, in Bridge Street, in less than three-quarters of an hour, skirting two sides of Hyde Park, and running through the entire length of Moore Park—a favourite resort of those who are given to athletics—and then between the Race Course and the Water Reserve, so that the journey is a pleasure in itself. Passing through Randwick, which will be afterwards described, the tram soon commences to descend the easy slopes of the hills which run down to the sea. A sudden curve, and the beautiful Bay of Coogee is displayed. The beach itself is small—barely half a mile in length—but composed of the finest golden sand, with a gentle slope down to the water. Looking out to sea on the left, to the north of the Bay, one sees a rocky promontory running out into the water. It is of no great height, but is remarkable for its beauty. Under that overhanging ledge is a natural seat—a favourite resort, where one may sit in safety and watch the huge breakers dashing themselves upon the reef below. This reef runs out for some distance, and exactly parallel to it is another ledge of rocks of equal length, distant from the first some hundred feet. At the seaward end of these reefs a line of sunken rocks serves as a barrier to keep out the sharks and other things of danger, and within this, and between the reefs, lies the most charming basin which it has ever been the writer's lot to behold. No such bathing-places exists anywhere along this coast; and the old watering-places of the mother country, Brighton and Hastings, Ramsgate, Scarborough, and Tenby, have no place that can be compared with it. Whether in calm or storm this Coogee basin is equally delightful. Art has assisted Nature, and years ago the rocks were cut and hollowed out, and the depth of the basin much increased, so that now, even in the lowest tides, the bather can dive off the rocks into a good depth of water, while in a high tide there is not less, in some places, than from eighteen to twenty feet.

But the best time to see the basin is when there is a good wind from the south and east. After an easterly gale a long swell sets in, reaching right across the Bay from one of its headlands to the other. More than half a mile away the swell may be seen rolling in, and as it sweeps onward, the reef forming the seaward barrier of the bathing-place seems to brace itself up to receive the shock. The wave, upraised, dashes itself madly against the rocks, the water shoots up to a height of thirty or forty feet, and falls in snow-white foam into the basin. Tons of water thus falling at a time, it requires a moderately good swimmer to battle against the weight; but after the first fall there is little risk, and it is easy to avoid this first fall by diving to the bottom. Now and then an incautious or inexperienced bather is caught by such a wave, and is lifted like a straw and carried over the landward reef; but accidents are very rare, and the basin will always retain its supremacy over all the places along the coast. On the opposite side of the Bay is the ladies' bathing-place, where a lamentable accident once occurred, three ladies being washed out to sea by the rebound of a wave, and drowned. But all danger of such a casualty has now been provided against. Half a mile from the beach is a low rocky island, over which, after a gale, the seas completely sweep; thus it forms a most charming object in the general view. This island was evidently in former ages a part of the headland just to the south of the Bay, and in low tides a sunken reef may still be observed connecting the two, and affording an unmistakable indication of the extensive encroachments of the sea upon the land at this spot.

Pleasant villas are dotted everywhere on the surrounding hills, and half-way between Coogee and Randwick stands the palace of the Bishop of Sydney, nestling amid its leafy surroundings. Coogee in years to come will doubtless be thickly built over, but at present its residents have plenty of breathing space. All round it there are most delightful walks and drives. Take, for instance, the walk to the South Head of Maroubra

Bay. Both headlands of Maroubra Bay are noted for the grandeur of their rock scenery. The sandstone here is the same as it is along the coast to the north, but for some reason which it would be difficult to explain the sea has washed it into more fantastic shapes and bolder faces. The North Head is fully three hundred feet high, coming down sheer into deep water. At its base, in a position which is hardly accessible even in the lowest tide, is a large, low cavern, reaching far back into the recesses of the rock, and the resort of creatures to which imagination may lend terrific attributes. Above the entrance to this cave, and about half-way up the face of the rock, is a sloping ledge, which juts out further than the rest of the promontory. This is the favourite spot of the most intrepid of the coast fishermen, for from this ledge a man may throw his weighted line far into the depths of water, and into a well-known fishing-ground. The wonder is that the man himself ever gets back alive, for, looked at from one side, it appears impossible for him to keep his footing, and if he once lost it nothing could save him. Not far above his head, at the very verge of the summit, is a monumental stone to mark the spot where a woman slipped and was launched into eternity. Many schnappers and other fish are caught both here and on the Southern Headland, while the long stretch of sand between the two is the place for mullet and whiting. The South Headland is barely so high as that to the North, but is still more curiously marked; and whilst it is impossible, save to a man with the agility of a goat or chamois, to pass round the face of the latter, in the

COOGEE BAY.

AT COOGEE.

former a path, cut by the waves, winds for a full half-mile under overhanging mountains of rock. There is one spot here which is known as "The Blessings," and this is particularly worthy of a visit. The name is a somewhat fanciful one, the place poetically taking its designation from the showers of silver spray which are constantly falling here. The sandstone blocks are jointed with great uniformity, and have worked into immense masses, with flat faces, placed at right angles to each other. The effect of this is that a huge perpendicular shoot has been formed, so that even on a calm day, when there is but slight motion in the water, the waves rushing against the faces of the rock find here a vent, and are thrown up to a considerable height, affording a beautiful sight as they fall and rise again. In rough weather it is unsafe to go near the place, for the high seas sweep not only here, but far overhead, and the bare tables of water-worn rock above show the height to which the water reaches.

A steep climb now brings us to the top, and a good scramble through the scrub for something like a mile will suffice to reach the calmer shores of Long Bay. This, as its name implies, is an inlet of unusual length, and somewhat narrow. In consequence of its peculiar shape, the seas which lash the shores of Maroubra, Coogee, and Bondi Bays are here somewhat quieted, and this circumstance gives a peaceful character to the scenery. The southern and western shores are well wooded, and through the woods a good military road leads down to the very beach. Thick beds of bracken line the sides of the road, a small cottage or two peeping through the woods show signs of encroaching civilisation, and the fisherman's boats rock themselves invitingly upon the waters. Following the southern shore for a short distance, the visitor will find one of the few memorials of the time, not very long ago, when all these shores, from South Head to Long Bay and beyond to Botany, were the favourite haunts of the aborigines. Here, under an overhanging ledge of sandstone, which crops out strangely in the middle of a grassy slope in the wood, was the "gibber-gunyah," or stone dwelling, of the black fellows. When, not long ago, the floor of this "gunyah" was dug up with pickaxe and shovel, many stone axes and spear-heads, together with bones of various descriptions, were discovered. In all probability many still would be found there if close search were made. At Bondi similar weapons, with skulls and other remains, have frequently been dug up; and the collector of curiosities of this sort would find all this coast a good hunting-ground.

Leaving the Cove behind, and following the coast-line, the visitor soon arrives within sight of Little Bay, the smallest and prettiest of all the bays along this part of the coast. The coast-line trends down on either side to a point, and when the two sides have approached within thirty or forty yards of each other they suddenly open out on the land side into the form of a large horseshoe, girdled with a strip of beautiful sand. Here the Coast Hospital has been built. Fronting the sea stand the neat wood and iron buildings, with their broad verandahs, designed for the patients. The thought occurs that here a man might make himself very much at home, and enjoy his quiet holiday, even though in quarantine. The patients, indeed, do enjoy themselves, and find amusement in bathing, and also in fishing, for there is much of this to be done. One part of the ground alone preserves a sombre and most melancholy interest, namely, that devoted to the lepers, who, fortunately, are few in number. The whole establishment, at the time of my visit, consisted of some six individuals, all Chinese. These, in all stages of the dread disease, live in small corrugated iron houses, and are supposed to cook and generally manage for themselves. Those in the early stages of the malady would by the ordinary observer be hardly recognised as ill at all, but the nervous twitchings and the reddened skin drawn tightly over the joints tell their tale to the seeing eye. That old man lying on the bed has lost the use of his limbs, which are drawn together convulsively, while the hands are bent and twisted into claws. His eyes start from their sockets in agony, and his lips refuse all utterance, but still can mumble a doubtful prayer for rum. Rum is a great treat to these poor outcasts, and they get a little of it every day. There is no hope for them: the disease is absolutely incurable, and they know it.

Still on and on, over the breezy hill-sides knee deep in the ti-tree scrub, and in less than an hour we are on the borders of Botany Bay. A few minutes' walk brings us to the monument erected to the great French explorer, the brave, gallant, and sad-fated La Pérouse. This monument, standing on the very shores of the Bay, and surrounded with trees and flowers, marks the last spot whence La Pérouse was heard of. Hard by lie the remains of the naturalist attached to the *Astrolabe*, the scientific Abbé Réceveur, who was one of the first white men who left their bones on Australian soil.

From these memorial grounds an uninterrupted view is obtained of the large expanse of the Bay, with the immense length of Lady Robinson's Beach on the right hand; opposite, on the far side of the Bay, are the leafy knolls of the National Park, and to the left of this the entrance between the Heads, while just inside the South Head is the historic Point Sutherland. After feasting the eyes on this extensive view, it is interesting to refer to the account given by Governor Phillip of his landing in January, 1788. "At the very first landing," he writes, "an interview with the natives took place. They were all armed, but on seeing the Governor approach with signs of friendship alone and unarmed, they readily returned his confidence by laying down their weapons. They were perfectly devoid of clothing, yet seemed fond of ornaments, putting the beads and red baize that were given them on their heads or necks, and appearing pleased to wear them." From other sources also we learn that the shores of this Bay were much frequented in early times by the natives, whereas now, throughout the colony of New South Wales, they have almost wholly disappeared. Very rarely are they seen anywhere along this coast or near Sydney, except on those periodical occasions when a few of them come in to obtain yearly gifts of blankets and other necessaries. Probably in the old days they were attracted to this Bay by the excellent fishing-grounds which still exist.

Boats are kept at various places along its shores, and weather-beaten ancient mariners are constantly ready, for a valuable consideration, to show the inexperienced where to throw the line. While in the boat it is well to row over to the other side and see Point Sutherland, a place named after one of Captain Cook's seamen who happened to die here. Here it was that, in 1770, Cook first unfurled the British flag, and the spot is marked by a small obelisk bearing as an inscription a short extract from the explorer's journal, in the following words: "28th April, A.D. 1770. We discovered a bay and anchored under the south shore, about two miles within the entrance, in six fathoms of water, the south point bearing S.E. and the north point E." All the ground round this spot, before many years are past, will probably be covered by the rapidly approaching tide of population. Already large blocks of land have been cut up and sold, and as the district immediately surrounding the city is too much crowded, the surplus population is sure to distribute itself along the shores. Between half a mile and a mile inland from the western shore of Botany Bay runs the Illawarra Railway Line, and all along this line, as far as the National Park and the Waterfall, settlement has commenced, whilst Hurstville and Kogarah have already grown into suburbs of no slight importance.

It may be said of almost any of the suburbs of Sydney that they are capable, in a similar manner, of indefinite extension, and in this fact lies rich promise of future greatness. To illustrate this characteristic of Sydney, imagine a common carriage-wheel. Let the axle represent the waters of the Harbour, and the spokes so many long arms of sea running up into the land, and the spaces between the spokes the land itself. Sydney and its suburbs are at present gathered close around the axle, and all the remainder of the spaces is naturally perfectly adapted for expansion. For example, this Illawarra Railway has opened up the magnificent district of the Illawarra, with soil and natural characteristics quite different from those of the country round Sydney.

"The Garden of New South Wales" is the name which, by common consent, has been given to this district, which consists of a more or less narrow strip of agricultural and pastoral land, lying between the hills and the sea. Its northern end may well be reckoned among the suburbs of Sydney. Stanwell Park, the northernmost part of the Illawarra district, is a most delightful spot. Here the sandstone hills, instead of descending by gradual decline to the sea, send out their bold faces from three to six hundred feet or more in the sheer. Two of these bold promontories enclose a gentle curve of silvery sand, which alone divides the boisterous sea from the still waters of the lagoon on the landward side. Standing on the sandy beach, and looking to the south, the eye can, on a clear day, easily discern the five rocky islands of Kiama on the distant horizon. Between them and the spectator innumerable points of land oppose themselves to the snowy breakers, while hard by he sees the most dangerous part of the coach road to Bulli, as it winds round the perpendicular face of the Coal Cliff. Let him turn round now and look inland, to the west. The unrippled waters of the lagoon reflect every detail of the sky and the well-timbered hills beyond: the tall, blue gums point downwards to the apparently unfathomable depths, the fairy tree-ferns, the brilliant cabbage palms, the giant lilies are all mirrored there; and so beautiful is the

THE UNIVERSITY.

sight that the eye lingers, and hesitates to look beyond. But when the face is lifted there are the hills, stately and supreme, capped with the forms of ruined battlements and turrets, such as this sandstone so frequently assumes. Such a scene makes the heart glad. As yet, too, the place possesses a charm which, it is to be feared, it must shortly lose—the charm of perfect rest and quiet. Although it is only some thirty or forty miles from Sydney, civilisation has not yet become obtrusive, and the dweller in towns, harassed by the anxiety of business, can here obtain the repose of which he stands in need. Certainly there is nothing like it anywhere nearer Sydney, for the altogether sufficient reason that everywhere round Sydney the sandstone reigns supreme.

But let us return to the city by rail, passing over the Cook's River Bridge, and into the Sydney terminus, which lies in the middle of the suburb of Redfern. Hard

1. CLONTARF, FROM SHELL COVE. 2. MRS. MACQUARIE'S CHAIR. 3. A SYDNEY FERRY STEAMER.
4. PARRAMATTA, FROM THE PARK.

by stand the old Exhibition buildings, surrounded by the grounds of Prince Alfred Park, and opposite to the old burying-ground of Sydney. The Park is much needed here, for the whole surrounding district is far too thickly populated, and many of the houses of the poor are little better than hovels. About half a mile farther from Sydney are the University Grounds, enclosing the extensive University Buildings, which undoubtedly deserve more than a mere casual mention. The building is in the Elizabethan style, and consists of a large centre and wings. Placed on a slight eminence, it is one of the most remarkable objects presented to the eye in any general view of the city. The Institution itself dates from the year 1850, when it was incorporated by Act of Parliament. Very large sums of money have already been spent upon it, and, while principally endowed by the State, it has been most generously supported by private donations and

THE CHAMPION COURSE.

bequests, one bequest alone, that of Mr. Challis, amounting to no less than £180,000. To any visitor the Museum of Antiquities must prove an object of interest, and the Great Hall will always be a sight worth seeing. In it is a very fine, large organ, with some three thousand pipes, and frequent recitals are given here on Saturday afternoons for the public benefit.

A very little distance south of the University Reserve is the suburb of Newtown, dusty and populous; and beyond that again, Enmore, Petersham, and Marrickville, of all of which little need be said; for, though these places may serve a useful purpose, they are none of them picturesque or delightful to the eye. Probably, the chief reason why so many people have come to live in these suburbs is that they are so readily accessible, tramways, trains, and omnibuses all running there frequently. A little farther along the line of the main Southern Railway lies Ashfield, then Burwood, and beyond that Parramatta. Now in the old days this last was a place of considerable importance. It is almost as old as Sydney itself, dating from the month of November, 1788, when, as Collins tells the story, "His Excellency the Governor, with the Surveyor-General, two officers, and a small party of marines, went up to choose the spot, and to mark out the ground for a redoubt and other necessary buildings; and, two days after, a party of ten convicts, being chiefly people who understood the business of cultivation, were sent up to him, and a spot upon a rising ground, which His Excellency named Rose Hill, was ordered to be cleared for the first habitations. The soil at this spot was of a stiff clayey nature, free from that rock which everywhere obstructed the surface at Sydney Cove, well clothed with timber, and unobstructed by underwood." The place still presents the same characteristics, and the country immediately surrounding is occupied by farms and orchards and country seats in great numbers. But, though the distance from Sydney is only some fifteen miles, and though a pleasanter place could not be desired, Parramatta is not much used for residence by business men, because of the delays of the journey. On account of the *détour* which the railway is compelled to make, and because of the many intervening stoppages, the trains take nearly three-quarters of an hour to perform the journey, while the trip down the river by steamer, although a very pleasant excursion, takes a full hour and a half. Starting either from the bottom of King Street, or from the Circular Quay, the boat passes close to Goat Island, rounds Long Nose Point, and then, taking a turn, skirts along by Cockatoo Island, on which stands the reformatory for girls, nears Spectacle Island, with its powder magazine, and soon enters on the waters of the Champion Course, the scene of the world-famed sculling matches between Hanlan and Beach. When such a race takes place, the scene here presented is almost unique, for everyone comes by water, and hundreds of private steam-launches and sailing yachts, with large public steamers, rowing-boats, and every description of craft, crowd up this river, which, about this point, is from a quarter to half a mile across, while the low, rocky shores on either side are as one long ant-heap in appearance. Near here is a large iron bridge, connecting the two shores. On either bank pleasant villas, with long, smooth, emerald lawns, descending to the water, are seen in considerable numbers, while in the background the large extent of country, covered with its original wood, gives some idea of the quantity of space still left for the encroachment of the Sydney population.

OLD GOVERNMENT HOUSE, PARRAMATTA

A little further up the river comes Ryde, a small village on the northern bank, and here the eye is caught by the beautiful dark green of the orange orchards. In the orange season one is reminded of Andrew Marvell's line—

"Like golden lamps in a green night."

The river is widening out to a considerable breadth, and extensive growths of the mangrove mark the many shallows. The steamer seems to turn towards every point of the compass until now it appears as if there were no outlet; but as the vessel advances an opening is perceived, and, passing through this, we are soon at our

LIGHTHOUSE ON SOUTH HEAD.

destination. This, however, is not yet Parramatta. A small but comfortable private tramway meets the steamer, and, after a run of a few minutes, lands the passengers in the very heart of the town. This line ends at the gates of the Public Park, and, after passing through these, a short walk along the pleasant avenue, by the water-side, brings the pedestrian to the old Government House, now degraded into a lodging-house. This venerable place is pictured in Collins's History, and, putting aside the modern improvements which have been made to the house, the general appearance of the site is very similar now to what it was nearly a century ago.

Soon the road curves and leads back to the town, and now a short drive takes us to the orange orchards. These orchards, which extend for a considerable distance on both banks of the river, are all arranged on much the same pattern. The trees are planted in regular rows, carefully dug and manured, and the dark green foliage, aided by the contrasted colour of the fruit, always makes a pleasing picture.

Returning to Sydney by train, all the principal railway suburbs are passed through; but there is very little of beauty to be seen, and after the monotony of the journey, the

to force its way through, the place has received the name of the "Gap," as prophetic, probably, of what will be in years to come. This Gap is one of the few historical spots around Sydney. To it will always attach a mournful interest, as the scene of perhaps the most fearful wreck that has ever occurred on this coast since first the colony was founded. It was in the month of August, in the year 1857. On Thursday, the 20th, about 10 o'clock in the morning, the man on the look-out at the South Head descried a sail in the offing. It was the *Dunbar*. The people on board, who were chiefly emigrants from the home country, gathered at the bulwarks to see that land which they had chosen for a new home. As the day wore on the land was approached more nearly, and point after point disclosed to the view, until, at about seven o'clock, the light at the South Head was seen. Previously to this the vessel had been lying a course N.E. by N., and was coming along under easy sail, sail having been shortened after the first sighting of the land. The weather was now thick with rain squalls, the wind blowing dead on land. Darkness had set in, yet many remained on deck, expecting every moment to pass through the Heads into the smooth waters beyond, and to see the lights of the city.

The light from the Lighthouse was shining brightly, but served only to render the surrounding darkness still more terrible, and nothing could be seen of the land but a dark mass looming on either bow. The captain of the vessel now judged that he was well between the Heads, and a slight break in the darkness right ahead confirmed him in this opinion. He accordingly gave the order to square the mainsail, and with the wind right astern the large canvas filled out. The good ship lifted, and at the rate of some fifteen knots an hour rushed headlong, and, ploughing up the white seas, and dashing the swirling foam from her sides, hurled herself with one awful and gigantic blow against the rocks. A moment longer, and the *Dunbar* had ceased to exist. The masts went by the board, every timber was loosened, every plank parted, and in the same instant of time several hundred souls, with all the *débris* of the wreck, were plunged into the water, with the black darkness overhead, and before them the perpendicular cliff, which even here, at its lowest point, is some two hundred feet high. A few seconds of time, a few weak cries for help where no help was, and all life had fled from those already shapeless forms. One man alone crouched there under an overhanging ledge of rock just beyond reach of the waves. This was Johnson, one of the sailors, who, by some wonderful means—partly by the shock of the blow and partly by the impetus of a huge wave—was cast up there while all the rest were drowned. Below him the battered corpses of his comrades float—welcome morsels for the sharks, which pull them down and tear limb from limb. During the whole of the Friday this continued, and from all sides these tigers of the sea, scenting the pleasant feast, hastened to join in the scramble. The next morning, Saturday, the sea went down, and with its quiet repose tempted poor Johnson, who had been on that ledge for some thirty hours without food or water, and without rest or hope. All seemed well-nigh over, and he thought that it was useless to struggle any longer for his life. But in the meantime the planks and other portions of the wreck had floated away on the waters and been sighted, and the news carried into Sydney, so that it became known that there had been a wreck along the coast. Search parties were sent out, and suddenly there is a shout above, and then another, and Johnson, looking up, sees whence the shouting comes, and a young man, risking his own life, slides down a rope two hundred feet from the top, seizes the poor, famished, almost senseless sailor, takes him in his arms, and both are raised to the top.

Any such calamity would now be well-nigh impossible, for a wonderful electric flash light, which can always be seen for many miles around, is exhibited immediately south of the Gap. The new lighthouse, in which this light is placed, is a most substantial stone structure; and well it need be, for on stormy days, when the gale is blowing from the south and east, the waves dash over the cliffs and over the lighthouse too. Up on that circular platform at the top, how glorious the view!—glorious in its details, in the brightness of its colours, and in its extent. No words can possibly describe the wonders and delights of the place: northward the hilly ground round Broken Bay, and the shores about the mouth of the Hawkesbury River, are well in sight; westward lie all the familiar glories of the Harbour, with the blue mountains beyond; and to the south stretches point beyond point of all the picturesque eastern coast. Bondi Bay is the nearest, with its sand-dunes and wide expanse of blown sand; and, beyond that, Waverley and Randwick, and Coogee, Little Bay, and Botany, already described.

If, on returning, a row-boat be taken from Watson's Bay across the Harbour, a good opportunity is afforded of seeing Middle Harbour and the north shore. Of the Middle Harbour scenery typical views are given on the following pages, one taken from a spot a little inside the entrance in Hunter's Bay, and the other of Clontarf from Shell Cove. In the immediate foreground of the former is a broad table of that sandstone which is characteristic of the country round Sydney, cropping out everywhere, and lying in boulders and in huge slabs. On the right a point of land, part of the Middle Head, covered with thick bush, projects into the water, and in the left distance the North Head shows its bold profile. A little to the left of this, as one looks out to sea, lies Manly Cove and the little village of Manly. This, of all the suburbs, can most be likened to the English Brighton. Here settlement has advanced more quickly than in the other coast suburbs, so that the place is now becoming crowded. Certainly it possesses immense natural advantages. The North Head itself is only a part, the extreme point, of a very large promontory, which at Manly is narrowed down to a small neck of land not more than a quarter of a mile across. On either side, this neck is bordered by a pleasant sandy beach, one beach looking across the quiet waters of the Harbour, the other receiving the thundering surges of the ocean. The neck itself is comparatively flat land, and is completely built over, and occupied chiefly by business houses; but the gently-rising grounds on either side are dotted with delightful villas and gardens. A little to the south-east is the site of a large residence for the Head of the Roman Catholic Church in Sydney, and, still further south, is the principal quarantine station of the port, occupying a beautiful site, and from a slight distance looking comfortable and tempting. From this point it is possible to obtain an uninterrupted outlook for some five miles across the Harbour, and the Middle Harbour on the west, and Double Bay and Rose Bay on the south and west, are amply extended to the view. As a final word of praise, it may fairly be said, at least of these water suburbs, that each one is a glory in itself. In some cases unqualified praise may seem to approach exaggeration, but to such an extent does this

MIDDLE HARBOUR.

city and country seize hold of the very heart of a man, that the place almost assumes the attribute of personality, and induces affection of the very strongest kind. Sydney is a place which, to be loved, needs but to be seen.

THE BOTANICAL GARDENS (p. 2)

# SYDNEY: ITS ORIGIN.

Discovery of Sydney Harbour—Botany Bay—Landing at Sydney Cove—Sickness—The Aborigines—Loss of the *Sirius*—Famine—Martial Law—Despair—Relief —Better Days—Past and Present.

AFTER what has been said of Sydney, it will not be easy for the reader to realise that in the pleasant month of January, in the year 1788, this favoured spot of God's earth was unknown to civilised man. On the 22nd of that month there came three small boats sailing north from Botany Bay, and keeping almost under the shadow of those rugged sandstone cliffs, until, as they rounded the South Head, they left behind them the heavy swell of the Pacific Ocean, and glided smoothly to the west and south over the wide waters of Sydney Harbour. These boats were the advance-guard of that fleet, consisting of the *Sirius* man-of-war and ten other vessels, which in May of the preceding year had sailed from Portsmouth with the express object of founding here a new penal settlement. Botany Bay had been visited by Captain Cook some eight years previously, and that great navigator had on his return to England given such a glowing account of the country of "New South Wales," as he himself had named it, that the Bay was chosen as the destination of this first fleet. But Botany Bay was found not all that Cook's fancy had pictured. For the purposes of a permanent settlement it was altogether unfit, for although the Bay includes an immense expanse of waters, these waters are not only too shallow for the anchorage of large vessels, but are also exposed to the full force of the prevailing winds. Captain Arthur Phillip, R.N., the commander of the first fleet and the Governor of the new settlement, after making an examination of the surroundings of the Bay, decided that the place was unsuitable to his purpose. He therefore ordered the fleet to remain at anchor, while he himself set out in an open boat to explore the coast and to look for a home.

The undertaking was a bold one. The coast was wild and surf-beaten. Its dangers were many and unknown. Immense rollers broke upon the rugged shore, and seemed to leave no safe landing-place for any boat. The shores were peopled by unfriendly natives, who, standing in large numbers on the tops of the cliffs, hurled threats and defiance at the boats as they approached.

Suddenly, after sailing north for about twelve miles, there came a break in the coast-line about a mile in length from headland to headland. Seen from the open sea, this opening appeared of little size, but as the boats rounded the inner head the immense extent of the harbour was displayed. After exploring the different bays, that which showed the deepest soundings was selected. "The different coves of this harbour," says Captain Phillip himself,* "were examined with all possible expedition, and the preference was given to one which had the finest spring of water, and in which ships can anchor so close to the shore that at a very small expense quays may be constructed at which the largest vessels may unload. In honour of Lord Sydney the Governor distinguished it by the name of Sydney Cove." Two days afterwards Captain Phillip returned to Botany Bay, and on the 25th of the same month, seven days after the arrival of the *Supply*, he left Botany and sailed to Port Jackson.

As at that time it happened to be blowing a strong gale, the rest of the fleet was left under convoy of the *Sirius*, with orders to proceed to Sydney as soon as the gale abated. Scarcely were the leading vessels out of sight when a strange sight appeared. "About daylight, just as they were preparing for a start," two strange sail showed themselves on the horizon. These gradually approached, and as they came nearer it was seen that they were the *Boussole* and *Astrolabe*, ships of the great French explorer La Pérouse.

On the 26th of the month, according to Captain Phillip, the transports and store-ships under convoy of the *Sirius* finally evacuated Botany Bay, and as in a fair wind the journey only occupies a few hours they were soon all safely anchored in Sydney Cove. Without any delay the disembarkation was commenced, and all persons able to work were set to clear the ground for the camp and to cut wood for the buildings. The clearing of the bush was then, as it has always been, a task of great difficulty. "The labour," says the Governor, "which attended this necessary operation was greater than can easily be imagined by those who were not spectators of it. The coast, as well as the neighbouring country in general, is covered with wood, and though in this spot the trees stood more apart, and were less encumbered with underwood than in many

* "The Voyage of Governor Phillip to Botany Bay, with an Account of the Establishment of the Colonies of Port Jackson and Norfolk Island." London, 1789.

SYDNEY HARBOUR, FROM BELLE VUE HILL.

other places, yet their magnitude was such as to render not only the felling but the removal of them afterwards extremely difficult. By the habitual indolence of the convicts, and the want of proper overseers to keep them to their duty, their labour was rendered less efficient than it might have been. In the evening of the 26th the colours were displayed on shore, and the Governor, with several of his principal officers and others, assembled round the flagstaff, drank the King's health" (George III.), "and success to the settlement." The first house to be completed was that of the Governor, the materials and framework of which had been brought out ready-worked from England. Other houses and huts of various sizes soon appeared, and all seemed fairly in progress, when a dread enemy appeared in the midst of the camp.

On the voyage out there had been very little sickness, but now dysentery showed itself, and soon took hold of a large number. Of the sufferers many died. Scurvy also attacked the little colony, the members of which had for months been deprived of fresh food. Even after landing, fish or other fresh provisions or vegetables could rarely be procured. For the dysentery the red gum was found to be useful, while for the scurvy the chief thing that could be done was to grow vegetables and fruits with as little delay as possible. Very little, however, could yet be done in this direction, and, meanwhile, recourse was had to the various species of plants that were growing wild— celery, spinach, and parsley—all of which, fortunately, were found in abundance round the settlement.

At that time, according to the historians of the young colony, the public stock consisted of one bull, four cows, one bull calf, one stallion, three mares, and three colts. These were carefully preserved for breeding, and were shortly removed to the bay adjoining Sydney Cove, which bay was none other than Farm Cove. Here, where the Botanical Gardens now extend their pleasant glades, a small farm was started, from which Farm Cove took its name. After strenuous efforts, matters began to improve a little, and by the end of February or beginning of March the settlement was in fair progress. The public storehouses had been well begun, and although the stumps of the trees had not been removed, the ground was cleared over a considerable extent, and Sydney town was no longer a mere hope, but had become an accomplished fact.

Before this time, that is, very shortly after the disembarkation, several of the convicts had attempted to escape. On the very morning after the reading of the formal proclamation nine convicts were found to be missing, and at various other times, owing to the want of overseers, small batches of prisoners took themselves off. Being without provisions, and amongst hostile natives, the fugitives must soon have perished.

As to the dangers arising from the natives, many instances occurred to warn the settlers. One evening a convict who had been working as a labourer on the farm was brought in seriously wounded. A barbed spear had entered his back between the shoulders to about the depth of three inches. The account he gave of the occurrence was that having strayed beyond the limits of the farm with another man, he had suddenly felt this wound in his back, but had seen no natives. The other European had immediately run away. A day or two afterwards, adds Collins, the clothes of the missing man were found, torn, bloody, and pierced with spears.

A similar incident is added, and is interesting as giving its name to what is now a favourite and well-known part of Sydney. "An officer who had been exploring the Harbour came suddenly on the bodies of two convicts who had been employed for some time in cutting rushes in what is now known as Rushcutters' Bay. These bodies were pierced through in many places with spears, and the head of one was beaten to a jelly. As it seemed improbable that these murders should have been committed without provocation, inquiry was made. It then appeared that these unfortunate men had a few days previously taken away a canoe belonging to the natives, for which act of violence and injustice they paid with their lives."

Many similar instances are recorded in the old histories to which we have referred, and there can be little doubt that the original number of the persons who landed, namely, one thousand and thirty, was from this and other causes considerably reduced. But as it was, the people were too many, and the supply of food too scanty. No sufficient provision had been made for supplying food from the fruits of the land. Large dependence had been placed on the storeships which had been anxiously looked for, and were daily expected to arrive. The seed-wheat that had been sown turned out badly. The *Sirius* and the *Golden Grove* storeships had been despatched for the purpose of obtaining stores, and a week after the departure of the former a fixed deduction was, from motives of economy, made from the public rations. Shortly afterwards the amount was still further reduced, and as a consequence of "short commons" various attempts were made to commit thefts from the general stores. The thieves were brought up and severely dealt with. The *Sirius* and *Golden Grove* returned, bringing but small additions to the public stock. "The Governor, whose humanity was at all times conspicuous, directed that no alteration should be made in the ration to be issued to the women. They were already upon two-thirds of the men's allowance, and many of them either had children who could very well have eaten their own and part of their mother's ration, or they had

DOUBLE BAY (p. 27).

THE OBSERVATORY.

children at the breast; and although they did not labour, yet their appetites were never so delicate as to have found the full ration too much had it been issued to them."

In this state of affairs, a great and distressing calamity fell upon the little community in the loss of the *Sirius* upon a reef at Norfolk Island. This vessel had been again despatched to obtain relief for the already hunger-smitten people, and upon news of this calamity being received, it became necessary to adopt the most stringent measures in order to preserve the lives of the people.

Accordingly, a Council was called by the Lieutenant-Governor, and important resolutions were arrived at. We are told that it was unanimously determined "that martial law should be proclaimed; that all private stock, poultry excepted, should be considered the property of the State; that justice should be administered by a court-martial, to be composed of seven officers, five of whom were to concur in a sentence of death; and that there should be two locks upon the door of the public store, whereof one key was to be in the keeping of a person to be appointed by Captain Hunter on behalf of the seamen, the other to be kept by a person appointed on behalf of the military." The day after the meeting of this Council, the whole community—soldiers, seamen, and convicts—were assembled; these resolutions were publicly read, and all present confirmed their acceptance of them, and their determination to abide by the conditions. This was shown by all passing under the King's colours, which were displayed on this occasion.

These stringent measures could merely check, not remedy, the evil, and at one time it seemed as if the unfortunate colonists had little to look forward to but a lingering and miserable death from starvation. The rations were still further reduced, and now the amount was no more than two pounds and a half of flour, two pounds of pork, one pint of peas, and one pound of rice for each person for seven days. "Was this," exclaims the historian of that day, "a ration for a labouring man? The two pounds of pork when boiled, from the length of time it had been in store, shrank away to nothing, and when divided among seven people for their day's sustenance barely afforded three or four mouthfuls to each." The natural result was that labour ended. The men were too weak to work, and matters at length reached such a pass that even the convicts, such was their physical prostration, were permitted to remain idle. Amid such extreme privation, it became necessary in the interest of the public safety to inflict very severe penalties on all who attempted to steal from the public stores. Many received for such offences three hundred, four hundred, and as many as five hundred lashes. Yet even these most severe punishments failed altogether to check the crimes to which these poor people were impelled by the dire necessities of their position. "The latter part of 1788," writes one historian, "and the first four months of the following year, was one of the darkest periods ever experienced in the history of the settlement. The gloomy prospect before the people, the decrease in their rations, the severity and frequency of their punishments, and the strictness with which the Governor found it necessary to husband every resource, bred in the minds of the thoughtless and improvident feelings of recklessness and despair. The stock of provisions brought out from England was well-nigh exhausted; the few head of cattle also brought out had disappeared, no one knew where; and nothing eatable had yet been produced in the colony, with the exception of a few vegetables. Many of the prisoners straying into the bush to search for edible roots or herbs were killed by the natives. Seven soldiers detected in the act of plundering the public stores were hanged without mercy. The case of the young settlement was daily becoming desperate."

All this time Governor Phillip was behaving with great generosity, and setting the people a wonderful example of self-denial. Collins seems never tired of recording this disinterested and self-sacrificing behaviour on the part of the Governor. "The Governor," he writes in one place, "from a motive that did him immortal honour in this season of general distress, gave up three hundredweight of flour that was his Excellency's private property, declaring that he wished not to see any more at his table than the ration which was received in common from the public store, without any distinction of persons. To this resolution he rigidly adhered, wishing that if a convict complained he might see that want was not unfelt even at Government House."

So excellent and noble an example was certainly not without its effect in assisting many to keep heart and to struggle manfully through their distresses. And soon the unexpected arrival of two storeships from England infused new hope and vigour into the almost starving people.

About half-past three in the afternoon of the 3rd of June, "to the inexpressible satisfaction of every heart in the settlement," a sail was sighted from the South Head. At once, although a very strong wind was blowing, the Governor's secretary and two other officers went off, and at considerable risk—for there was a heavy sea running through the Heads—reached the ship, and brought her in safety into Spring Cove. She proved to be the *Lady Juliana*, from London. She had been much delayed, having been not less than ten months on the voyage. The *Guardian*, a much larger vessel, which had sailed from England about the same time, had been wrecked on an iceberg in 45° south, and all her stores lost. About a fortnight after the arrival of the *Juliana* the storeship *Justinian* also arrived, five months out from England. The stores brought by these two vessels altogether altered the complexion of affairs, and the more immediate fear of starvation being removed, the people were enabled again to go about their proper business, to till and improve the land, and by various methods to gain a subsistence from the soil. It seemed that a more friendly fortune was smiling upon the colony; but there were still further difficulties at that very time approaching the shores of the settlement. Three transports, the *Surprise*, the *Neptune*, and the *Scarborough*, arrived, one after the other, with large numbers of convicts, and with much sickness prevailing amongst them. By the 13th of the next month there were no fewer than four hundred and eighty-eight persons laid up under medical treatment at the hospital.

Among some new regulations issued about this time by the Governor was one the object of which was to enforce the attendance of the people at Divine Service on Sundays. A large proportion of the rations was deducted from the share of each person who absented himself from prayers on that day. Up to this time no very serious evils had arisen from intercourse with the natives. A few stragglers, and some who had wantonly interfered with the goods or persons of the aboriginal inhabitants, had lost their lives, but as a rule the intercourse had been more or less of an amicable description. The Governor had especially endeavoured to conciliate the blacks, and to show them that he wished above all things to be their friend. Two young natives, one of whom was named Bennilong, had been taken by him into his own house, and kept there for some little time, in order that they might learn something of the habits and comforts of civilised life. Both, however, preferred liberty to everything else, and took an early opportunity to escape. The Governor, after this, hearing that Bennilong had been seen in company with some natives in one of the numerous coves of the Harbour, determined, regardless of the personal risk, to visit and again endeavour to conciliate him. The cove was full of natives allured by the attractions of a whale feast, for a whale a short time before had entered the Harbour and been unable to find its way out again. The Governor had distributed various tomahawks and other articles as presents to the natives, and he was approaching one man with arms extended in a friendly manner; but the black, misunderstanding his intentions, and probably imagining that the Governor was intending to seize him, raised his spear, and hurriedly bringing his throwing-stick into use, hurled the weapon at Captain Phillip. He had employed such force that the spear went through the Governor's body, entering a little above the collar-bone, and coming through on the other side. Several other spears were thrown at the rest of the party, but fortunately without doing much

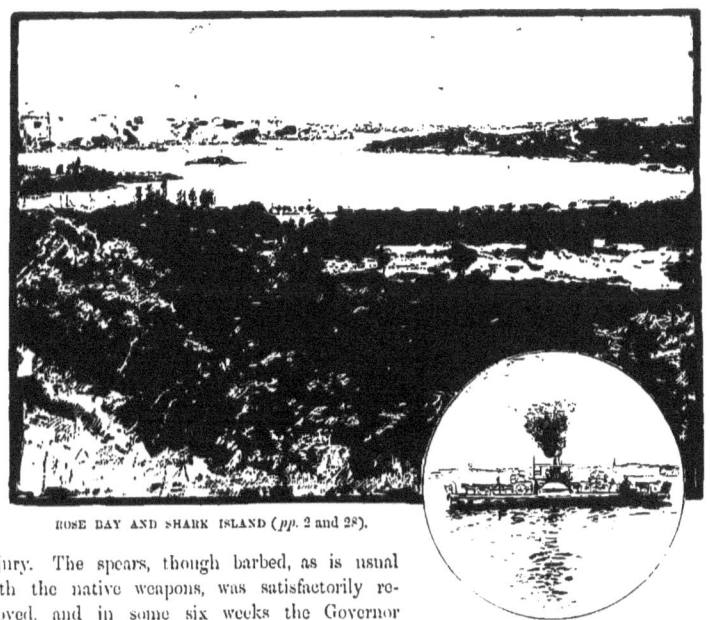

ROSE BAY AND SHARK ISLAND (*pp.* 2 and 28).

injury. The spears, though barbed, as is usual with the native weapons, was satisfactorily removed, and in some six weeks the Governor had quite recovered. This adventure was not without good effect, for Bennilong, grateful for

STEAM FERRY.

past favours, displayed much anxiety about Captain Phillip's well-being. By his means friendly communication was afterwards opened up with the natives.

It is worthy of record that in March of the year 1791 James Ruse, the first man to whom land had been granted by the Government, announced to the Governor that he would from that time be able to live on the fruits of his land without assistance from the public stores. At the end of the same year it was found that there were in all some thousand acres under cultivation, giving good promise for the years to come. Four years later, in 1795, it was calculated that there were five thousand acres cultivated, and after that the quantity steadily increased. There was no more fear of general starvation, but the early privations of the settlers will never be forgotten. A wealthy citizen, who arrived in the colony as a free person, told Dr. Lang, who gives the statement in his "History of New South Wales," that "his ration for a long period was merely a cob or single head of maize or Indian corn a day, and that for three years he had lived in the colony in the constant belief that he should one day perish of hunger."

But these old times have long been left behind; privation, and the fear of it, are things of the past. It will, however, always interest an English people, whether in New South Wales, or in the old country, or elsewhere, to read of the early struggles of the founders of this flourishing city; and the interest is increased when one considers the singularly rapid progress which it has made in commerce and in every other feature of civilisation. To prosecute a careful inquiry into its history is not our present object, nor would the general reader greatly care for an account of the reigns of the different Governors, or of the rise and fall of political Administrations. Suffice it to say, that the mutiny of the convicts, the deposition and expulsion of Governor Bligh by the New South Wales corps, and the first discoveries of gold, form the most important events in the city's career.

GARDEN ISLAND BY MOONLIGHT.

DISTANT VIEW OF MELBOURNE FROM DONCASTER TOWER.

## MELBOURNE PROPER.

General Features of the City and the Suburbs—Elizabeth Street—Australian Creeks—The Cathedrals—The Churches—Government House—Princes Bridge—The Town Hall—The Wards—The Hospital—The Public Library—The Working Man's College—The Old and the New Law Courts—The Royal Mint—Collins Street—Flinders Street—Little Collins Street—Bourke Street—The Post Office and the Eastern Market—Parliament House—Little Bourke Street.

TO the visitor who comes to Melbourne after Sydney, and to the reader who has been hearing of the beauties of Sydney Harbour, it is necessary at once to say that on the score of natural beauty Melbourne must own its inferiority to Sydney. The shores of Port Phillip are not interesting in themselves, and they can ill bear comparison with the infinite variety of coast-line, the constant interchange of point and cove that forms the charm of Sydney Harbour, so different to the flat, low-lying expanses of sand that skirt the upper end of Port Phillip, known as Hobson's Bay. Friends of Melbourne may fairly contend that it has its pretty spots, and some even that seem fairly blessed by nature, as, for instance, the Botanical Gardens; but without the hand of the gardener making smooth, sloping lawns, graceful curves, and richly-coloured flower-beds, even the charming situation of the ground would have escaped the observation of ordinary eyes. In Melbourne it is man's work, not nature's, that invites admiration; and it is from this point of view that a traveller characterised Melbourne as "marvellous." No two places, be they regarded as rivals or as sisters, could present greater contrasts than Melbourne and Sydney. Some cities are founded, others grow. Some seem to have been arranged and built according to a plan, others to grow according to their needs, seemingly following their own sweet will. With certain limitations, Melbourne belongs to the former class: Sydney, from the very nature of its position, to the latter.

The City of Melbourne has been so carefully and regularly laid out that it is very easy for a stranger to remember its plan, and to find his way about. It may be said to consist of a square and two offshoots. One of these is the only suburb lying wholly within the municipal bounds of the city, the fashionable suburb of East Melbourne,

PLAN OF THE CITY OF MELBOURNE.

held at arm's length from the city by the beautiful Fitzroy Gardens. Here is Bishopscourt, the residence of the Anglican bishop, and here, too, stand many comfortable villas and large private houses. The other offshoot is south of the Yarra, and consists of the Domain which includes the Botanical Gardens, and of the Fawkner Park. A small portion of the suburb, also fashionable, of South Yarra, is thus included in the city for municipal purposes, though, curiously enough, this fragment is in the Parliamentary borough of St. Kilda. Probably the reason for carrying the boundary of the city so far to the south is to secure that the richest municipality should retain its share of the burden of park-maintenance.

East Melbourne and South Yarra are places of residence, whereas what may be called Melbourne proper is chiefly a place of business. Business, however, is not quite so absorbing as in London, for the chief hotels, the theatres, and the clubs, fall within this business area. The larger the size of a town, the more complete is likely to be the division between the functions of its different quarters. The "City" of London is wholly given up to shops, warehouses, banks, and places of business. When these are closed, the City is deserted. On a Sunday, if it were not for the attractions of St. Paul's Cathedral, there would be hardly a soul in the City except the caretakers. Melbourne is never so completely deserted as this. It has well-marked divisions into quarters, but these lie cheek by jowl. Yet Melbourne proper is not a place of residence. In old days a tradesman lived over his shop, but modern conveniences of travel enable him to live in a suburb, to surround himself with a garden, and separate himself each evening from the outward signs of his business. A jolting in the train, lasting each morning and evening from ten to forty minutes, as the case may be, is the price that he pays for the fresh air and the freedom.

Melbourne proper was to have been one mile square. Eight streets, running north and south, divide the more famous streets that run east and west. Collins and Bourke Streets are exactly a mile long, and each block in them is one-eighth of a mile. The pedestrian can time himself on a measured mile. Even the very names begin most regularly, and as if to form a *memoria technica*—King, William, Queen, Elizabeth; but here the limits of mnemonic invention appear, and distinguished colonists, and even those not very well known, claim their due. When we turn the other way the symmetry is not so complete, but a new element comes in. The southernmost street, more or less parallel to the river Yarra, is Flinders Street, called after the navigating explorer, famous in early Australian history. Between Flinders and the next street, Collins, comes Little Flinders Street, otherwise called Flinders Lane. So, also, Collins and Bourke Streets have each a little namesake lying to the immediate north. The idea in the original scheme was that these should be really lanes leading to the back doors of the houses in the larger streets. But land became too valuable for this luxury, and the smaller streets soon won an existence of their own. Their narrowness, thus explained by their history, forms an exception to the general rule of wide and airy streets so characteristic of Melbourne.

Elizabeth Street, which, continued northwards though not exactly in a straight line, becomes the Sydney Road, divides Melbourne proper into two nearly equal parts. There is no doubt that the lower end of Elizabeth Street was originally a creek or small brook, a branch of the Yarra. If a man takes his stand at the crossing of Collins and Elizabeth Streets, the most crowded and busiest crossing in Melbourne, on each side he looks up-hill. It is not very long since each Melbourne street had very wide gutters on each side, with wooden bridges across them for the use of foot passengers wishing to pass into the roadway. In the more important streets there has been lately substituted a complete system of underground drainage. Before this change, however, there was plenty of evidence that Elizabeth Street occupied the place of a stream. Whenever a shower of rain fell, the water came streaming down this street. All the streets that led out of it were contributory, and the gutters were soon full. When the rain was heavier than a shower, and the town was favoured with long rain or a tropical downpour, it very soon became impossible to cross the road. So swift ran the stream in the gutters, that in the early days, when the streets were not full of people, the drowning of a child in a gutter is said to have been no uncommon occurrence.

IN THE BOTANICAL GARDENS.

The swollen streams in the gutters sometimes even joined across the roadway, and for a while the street became a river again. Shopkeepers naturally complained, and this ultimately led the city authorities to adopt the underground drainage. It was long argued that no pipes would be large enough to carry off the storm water, and an arrangement has been made by which an overflow from the pipes will, if necessary, still be carried along the modern and moderate-sized gutters. The sight of this main street flooded will be rarer in the future than in the past, but a very heavy rain will probably yet enable it to be seen. Nothing less like an Australian creek debouching

A MELBOURNE GUTTER IN EARLIER DAYS.

into a river could well be imagined than this prosperous street, with its large and lofty houses, ended by a spacious but not very sightly railway station. Yet those who know what Australian creeks are like ought not to find a difficulty in bringing back the scene. Scattered over the bush there are thousands of them. Generally, where the English language is spoken, a creek means a small inlet of the sea, but in Australia a creek is literally what it is etymologically, a crack in the ground. In dry weather there is very little water; perhaps in the height of summer the stream altogether ceases to run, and the creek becomes a string of water holes; but when the heavens are opened, and the rain falls, it reappears a river. All around, the ground is uneven, and smaller creeks drain into the larger. Great gaunt gum-trees fill up the landscape.

It comes natural to cities to swallow up streams, and to turn brooks into main drains. Melbourne has only done with this nameless creek what London did with the Fleet and with the Ty-burn. Londoners grumble because their streets are always "up" for repairs, and Melbourne people make the same complaint. On one occasion a curious relic of antiquity was brought to light by the picks of the workmen. At some distance below the level of the road the wooden planks were found that used to form the simple bridge by which the early settlers crossed this very creek. An interested crowd soon collected, and many of the bystanders cut themselves chips to serve as mementoes. Fancy the excitement among English antiquaries if such a find had been made of an old bridge across the Fleet or the Ty! But in the case of Melbourne, it is not forty years since the simple bridge was in use, and an antiquary is hardly needed.

If the old idea be adopted, and the possession of a cathedral and a bishop be regarded as that which constitutes a city, then is Melbourne fortunate, for it has two cathedrals. The Roman Catholic cathedral on the summit of the Eastern Hill has the pride of place. It is already a beautiful Gothic church, and, when finished, it will be certainly the chief architectural ornament of the city. The architect is Mr. Wardell, who is allowed by all who know anything of the subject to have a true feeling for the beautiful in Gothic architecture. With respect to the site of the Anglican cathedral, which was commenced much more recently, a very fierce battle was waged. There were those who maintained that a cathedral ought always to be built upon a hill; and these were divided into two parties, advocates for the Eastern Hill and advocates for the western heights. Others maintained that the cathedral should be in the true centre of city life, and it was this party, strengthened by the vigorous eloquence of Dr. Moorhouse, the then Bishop, since transferred to the see of Manchester, England, as successor to Dr. Fraser—that carried the day. The St. Paul's site, which was then selected, is undeniably in the flattest part of the city, but the fact remains that it is in the centre, if by centre we mean the point most easily accessible from all parts of Greater Melbourne, that is, Melbourne and its suburbs. It is very close to two railway stations to which gathers the traffic from by far the larger number of suburbs, and it is not far from the starting-point of the northern omnibus and tramway systems. Standing opposite the great bridge over the Yarra, it is at the entrance of the city by its chief southern road. There is no site to which on week-days so many business men could so easily collect, whether for a few minutes of quiet devotion or to listen to an eloquent preacher; no site to which on Sundays so many could so easily gather by rail or road from their more distant homes. Arguments like these prevailed, and the lowness of the position was atoned for by an instruction to the architect to make the building itself lofty.

There are great differences of opinion with respect to the architecture, which is strongly characteristic of the eminent English architect who designed it. "Oh, if Butterfield is building your cathedral, he will afflict you with many stripes," was the comment of a Rugby master, whose knowledge of what Melbourne might expect was drawn from the magnificent school chapel which Mr. Butterfield built at Rugby. In the selection of materials for the Melbourne Cathedral, the architect took the utmost pains, having large specimens of the stone sent to him, but there are many unaccustomed to the variety introduced who regard with a feeling almost of horror the different coloured bands of which the pillars are composed, and the diaper work in the gables.

It is unfortunate that disagreements arose at an early period between the architect and the building committee, with the result that Mr. Butterfield declined to have anything further to do with the building. It is necessary to mention this dispute because Mr. Butterfield cannot be held wholly responsible for a building for which he only furnished general designs, and the construction of which he only superintended up to a certain point. The local architects, who have taken up the work of construction, maintain that they have sufficient clue for the completion of the building in keeping with the design; and, at any rate, it is not the first cathedral begun under one architect and finished under very different superintendence.

Many of the Melbourne churches are the reverse of beautiful. They were built after the revival of Gothic architecture in England, but before that influence was very widely spread. It must be allowed that the times just before Pugin and Gilbert Scott were specially bad times for church architecture. Moreover, intercourse with England was much more rare and difficult then than now, and the early days of a colony cannot be expected to be days of good taste; Nature has first to be conquered, and necessaries come before ornaments. But much more attention is now being paid to ecclesiastical architecture. The leading denominations are very evenly matched in numbers and wealth, and they vie with each other in their church building, as in other matters. After the cathedral, St. Francis is the best of the Roman Catholic churches, both for architecture and music. Wesley Church, in Lonsdale Street, is a very good

BURKE AND WILLS MONUMENT.

building, well proportioned throughout, and with a beautiful spire; but, probably, most people will consider the Scots Church, in Collins Street, the gem of church architecture in Melbourne. The style of architecture is Early English; the material, a brown freestone, faced with a white stone from Kakanui, in New Zealand. The spire has very graceful proportions, and its 212 feet of height make it the tallest in Melbourne and suburbs. Inside the church there is an air of great wealth and comfort. Its carpeted passages and well-upholstered pews make it a drawing-room amongst churches. The floor rises gradually to the end furthest from the pulpit. This fact, and the central position of the handsome pulpit, show a visitor at once that pulpit ministrations occupy the most important place in the services of the church. There is a fine organ, however, and the music, until differences unhappily arose which divided the congregation into sections, had a great reputation—evidence of a change in Presbyterianism since the days when an organ was condemned as a "kist o' whustles." The Independent Church does not look very much like an ecclesiastical edifice, but it has the great advantage of being admirably adapted for hearing. Wicked wags say that the intention of the founder was to turn the building to some other purpose, if it failed as a church. Of such failure there seems little prospect; the pulpit of this church has had some of the best preachers of the colony.

At the intersection of the streets, opposite these two churches, used to stand the Burke and Wills monument, but the exigencies of the tramways drove it from its position. The old site was certainly splendidly central; the new site for this monument is in Spring Street, at the north-eastern corner of the city. Melbourne is not at all rich in statues, and cannot afford to put a fine monument like this out of the way. A history of the exploring expedition in 1860, in commemoration of which this monument was erected, will be found elsewhere in this work. The preparations for the exploration, and its fatal termination, caused a great excitement in the public mind. At a later day, the enthusiasm that was created in Victoria by the heroic endurance and manly Christian character of General Gordon led to the determination to give to the Melbourne streets a second statue, worthy of its predecessor.

Government House, which occupies a fine site in the Domain, to the south of the city, is a building not much admired by people of taste. It has often been compared

THE SCOTS AND INDEPENDENT CHURCHES, COLLINS STREET.

GOVERNMENT HOUSE, FROM BOTANICAL GARDENS.

to a workhouse or to a factory. The story goes that Mr. Wardell, then the architect of the Public Works Department, prepared a beautiful design for a Gothic house, but the Prime Minister of the day, like Lord Palmerston, did not appreciate Gothic architecture for domestic purposes. He was one of those who think that Gothic is all very well for churches, possibly even for public halls, but is not suitable for private buildings. So he exclaimed "Bring me a book of designs," and on the first page there happened to be a picture of Osborne, of which he said, in a manner that some might call despotic, some vigorous, "That's the sort of house we want; build a house like that." Certainly the present Government House is a fair general imitation of Osborne. But there is this difference. Osborne has a background of trees, and a slight elevation; the Melbourne Government House, built on the top of a rising ground, has its outline brought out by a clear and often cloudless sky. The Governor's residence is certainly not beautiful; it must be reckoned a lost opportunity, for the position is splendid, and commands one of the finest views of the city of Melbourne. The most that can be said for the appearance of the house is that it is not equally bad from all points of view. The worst views are those of the whole length; the best are those, as from the Yarra or the Botanical Gardens, where the building is seen nearly end-wise. If not beautiful, it is certainly commodious, and some people would say that is better. The state apartments, dining-room, and drawing-room are very roomy, and the ball-room is one of the largest in the world. It is said of the Town Hall that instructions were given to the architect to make it a little larger every way than the Guildhall in London. Similar instructions are not known to have been given in the case of Government House, but it is often repeated with pride that the dimensions are larger, even if only a little larger, than those of the ball-room at Windsor. The danger for a Governor of Victoria is rather that he should be over-housed than have too little accommodation, but that is a fault on the right side for one who, from the nature of his position, must entertain many visitors. The proportions of the ball-room are admirable, and it is a magnificent sight to see the apartment crowded on a ball night with handsomely dressed guests, the bright uniforms of many officers mingling with the varied colours of the ladies' dresses. In this room, too, the Governor holds a levee on the Queen's birthday in each year, when more than a thousand citizens usually attend to show their loyalty.

THE TOWN HALL.

Princes Bridge is a convenient starting-point for a walk through Melbourne. It is the entrance by road from the south, and it lies close to two railway stations, one called after itself, the Princes Bridge Station, and not very long built; the other named Hobson's Bay Station. There used to be a short railway that led to the Bay; and the name still clings to the station, though the lines of the company which worked it have been absorbed into the State system of railways. Old Princes Bridge, which spanned the Yarra with one fine arch, 150 feet wide, was long the pride of Melbourne. It was opened with great pomp and ceremony, but after thirty years it was thought too narrow and inadequate. Tiresome restrictions had to be placed on the traffic crossing the bridge. It was at length determined to have a new and broader bridge, with a viaduct to keep the roadway at the level that it has a few yards to the north and a few hundred yards to the south. Not without great regret did many of the inhabitants of Melbourne see the fine old arch pulled down. Swanston Street is in a line with the St. Kilda Road, and on nearly the same level. The Anglican Cathedral stands on the immediate right. The Town Hall is at the corner, where Collins crosses Swanston Street. Further to the north, the side of the Melbourne Hospital, and the front of the Public Library, are features in the same street.

The Town Hall is very spacious, as has already been implied. It is a fine sight when the Town Hall is thronged for a public meeting, and the audience is held spell-bound by an orator; or when it is occupied for a concert by a company of ladies and gentlemen in evening attire; or, again, filled with gay masqueraders at a fancy dress ball. It is generally said that the room will hold four thousand; it most assuredly will not seat that number. But when the public mind is agitated upon some political question, for instance, the German occupation of New Guinea, no doubt fully four thousand manage to find standing room. About two thousand four hundred can be comfortably seated for a concert. One of the musical societies, known here by the German name of Liedertafel, has sometimes a pretty way of arranging the room, breaking up the long lines of seats by tree-ferns and pot-plants, and grouping the seats round small tables. The acoustic properties of the room cannot conscientiously be praised, but architects generally, whether of churches or of lecture-halls, do not seem to pay enough attention to the laws of acoustics. The best advice that can be given to one who has to speak in the Town Hall is "Hold up your head, and speak straight to the farther end of the room; do not turn to right or left in the course of your speech, and do not try to speak too loud." Two speakers out of three, however, even when these rules are followed, will not be heard in large portions of the room. The Town Hall has other smaller rooms, the offices of the Corporation, as well as a very handsome and well-proportioned Council Chamber, ornamented with portraits of municipal celebrities.

The city of Melbourne, it may here be mentioned, is divided into seven wards, each represented by an alderman and three councillors. The names of the wards exhibit a combination of loyalty to the Crown with colonial patriotism. Victoria and Albert need no explanation. Lonsdale and Latrobe were Governors of Victoria, Bourke and Gipps, of New South Wales, when what is now Victoria was yet unseparated from the parent colony. Smith was a public-spirited man, seven times Mayor of Melbourne, and of him it is remembered that he imported the first jackass (not laughing) into the colony. Lovers of euphonious names, however, cannot repress a feeling that Smith ward is not to be regarded as a success in nomenclature. The Mayor of

INTERIOR OF THE TOWN HALL.

Melbourne holds so important a position that many can be found to think he ought to receive the distinctive title of "Lord Mayor."

The Melbourne Hospital was founded in 1846. It is a good specimen of what is known as the Queen Anne order of architecture. It looks very roomy, and stands in grounds of its own, which, for a town site, are certainly extensive; but it has been the subject of very serious complaints, partly the result of overcrowding. Upon high medical authority it is said to be "saturated with septic poison," and whether this strong statement can be proved or not, it is quite certain that the hospital is not large enough, and not such as would be constructed in the present day.

Beyond the hospital stands the Public Library, with its fine façade. This institution consists of four departments, under the control of the same body of trustees, though one of the four, the Natural History Museum, is situated elsewhere, being at the back of the University. The three departments housed on this large block of ground are the Public Library, the National Gallery, and the Industrial Museum. The Library has two large reading-rooms, the Queen's and the Barry Hall, besides a newspaper-room. It is much frequented, the average attendance numbering considerably over one thousand a day. Boast is made that it is the freest library in the world. Any one is admitted without recommendation or restriction, and readers are permitted to help themselves to books from the shelves, the only exceptions being with respect to expensive works of art and medical books. The collection is very extensive, and, according to the article on "Libraries" in the "Encyclopædia Britannica" (ninth edition), there are only nine larger libraries in the United Kingdom. The National Gallery is a collection of modern pictures, amongst which many old favourites at the Royal Academy may be seen. Long's "Esther" and Webb's "Rotterdam" are probably the most admired by those who know, and Mrs. Butler's "Quatre Bras" is, through engravings, the most widely known; but an enormous picture called the "Brigands" is the favourite with the general public. The gallery also possesses portraits, some of great interest in early Australian history, which are soon to be housed in separate rooms, and some reproductions of the most famous statues and busts. Attached to the gallery is a school of painting, which is already beginning to produce good fruit. The Industrial Museum is after the pattern of South Kensington, and contains models of the fruits of the earth, models of mining apparatus, and specimens of domestic appliances. As is natural in a young museum, articles of this sort are better represented than curiosities, except in the matter of aboriginal weapons and implements, Australian and from the South Sea Islands, of which the collection is one of the best in the world. An institution of this kind must grow slowly, and on every side an air of incompleteness hangs about the exterior of the buildings.

Across the street, from the back of the territory of the Public Library, stand the Working Man's College and the old Supreme Court. The Working Man's College is chiefly due to the liberality of one citizen, the Hon. Francis Ormond, who in this as in other ways has shown a wise interest in the progress of education. An unfortunate mistake was made by the Council responsible for its management, in not commencing the institution with lectures and teaching, and waiting to proceed with a building when the need of one was proved; nor is it quite clear whether the college is to be of a technical nature, or, like its London prototype, is to fill up the gaps in general education. At any rate, it is most satisfactory that on its finished side the building looks handsome, and that it is most conveniently arranged.

It would not be easy to find two buildings with the same purpose presenting a stronger contrast than the Old and the New Law Courts. The latter might fairly be described by the French name, "the Palace of Justice." No doubt it is right and there are palatial establishments in which modern banks delight to do their business. Banks, it must be mentioned, are a great element in Australian life. There is no country in the world in which, in proportion to the population, such a large banking business is done or so many accounts kept. What with branches in very small townships, and palaces in the large towns, this business has outward and visible signs which cannot be overlooked. From a few minutes after six in the evening until eight in the morning, and for the whole of Sunday, Collins Street is almost deserted.

Other parts of Melbourne have their special characters. At the west end of Flinders Street there is a strong nautical flavour. The houses there are opposite the wharves, though at a considerable interval; and it is natural that the sailors should frequent them, and that the shops should "cater" for the tastes of sailors. Little Flinders Street, or Flinders Lane, or "the Lane," as it is sometimes fondly called, is the street for large wholesale warehouses of ready-made clothing, woollen goods, and the like. The local name for all this is "soft-goods."

MELBOURNE HOSPITAL.

North of Collins Street is Little Collins Street, a part of which, lying well west of the centre, is known as Chancery Lane. It need hardly be explained that this is where the barristers' chambers are. On one side goes forth Temple Court, which has, however, of late been nearly deserted in favour of a set of chambers, more modern and more commodious, on the other side of Chancery Lane, called after Lord Chancellor Selborne, equally well known as Sir Roundell Palmer. Besides being more commodious, these chambers are somewhat nearer to the new Courts.

Bourke Street has a character of its own. It is a street devoted both to business and to pleasure. It has many large shops; but it is more important to notice that here are the theatres, and the *cafés* and the shops devoted to the theatre-frequenters.

In half the street—the eastern half—there is as much traffic an hour before midnight as at any period of the day. In the centre of Bourke Street is the General Post

THE NEW LAW COURTS.

Office, from the tower of which the arrival of mails from England is notified by flags in the day-time and by lanterns at night. The Post Office is not a small building; but it gradually became too small for its work, which, as in England, includes the Telegraph and Savings Banks, and must soon also include the carriage of parcels. In England the Post Office is a source of profit to the general revenue. In the colonies, because of sparser population and great distances, it is not. This colony, therefore, has no penny postage; but a generation that has seen the reduction on English letters from a shilling to half that price, with a proportionate increase in speed, lives in hope of further postal improvements. From the Post Office, by the way, distances are measured: the number on a milestone after "to Melbourne" meaning the number of miles to this centre.

Bourke Street has other sights. To the west of Elizabeth Street, the space for some distance seems devoted to horses. There are saddlers' shops in a row, and then great yards for the sale of horses, carriages, and carts. In the morning horses are being trotted in the street to show their paces. Nearly opposite the Post Office stands Cole's Book Arcade, an interesting place, with a brilliant-coloured rainbow for a sign. By the attractions of music people are encouraged to frequent the shop, and to read books in the hope that they will buy them. Mr. Froude was most struck with the number of young men engaged in skimming shilling dreadfuls and exciting novels. But had he known the shop well he would have found much else, solid food for the intellect as well as stimulants for the imagination. Passing further up Bourke Street, towards the Houses of Parliament, the visitor comes to the Eastern Market, a comparatively recent erection on the part of the City Corporation. This is commodious, and complete with modern appliances, including the electric light; and yet there are found those who regret the old and rougher Paddy's Market. Saturday night was the time to visit this in all its glory, when side by side with the genuine marketers there were found the quacks and the conjurers, who formed the attraction of an old English fair. But even though the fun may not now be so fast and furious, there is much that will interest a visitor to the Eastern Market. Even in the day-time it is well frequented; at night there is a much larger attendance; on Saturday it is so crowded that locomotion is difficult, and with the crowd there is such a noise that a lover of quiet had better stay away. Any one who wants a dog, or a canary, or a parrot, or any of the many Australian birds, can here find what he seeks. Every kind of article is being sold by cheap jacks, who shout at the top of their voices. Here men are trying their strength by blows upon a machine; others are testing their lungs, or being weighed. A little further on a man has charge of an electric machine, and is prepared to give a shock for a consideration. Vendors of vegetable pills, and other quack medicines, seem to be doing a roaring trade; and here stands an ardent disciple of phrenology, who, for a very small sum, is prepared to feel your bumps and tell your character therefrom, or will tell you how to educate your children in accordance with bump-lore, until one is reminded of the father of Mr. Midshipman Easy.

Leaving behind us—may we hope?—everything in the nature of nostrums, quackery, and the art of gulling fellow-creatures, we come to Parliament House. When this pile is completed, according to

MELBOURNE UNIVERSITY.

THE OLD LAW COURTS.

THE MINT.

its design, the great busy street will be worthily closed. On the granting of Parliamentary government to the colony, it was determined to have a noble plan for a building, and to carry out parts of the design. Melbourne has often been described as a city of unfinished buildings. The charge is true, but the incompleteness is based upon worthy reasons and a care for posterity. Better a part of a good design, than a whole building executed upon a plan which must in after days prove too small or too mean. The present generation suffers, but posterity gains. Parliament House has long looked very ugly, because unfinished. The inside has been attended to first, and the two Houses of Legislature have handsome debating chambers, separated by a very spacious and handsome lobby, with a well-arranged and well-stocked library. With the exception of their debating chambers all the arrangements of the building—library, refreshment-rooms, billiard-rooms, and the like—are shared in common by the members of both Houses. Following the precedent of the Lords, the Upper House has a far more gaily decorated apartment than the Lower; in it the ceremonies of opening and closing Parliament by His Excellency the Governor take place. In addition to the billiard-room, Parliament House has an open asphalt tennis-court and a large garden. When the tennis-court was first proposed, much fun was made of the proposal, which easily lends itself to ridicule. But, the idea is the same as in the case of a billiard-room—that it is desirable to keep members in the precincts of the House, though not necessarily in the House itself, when their attendance may at any time be required. Many would expect better legislation from legislators fresh from tennis, than from legislators fresh from billiards.

Not far from Parliament House are the Public Offices, with respect to which the question will arise whether they are not too large for a young country with a population of a million. When the answer is given that every nook and corner of the building is occupied, doubt still finds place whether the colony be not over-governed. Architecturally the old Treasury is the handsomest of the offices. As a building it is too thin, but it has an excellent front.

One other street in Melbourne has a very special character—Little Bourke Street, the Chinese quarter. There are a great many Chinese in Australia, and some few have risen to the position of wealthy merchants. As a rule which knows few exceptions, they are very industrious, and render good service to housekeepers as hawkers of fish and vegetables. In mining places they can make a living where no Englishman can. But they are not good colonists, because they come with the intention of saving as much money as they can scrape together, and then returning to China. Moreover, they bring no women with them, and by providing temptations to gambling, and in other ways, are the cause of not a little immorality. Our artists, under the protection of two policemen, ventured into the Chinese haunts in Little Bourke Street, and have reproduced some features of the strange life which is daily going on there within a few hundred yards of the Chambers of Legislature. But this subject is so strange and special that we have devoted to it a separate chapter.

EXHIBITION BUILDINGS, MELBOURNE.

## GREATER MELBOURNE.

Distinctive Features—Richmond Park—The Yarra Yarra—Rowing Clubs and River Picnics—Suburban Municipalities—Means of Locomotion—Collingwood—Prahran—Hotham—Exhibition Building and the "Zoo"—The Colonial Colney Hatch—Toorak—South Yarra—St. Kilda—Brighton—Flemington—Public Holidays—The Ports of Melbourne: Sandridge and Williamstown—Origin of Local Names—Admiral Collingwood.

IT will be of interest to consider what are the distinctive features of Melbourne. And herein we are speaking not only of the city, but of the city together with its suburbs, of what, following the precedent of the popular name "Greater Britain," has been called Greater Melbourne. The two features that will strike every stranger are spaciousness and variety. The first of these shows itself in the great extent of ground that is covered, the width of the streets and main roads, the large number of public parks and gardens by which over-building has been prevented, or, at any rate, its inconveniences modified. The width of the streets helps to give the city proper an air of magnificence. Where the traffic is considerable, a feeling of satisfaction arises that ample provision has been made for it. But the roads are too wide. In a country where violent wind is not unknown, and where dust rises even to the magnitude of a plague, very broad roads and wide street spaces are a real inconvenience. It is true that the dust nuisance would be much mitigated, though not altogether removed, whilst a decided improvement would be made in the general aspect, if the roads, being far too wide for the traffic, were made narrower by plantations of trees along their sides. These plantations should be fenced for the protection of the trees, and inside the enclosure there should be grass. This has been done with good effect at various points, but the misfortune of Melbourne roads lies in the variety of municipal government, and in the need of some central authority or metropolitan board of works.

It is unfortunately true that in the decade after 1876 little or no progress was made. One road which was formerly splendidly smooth has become a byword and a disgrace. The St. Kilda Road was kept in admirable order in the days of tolls, but tolls were abolished by the legislature without providing a substitute. This road suffers from a divided jurisdiction, for the division line between the city of Melbourne and Emerald Hill (or South Melbourne) is the middle of this road, and though the people of Melbourne are famed for their practical business qualities, they seem unable to discover a method of keeping this particular road in good repair. There are several places near Melbourne where the road is so broad as to be a simple nursery of dust, and where a wise municipality would have made a central plantation, circular or triangular. In Paris such spaces would have been seized for a little garden, with a fountain playing in the midst, and pleasant seats for the wayfarer. These little neglected opportunities are the more to be regretted because Melbourne has beautiful gardens on the large scale. The wise foresight which almost encircled Melbourne proper with public gardens, driving future suburbs further afield, and the skill with which these gardens have been laid out, have provided Melbourne with admirable places of public resort. Some of them are as delightful as any gardens in the world. There is shade in summer heat; there are spacious and inviting lawns; there are flowers and trees to charm the eye.

The view of the Fitzroy Gardens given below was taken on a lovely moonlight night worthy of the tropics, when it was so light that the artist could without difficulty

IN THE FITZROY GARDENS.

see to sketch. "Weeping willows," to use his own words, "giants compared with English willows, were trailing their branches; there were deep shadows with tender half-tones; the grass and fern-tree gully were filled with mystery; whilst glintings of silver, or rather golden, moonlight fell on edges of trunks, fronds, and leaves; and the whole scene was made musical by the plashing of a tiny stream hidden from view under a spreading greenery."

Passing, however, from poetry to measurements, the ordinary width of main roads is three chains, and an exaggerator, with a touch of American humour, once said that it took him half a day to cross the St. Kilda Road, which in parts is even wider than the orthodox three chains. Side roads often reach to two chains, and a man has been heard to urge it as a reproach against another that he "lived in a one-chain road" in much the same spirit as that in which the American tourist upbraided the Oxford traveller who stopped at the ancient city of Trent with "Surely you are not going to visit such a one-horse place!"

Although land is very expensive in the near neighbourhood of the city, and fetches a good price throughout the suburbs, private gardens abound, especially along the main highways. Villas stand in what Anglo-Indians call a "compound." This is a combination of shrubbery and garden; sometimes there is a grassy lawn, oftener a lawn-tennis ground, here generally, in spite of the prefix "lawn," laid in asphalt. The result of these large spaces is that the suburbs are far apart. One of the American cities is known as "the city of magnificent distances." A name of the kind would be not inappropriate to Melbourne; and the tax upon the ladies of visit-paying, which modern society demands, is made much heavier because of the distances that have to be traversed between friend and friend.

The second feature in the appearance of Melbourne is its diversity. A poor house stands side by side with a good house, a cottage, one might almost say a hovel, in close proximity to a palace. It is only fair to say that there is nothing in Melbourne like the "long, unlovely street" of London; nothing so hideous as Gower Street or Harley Street, neither of which expresses more, as has been caustically remarked, than "the impotence of the architect to express anything." There is nothing like Regent Street in London or the Rue Rivoli in Paris, for in the streets there has been very little continuous building, or building in a block upon the plans of a single architect. Subject to certain municipal restrictions, each man has built as seemed good in his own eyes or in the eyes of his architect. There are handsome individual buildings, some few in admirable taste, but the general effect is often marred by the surroundings. The eye at once marks a great difference in the height of the houses as well as in their architectural style.

In 1882 a traveller remarked that in this city there were no houses with more than two storeys, but, on account of the expense of the land, some of the newer shops in Melbourne proper have been built very tall, reminding a visitor of houses in older cities; and these shops have a tendency to look absurd, because their neighbours are so much shorter in stature. In time much of this inequality will be removed. The rapid growth of Melbourne partially explains it. But then it is not all new cities, or new parts of cities, that are built irregularly. The buildings that have been run up in the last decade in new parts of Paris, for example, are as regular as the houses in the older quarters of the city. We must seek the difference rather in the character of the people. The Victorians are great lovers of independence, and are, many of them, sprung from a stock that cherished as its principle what Burke describes as the "dissidence of dissent, and the Protestantism of our Protestant" character. And yet, early years spoke the native language fluently, maintains that this is a popular delusion, and that the name means "Big Gum Trees." Unfortunately, the native languages are fast disappearing, and will soon be "dead" in a sense other than that in which we apply this epithet to the classics.

Within the circuit of Greater Melbourne no fewer than seventeen boroughs are included. Of these, five are classed as cities, one is a town, and eleven are only boroughs. It may be asked wherein the distinction lies. If in England, according to the old doctrine, a bishop and cathedral made a city, what makes it in Victoria? The Local Government Act requires that a borough shall not exceed in area six square miles, that no point in such area shall be more than six miles distant from any other, and that there shall be not less than 300 inhabitant householders. All towns and cities are boroughs, distinguished from other boroughs by the amount of gross municipal revenue in the year preceding the declaration of them as such by the Governor in Council. A gross revenue of £10,000 makes a town, one of £20,000 a city.

The five cities are South Melbourne, or Emerald Hill (population, 32,500), Prahran (27,000), Richmond (26,503), Collingwood (25,500), and Fitzroy (23,500). Many an ancient and historic city in England has a smaller population than any of these. Hotham, with a population of a little under 20,000, is the solitary "town." And the eleven suburban boroughs, in order of population, are St. Kilda, Williamstown, Port Melbourne, or Sandridge, Brunswick, Hawthorn, Footscray, Kew, Brighton, Essendon, Flemington, with Kensington, whilst the latest declared is Northcote. Each of these has a mayor and corporation, with all the appurtenances of municipal government. Upon public occasions, as at a Governor's levee, the furs of mayors and aldermen are very conspicuous. These, with the wigs of judges and barristers, give rise to the reflection that the English are a very conservative race, or in a new country they would have devised new emblems. The tall black hat is still our badge of respectability, whilst furs and wigs have often to be worn in a summer heat which makes them quite intolerable. Another visible sign of municipal government is the large number of handsome town-halls, useful for public meetings, concerts, and balls, though dancers naturally object to a floor lately trodden by the ordinary working boot. With these town-halls are combined the municipal offices and council chambers. The neighbourhood of Melbourne reminds one of Belgium for the pride which is taken in the externals of municipal government.

We have already noticed the way in which towns expand into suburbs. Business and domestic life are nowadays quite distinct. This separation was common with the merchant before it was true of the tradesman, but now it is pretty general with all classes. The barrister lives away from his chambers, the solicitor from his office, and even in some cases the doctor from his consulting rooms. Melbourne is singularly well supplied with residential suburbs. Railway lines go out in different directions, and along all these lines there run many full up-trains in the morning and down-trains in the later part of the afternoon. There are no fewer than fifty suburban railway stations, and some fifteen more which lie a little beyond the radius that can be fairly called suburban. As far as Richmond six lines abreast (*i.e.*, three up and three down) have been laid, and at certain periods in the day, though trains run every ten minutes, every train is crowded.

Besides the trains, locomotion is assisted by omnibuses, trams, and cabs. In former

THE "EIGHT HOURS A DAY" PROCESSION PASSING THE TOWN HALL.

days the Melbourne cab was a kind of Irish car, popularly known as a "jingle." Most of the cab-drivers are still Irish, but the jingle has been ousted by the one-horse waggonette, holding six persons. These can either be hired separately or used in common as a kind of small omnibus. To many of the suburbs there is a line of waggonettes running at regular intervals, each passenger paying only threepence. In the

## MEANS OF LOCOMOTION.

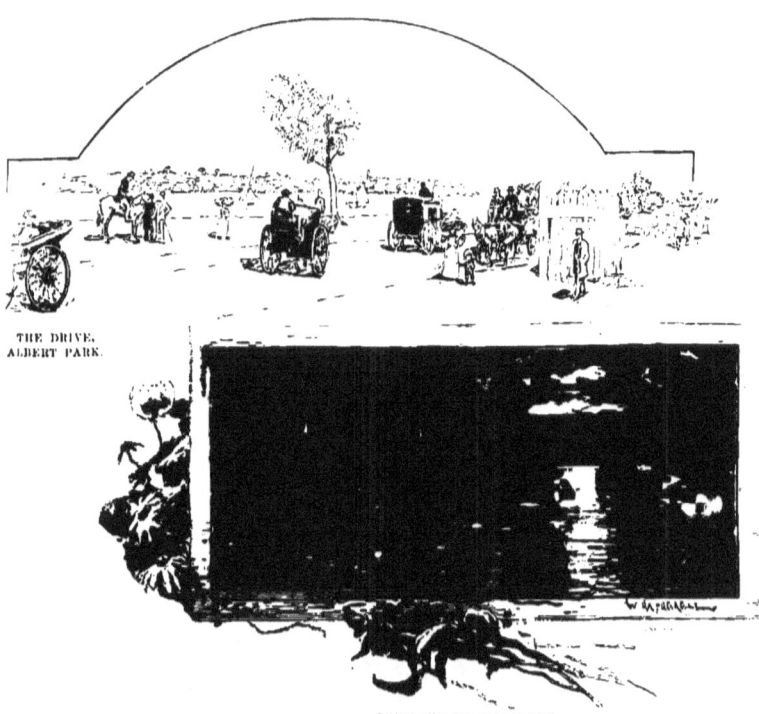

THE DRIVE, ALBERT PARK.

THE LAKE BY MOONLIGHT.

chief streets there are stands of comfortable hansoms. Stands of drays and furniture-waggons also are to be found. That Melbourne omnibuses do a good business is shown by the high price that shares in the Company fetch. The ordinary omnibus is in many cases being replaced by tram-cars. These are pulled by a continuous rope. Underground, between the tram-lines, is a cylinder in which a strong steel rope works. Near the middle of each line there is an engine-house, the steam machinery in which causes the rope to continuously revolve. Each passenger car is preceded by what is called a dummy, in which there is a gripping apparatus. When this has hold of the rope underneath, the car goes forward, at the same pace up-hill and down-hill. As the rope is let go, a break is put on, and the car stops. Since the break is very powerful, a car can be stopped in a very few feet. The gravest risk of accident is that when two cars are passing each other one may be hidden behind the other. A warning bell is, therefore, frequently employed, and at night very brilliant lights also.

The different suburbs have characters of their own. The working-men are most at home in Collingwood, Prahran, and Hotham. In certain streets in those places the cheapest shops are situated. In Collingwood the inhabitants are most crowded together, and some of the streets are as narrow as in an old English town. Prahran has in the last few years made great strides. Large spaces which had not a house are now covered. Many of the houses are small; but at the eastern end, at Hawksburn and Armadale, there are more of the kind described by auctioneers as desirable villa residences. Even the small houses of an Australian town do not in their variety look so mean as the rows of small houses in such towns as Sunderland or Hartlepool, or as the acres upon acres of monotonous rows that occupy the east and south-east of London. The houses of the Melbourne working-men have some little individuality; and though the extensive use of corrugated iron is not a picturesque feature of them, the verandas give a character lacking in the London houses. It is at once noted that a great many are built of wood, which is a clean material when new, but implies that long life is not intended for the house. Fires are frequent, and in the chief suburbs there are watch-towers erected, where a bell is rung the moment that a fire is seen; and devices are used in ringing the bell to denote the quarter in which the fire has been seen. Wood has the great advantage of cooling quickly. When a hot wind blows, as it sometimes does for three days, a stone or brick house is at first a great protection, but in the end it is an oven, and remains one for long after the wind has changed. A wooden house becomes quickly hot, but cools as evening comes on; and to be cool at night is of course a great boon. Hotham is a large working-men's suburb on the north-west of Melbourne. The Benevolent Asylum is partly in Hotham and partly in the city. Carlton and Fitzroy may be described as middle-class or bourgeois suburbs. Emerald Hill and Richmond might fall under the head either of middle-class or working-class cities. Between Emerald Hill and the St. Kilda Road is a large tract of low-lying land, on which Canvas Town used to stand. When the gold rush took place, enormous crowds came from all parts of the world to Melbourne. There were not sufficient houses to accommodate the new arrivals. Canvas Town, as its name implies, was a collection of tents, and many a one of the new-comers was glad enough to secure a tent, and ground on which to pitch it. The ground on which Canvas Town stood more than thirty years later was not occupied with houses, because the situation is so low that it is sometimes flooded by the Yarra. But it is hoped that Sir John Coode's improvements will prevent floods in the future. At the south side of Emerald Hill stands the Albert Park. This has a lagoon, partly natural, partly artificial, which gives opportunities for sailing and rowing. On certain days in the summer a fashionable gathering of carriages and riders assembles in the Albert Park, and regales itself with the music of a band. Some have tried to give to this assemblage the name of Rotten Row, but the name is exotic, and it is a question whether the institution will take root.

Carlton is a large suburb in the north of Melbourne. Part of it is becoming the smokiest of all quarters of Melbourne. There are huge factory chimneys which do not by any means consume their own smoke. Fortunately, they are rather intermittent in their action, but at times they send forth into the air volumes of smoke which threaten, unless legislation intervene, a reproduction of the English "black country." Here dwell the workers in iron, and here are certain very large mills, and there is a monster brewery, the proprietor of which is a public benefactor, who has set up a large town clock. Melbourne is becoming smoky, and sometimes the atmosphere, if the whole truth must be told, is positively murky. But let us add that it is only open to that grave accusation on exceptional occasions, for we should hardly like our English readers to think that we always, or even often, live in such an atmosphere as that. As a rule, Melbourne skies can be compared, for clearness, to Italian, but this character will not long be preserved unless something be soon done in the way of smoke prevention.

Carlton is a suburb that includes many institutions within its bound. Of these the largest is the Exhibition Building, in which the successful Victorian Exhibition of 1880 and 1881 was held. It occupies the middle of the large Carlton Gardens. The greater part of the building then erected was permanent, though for the Exhibition there were extensive annexes of a temporary nature. In the interval between exhibitions the great hall is used for various purposes—for monster bazaars, for dog and poultry shows, for very large meetings. Part of it has been used as a Government printing office, the former office having been burnt down, and part has been fitted up as an aquarium. In Carlton also the visitor will find the Cemetery, the University, and the Women's Hospital. The Cemetery is like unto most large town cemeteries, carefully portioned out amongst religious denominations, so that those who have been divided in life may be divided also in death. Beyond the University and its affiliated colleges, on the northwest of Melbourne, is the Royal Park, standing high and healthy. A portion of it has been set apart as the ground of the Acclimatisation Society, generally known as "the Zoo." The collection of animals to be seen here is well worth a visit. It is, of course, especially strong in native specimens. Most of the creatures have plenty of space. Kangaroos and wallaby may be seen in a paddock, and rabbits are not kept in hutches, nor rats in cages. Wild animals, however, are still housed in dens that must be to them inconveniently small. As London and Paris have been surpassed in the space given to many animals, it may be hoped that the lions and tigers will be granted space as large as they have in London, and perhaps a return compliment might be paid to our friends the kangaroos. Those in the Gardens in Regent's Park are so miserably cramped that they are much to be pitied.

Amongst other suburbs of a different character, Hawthorn and Kew may be mentioned as very pleasant residential suburbs, rich in villas and gardens. In Kew two lunatic asylums are situated, one called after the suburb, and the other Yarra Bend. In popular conversation the latter, perhaps from its peculiar name, takes the place occupied in England by Colney Hatch or Hanwell—"a joke worthy of Yarra Bend," "conduct of which no one would be guilty, except an inmate of Yarra Bend." Of the two asylums, one is a barrack, and the other is divided on the cottage system.

The suburb with the most magnificent mansions is Toorak, which is largely affected by wealthy squatters, especially successful Scotchmen. The question is often asked why

Australia does not devise an architecture suited to its own wants. Perhaps some day it will, and in such architecture of the future the verandah and the balcony will be found to play a prominent part. An outward sign of wealth can be seen in the two spires that ornament Toorak Hill. The place is still embosomed in trees that stand

THE PIER AND ESPLANADE, ST. KILDA.

round the big houses. The native name certainly has a somewhat uncouth sound, and the wife of a Presbyterian minister coming here from Scotland created some amusement by deploring that her husband was being "sent to a place called Toorak," when really the lines had fallen to them in about the pleasantest place in the colony. South Yarra, which has no independent municipal existence, has upon high authority been described as the place of residence of "curled darlings." Lying just beyond the precincts of

Government House, this suburb may be thought to gain some reflected glory from proximity to vice-royalty. St. Kilda is a favourite seaside place within easy reach of Melbourne, is provided with large hotels, and is proud of its baths, pier, and esplanade. The young Australian, it is well known, is not easily abashed, and a story is told of one on a visit to England who, being shown Brighton, with its four consecutive miles of substantial houses, only remarked to his host, "You should see St. Kilda." St. Kilda is within a very short distance of Melbourne, and its pier is a

THE PORTS OF MELBOURNE.

favourite resort on Sundays, its baths on any hot day in summer. Brighton lies further off, and is generally a quiet place, covering a large area, but with houses somewhat sparsely scattered over it. A man might still move out from a crowded suburb to Brighton to enjoy "three acres and a cow." No less than five suburban railway stations use the name of Brighton—surely a mark of poverty of invention. The parts of the Brighton district that lie furthest away from the sea are much affected by market gardeners, whose carts move marketwards in the night, especially of Fridays, returning laden with stable manure on Saturday afternoons. But the time to see Brighton is on a public holiday, when it is the favourite place of popular resort. The beach thronged with holiday-makers is a subject for an artist like Frith. The Chinaman in the foreground of the accompanying view is an Australian speciality; otherwise the scene might well be laid at some English watering-place. By-the-bye, the term "watering-place" is not generally used in this sense in the colony, but literally for a place where horses are taken to drink. A thoughtful boy once asked his master whether horses in England drank salt water, because he found in his geography that the watering-places were at the seaside.

On public holidays the trains are crowded in a way that to an Englishman brings back reminiscences of the Handel Festival at the Crystal Palace. He would be a churl indeed who objected to five additional persons standing in a railway compartment that has its usual complement of ten. It is often said that in Australia there are more public holidays than in England, and that when opportunities offer of holiday-making they are not neglected. Perhaps it is the sunnier climate, perhaps the higher average of prosperity, but loyalty gives two genuine holidays in Melbourne, where in England one only is observed, and that partially. Australians celebrate not only the Queen's birthday, but also that of the Prince of Wales. Many Englishmen do not even know when the Prince of Wales's birthday falls, but no Australian is ignorant of the date. The Lord Mayor's Show falls in London's foggiest month, but "the ninth" is in our bonny spring. Church festivals are respected by many who pay attention to no other ordinance of the Church. Christmas and New Year fall at a time of year when the weather is usually fine, tempting men out of doors. Up country, a race meeting is an excuse for the proclamation of a local holiday, and on the occasion of the Melbourne Cup all the shops, and most of the schools in Melbourne, are closed. Fancy an English school with a holiday for Derby Day! Here the practice is defended on the ground that discipline is sure to be broken by parents taking some of the children with them; and parents who think races dangerous have holidays themselves, and take their children elsewhere to avoid contamination. It should be added that in our holiday crowds there is a good deal of noise and merriment, but that few of the pleasure-seekers are seen under the influence of alcohol.

The most horsey part of the neighbourhood of Melbourne is Flemington, where is the great racecourse, that has been so often favourably compared with the English racecourses. Trainers and training stables are not far off. Of late years a second racing colony has appeared at the other side of Melbourne, near the racecourse at Caulfield. To a non-racing man it seems as if every week there were some races or other at no great distance from Melbourne. Almost every Saturday little boys in the streets solicit him to buy "correct cards."

At Flemington great attention is paid to the comfort of visitors. A magnificent grand stand has been erected, capable of holding 15,000 spectators, and in front of it a large and prettily-arranged lawn. The great day in the year is the Melbourne Cup, a race which does not depend on any ecclesiastical festival, but is generally run on the first Tuesday in November. Visitors come from all parts of the colonies, from Queensland, New Zealand, Western Australia; and many go to the races on that day who

# THE PORTS OF MELBOURNE.

never attend a racecourse on any other day in the year. Ignorant even of the horses' names, some go to meet friends, or to see the spectators. The ladies' dresses are observed quite as much as the races, and many ladies spend fabulous sums on the toilets that are there closely inspected. Mr. Worth, of Paris, is believed to know the importance of the Melbourne Cup. In the year 1885 it was estimated that 123,000 persons were present. The Racing Club gives away annually no less a sum than £19,000; and since the establishment of the Club a total of £217,900 has through its agency been distributed.

It would be absurd to describe either Sandridge or Williamstown as simply a suburb of Melbourne, yet both are very important adjuncts to the city. They are the ports of Melbourne, though it must be remembered that Melbourne is itself a port. It has been already stated that the advice of the distinguished engineer, Sir John Coode, has been obtained by the Melbourne Harbour Trust; and that when all his improvements have been carried out, the passage up the Yarra will be made easier, and open to larger vessels. These at present stay at Williamstown or Sandridge, the large steamers, as a rule, at the former place, and the large sailing-vessels at the latter. The large ocean steamers belonging to the Peninsular and Oriental Company, those of the Orient line, and the French Messagerie steamers, all of which carry mails, now come alongside the Williamstown Pier. When one of the mail steamers is departing, especially if it carries away some very popular citizen, the pier is even dangerously crowded, and the whole scene singularly animated. Not a few tears have been shed on Williamstown Pier; and it has been the place of not a few joyous meetings. When a popular sailing ship departs, it is generally drawn off into the open roadstead of Hobson's Bay, and those who wish to see their friends off go to and fro in a small steamer. A charge of a florin damps the enthusiasm, and diminishes, if it does not altogether prevent, overcrowding. And if the departing guest be very popular, with a reputation for horses or dogs, or is some "potent voice of Parliament," a special tug or steamer will be hired by his friends. And if he be of Scotch extraction, the bagpipes will be requisitioned for the occasion, to the discomfiture of mere Saxons. Sandridge is nearer Melbourne, but Williamstown has the advantage of its rival in the possession of a large dry dock, into which so large a ship as H.M.S. *Nelson* can pass, and there be thoroughly overhauled. Not only Williamstown, but all Melbourne, may be proud of this dry dock. Its proper title is the Alfred Graving Dock. It is the first sight that, on arrival, many a visitor is taken to see. On a Sunday a great crowd always gathers at both the ports. Sight-seers now claim it as a right to be allowed to go over the ships and steamers that lie alongside the piers. The result is that they swarm over them, sometimes not quietly, nor without mischief. Sunday is by no means a popular day with captains and officers in port.

At Williamstown there is to be seen a little white tower, formerly a lighthouse, and now used chiefly to mark the time by the descent of a ball when the hour of noon is telegraphed from the Melbourne Observatory.

Probably most visitors reach Melbourne by one of the mail steamers, and therefore approach by way of Williamstown, and thence by rail. Unfortunately, the railway journey from Williamstown is tedious, because the line has to skirt round the north of Hobson's Bay, and through country so dull and uninteresting that the visitor is to be congratulated who makes his first acquaintance with it after dark. The most thriving suburbs through which the line runs are Yarraville and Footscray. Though not amongst the most fashionable, they are yet very prosperous places. The former name is an unsatisfactory compound of French with the aboriginal language, and permits the inhabitants to pass under the unfortunate soubriquet of "Yarravillains."

The names of the suburbs can be grouped under four heads—native names, names of places elsewhere, names of people, and fancy names. Of these, the first are the best and most distinctive, but there are, unfortunately, very few of them—Prahran, Toorak, and South Yarra. The first of these used to be accented on the first syllable; the accent now always falls on the last. Some say the waggonette drivers hailing for passengers altered the pronunciation, finding the name easier to pronounce with the accent on the second syllable. The names of places elsewhere are the least satisfactory, for they invite comparison, or at least introduce associations, and seem generally due to poverty of invention on the part of the namer. Such English names as Windsor and Kew make a new arrival look out for the castle or the famous gardens. Brighton, Malvern, and Richmond suggest comparisons which cannot be sustained. Sometimes we have foreign towns like Coburg and Brunswick. Balaclava is one of a batch of Crimean names that mark the date of the laying out of the suburb; others, applied to roads and streets, are Alma, Inkerman, and Redan. Balaclava has been promoted from a road to a district. Amongst the fanciful names are Hawthorn, (called after the bush, and not after the American novelist), Hawksburn, Armadale, and St. Kilda. There is good authority for saying that the last of these was named after a yacht, *The Lady of St. Kilda*, the property of Sir Thomas Acland, and not directly after the seldom-visited island that lies beyond the Western Hebrides.

Two suburbs with fanciful, but distinctive designations, Emerald Hill and Sandridge, have lately thought it worth while to shed their names, and ring confusing changes on the name of Melbourne. It may be quite true that the former was no longer on a green hill, just as Newcastle dates from the time of William Rufus. But "South Melbourne," the new style and title of Emerald Hill, sounds like a denial of the separate existence of the suburb. Port Melbourne, the new name for Sandridge, seems to suggest that when the weary traveller to Melbourne has reached the pier he has reached his goal, which is not quite the case.

Williamstown is evidently named from Queen Victoria's predecessor. Hotham and Fitzroy are called after Governors of the colony; Northcote, after Sir Stafford Northcote, the late Lord Iddesleigh. One of the most populous of the suburban cities has honoured itself by assuming the name of a great English sailor. The name of Nelson is used frequently in these colonies, and so is that of Wellington: they stand for towns and provinces in New Zealand, and for legislative provinces in Victoria. Wellington is a mountain in Tasmania, as well as a small town in New South Wales.

Nelson's companion in arms is held in memory in the city of Collingwood; and as this worthy's memory seems to be growing somewhat dim with this later generation, it

## LITTLE BOURKE STREET.

Among the Chinese at Midnight—Lotteries—Chinese Shops—A Typical Cookshop—"The Grand Secret"—A Gambling Hell—A Barber at Work—"Nance" going Home—Opium Dens—Taking a "Pull"—Vice in a Veil—Pandemonium—Philosophy under Difficulties—A Devoted Housebreaker.

LITTLE BOURKE STREET is a world apart from the city of Melbourne, and the race which occupies its crowded courts seems to have no connection with the other people who by day or night promenade along the pavements of Bourke Street proper. Few Victorians who look with just pride upon the vast, clean-kept streets and lofty buildings of their monster city know or dream of the life so far removed from all their ideals of home comfort which is seething quietly a few feet from where they are walking and laughing in happy ignorance. Let me begin by lifting a single corner of the veil which nicely covers up all, and show a scene or two from the Chinese quarter.

With two detectives as our guides, for no sane man would think of venturing into those quarters alone, particularly at night, we did the round, and as might be expected under the circumstances, saw everything *couleur de rose*. Our visit had evidently been expected. Men talk of the advances of civilisation, of telephones, and the like, but the rapidity with which news can circulate through thieves' quarters surpasses all the inventions of modern science. We began our walk at 9 p.m., having made our arrangements with the courteous head of the police about five hours before; but we had not advanced ten yards into the street before a woman hailed one of the guides with the cheerful words, "They all know you are coming down to-night with two gentlemen, so you won't see much fun." Possibly we had been seen and watched coming from the detective station, and so the password had travelled to and through the whole district.

First we visited the shops where lottery tickets are sold to the Chinese. The law prohibits any being sold to Europeans, therefore we had no chance of testing Dame Fortune, but the system was thoroughly explained by our friends, and the lottery vendors were "child-like and bland," most politely allowing us to see and handle everything, regarding us the while with that placid air and gentle smile so characteristic of the Celestials. The mysteries of the lottery ticket systems are too intricate to enter upon now, but everything seemed fair and above board. Regret would cross the mind that we were not permitted to purchase a few—a regret which was somewhat diminished when we heard so much of the losses, and so little of the gains, of this very openhanded game of Chinese lottery. It seems a strange combination, but all the Chinese gamble, and all smoke opium, yet they are industrious and cleanly, rising early and working late, and on Saturdays their week's savings go to the Lottery Bank or the Fan-Tan. Some people deny the cleanliness, but writing from personal experiences of the Melbourne Chinese, I boldly affirm that cleanly they are.

Some of these Chinese shops are delicious in colour and picturesqueness—lanterns swinging about, throwing down soft light on the assembled figures; jars and grotesque china monsters standing on the shelves; bills, boxes, and packages; vermilion labelled with quaint Chinese characters; rice books set before the markers, who were dotting off tickets with their vermilion or black paint pots and pointed poonah-brushes. Groups of forbidding-looking Europeans, or rather a conglomeration of nationalities, half-castes and white men, were lounging about, casting scowling, yet timid, hangdog glances on the intruders, muttering sounds like maledictions, yet not plain enough to be resented. Above the counter-top stood an altar-piece with its hideous god, or rather complex symbol of Nature, and before it the daily offering, a cup of tea, which no European is allowed to touch. All was cleanly and sweet-smelling, except when the filthy European mongrels chewed tobacco and spat about the floor. The shopkeepers and their friends, open-faced and placid, wore a quiet and unobtrusive air, whether clad in their own blue nankeens, or in English fashion, showing a neatness of attire very different from the Europeans around. We prefer to see them in the costume of their own country: like a cooked tomato, a Chinaman *à l'Anglaise* is a Chinaman spoilt.

From the lottery ticket-shop, with its jacket-loafers, we next enter the cookshops, and watch the dough being rolled into long, thin ribbons, and afterwards chopped up into squares so exactly correct in size that it seems a marvel how such skill can be acquired. One man made the dough on a flat table, and rolled it out by the yard about an inch wide, another cut it into little squares, while a third filled each square with pork and folded it up into rolls. This is next put into a pot by the cook and made into delicious soup; long soup they called it. Up aloft are berths like ship-bunks, the sleeping quarters of the Chinese, and inside are the dining-rooms. It is wonderful what a limited space can hold these people. In a room about twelve feet square a dozen Chinamen can exist comfortably. We went into one house, a hovel from the outside, with little windows like pigeon-holes, yet inside clean and comfortable. It was one o'clock on Good Friday morning, and these were decent, hard-working fellows, at least, Chinese who had never been convicted. One lay in a bed like a shelf, tired, as the other Chinamen observed, while our informant was just beginning to hang his line across the five-feet general apartment preparatory to doing his daily washing; and above him, reaching to a little loft, were placed rows of shelves, the couches of Chinamen not yet home. The detectives told me that these were good specimens, and that this one now awake would be up by daybreak and away on his rounds with his pack—he is a licensed hawker—that from early morning of the day before till late at night he had been tramping over miles of ground, and from late at night till this hour had been summing up his day's expenses and gains, and sorting his merchandise against the morrow; that he would do his washing before going to bed, and perhaps scrub out his cabin; and all this from Monday till Saturday, week after week, and year after year.

"But how can they stand the strain and want of sleep?"

# A COOK-HOUSE.

"Opium, that's the grand secret. Of course they don't last long, and don't want to."

The kitchen of the cook-house was a rare treat for us, and the cook an object not to be easily forgotten. On one stove pots were bubbling away, some filled with water, others with long and short soup. Beside the oven stood the cook, shrivelled and lean,

A TYPICAL SCENE.

with parchment visage and lank pigtail. On another side stood an immense boiler, and near by hung the carcass of a pig very carefully scraped, and entire. Chinamen are splendid customers to the butchers, but they must have their pigs killed and dressed in their own way, i.e., with the head, and all complete and undamaged. On the ground was placed a low iron stove with tea, a free gift to any one coming in, and always ready—delicious tea, taken without sugar or milk, and always fresh drawn, without much colour. Two or three Chinese sat on the ground squatting and sucking their opium pipes.

"By whom are these shops mostly patronised?"

"Thieves, garrotters, housebreakers, pickpockets, and women of all sorts, most of them being addicted to the habit."

"What habit?"

"Opium; but you'll see presently."

As we passed out of the shop we saw in one little den a Celestial regaling himself on the long soup; it was boiling hot, yet he supped it up without pausing. Further down the passages we gained a glimpse of another room where two genteel-looking, well-dressed young ladies sat eating a plate of cut chicken. They nodded to the detective as we passed, and he remarked laconically, "Clever girls, these, both thieves." The outside shop was crammed with quaint jars, ornamental vases, bottles of sauce and pickles; and on the ground, counters, and low shelves, were splendid vegetables—cabbages, leeks, parsnips, potatoes, &c., of such development as we could find in no other place than a Chinese vegetable shop.

Our next visit was to the Fan-Tan shop, where heavy stakes are laid and lost, or won. Here a large crowd was assembled, mostly Chinese, with a slight sprinkling of the wolf and jackal species of white men, and a few darkies. The excitement was great. We stood in the shadow watching the faces and backs of the players. The light above the coin-covered table was bright, and streamed upon the yellow heads of the banker and his colleagues, with their coiled-up black plaits, on the shining, evil faces of the gamblers, on the gold, silver, and copper coins, and strings of leaden counters before the banker; the wall was bare and whitewashed, and the ceiling was destitute of ornament, and by no means clean. Between us and the bright gaslights most expressive backs could be seen in shadow relief.

Passing through the lobby into the street, we came upon the barber waiting at this early hour on customers, and as we repassed the window outside in the dark lane we saw the barber standing, and his customer sitting, with a luminous glow of colour, framed by the blackness of that little window-sash. The barber stood behind the chair plaintively unplaiting the tail, and laying on one side the horsehair additions, while the customer sat with drooping, melancholy head, the coloured lantern above his head, and on the wall gay-coloured Chinese designs on screens. Although it was early morning, there seemed no signs of shutting up.

Into alleys where no one could dream of finding a passage we stumbled, every little hole and corner laden with its own burden of depravity and crime. Here, in a dark corner, with fearful-looking, tumble-down sheds on three sides of the yard, and the damps and chills of foulness underground, one of my guides had lain a whole night watching for some daring burglars, and had been rewarded by catching them. Lighting a match, he pointed out to me strange dens and hiding-places. In one an old sack and some straw flung in a corner on the bare floor told us that the birds had not yet forsaken their vile nest. In another alley the policeman showed us where he had recovered a large "plant" of jewellery. In capturing the Chinese receiver he had nearly been killed by a blow on the head with a cleaver. As we were standing listening a figure slid softly past, yet not too softly to evade the sharp ears of the detective, who called out the name, and received in reply, "Good night." Shifting a loose paling aside, our guide crushed through; we followed, and lo, another land lay revealed. It was no longer Little Bourke Street, but a vast territory of horrible dens of infamy. What we saw was vile enough, but yet innocence itself to what we could not see, as our visit had been notified, and the inmates were mostly out, or if in, hiding and pretending to be out. Most of these dens had Chinese characters upon the lintels; and as we went on we passed shambling, indistinct figures, who kept to the shadow side of the wall, and tried to move past unseen, yet all had to announce some errand to the vigilant policeman. The graceful outline of a well-dressed girl brushed me in passing, and she tendered her excuse for coming against me in a soft tone and educated accent. "Going home, Nance?" inquired the detective. "Yes, sir," sweetly returned the young girl, and became lost in the obscurity. "That girl is a perfect slave to the opium-habit," I was informed by my guides.

Presently we came to another wooden building, on its last legs, or, rather, piles. It slanted down sideways amidst the mud, and rags filled up the holes of windows, while the thin morning breeze flapped some loose boards with a dismal sound. A loud knock against the door, to which no reply was given; then a rough shove, and the door yielded, and we entered an apartment pitch-dark.

"Take care of your feet," muttered our guides, "and walk softly." We groped our way along until a turn revealed to us a low light burning in a far-off room, like a candle in a fog, while the pungent odour of opium-smoke filled our nostrils with its rather pleasant perfume. On we went, and presently entered quickly upon the scene where the habit was being indulged. Here we saw a hideous, yellow-visaged, shrunken-eyed Chinaman, and a young woman about twenty, neatly dressed and comely, while between them stood a tiny oil-lamp, the light of which had shown us the way in, and near the lamp a little saucer with a dark, treacly substance at the bottom. She held the long opium-pipe to her lips, and waited; he slowly extracted a small quantity of the glutinous liquor from the saucer on the point of a needle, and, rolling it round like a pea, held it over the lamp-flame. He rolled it round and round until it frizzled, swelled, and then became reduced in size, so as to fit into the tiny aperture of the pipe which the woman held glued to her lips. As he pushed it in, and held the filled pipe over the flame, the girl inhaled one long, sucking breath, which she swallowed, and then it was all over—to begin again after we left, pipe after pipe—one long suck to each elaborately-prepared pipe.

We went into other dens. In some we saw Englishmen indulging in the pernicious habit; in others young females, with sweet, pure-looking faces and gentle manners, who would have deceived me as to their vocation if seen elsewhere. Yet others there were in which Chinese alone congregated, to prepare and smoke their evil pipes; and these dens were invariably clean. In one I tried four pipes; but evidently I had not done the business right, for I felt none of the delightful sensations which De Quincey so vividly describes. I only rose with a dry, nasty taste in my mouth, feeling nothing more than I felt before; and the taste was only in a measure removed by a visit to the cookshop, and a plate of long soup, with the native sauce added to it, followed by a saucer of cut chicken. The Chinese, it should be mentioned, cut their chickens into square pieces, bones and all, and roast them perfectly, but do not indulge in stuffing. This feast cost us the sum of sixpence per head.

In one English house which we entered—filled to the door with harsh-voiced women and coarse-looking men—I seemed to recognise for the first time the noisy vice of London slums. In all the other places we had seen refinement and gentleness—the gentleness of demons—an air of courtesy and education which appalled me more than the worst language of Billingsgate. We are accustomed to associate vice with curses and blasphemy; but it seemed more hideous and revolting when accompanied by gentle tones and educated language. Victoria swarms with State schools and free education, and yet villainy is not stamped out, but rather intensified, by the power which books have given. There were no brutal ruffians in the dens I saw, with the exception of this one house. I heard no vulgar jests or blood-curdling oaths. Those of English race spoke gently, as the Chinese did, and in set phrases, the men looking like world-worn gentlemen, while the women spoke like blasé ladies, with modest attire and girlish figures; only here and there in the lanes might be seen a recognisable blackguard, smoking coarse tobacco, or a bloated, unmistakable night-bird; and these were merely the prowlers of the dark outside. Inside, refinement and villainy blent too readily not to be suggestive of a poetic ideal of the damned.

But in this one dark-covered house were assembled larrikins and females with coarse features and corresponding figures. Here were arms tattooed, scowling faces, unkempt locks. We were prepared at a glance for anything, from the garrotter down to the kinchin-layer, and left with the feeling that all the surroundings were in accordance with the proper fitness of natural laws outraged. This was ordinary vice, and about it we thought no more. Does not the poet say

"Vice is a monster of so frightful mien,
As, to be hated, needs but to be seen"?

And this was a case in point. But the Chinese lepers of morality gave us more concern. We could not but wish Little Bourke Street demolished and the plague-spot wiped out altogether, warehouses built in the dilapidated quarter, crime crushed and the vermin driven out.

How calmly and philosophically these Chinese bear losses and gains! In one house, called a lodging-house, we found the keeper, a splendidly-developed animal of a Chinaman. We were told that he had broken the banks several times, and only last week had lost at Fan-Tan over £2,000, his whole filthy earnings. He showed us over his premises, kept and cleaned by him alone, and looking like a man-of-war for order and neatness, with one narrow stair like an upright ladder. Men could be pitched down, and their necks broken very easily. He was proud of his establishment, and showed no regret over his losses. "As well spend it that way as any other: a man cannot take it with him when he leaves this world." Thus the creed of Confucius consoled him, and

# A SAD SCENE.

AT PLAY.

AT WORK: A CHINESE KITCHEN.

rendered him happy and contented even in poverty and utter vice.

It was growing very near daylight, and we were utterly tired out, and disgusted to the heart's core with our eight hours' experiences. In the last house that we visited, we saw on one bed of the opium den three young colonials lying making up their own pills, and languidly sucking at the pipe-stems one after another. Here also we saw a Chinaman and a lovely girl of about sixteen years, while her companion, also about the same age, with a bundle of purchases at her side, was sitting down. Behind the door on a chair, in half shadow, sat a most lady-like woman of about twenty-five. As our eyes grew accustomed to the dim light, we saw a blear-eyed old hag with a face wrinkled and marked like a parchment record of iniquity, and, most pathetic sight of all, a young man tenderly nursing a baby.

"Ha! Tom, lad, is the youngster any better?" inquired one of the detectives.

"Not much, sir," quietly replied the young man. "Yet since Nelly came out he has been easier with his cough."

"So you are there, Nell?" asked the detective, looking at the woman behind the door.

"Yes, sir."

"Nice girl, isn't she, gentlemen," he continued, waving his hand carelessly, with the air of the proprietor of a wild beast show, "and the smartest pickpocket in Melbourne, ay, or the world either, for that part, as I think we can nearly beat Creation in the way of the under professions."

"Yes, I think I have seen more of real blackguardism to-night than in my previous life's experience, and I have seen a few places pretty bad."

The woman sat with her hands folded on her knees, and gently smiled, while the three young colonials made a motion as if to rise.

"Don't stir, gentlemen, we are going in a moment."

The three young men sank back languidly on the bed, and prepared another opium puff.

"Where is the pleasure in this?" I asked one of the pleasantest faced, as he lay back looking passively at me with half-closed eyelids.

"Well, you see, when a working man like myself"—he certainly did not appear like a hard worker—"comes home of a night too tired to eat or sleep, we come here and take a pipe or two, and feel as if we could go fresh to work once again without needing either to sleep or to eat. You have read De Quincey, haven't you?"

"Yes," I replied, feeling a sudden interest in this opium victim.

"Well, he tells you all about it."

"But are you all working men?"

"Certainly," replied the other two young fellows, who had not spoken before.

"None of your lies!" harshly broke in one of the detectives, with a sudden scowl; and at his voice the young man seemed to shrivel up. "I'll tell you what they are. That fellow you have been speaking to is not two days out of gaol for a case of burglary and violence. The other two were in the same haul, only we hadn't evidence enough to convict them. Better luck next time. This young man is a sort of all-round man, although I know his tricks best in shoplifting. He is the friend of Nelly over there, and the baby he is nursing is hers, before she took up with him."

"And the others?"

"Old Mother Murphy, with crimes enough to sink a frigate, past all use except opium-sucking now; and these two on the bed—well, they are called ladies by day, and keep a villa in one of the fashionable outskirts of Melbourne: only they cannot exist without their pipe, and come here under cover of the night to enjoy it quietly."

# THE FIRST LORD.

Sir Peniston Lamb had two country seats, Brocket Hall, near Hertford, afterwards famous as the seat of Lord Palmerston, and one in Derbyshire, near a village which, fortunately for us, bears the melodious name of Melbourne. His first title was Lord Melbourne of Melbourne, *in Ireland*, whereas, we believe, there is no place called Melbourne in Ireland; but sometimes, when an Englishman was rewarded with an Irish peerage, it was the practice for him to take his title from some place in England, representing it as "in Ireland." This was in the days before the Union, and it was manifestly unfair that a peerage should be given for services that had nothing to do with Ireland, with

LORD MELBOURNE.

which country it seems that Lord Melbourne had no connection. If the Irish peerage roll had not been unfairly stuffed, it would not, perhaps, at the Union have been necessary to resort to the expedient of representative peers.

In 1815, the Waterloo year, Sir Peniston was made a peer of the United Kingdom, Viscount Melbourne, of Melbourne, in the county of Derby. His son, William Lamb, our Lord Melbourne, was educated at Eton, from which he passed to Trinity College, Cambridge. As the English Universities in those days made no provision for education beyond classics and mathematics, he passed from Cambridge to Glasgow, in order to study law and political science under an eminent professor at that University.

In 1805 he entered the House of Commons, being elected for Leominster. He ranked himself amongst the Whigs under the leadership of Charles James Fox, a brilliant phalanx but in a decided minority. One may almost say that during the whole of George III.'s reign, and until the passing of the Reform Bill, in 1832, the Tories were in office. Now and then, of course, there were short breaks. From Waterloo, however, to the Reform Bill, the Whigs were growing in strength. When Lord Liverpool, in 1827, was struck with paralysis and compelled to resign, King George IV., after much hesitation, and what with a less exalted personage would be called "shilly-shallying," appointed Mr. Canning Premier. Mr. Canning, clever, brilliant, witty, was little prepared to join those who blindly resisted all change. He was therefore distasteful to high Tories such as the Duke of Wellington, who held aloof from him, but, obtaining the support of many Whigs, he formed a ministry from the moderate men. Mr. Lamb joined him, accepting the office of Secretary for Ireland. Canning was soon worn out by the labours, anxieties, and annoyances of office. Four months of it killed him. After a short interval of government in the weak hands of Lord Goderich, in January, 1828, the Duke of Wellington became Prime Minister. During all these changes Mr. Lamb remained in office, but the Duke did not like the more Liberal or Canningite section of his Cabinet, and quarrelled with them; and in May of that year Mr. Huskisson, Lord Palmerston, and others resigned, amongst these others being Mr. Lamb, who soon afterwards succeeded his father, and became Lord Melbourne.

The particular matter which caused a split in the Tory Cabinet was a question of Parliamentary Reform. Two boroughs, convicted of corruption, having been condemned to lose their representatives, Mr. Huskisson and the so-called Canningites voted that the right of election should be transferred to Manchester. Indeed, the feeling for Parliamentary Reform was growing in the public mind. The Duke of Wellington, the Prime Minister, said that the representation could not possibly be improved, and, as a result, the Ministry was upset. The Canningites mostly joined Lord Grey, in whose administration, formed in the autumn of that year, Viscount Melbourne was Home Secretary and Lord Palmerston Secretary for Foreign Affairs. Mr. Huskisson was no more. Two months previously he had attended the opening of the Manchester and Liverpool Railway, the first passenger line opened in England. Seeing the Duke of Wellington, with whom he had not been on friendly terms since the split in the Ministry, he stepped out of the railway carriage to shake hands, and was killed by an engine coming up suddenly — the first of a long list of victims to accidents on English railways.

For four years Melbourne remained at the head of the Home Office, and during that time the great Reform Bill was carried. About his administration of his office there is a great difference of opinion. It was a time of great excitement. Reformers called Lord Grey's coming into office "the year One of the people's cause." Expecting too much—a sort of return of the Golden Age—they were naturally disappointed, and have vented their disappointment on ministers for ills that they could not cure. It was creditable to English good sense that, with much excitement, there was little disturbance; but there were riots in some towns, and rick-burnings in various parts of the country. The maintenance of order is in the hands of the Home Secretary, and the friends of order complained, but apparently without much ground, that Lord Melbourne lacked vigour in this work.

In August, 1834, Lord Melbourne became Prime Minister. William IV., who had supported the Whigs in the matter of reform, was beginning to turn against them; and Lord Melbourne accepted office upon the resignation of his late chief, Lord Grey, because the majority in Parliament were prepared to support him, and not because he had the confidence of the king. In December the king, in summary, almost in sailor fashion, dismissed his Ministers, and consulted the Duke of Wellington about the formation of a Tory Ministry. "H. B.," the great caricaturist of the day, has a picture of a Cabinet meeting, into which Lord Melbourne rushes, in great excitement, shouting, "We're kicked out! we're kicked out!" By way of salve for the sore that the kick produced, my lord was offered an Earldom and a Garter, but he had the self-respect to decline both.

The Duke of Wellington advised King William to make Sir Robert Peel Prime Minister; but he was enjoying a holiday in Italy, and had to be sent for. Meanwhile, how was the king's Government to be carried on? Always fertile in resource, and not caring what people thought or said, the Iron Duke took the whole government on himself. Accordingly "H. B." has another picture of a Cabinet meeting, with the duke himself occupying all the chairs. It was a very united Cabinet—in fact, literally unanimous.

Sir Robert Peel, on returning to England, became Premier, and, to help him, Parliament was dissolved. But the new Parliament still showed a majority against him, angry at the way in which the Whigs had been treated, and Peel finding it quite impossible to remain in office, Lord Melbourne was reinstated in April, 1835, and remained in power until September, 1841.

In June, 1837, William IV. died, and was succeeded by his niece, the present Queen. It is said that her Majesty liked her first Prime Minister very much, but out of doors his popularity was not great. He was careless in his manner of receiving deputations. When his visitors were discoursing learnedly and gravely, he would blow a feather into the air and watch it with delight; or he would place a cushion on his knee and seem to concentrate all his attention on nursing it. The impetus of reform was spent, and Melbourne's star was waning before the growing influence of Peel. In May, 1839, on an important division on a colonial question, the ministers could only obtain a majority of five in the House of Commons and therefore resigned. This led to what is known as the "Bedchamber Question." The great ladies of the Queen's household, appointed at her accession, were relatives of the retiring ministers. Sir Robert Peel informed the Queen that he could not take office unless he were permitted to change these. The Queen refused, and Lord Melbourne and his colleagues, "sheltered behind the petticoats of their wives and sisters," returned to office for two and a half more years, when, at length, their opponents, the followers of Sir Robert Peel, had so large a majority that they had to give up office. Melbourne now practically retired from politics, although he did not die until November, 1848.

One cannot finish this sketch without a quotation from Sydney Smith's famous character, which may stand in place of estimate of our own. "If the truth must be told," says the witty dean of St. Paul's, "our Viscount is somewhat of an impostor. Everything about him seems to betoken careless desolation; any one would suppose from his manner that he was playing at chuck-farthing with human happiness; that he would giggle away the Great Charter, and decide by the method of teetotum whether my lords the bishops should or should not retain their seats in the House of Lords. I am sorry to hurt any man's feelings, and to brush away the magnificent fabric of levity and gaiety that he has reared; but I accuse our minister of honesty and diligence; I deny that he is careless or rash. He is nothing more than a man of good understanding and good principle, disguised in the eternal and somewhat wearisome affectation of a political *roué*."

MELBOURNE HALL, MELBOURNE, ENGLAND.

OHINEMUTU.
(From a Photograph by Messrs. Burton Bros., Dunedin.)

## A VANISHED WONDERLAND.

The Hot Lakes—A Terrible Catastrophe—Oxford and Cambridge—Rotorua—The Boiling Springs—Ohinemutu—Whakarewarewa—Wairoa - Lake Tarawera—Lake Rotomahana—The Wonderland—The White Terrace—The Steam Demon—The Pink Terrace—Vanished!—A New Wonderland.

THE Hot Lake district of New Zealand lies in the Auckland province, about one hundred and fifty miles south-east of the city of that name, and forty-five miles south from the port of Tauranga, on the Bay of Plenty. Setting aside the giant lake of Taupo, which should be treated alone, the thermal region includes Lakes Rotorua, Roto-iti, Roto-ehu, Roto-ma, Tarawera, and numerous other *rotos* of smaller extent. All these have their charms of position or of shape, if not their volcanic wonders, but the large lake of Rotorua and the little lake of Rotomahana are the chief centres of interest. There are two inducements to visit the region, cure-seeking and sight-seeing. For the former purpose the township of Ohinemutu, on Rotorua, with its hot-springs and sulphur-baths, is the special resort; for the latter all the interest culminates upon the terraces and geysers of Rotomahana. Or rather *did* culminate; for though Rotorua and its medicinal springs remain very much as they were, Rotomahana, with its terraces and fumaroles, is now represented, so far as can be ascertained, by a vast and awful crater, or assemblage of craters, active and unapproachable.

All the world has heard of the marvels of this mysterious region, and all the world has heard, too, of the catastrophe which befell it on June 10th, 1886. On that day Mount Tarawera, a hill some two thousand feet in height, and situated at the south-east corner of the lake of the same name, suddenly burst into violent eruption. It startled the good people from their beds in Auckland, a hundred and fifty miles away. It strewed the earth with a thick coat of ashes all along the Bay of Plenty, forty or fifty miles distant. It vomited mud and scoria in tons over all the surrounding country, burying the European village of Wairoa, nine miles off, and blotting from the face of the earth several picturesque Maori hamlets, along with their luckless inhabitants. Standing, as it did, just behind the famous terraces of Lake Rotomahana, it naturally enough made an end of those wonders which Nature had been accumulating for thousands of years. The whole region was for some time turned into a scene of panic and of the wildest desolation. But at length we are in a fair position to estimate what has been lost, even if we cannot as yet say definitely what has been gained in its place. Such volcanic outbreaks, however, seldom destroy without also creating.

Those who had the good fortune to visit the Wonderland of New Zealand before this awful calamity robbed it of its most delightful, if not of its most marvellous, features, will be more overwhelmed by the present reality of the catastrophe than astonished at the fact that it should have occurred at all. No one gifted with the least imagination could walk warily among those seething cauldrons, those pools of boiling mud, and those unnumbered jets of steam, without realising something of what was going on beneath; and occasionally a disturbing thought would steal into the mind, and grow and grow—"What if *this* should be the moment of an outburst?" Yet familiarity bred contempt, and whenever at Rotorua a new mud-spring burst up suddenly through a cottage floor, it would cause but a mild surprise, and in a day or two the occupant of the domicile would be utilising it for the cooking of his potatoes or the curing of his rheumatism. At rare intervals a human being, a cow, or a horse would through some slight inadvertence fall into a boiling pool, and only be recovered thence in ghastly shreds. A newspaper paragraph might record the fact, the Maories would hold a *tangi*, and then men and women would go on cooking their food in convenient holes, and the children would go on playing upon isthmuses of questionable thickness which separated cauldrons unquestionably fatal. And all this was perfectly natural. Any accidents which occurred had been due to carelessness. Mother Earth herself had never been treacherous; she had, indeed, occasionally developed a new hole here and a fresh pipe of steam there, but she had let the roads and townships alone.

And even now, after the warning which was given on the 10th of June, and after finding day turned into night, and feeling all the thin earth beneath quake and shiver for hour after hour, the ordinary resident goes about his avocations, and the tourists flock to the scene, just as if the event had been one of a century ago.

There are two routes to Ohinemutu, which is the central starting-point for viewing the whole district. The one is overland from Auckland, the other by sea to Tauranga, and thence by road. It was only a few short months before the catastrophe that the present writer was amid the scene. We chose the overland route, which is now admittedly superior to that by way of Tauranga. The latter is not indeed without very great attractions, passing as it does through many miles of magnificent bush, and through the Mangarewa Gorge. Yet the sea voyage to Tauranga in a comparatively small vessel, and on a rough coast, is apt to be unpleasant and monotonous. The railway, on the contrary, passes through varied scenery in the plain of the large Waikato River, which was once the great field of campaigning, but now smiles with prosperous agriculture. Cattle may be seen browsing quietly by the remains of the

THE PINK TERRACE, ROTOMAHANA.

Maori *pa* and the British redoubt; and Maori faces may be seen grinning a cheerful recognition where once they gloated over the slain.

For those who would make the journey with the greatest comfort and satisfaction, the way lies by rail from Auckland to Cambridge, distant about a hundred miles; and thence by special vehicle through Oxford to Ohinemutu, the main township of the Lake District, which lies upon Lake Rotorua, fifty-five miles distant. Of the above-named places, Cambridge is but a little agricultural village, and Oxford but a place of entertainment for man and beast; but where there is a Cambridge there must be an Oxford, and no doubt both will in due time become places of importance. The carriage drive from Oxford to Ohinemutu is itself worth all the trouble, the road being diversified enough for every taste. The best part of it is, perhaps, the eleven miles of "forest primeval," where on both sides of the winding track there is an infinity of dense jungle, full of that luxuriant growth which distinguishes the North Island of New Zealand. The tall kauris, the puriri, the rimu, the stealthy merciless rata-vine, winding itself like a baleful serpent round the trees from which it sucks the life-blood, the thick undergrowth of rampo and fern—all this reminded one more of the Amazon or the Orinoco than of anything else in Australasia. Gigantic tree-ferns and graceful nikau-palms edged the road, while curious parasites bulged out here and there upon the tree-trunks, as if the growth were not already thick enough without them. Sometimes the buggy would sway for a mile or so along the edge of the precipice, where we could, if we had nerve enough, gaze down upon gullies which were the consummation of sylvan beauty.

Emerging from this piece of bush, we descend into the plain of Rotorua. The lake itself is at this point uninteresting, nor, for some few miles, does there seem to be anything particularly attractive or wonderful. A long, flat stretch of clayey soil, covered with monotonous ti-scrub, lies between the hills to the right and the lake to the left; and ahead, upon a kind of promontory, we catch sight of the low-lying township of Ohinemutu. As we draw nearer along the dusty road, our first perception is one of the nose. There comes upon the breeze a perfume which is not balmy, and yet is not strong enough to be called detestable. Gradually it grows more pronounced, and emphatically suggests over-ripe eggs, or those matches which unblushingly describe themselves as *ohne phosphor*. The inhabitants say that one grows to like this sulphurous odour. For our part, we never got beyond toleration.

Here and there, amid the ti-scrub, we notice a kind of bald patch, with a yellowish covering, which will, on inspection, turn out to be composed of stones coated with sulphur. Next, we become aware of numerous small columns of steam rising by the roadside, or issuing here and there amid the ti-trees, and these grow more and more frequent as we near the town. An exaggerated idea may perhaps be entertained of the size and appearance of the boiling springs, whose presence these columns of steam betoken. In size and shape they are like an ordinary pool which forms itself in the fields after heavy rain, being of an irregular edge, and of all sizes, from a square foot to many square yards. Somewhere towards the middle of them bubbles may be detected rising from a "pipe" which communicates with an unknown depth of volcanic mystery.

Sometimes one of them steams away all alone, like an exile, far away in the scrub, but generally they are in clusters, with only a foot or two of ground between, and how solid that ground may be no man knoweth.

The little township, half native, half European, stood calmly that day amid the springs, just as if they were things that "no family should be without." Between house and house a disregarded cauldron or two steamed and steamed, so that the general appearance of the settlement from a distance was as if every householder were burning

WATERFALL AT WAIRBA.
(From a Photograph by Messrs. Burton & )

a few heaps of garden rubbish. The springs were not provided with any fence, and the tourist had need to accept the warnings he received at his hotel to keep his eyes well upon the ground, never to wander from the main road after dark, and to beware of putting an enemy into his mouth to steal away his control over his feet. Accidents did occur from time to time, but fencing was no one's business in particular, and as no Cabinet Minister or bishop had ever been boiled alive, the danger was allowed to remain. It may be observed that the "hot" springs are really hot, the water having a genuine record of 212 degrees. The first sensation in walking amid all these wonders was rather disappointing, for the simple reason that there was so much of them, and the residents took all so much as a matter of course. They went to their baths—especially to the one which turned them red, and which was called the lobster-bath—and they discussed the effect on their rheumatism or sciatica, but nothing

FISSURE IN ROAD NEAR THE TIKITAPU BUSH, AFTER THE ERUPTION

was said of the wonder or the awe. Even the new-comer was more amused with dropping a sixpence into a shallow pool, and fishing it out again as black as ink, than astonished at these marvels of Vulcan.

Though many of the springs keep at nothing less than boiling point, others are of a milder temperature. Nature seems to have graduated them to suit all requirements, balneatory or culinary. But by a peculiar coincidence, the hottest and largest pools are to be met with exactly where they are likely to prove most dangerous. From a medicinal point of view, the merits of some of the baths constructed from these natural thermal springs are incapable of exaggeration. The faith in their potency displayed by sufferers from all parts of the world must be most unaccountable if it is baseless, most touching if it is a delusion. The Government has declared its belief in them by establishing a sanatorium on Sulphur Point. Many a cripple is said to have been able to take up his bed and walk after due treatment in the baths of Rotorua.

There are, therefore, good hotels at Ohinemutu, and much company of a cosmopolitan nature. There is, moreover, a delightful blending of civilisation and barbarism. As one roams through the village, keeping a wary eye upon the ground, he stumbles against old Maori carvings of the most grotesque description. He will not be surprised to behold an English church here, an English store there, and a Maori *whare*, or a Maori meeting-house, in another direction. Ohinemutu was one of the earliest fields of missionary work, and a Maori may be beheld conducting a service or a catechism, in his soft native tongue, inside a building which was once used for councils of war and other pagan purposes. All around, the rudely-carved figures of Maori ancestors, with eyes of shell, protruding tongues, and three-fingered hands crossed over the stomach, look on benignantly, if leeringly. The visitor will not be astonished to meet with a neatly-railed tomb, which sets forth, by means of its headstone, how "Helen Hinemoa Wilson was accidentally scalded to death" in such and such a year. He will, if he takes care of his steps, arrive safely on a little promontory, where stand the tokens of an old *pa*, which formerly stood high and dry, but lies now beneath the water. The point has sunk still lower of late, and its total disappearance is but a question of time.

Beyond curiosities such as these, and its medicinal advantages, Ohinemutu offers no charms to detain the visitor. It is the head-quarters of the whole district, and it gives a foretaste of the expected marvels: but the air is heavy with sulphur, and the scenery of little value. As a starting-point for expeditions on Rotorua, to the island of Mokoia, rich in legend, to Roto-Iti on the north-east, and to Rotomahana east by south, the town is something as Keswick is to the English lakes, though without any pretensions to the beauty of that place.

We mount our buggy again, and as the sulphurous odour grows fainter and fainter behind us, we make for Wairoa, over the hills. Wairoa is the settlement which has played the part of Pompeii in the late catastrophe. We have some eleven miles up and down hill to drive, and the last half of them shall not yield the palm of beauty to any Trosachs or Yosemites you can name.

The first half of the journey is not interesting. A little to the right we pass Whakarewarewa, with its mud-pools and geysers. Whakarewarewa is a Maori hamlet of a size by no means commensurate with that of its name. Its mud-springs form an agreeable change from the Ohinemutu fumaroles. They are more alive, and show more varied phenomena than those everlasting water-holes. Generally speaking, they resemble so many porridge-pots, set over a slow fire. To sit up to the neck in a bath of the buttery mud, that laps and hugs the limbs with a pleasant tenacity, is a luxury highly appreciated by the natives, and not altogether despised of the European. The same mud is said to be edible, and the Maori smacks his lips and cries "Kapai" ("First-rate") as he attempts to swallow it. It appears, however, to be caviare to the general. Unfortunately our recollections of Whakarewarewa are not of the most pleasant. It is a kind of private reserve, whose owners are absurdly extortionate natives; for be it known that the Maori soon learns to higgle for the means wherewith to purchase gin.

The journey to Wairoa should be made both by day and by night. No more bewitching drive can be imagined in the broad light of day than to plunge downward through the dim twilight of the Tikitapu bush, and then out upon the road which winds by the shores of Tikitapu, the lake whose waters are blue, and Rotokakahi, the lake whose waters are green. The Blue and Green lakes are undeniably what they call themselves. Yet, beautiful as they are, there is something weird about them: an air of mystery, suggesting a secret preserved from a wondrous past. And what of the future?

During the late outburst the road along which we passed was rent across with a yawning gulf, the bush was overwhelmed and broken down with a foul weight of mud and ashes, and the shores of the lakes were stripped of all their marge of verdure, till Tikitapu became desolate as Avernus.

Then the drive at night, with a faint moon peering through the arboreal canopy! Nothing was ever more fascinating. Along the roadside, under the ferns, tens of thousands of little lanterns were brightly burning. They were only the glow-worms, but the bank was as beautiful as if strewn with diamonds. And now the bush is "uprooted," and all the foliage and the glow-worms covered with scoria and mud. Along we go, under the moon, with the Blue lake and the Green turned each to burnished silver, and finally, through a noisy crowd of natives, we dash up to the door of that hospitable hotel which we now know is "wrecked," and its surroundings buried under ten feet of blue mud and ashes.

It is inconceivable. The little township of Wairoa, almost entirely native, lay in a narrow glen some hundred feet or so above the head of Lake Tarawera. It was one of the most picturesque spots in the world, with its half-civilised inhabitants grouped about in their parti-coloured attire, with its wattled *whares* built on the hillsides amid the eternal green, and with its *haka* dances and *tangi* wakes. And now many of these tattooed denizens are overwhelmed, the vegetation and the *whares* are ten feet deep in mud: a foul-smelling, desolate stretch of ashes covers the most romantic spot on the earth! Where is the genial M'Crae, our guide, philosopher, and friend? Where is the sturdy guide Kate, with her Humane Society's medal? Their occupation has gone for many a day, unless they are following it in other fields of wonder and mystery. A beautiful spot was this Wairoa, with its waterfall in the bush, its peeps through frames of foliage on to the Lake Tarawera below, its jovial Maori life, its apparent separation from all the rest of the world and the world's cares. No doubt in a few years the mud will have cleared away, the vegetation will have been renewed, and that most charming nook will again be filled with a joyous, careless population of the two races.

Descending in the early morn along a winding path, we reach an arm of Tarawera Lake, whereon we embark in a boat manned by eight stalwart Maoris. The lake broadens

LAKE TARAWERA BEFORE THE ERUPTION.
(From a Photograph by Messrs. Burton Bros.)

into a little sea, rimmed in with harmless-looking hills, but we keep always near the shore on our right, under the pohutukawas which hang tenaciously from the fire-seared rocks. Our Maoris chant as they row, and ever and anon stop to perform a rhythmical gesticulation, which vastly amuses them and does not hurt us.

Two-thirds of the journey are over when we touch at a tiny native settlement called Te Moura—now, alas! swept away, along with its little population of thirty. To have refused to call there would have been to violate all the traditions. Ever since strangers first rowed across Tarawera, they have by prescription been compelled to purchase at Te Moura a certain kind of diminutive crayfish. These provisions are subsequently to be cooked in the boiling water close by the Terraces, and their consumption is a necessary part of the programme. There are hundreds of people in every part of the world who will recollect and grieve for the sociable people of this little place of call. Its place knows it no more, and they would not so much as recognise the sheltered corner in which it stood.

Another chant, a short race with a rival boat, and at eight miles from Wairoa we reach another now vanished settlement called Te Ariki. At the mouth of a tepid little stream we disembark. The stream runs out of Lake Rotomahana, which is but half a mile distant, and it is usual to descend it in a canoe, but as the current is strong, and the course winding, tourists in going upwards make a short cut on foot through the scrub. Suddenly we come on the crest of a little hill, and lo! the Wonderland of the World lies before us. The scene has often been described, but never in such a way as to fully satisfy those who have beheld it. We cannot here do it justice, and must content ourselves with an outline, necessarily inadequate even as a sketch.

Before us, towards the right, lies a lake of something over a mile in diameter, and just at our feet is what may be called the bottom step of the belauded and bepoemed Te Tarata, the White Terrace. It is only separated from us by the little stream aforementioned. Stretching away along the shore of the lake is the realisation partly of Inferno, partly of Paradise. The awe, perhaps, exceeds the beauty. The White Terrace,

LAKE TARAWERA AFTER THE ERUPTION.

a mass of silica, rises tier above tier, and culminates in an impenetrable mystery of steam. To the right of it the low hills are all alive with jets of vapour. The whole side of the range seems to smoke. We must look at the terrace from every part, and the nearer the better. On every stage of its white surface there are pools of water of a celestial blue, while the edge of each platform is embroidered with curious incrustations, and its surface strewn with petrifactions of much beauty. Higher and higher we mount, and the water that trickles over grows hotter and hotter, until we reach the topmost level, and there take our stand on the edge of a boiling horror. We cannot see across it for the dense steam; we cannot sound it; we can only gaze in wonder. Well do we remember two figures which had approached from a different side, and had taken up their position upon a peak of rock, where they loomed of more than mortal size: Dante and Virgil to the life, from Doré's cartoons. Then we turn and gaze down upon the ever-widening expanse of white and blue below us, and we feel that we never knew colour before, and that the beauty, the grandeur, the awfulness, are too much for the soul to feel at once.

The impressions formed of the Terrace from different points of view were very various. At one time it seemed as if we were walking over snow, marked with those curious and fantastic patterns which frost creates. Here we took delight in the more minute work, the little silicious fretworks spread over the surface of a platform, or the delicate lacework which fell over its edge. In another place it was the regular sweep of the arcs, as stage rose above stage, that called forth our admiration. Again, we met with a space which seemed broken up into a series of pockets, whose white depths were filled with baths of azure water of every degree of temperature. Nearer the summit the gradation was less regular, the formations less symmetrical, and buttresses had formed themselves upon the vertical walls. And this we might expect, for at different times the angle of ejection of the silicated water inclined in different directions; and while this would give irregularity to the shape of the upper platforms, the lower and wider stages would receive a more even distribution of the deposit.

Perhaps the English language never was so ransacked as for terms adequate to the description of this Terrace. How shall we give a simple understanding of the formation as a whole? Perhaps thus: From the summit downwards it spread itself, in shape like an enormous fan, in build like a vast flight of alabaster steps rising to a throne—the throne of Nature: not the benignant, life-giving Nature, but the Titanic Nature which sent its giant brood to war with the gods at Phlegra. Where the throne should stand, was a hissing cauldron, and the scorching vapour hid the ruling majesty from human sight.

These vast steps had taken myriads of years to form, for the plebeian names which those pigmy barbarians Smith and Jones inscribed, according to their Vandal wont, upon these great white platforms in the year 1860, were to the last as visible as when they were first scrawled: a quarter of a century had not contrived to blot them out with an appreciable fraction of an inch of deposit.

Over all the steps a film of water, as soft to the touch as satin, glides incessantly, and trickles into the lake till it gives it its name, Rotomahana—the Warm Lake. Descending, and entering the neighbouring scrub, we pass warily among holes in which mud boils and leaps up, subsides again, again leaps up, and forms huge bubbles, which explode with a "flopping" sound. We stand beside a basin of rock in whose depths we hear ominous rumblings and seethings. Suddenly comes a rush of water, and we flee to a safe distance, turning round in time to see a column of water spout up and

## THE PINK TERRACE.

fall again with a most gruesome swirl. Yet further, and we become conscious of a loud and sustained roaring, like that of a hoarse steam-whistle, proceeding from a hole or tube of rock some two or three yards square. There is no water or steam visible, but I know nothing more fearsome than that hole. You can look into it, and hear the roaring deeper and deeper down. The suggestion is of an unfathomable depth, but that hoarse voice of the steam demon is the most terrible of earthly sounds. And all the while a muffled noise is heard as if a diabolic steam-hammer were working deep, deep down in the earth.

Standing on the side of this ridge, putting our fingers in our ears, and turning our backs upon the screaming depth, we look out through the trees over the peaceful little lake and its brilliant shore, thinking it a scene of retirement fit for a *Sans-Souci*. But turn once more, and there are the steaming breath and the horrible yell of the volcanic demon. The sounds and sights are apt to haunt one's dreams for many a day.

It took long to examine all these things so new and strange; and it was not uncommon for tourists to camp for some days upon the scene. When curiosity was appeased on this side, it was customary to enter a canoe and be shot swiftly across a corner of the lake to the Pink Terrace, Otukapuarangi, in all respects like the White, except in colour and size. It is smaller, more comprehensible, so to speak. Compared with the White Terrace, it was a toy; yet it was necessary to complete the picture. It derived its name from a coloured deposit found among the white silica, and to be seen in perfection it required one of the brightest of New Zealand days. Ah! its sapphire pools were the most delicious baths that man ever knew, soothing the sense, and yet filling the soul with ecstasy! Now a frightful cavern is belching and vomiting where that work of beauty was. Let us row off into the lake, and post ourselves where we can see on the one hand the White Terrace, and on the other the Pink. An azure sky is above us, the sun-lit lake before us; the leafage around is of a glorious green, and here and there we catch sight of a native in gay attire. Let no man deny the truth of any painting he may hereafter see of the terraces of which New Zealand was so proud. Imagination deserts us when we think of them as gone, and for ever. Yonder Mount Tarawera looked as if his day was done; but so did Vesuvius in the year of grace 79. Yet Pompeii and Herculaneum were but commonplace cities, and might, perhaps, have been spared. The terraces of New Zealand were unique, unparalleled. They are now only, or little more than, a tradition. That awful roaring in the "Devil's Hole" meant something, a perpetual warning, as awful as it sounded. Little did we think, as we paddled down the stream on our way back from Rotomahana, trying to think we had fully appreciated what was past appreciation, that another year would see the whole of this wonder and magnificence wiped from the face of the earth. Nature truly is cruel to her own works. One who has never visited the scene can scarcely understand the grief and wonder of the New Zealander who knows it well. The Wairoa Valley, the little tepid stream, the terraces, all the wonderful places, sights, and sounds, gone, and something, perhaps more awful, but not for centuries as beautiful, left in its place! The children of the future will see the terraces only in pictures, which they will call exaggerated. Truly this was the event of a century. Similar events will no doubt occur in time to come. The Maoris have long had traditions of lost mountains and other wondrous changes, and a Maori tradition always rests upon some basis. Yet we may imagine that the feeling of awe will soon subside, and that the neighbourhood will quickly become inhabited again.

Since the above words were written there comes the news that another Wonderland has been discovered, or rather opened up. A few miles to the south of the old Wonderland, and within the same immediate volcanic radius, lies a mysterious valley

THE WHITE TERRACE, ROTOMAHANA, BEFORE THE ERUPTION.
(From a Photograph by Messrs. Burton Bros.)

named Waiotapu, which, though known to surveyors, was otherwise unvisited of white feet. That it had its volcanic phenomena was suspected, as being a matter of course, yet, lying away from the broad and beaten road, it was neglected for its inconvenience sake. But when such a loss as the one we have been describing befalls a country, it is not to be expected that the enterprising explorer will sit still. The colonist is confident of his resources, and therein he is justified. This solitary valley, guarded by two hills of the awe-inspiring names of Maungaongaonga and Maungakakaramea, is, we are told, as full of its geysers and its "Devil's Holes" as were the shores of Rotomahana. Nay, it even possesses its incipient terrace; and there is every reason to expect that "Ichabod" will sound but for a little while in the province of Auckland, and that "Eureka" will triumph in its stead.

BRISBANE FROM BOWEN TERRACE.

## BRISBANE.

The Approach by River—North Brisbane—Victoria Bridge—Stanley Street—The Breweries—The Gaol—The Water Supply—City Charities—Grammar Schools—The Botanical Gardens—Government and Parliament Houses—The Churches—Exhibition Buildings and Places of Amusement—Newspapers—'Buses and Trams—The Ferries.

IN the visitor reaching Brisbane by steamer, the first object that excites attention and elicits admiration is the noble stream on which the city stands, and after which it is named. From the mouth of the river, at the township of Lytton, the distance to the wharves is about fifteen miles. After the halfway point is reached, not far below the Hamilton Pavilion, the stream begins to narrow to a breadth of about a quarter of a mile, whilst the swampy mangrove banks give place to high ridges, rising here and there into pretty wooded crests, on which are perched many handsome private residences. Owing to some sharp bends in the river, the journey up from Breakfast Creek (about four miles from town) occupies more than half-an-hour. Rounding the last corner, we see to the right some imposing residences; on the left is the Kangaroo Point Slip, and further on, facing the stone quarries that nestle beneath the heights of Bowen Terrace, the new Immigration Depôt Reserve. With some difficulty, and at a very slow pace, the vessel swings round Kangaroo Point Corner, and the main portion of the city is before us. The British India Steam Navigation Company, which is subsidised by the Queensland Government to carry the European mails *via* Torres Straits, has lately built the only wharf on the Kangaroo Point side. With the exception of the narrow tongue of land that constitutes the "Point" proper, this bank is too steep to be favourable for wharf construction, and the river frontage is chiefly occupied by private residences. On the opposite side are the wharves of Howard, Smith, and Co., of Gibbs, Bright, and Co., of the Queensland Shipping Company, and the two Australian Steam Navigation wharves, in the order named. Further on is the office of the Inspector of Harbours and Rivers, with a small wharf attached; and the Botanical Gardens end the reach. In the next one is the Government House Domain on the north side, and further up, about two hundred yards below the Victoria Bridge, is the wharf of the Government steamer *Lucinda*, in which the members of the Ministry are wont to hold cabinet meetings and picnics. On the opposite or South Brisbane bank a fine wharf has been erected for the Corporation, near the Dry Dock; hard by is the terminus of the South Brisbane Railway, which brings coal down to the vessels from the neighbourhood of Ipswich.

The city of North Brisbane proper lies in an almost perfect triangle, of which two sides are formed by the river, and the third by Ann Street, which runs from Petrie's Bight, opposite the Kangaroo Point Corner, to a point on the river about two hundred yards above the Victoria Bridge. If we cut off from this triangle the smaller triangle embracing the Botanical Gardens and the land attached to Government House and the Parliament Buildings, we have left a figure with two parallel sides—Ann and Alice Streets. The principal thoroughfare is Queen Street; all the streets parallel with it are named after ladies whose surnames have not been preserved, and are, on the north, Ann and Adelaide Streets; on the south, Elizabeth, Charlotte, Mary, Margaret, and Alice Streets. The cross streets are, starting from the west, William, George, Albert, Edward, Creek, and Eagle Streets. The last-named, however, is not at right angles to Queen Street, but runs alongside the wharves. For breadth, the streets will compare favourably with those of Sydney, though this, perhaps, is not saying a great deal. From Queen Street to Ann Street there is a gradual rise, which continues till we reach the Observatory Hill and Wickham Terrace. Brisbane, surrounded as it is by hills, possesses a series of what are called "Terraces," high ridges surmounted each by a winding road, on one side of which (the upper) are long rows of private houses. Of these, Wickham Terrace is nearest to the city. In the hollow between Wickham and Petrie Terraces are a public park and the Railway Station Reserve; the Sandgate railway passes by the Grammar School into Victoria Park, through which it runs. The Southern and Western Railway runs between Petrie Terrace on the right, and the North Quay, which lies on the river's bank to the left, and so passes westwards towards Milton and Towong, where One-tree Hill stands out clearly in the distance.

At the western extremity of Queen Street is the Victoria Bridge, a magnificent structure, spanning the river between North and South Brisbane. It is nearly a quarter of a mile long, and was only completed after many futile attempts to obtain a safe foundation. More than once during its erection the strong floods which at that time flushed the river, undermined the piles; and though begun in the year 1863, it was not finished until 1875. For the first year after its opening a toll was levied on traffic, but the bridge is now entirely supported by the Corporation funds. It was fitted with a swinging girder to allow the passage of vessels with tall masts; beyond this point, however, the river is now navigated only by small craft, and at the time when tramway lines were laid across the bridge, this girder was permanently fixed. In the "good old times" before the extension of the railway system to Brisbane, the greater part of the traffic to Ipswich and the interior went by water, and this beautiful stretch of forty miles was a second Mississippi, with small Mississippi steamers doing a brisk and profitable trade.

The chief street in South Brisbane is that nearest to the bridge, and running along the river bank—Stanley Street. Melbourne Street is the one leading to the bridge;

it stretches out in the direction of West End. Stanley Street is the business centre of South Brisbane; the others are mostly occupied by private houses. At its southern end are the Dry Dock and the terminus of the South Coast and Oxley Railways. Near the Railway Station it is crossed by Vulture Street, which runs along the chain of hills that flanks this portion of the city, and leads into River Terrace, where the beetling cliffs tower over Government House Domain and the Botanical Gardens on the opposite side of the river. River Terrace terminates in Main Street, which runs downhill to Kangaroo Point Corner; and now there is only the river between us and Ann Street.

We have supposed a visitor coming to Brisbane. His first care is to select his hotel; and we shall find that in describing Brisbane its hotels constitute a good starting-point. The difficulty in choosing an hotel arises more from an *embarras de richesses* than from any other cause, the number of such establishments being very large; larger, probably, in proportion to the population than in Sydney and Melbourne. For Brisbane in the summer is, indeed, a thirsty place, and the breweries do a fine trade. Until the year 1878 Perkins' City Brewery was the only one in existence. It is now a compact pile of buildings, with capacious cellarage,

MAP OF BRISBANE.

extending from Mary Street to Margaret Street, in a wide block, and with a five-storeyed tower for the brewing process. In the year mentioned, Messrs. Fitzgerald, of the Castlemaine Brewery Company, erected premises for brewing purposes at Milton, about a mile from the city, on the Southern and Western Railway. Still later (about 1884), the Queensland Brewing Company commenced operations on the river bank at Bulimba, near Breakfast Creek. Besides the hotels there are clubs, where bachelors can find accommodation — the newly-erected Queensland Club, the town-house of squatters, and of country members of Parliament, who are here situated close to the scene of their labours; the Union, in Charlotte Street; and the Johnsonian (Literary), in William Street, presided over by Australia's foremost living poet, Mr. J. Brunton Stephens.

In Brisbane the working man holds a strong position. He works eight hours on five days of the week, five on Saturdays, and has a special annual holiday (Eight Hours' day) all to himself. On this occasion he makes a grand display, and walks in a procession, with numerous banners. The chief trades of the city are represented by iron foundries, shipbuilding yards, saw-mills, masonry and rope-works; ice-works also are naturally numerous. The wood and coal consumed in the city come chiefly by rail from the neighbourhood of Oxley and of Ipswich. The absence of fish in the river for some years past has been attributed to the effect on the river water of the refuse from the gasworks.

The prisoners formerly had their home near the Police Barracks on Petrie Terrace,

STEAMER LEAVING BRISBANE WITH MINERS.

until it was transferred to a position near Woolloongabba, South Brisbane, where it is the scene of a variety of industries; while the penal establishment at St. Helena, a small island in Moreton Bay, set apart for long-sentence prisoners, bears evidence, in its flourishing crops of sugar-cane, and in a pier erected for the accommodation of steamers, of the enforced diligence of its population. Its insular position and considerable distance from the mainland have not prevented escapes being frequently attempted and sometimes accomplished. The venturesome swimmer has, however, more than once fallen a victim to the sharks that abound in the locality.

The Brisbane water supply is drawn from an artificial lake at Enoggera, about eight miles north-west of the city. This lake is fed by a number of pretty creeks that flow down from the range of mountains by which it is encircled. Some years ago it was the favourite haunt of the sportsman who was lucky enough to come armed with a permit from the Board of Waterworks, which licensed him to use the official boat and

## THE SCHOOLS.

schools of the colony. The competitors must be under the age of fourteen. A number of scholarships are awarded annually by the Grammar School Trustees (at the Brisbane Grammar School the number is six), by which the term of the State School Scholarship is continued for two years longer, so that the foremost boys obtain five years' grammar-school education free of charge. Finally, three exhibitions (each worth £300), are annually awarded by the Government, and are open for competition to those under the age of nineteen who wish to proceed from any grammar-school to any university.

The chief Primary School in Brisbane is the "Normal School," a stone building at the corner of Edward and Adelaide Streets, which has a daily attendance of over five hundred. There are other large primary schools in both North and South Brisbane. The Boys' and Girls' Grammar Schools are in close proximity in the Victoria Park, opposite Gregory Terrace. The Boys' School was built in 1880, when it was found that the old building in Roma Street would be needed by the railway authorities; the Girls' School is still more recent. The former is a handsome brick edifice in the Gothic style, and consists of a main building, with two cross buildings at its ends and a large hall across the centre. The hall is fitted with two large stained-glass windows, one of which contains pictures of the Queen and prominent English worthies. The grounds are attractively planted with English and tropical flowers and trees; two Moreton Bay figs, planted by the two sons of

DRY DOCK.

the Prince of Wales on their visit in 1881, are especially handsome, and thrive vigorously. In the school ground are a gymnasium and several lawn-tennis courts, while at the other side of the Sandgate Railway, about three hundred yards off, is a turfed cricket ground.

Not far away, further round Gregory Terrace, is the Christian Brothers' Catholic School, a flourishing institution with about two hundred pupils. There are innumerable private schools in town and suburbs for the education of both sexes; one of the most important being All-Hallows' Convent, which is built on perhaps the finest of the many fine sites in Brisbane. Situate at the river end of Bowen Terrace, the convent towers over Petrie's Bight and Kangaroo Point Corner on the opposite side of the river; it is visible from almost every part of the town, and is the first object in the city that meets the eye of the visitor who arrives by steamer. It is a two-storeyed building, in the simplest possible style.

Important adjuncts to a popular education exist in the School of Arts and the Museum. The former is a spacious building, with wide verandas suitable to the climate, and is situate in Ann Street. The upper floor is occupied by ladies' and gentlemen's reading-rooms, where Colonial and English newspapers are to be found.

1. THE CITY FROM ONE TREE HILL.
2. THE RIVER FROM ONE TREE HILL.

Downstairs is a circulating library of several thousand volumes. The Museum is in William Street, on the river's bank, below the bridge; its specimens of mineralogy and natural history, its stuffed quadrupeds and bipeds, and the live cobras in their glass cases always prove attractive to the country visitor. Almost next door to this building is the Immigration Depôt, a scene of great bustle and excitement when every fresh batch of immigrants arrives, and would-be masters and mistresses assemble to select or be selected by their future "assistants," as the term goes.

The chief place of recreation in the city is the Botanical Gardens. The portion of these gardens nearest to the city is called the Queen's Park, and is not planted like

VIEW FROM THE BOTANICAL GARDENS.

the rest, but kept as a reserve for tennis, cricket, and football. Upon entering by the principal gate (at the end of Albert Street), the visitor is under a huge canopy of the evergreen bamboo, which affords in summer delightful shade to the weary citizen and his untiring companion—the mosquito. To the right is a small lake, whose bank is lined with bamboos, and whose surface is decked with pink and white water-lilies; beyond this are the tennis courts, where the bank clerk and the law student may be seen taking their exercise between four and six in the afternoon. To the left of the entrance is a wide space, turfed in the centre, where three cricket clubs practise in the summer months; during the winter it serves the same purpose for footballers. Brisbane produces some good footballing talent, and has bravely held its own with Sydney during the last few years; but cricket is not what it should be, owing partly to the inferior quality of the wickets, which results chiefly from the lengthened droughts, and partly, perhaps, to the enervating effect on the players of a Queensland summer. There are various other cricket and football grounds at a little distance from the town—the Union Ground at Toowong, the Albert Sports Ground at Bowen Hills, and Kedron Park, near Lutwyche; all of these are well patronised on Saturday afternoons.

The possession of such a splendid river ought to be a great incentive to rowing men, and there are some half-dozen rowing clubs in Brisbane; but the city has not yet produced a Beach or a Laycock, and does not seem likely to, for training in the summer months would be too great a punishment even for the athlete. Sailing, however, is extremely popular, and many delightful trips are made to the Bay for fishing purposes between Saturday and Monday. There are several fine yachts on the river, and the Brisbane larrikin, when he hoists his shoulder-of-mutton sail on his flat-bottomed and square-nosed "punt," may be seen scudding before the wind at a high rate of speed. But let us go back to the Gardens.

The ground occupied by the Botanical and Government House Gardens, and the land attached to the Houses of Legislature, occupies the river frontage for a distance of about two miles. The Botanical Gardens are tastefully laid out with walks, flower-beds, shrubberies, and groves of trees, native and tropical trees being predominant. The whole of what now forms these Gardens was once an immense swamp, of which the only remaining relics are some half-dozen pretty lakes, overgrown with lilies, and hidden beneath clumps of the umbrageous bamboo. The curator's house stands on a gentle rise at the far end: between it and the river is a small aviary. Altogether, these Gardens, though small in comparison with some in the southern colonies, are in point of situation and general attractiveness surpassed by none.

Government House Domain is entered by way of George Street—the lodge is just beside the Parliament Buildings. Government House itself is pretty, but exceedingly small; indeed, from the cliff, on the opposite side of the river, it looks quite insignificant. As a matter of fact, the extensive hospitality demanded from it has on several interesting occasions of late years caused the erection of marquees and annexes. The Governor has a summer residence at Southport, while his predecessor bestowed some *éclat* on Toowoomba by selecting his summer seat near that town, on the summit of the Main Range.

Parliament House is a substantial block of stone buildings, rising to three storeys, and capped with little turrets of galvanised iron. Besides the two Legislative Chambers, with their galleries for reporters and the public, there is a magnificent Parliamentary Library, and also a dining-hall.

Two important public buildings stand close together in George Street—the Land

Office and the Supreme Court. The former is a brick building, chiefly noticeable to one walking along the street by reason of the large clock which stands out from the front door. The Supreme Court buildings are well removed from the street, and occupy the whole block between George and William Streets. The courts proper are on the second floor; downstairs are comfortable chambers for the three judges and their associates, as well as for the registrar and other functionaries.

There is one cathedral in Brisbane, and one pro-cathedral, besides a goodly number of churches. St. Stephen's Roman Catholic Cathedral is in Elizabeth Street, opposite the City Police Court, and behind the Post Office; it is a handsome stone building, with an elegant steeple and artistic stained-glass windows. It is especially noted for possessing a fine choir. St. John's Anglican Pro-Cathedral, between George and William Streets, has attached to it a splendid peal of eight bells, which is heard to great advantage, especially by those in the immediate neighbourhood, on Sundays, and on one evening in the week, when there is a practice. The other principal Anglican Church is All Saints, at the junction of Creek Street and Wickham Terrace, and next to it is a Presbyterian church; this denomination possesses another further down Creek Street, with a spire one hundred and twenty feet high. St. Mary's (Anglican), Kangaroo Point, is a pretty little church, perched on the high cliff that rises from the water's edge.

The chief places of amusement in town are the Theatre Royal, in Elizabeth Street, and the Albert Hall, in Adelaide Street. The latter is much used for concerts and balls; the theatre, though an immense improvement on the wretched wooden building that did duty in that capacity less than eight years ago, is still not good enough to satisfy the growing theatrical taste of the Brisbane public. Shakespearean representations, and the better class of comedy, are at present rarely put upon the boards. The chief English and Comic Opera Companies, however, generally spend a couple of months in the year at Brisbane. The Exhibition Building, apart from the prominence into which it rises every August, when the Queensland National Association holds its annual show, is much used for tea-meetings and large balls, such as the Mayor's annual ball. The Brisbane people, perhaps because the community is small—the last census returns show a population of fifty-two thousand inhabitants—are extremely sociable, and notwithstanding the warm weather that prevails even in the winter months, the "season" lasts for more than six months of the year. At Christmas and Easter many of the citizens proceed to Southport and Sandgate, to recruit themselves with sea-breezes and salt-water, and at these places, even in the middle of summer, dancing is not unknown.

The chief of the city streets is Queen Street; and this we have left to form the conclusion of our sketch of Brisbane. At the corner of George and Queen Streets stands the Bank of New South Wales, the first of a series of banks that we shall meet. Further down Queen Street, on the left hand side, is the Town Hall, a building of considerable age, and showing signs of wear. The upper floor, at the rear of the building, is occupied by barristers' chambers. On the ground floor is an open quadrangle, around which are the small offices of accountants and commission agents;

those of the mayor and the other municipal authorities are nearer the street. The acoustic properties of the large hall are very deficient, though it is chiefly used for public meetings; and a site for a new Town Hall has been selected at the corner of Albert and Roma Streets (the latter is a wide thoroughfare leading out to the railway station). On the same side of Queen Street, and at the corner of Albert Street, is a pile of buildings that would do credit to any city in Australasia, occupied by shops of drapers, booksellers, and photographers. Passing

IN THE BOTANICAL GARDENS.

on, still eastwards, at the corner of Queen and Edward Streets we have four important buildings. The first is the largest draper's shop in Brisbane. The second, on the opposite side of Queen Street, is the recently-erected Brisbane Arcade, which runs in a curve from Queen Street to Edward Street. The lower storey is divided, as is the manner of arcades, into a number of tasteful shops; the upper balcony opens into the offices of various commission agents. On one of the two remaining corners are the premises of the Australian Mutual Provident Society; on the other is the immense seven-storeyed pile of the Brisbane Newspaper Company. This Company issues three papers—*The Brisbane Courier* (price 2d.), the only morning daily, of which the *Observer* is an evening edition (price 1d.), intended chiefly

1. A BIT OF THE BUSH HOUSE ACCLIMATISATION GARDENS.
2. FOUNTAINS.  3. THE AVIARY.

for the working man, as a rival to the Liberal organ, *The Daily Telegraph*; the weekly journal of the Company is the *Queenslander*. Further down, on our left, is a stately block containing the shops of a jeweller, a tailor, and an ironmonger; further still is the Joint Stock Bank. Opposite the "Royal" are the Post and Telegraph Offices. The *locale* of the latter was formerly in William Street, but some years ago it was found more convenient to have the two establishments together, and a second building was erected alongside the first, and a *fac-simile* of it. There is often a considerable difference between the time indicated by the Post Office clock and that recorded by the gun fired from the Observatory at 1 P.M. on six days in the week, which is supposed to represent standard time. Brisbane time, it may be mentioned, is about five minutes faster than Sydney, and thirty minutes faster than Melbourne, time. Adjoining the Royal Hotel is the Brisbane Exchange, which has been removed from its former position, at the corner of Queen and Albert Streets. In the reading-room, downstairs, weather and business telegrams are to be seen. The rest of the building is taken up with the office of the Secretary and those of many prominent business men.

The last, but by no means the least, notable edifice is at the corner of Creek Street—the newly-erected and splendidly finished premises of the Queensland National Bank, certainly the finest, though not the largest, building in the city, and one of the handsomest banks in the colonies. It is built in the classical Italian style, and the stonework is highly ornamental. This bank has the custody of the Government moneys, and its half-yearly balance-sheets show a progressive development since its foundation unsurpassed by that of any bank in Australia. At the opposite corners are other large banks.

At the corner of Queen and Eagle Streets is the omnibus stand, from which 'buses run to South Brisbane and Woolloongabba, West End, Toowong (a pretty but usually dusty drive as far as the general cemetery, along the river's bank nearly the whole way), and likewise to Petrie Terrace and Kelvin Grove; others run along the Enoggera (Waterworks) road. From the other end of Queen Street 'buses ply to Gregory Terrace, the Valley and New Farm, Breakfast Creek and the Hamilton. The introduction of tramways has considerably diminished the business of the 'bus proprietor. The tram-cars are roomy, and generally well built; some have the top storey.

We shall conclude with a short reference to another important means of public conveyance—the ferries, which are invaluable to the residents of Kangaroo Point and some parts of South Brisbane. Kangaroo Point possesses one steam ferry, owned by a company, and three boat ferries, leased by the Corporation. The former runs from the foot of Elizabeth Street, North Brisbane, at regular intervals between 7 A.M. and 7 P.M. Since the construction of the British India Steam Navigation wharf on the Point side, the dray traffic by this route has been very large, while it is generally preferred for personal transit to the slow and somewhat unwieldy ferry-boats. The "lower" ferry runs from the foot of Queen Street to the end of Main Street, Kangaroo Point; the "middle" ferry, from Alice Street; and the "upper" ferry, from the far end of the Gardens to the rocks below River Terrace; the journey by this route involves the passenger in an arduous climb. Other ferries run to South Brisbane from the western end of Alice Street and the North Quay.

Sandgate, to which reference has already been made, is a rising watering-place prettily situate on the shores of Moreton Bay and Cabbage Tree Creek, some twelve miles north of Brisbane, with which it has intimate railway communication. The enterprise of its inhabitants has provided a pier of no mean pretensions for the accommodation of visitors from the capital; the Corporation—for although the population at the last census was only about 1,500, the town has for several years been under municipal government—has also greatly improved the facilities for bathing, by erecting several public bathing-houses and shelter-sheds. With these and other attractions, it is not surprising that the place should be so largely resorted to by the citizens of Brisbane, pining for breezes that are as the breath of life to lungs which, in the heated air of the capital, have almost forgotten their office.

SANDGATE PIER.

NEAR SUVA.
(From a Photograph by Burton Bros., Dunedin.)

## UNTRODDEN TRACKS IN FIJI.

Fiji—Its History—Suva—Government House—Cricket and Tinka—Armstrong's Point—The Botanical Gardens—Viti Levu—Sugar Plantations—Nandronga—A Fijian House—Fijian Comestibles—A Dance—Yangona—An Early Start—Refreshments—A Native Hut—Photographing—Mount Tomainivi—Hairdressing—Halts—The Summit—Na Matakula—Fijian Boats—A Moonlight Dance—A Fish Weir—Levuka.

I WANTED a holiday, I wanted to get away from letters, from work, from the worry of business and the worry of pleasure. I longed to see something of the tropics, and, much as I love England, to view her from the greatest possible distance. So I started for the Pacific, taking my passage to Auckland, by direct steamer to New Zealand round the Cape, as it would have been unpleasantly hot by "the Canal" in August. From Auckland I took a passage to Suva in the Union Steamship Company's steamer *Arawata*, of over one thousand tons; and after running up to the picturesque Bay of Islands to coal, we steered straight for our destination.

Before going further with my story, it may be as well to say that the Crown Colony of Fiji consists of over two hundred and fifty islands, nearly a hundred of which are inhabited, situated in the tropics between 15° and 22° S. latitude, and 177 W. and 175 E. longitude, the opposite meridian to that of Greenwich passing through the middle of them. They are dotted about over an area of two hundred miles from north to south, and three hundred from east to west, and are midway between New Caledonia and the Tongan (or Friendly Island) group. Their estimated area is a little over eight thousand square miles, or rather larger than that of Wales. Viti Levu, the principal island, in which the present capital, Suva, is situated, contains about half this area. The population of the whole is estimated to be nearly 127,500, of whom about 115,000 are Fijians, 5,700 Polynesians, 2,500 Asiatics, 800 half-castes, and 3,500 Europeans.

Tasman, the great Dutch navigator, discovered the islands in 1643, and was the first to make them known to Europeans. He called them Prins Wilhelm's Eylanden. After this they appear to have been unvisited for upwards of a century, when Captain Cook touched at one of them. In 1804 twenty-seven convicts, who appear to have been monsters of iniquity, escaped from New South Wales and settled here, chiefly at Rewa and Bau. In 1859, King Thakombau offered the sovereignty of the islands, under certain conditions, to Great Britain, but it was declined then, as was also a similar offer made in March, 1874; but by a deed of cession dated the 10th of October, 1874, the islands were ceded to the British Crown, and a Charter was soon afterwards issued making them into a separate colony. Sir A. H. Gordon, G.C.M.G., arrived in June, 1875, and on the 1st of September assumed the Governorship. He was succeeded by Sir G. W. Des Vœux, K.C.M.G., and during his absence from the colony the Hon. J. B. Thurston, C.M.G., was appointed Administrator; his successor was Sir C. B. H. Mitchell, K.C.M.G. The affairs of the colony are administered by a Governor and Executive Council. The laws are prepared by a Legislative Council of thirteen members, of whom seven are official, and six nominated by the Governor. The Imperial laws are followed, except where there has been local legislation. Trial by jury has been abolished, and jury cases are decided by the judge and two assessors.

The *Arawata* had a fair passage across the thousand miles of calm sea that separate

VIEW OF THE REWA RIVER.

New Zealand from Fiji, and we obtained a glimpse of Gondavo, the most southerly island, soon after sunset on the fourth day after leaving the Bay of Islands. We then steamed slowly towards Suva so as to enter the channel through the reefs by daylight.

These are the latitudes where life on a steamer is a real pleasure, for it is warm enough to sit constantly on deck, to revel under the awning by day, and in the evening, after dinner, to sit chatting at intervals with our captain and fellow-passengers while we gaze at the glorious sunset clouds. Later on, songs and yarns are the order of the evening.

As we pass through the narrow channel in the reef opposite Suva, and approach the pier, the long roofs of Government House are visible about a mile to the right. In front is the town of Suva, spread along close to the shore, with a road in front of the houses just above the beach. Dotted about the hills are wooden villas with spacious verandas, and away on the left, unbroken forest, stretching away to a range of mountains. On the pier there is a gay crowd to meet us—Europeans who have sauntered down to hear the news and look at the new arrivals, and Fijians, Samoans, Tongans, and Indian natives, people of all colours, from white through every shade of brown to black, all laughing and chatting together.

A couple of stalwart natives carrying my baggage precede me to the hotel, and on the way I have time to revel in the gay colouring and sunny aspect of the place, to admire the fern-like grace of the cocoanut palms, with their great fronds trembling in the breeze, and to get my first glimpse of the curious native canoes, with their outriggers of wood. There are good hotels here, and the charges are reasonable; and we soon find our way to one of the best, where we found that there was plenty of good society to be had. Many of those employed in the different Government departments reside here, and others who have houses come to it for meals, as it saves them many of the troubles of housekeeping.

A mile or so away, near Government House, is the native village, the houses made of reeds and leaves. In close neighbourhood are one or two good houses of high officials, surrounded, as most of the houses are, with gardens, gay with crotons and other "foliage" plants. A fine airy building, this Government House, long and irregular, built of wood, and covered with shingles instead of the eternal corrugated iron, with, of course, plenty of veranda space, a bold flight of steps leading up to it, and a sentry pacing to and fro at the bottom—a fine fellow with a white sulu (a cloth from the waist to the knee) and jersey, and red sash round the waist, and carrying a rifle. He is one of the armed native constabulary.

Passing through the gardens of Government House, we came upon a grass field with a few native houses round the sides, and entered one to call on the wife of the native officer of the armed constabulary. My companion, who talks Fijian fluently, introduced me, and we sat down on the mats spread all over the floor, and found the good lady very pleased to see us, while her jolly little boy, about twelve months old, came and "tamaed" to us, taking our hands and putting them to his lips, making a peculiar guttural noise. Another day, when I came here, I found the men playing cricket with great zest, and delighted at my joining in and "fielding out." One or two wore a jersey, but most of them only a sulu round the waist, and one fellow with pads on his bare legs looked very comical. One of the men, who was bowling, had his face blackened to look smart, but though he was such a dandy he bowled well, and was soon able to get me out.

In another part of the ground some of the men and a fine lad of sixteen or so were playing tinka. This is a very favourite game with Fijians. It consists in throwing a bamboo or reed spear with a head of hard wood of an elongated oval shape. It is held between the fingers and thumb, with the forefinger on the end, and a short run is taken to throw it. It strikes the ground ten or twenty yards away, and then bounds up and goes a long way in the air, at a height of three or four feet from the ground.

Further on we come to Armstrong's Point, near which Mr. Armstrong has a plantation of nearly a hundred acres of bananas. These are brought down by a tram to a creek, where they are loaded into barges, in which they are afterwards taken round to the harbour and sent by steamer to Sydney or New Zealand. The current price here is one shilling a bunch, and the freight is one shilling, but in Sydney they fetch four or five shillings. A good many cases of pineapples are sent too, and an amusing sight it is to go out to the Sydney steamer just before she sails, and to watch the boats, chiefly cutters and large canoes, owned by natives, crowding round waiting their turn to unload, amid a babel of voices.

From the Point we get a view of the opening to the Rewa river, where we see a three-masted ship anchored, waiting to take its load of sugar from the huge sugar-mill up the river. The mill belongs to the Colonial Sugar Company, and is said to be the largest in the world. As we recross the little bridge over the creek, we notice the long seeds or seed-pods of the mangrove, like very long, narrow cigars, floating away upright in the water with the root end down, ready to found a new plantation of mangroves wherever the current may drift them.

On the other side of Suva a walk of a mile or so brings one to the Botanical Gardens, which, though only in their infancy, are well worth seeing, for they contain many fine trees and shrubs, among them being cinnamon, with its branches terminating in pale-red foliage, cacao, sarsaparilla, candle-nuts, &c.; but towering above all, and worth going far to see, is a magnificent banyan tree. It is apparently pushed high above the earth by its roots, and the proper trunk of the tree commences many feet above the ground. Near it there is a path, on each side of which are a few graves, one of which is marked only by a great bush of gardenia covered with flowers.

In the year 1875 there was a war in Viti Levu, in a district called Tholo. The natives had not then asked for English rule, and they fought against it. Their rising was treated as a rebellion, which after some fighting was put down by Sir Arthur Gordon, some of the leaders being shot as rebels. Now the district is quiet enough, but the authorities watch it carefully, knowing that the old wild spirit might be again roused in some paltry quarrel, and when once excited might be difficult to quell. It is a mountainous tract of country, and the natives have little intercourse with white men, and live here much in their old state, though they have given up cannibalism and club-law and devil worship. Some, no doubt, still hanker after cannibalism, and there seems to have been a little relapse in that direction during the war.

This district seemed to be the most interesting to visit, and I applied for permission to travel there—for no one can do so without permission of the Government. I was given the necessary authorisation by the Acting Colonial Secretary, who at the same time conveyed to me a gracious invitation from the Hon. J. B. Thurston, the

A SUGAR-CANE PLANTATION.
(From a Photograph by Messrs. Burton Bros.)

Administrator, to accompany him, as he was going to visit the district, and, if possible, make the ascent of Tomainivi, the highest mountain in the Fiji group.

On the morning we were to start I met Mr. Thurston at Government House, and at the jetty below we were joined by the Chief Justice (Mr. Fielding Clarke) and Lieutenant Malan, R.N. Half-a-dozen of the native constabulary soon pulled us out to the *Clyde*, the Government steamer. Our plan was to go some sixty miles down the coast-land, and cross the island from south to north, stopping at Fort Carnarvon, in the middle of the island, for a few days, and ascending Tomainivi on our way from the Fort to the coast, where the *Clyde* was to meet us.

## SUGAR PLANTATIONS.

After coasting slowly along for two or three hours, most of the time inside the reef, and with the captain or one of the men most uncomfortably perched on an iron bar nearly at the top of the foremast, looking out for isolated patches of reef, we reached Naitonitoni, and went ashore to visit the sugar plantations near the mouth of the Navuo river. We first passed through one which had failed, and was a melancholy sight, with the cane not properly attended to, and costly tramrails, machinery, and buildings going to ruin. We then crossed the river by boat to the flourishing sugar plantation of the Fiji SugarCompany. Here

FIJIAN HOUSES.

everything looked prosperous and well managed. In this plantation there are some seven hundred acres of cane, but cane from more than twice that number of acres is crushed here. The labour employed is chiefly that of coolies; the number of these in Fiji is surprising, and one would have supposed that the large population of these islands, and of the countless islands of the Pacific, would have sufficed. But as one cannot "indenture" the natives for a term of years, and so insure regular labour, the Government imports coolies from India, who are indentured for ten years to the planters. They have to give £21 for each coolie, find hospitals and lodgings, and pay wages. The pay averages about one shilling a day for men, and ninepence for women. We got on a sugar truck, and were run gaily up the plantation behind a little engine of French make. There was cane ready to cut, cane cut, and cane being planted, everything apparently going on at once. The soil was red and hard, like burnt clay, so that it was presumably of comparatively recent volcanic origin. We had a pretty view looking over a considerable extent of sugar-cane and fields, with the coolies working like bees below, the bends of the river visible here and there, and hilly country in the distance.

The next day we made an early start, and steamed most of the time just outside the reef, and though apparently there was hardly any swell, and there were no waves where we were, on the reef there were fine breakers, which rose in some places several feet, and then fell on the reef in splendid cataracts of foam. Opposite Naudronga, a native town, there was an entrance in the reef, and we were "pulled" in by some of the native constabulary in the galley, and a hard pull they had, for we had to go between a small island and the mainland, and the tide was racing out of the channel.

We landed at a little jetty near Naudronga. Round the town was a high bamboo fence, but over the entrance one or two bamboos were tied at a height of about four or five feet. I thought this an inconvenient sort of entrance, but was told it was to insure everybody's stooping on entering, as a mark of respect to the chief. We found the latter—the roko of Naudronga is his title—and the principal men of the town sitting on the ground, or on their heels; on the Administrator approaching they "tamaed" to him. The "tama" is a mark of respect, and varies in different parts of the colony. Here the natives give guttural noises like "Oe, ugh," pronounced slowly, and then hit their hands together—I can hardly call it clapping them—striking the palm of the left hand rather slowly, and all at the same time.

Then the roko rose and shook hands, a custom to which the natives have taken very kindly. Sometimes it is amusing to see them shaking hands with one another, and also to see them dawdling down the streets at Suva or Levuka, one man with his little finger linked in that of another.

After the interchange of a few words we went to the roko's house and shook hands with his wife, who was lying full length on the floor with her little boy beside her; and then we all sat down on the floor, or lay down and gazed up at the roof. There are quantities of cocoanut leaves under the mats, and on a hot day one can lie there, taking no notice of anything, for an hour or two with great comfort, and at the same time with the happy consciousness that he is doing the right thing. Mr. Thurston conversed with the roko, and some of the older men came in and sat at a respectful distance and listened. Smoking goes on on these occasions, with the aid of seleukas, as they are called, of native tobacco, rolled up into a piece of banana leaf, and handed to you in a split reed; one often sees a native with one or two ready in advance, stuck through the hole in his ear. The house is built on a very high platform of stones, eight feet above the ground, with a log placed at an angle of about forty-five degrees reaching up to the entrance. There were niches cut in it for the feet, and in this case the unusual help of a long pole stuck in the ground was provided, but even thus one had to be careful, for a fall from near the top would be no slight matter. The house is oblong, with a roof-tree supported on two big posts, one near each end of the dwelling. The measurements would be about forty feet long by twenty wide, and perhaps thirty high.

Near the coast the houses are generally oblong, with a ridge, and the roof-tree or ridge-pole sometimes projects a yard at each end, and is very often ornamented with large white cowrie shells. In the interior they are generally nearly square, with rounded corners; they have a huge post in the centre, inside, and the roof rises in a conical shape to a great height, while the sides or walls, of a sort of wicker-work, are not more than about five feet high. There are no nails used in building, but the houses are put together either with creepers bound round where the timbers, poles, or bamboos join or abut against each other, or with sinnet, which is a stout string made by the natives. The best house which I saw had walls—as I must call them, though they were made of reeds—interwoven with sinnet, with sixteen posts of greenwood inside, to which the wall-plates were tied. Then near each end of the house were two large posts tapering to the top, and about two feet in diameter, supporting a long roof-tree nearly a foot in diameter, which projected about three feet beyond the roof outside the thatch, and the rafters, in this case of poles, but very commonly of bamboo, were tied at one end to the wall-plate, and at the top to the roof-tree, and supported at three different points by purlins. Wherever two pieces of timber cross one another they are bound together by black and yellow sinnet, wound round so that the colours form bold patterns. The doorways are closed by mats hung on sinnet, and the roof is covered with a broad-leaved grass, with wild sugar-cane plaited on the inside, and the walls outside with reddish-brown leaves about the size and shape of Spanish chestnut leaves. The floors are covered with mats spread on cocoanut leaves. Better mats indicate the sleeping-place, while a hollow sunk in the floor, and a frame round it of heavy wood, with smoke wreathing slowly upwards, mark the fireplace.

In the evening we had a present of food called a mangete, and after that a yangona meke, or formal yangona drinking. Yangona, or kava, is the root of the yangona tree, and a very important ceremony is made of drinking it. All the principal men in the village came in, and sat down on the floor at the sides and one end of the house, while the Administrator sat at the other end on a chair, and we round him. A yangona bowl, a big wooden basin on four dwarf legs, with a rope attached to one side, was brought out and placed at the end of the house furthest from us, with the rope carefully arranged so that the end should point towards Mr. Thurston. A matter of particular importance is this of the rope, and we were told that in the old days anyone passing between the chief and the bowl, or across the rope, would have received a finishing touch with a club. A root of yangona, which was presented with great ceremony, was then scraped and cut into great mouthfuls by one of the men, and handed to some young men to chew. They sat near the yangona bowl at the end, slowly munching away at their enormous mouthfuls, and when they had done this for some time, they took the chewed root out of their mouths and placed it in the bowl. Water was then added, being ladled into the bowl in a cup made of cocoanut shell, and the yangona maker commenced his apparently arduous labours.

Two men now began to sing, and after they had sung a few words, the strain was repeated by the rest, while all swayed their bodies, first in one direction, then in another, stretching out their arms, and striking their hands together at intervals, and all simultaneously, and ending the chorus with a sort of grunt. At the same time a tinkling was made on a drum, which consisted of a length of bamboo. Then there was a pause for a minute or so, when the two men began again, and the rest struck in as before.

All the time this was going on, the man at the bowl was working hard stirring the yangona about with a swab made of fibre. When it was ready to be drunk there was a great noise, the lali, or wooden drum, which is a piece of a big tree with a hole dug out of it with an adze, being beaten, and conches, which look like gigantic whelk shells, being blown. The fine deep note of these shells can be heard a great distance. A cup of cocoanut shell was next filled, and a man carried it, half-stooping and half-crawling, until he came within about five feet of Mr. Thurston, when, resting on his knees and one hand, he stretched the other with the yangona towards Mr. Thurston, who by dint of a great stretch got hold of it and drank it off. Afterwards we came in for our cup, and then the natives, in order of precedence, except the young men, who are not allowed to drink it, as it is apt to excite them and lead to mischief. There is, by-the-bye, a heavy fine for supplying the natives with intoxicating liquor, which seems to have a good effect.

I had made up my mind to drink yangona, though, of course, one is not prepossessed in its favour by witnessing the mode of its preparation. The cup, half of an enormous cocoanut shell, nearly full, was handed to me by the native sprawling below me. I just saw that the liquid was thick-looking, like coffee, with a little milk in it —sighed, breathed an inward aspiration that I might behave like a dauntless Englishman, took a deep inhalation, so as to finish it at one draught if I could, as that is the correct thing, and went at it. I was agreeably relieved at finding it of a clean, subacid nature, without much flavour, and finishing it, took the cup between my finger and thumb, and gave it a little spin on the mats near my grovelling friend. A few claps followed, which I took as applause, though, of course, they were not meant so, and then I began to experience a rather pleasant astringent feeling in the throat. Many Europeans are very fond of yangona, as it has a slightly exhilarating effect, and is a decided "pick-me-up," they say, for a tired person. Two or three cups, however, produce intoxication, if that may be called intoxication which does not attack the brain. The head is perfectly clear and unclouded, but is made only too well aware, if it directs a movement, that it has absolutely no control over the legs. Continued excess in yangona drinking—and some Europeans drink half a gallon a day—sometimes destroys the eyesight, and usually causes a deplorable wreck of the whole system. One doctor told me he considered persistent yangona drinking worse than the excessive use of opium or of alcohol.

A FIJIAN VILLAGE NEAR LEVUKA.

The following morning we made an early start, and a fine procession we were, ourselves and Mr. Thompson—the magistrate from Nandronga—with horses, then some half a score of native constabulary from Suva, with the Administrator's master of ceremonies, as I must call him, and his servant, a native who could cook a little, and about thirty prisoners sent down with one or two constables from Fort Carnarvon as carriers. We had to furnish ourselves with rugs and mosquito nets, native mats for sleeping on, some clothes, and a large amount of biscuits, tinned meat and soup, bacon, whisky, and tea. As enough provisions had to be taken for a fortnight, and all this had to be carried swung on bamboos between two men over narrow paths, often very steep, our escort can hardly be thought excessive. We started in heavy rain, and as we left the village we saw the yellow flowers of the cotton plant, the remains of an old plantation. At one time everybody was to make his fortune with cotton. And this is all that is left!

After skirting the shore for some way, our path led inland across rather bare undulating ground, but presently we saw the river and village of Singatoka below us, with its plantations of plantains and its thatched roofs, overshadowed with cocoa palms. Here we had a mangeto presented to us. The arrival of the Administrator is greeted by the "tama," or double grunt, and the formal clapping of hands after it. He shakes hands with the chief, and then we have to sit down, very often on the edge of the raised platform surrounding a house, or on a log. Perhaps the first thing that is offered is a young cocoanut for each of us to drink. Oh! how deliciously cool this draught is after a hot ride. If the nuts are not ready, up goes an agile fellow, not swarming, but almost walking, up the rough bark of the bare stem, and throws them down; then the outer rind is struck on the end of a pointed stick, and torn off with hands and teeth, then four taps with the edge of a long knife, and a neat little piece is cut out of the top, and it is ready. Now the women appear, with cooked yams and taro, the root of a sort of lily (*Caladium esculentum*). How funny they look with either a sulu or a niko, or fringe of fibre, from a few inches up to, perhaps, eighteen inches wide, tied round them. They come bending forward, carrying the food, put it on the ground, then fold their arms behind their backs, and go away, still bending, as a mark of respect. Next come men with great wooden trays with cooked pigs—enormous pigs, and little pigs, and pigs of all sorts and sizes, but all looking ghastly. The bones of their snouts are all bare from being cooked, and huge bits of stone and leaves have been placed inside them to keep them warm. The men bring forward the things the women have borne in, and pile them up, and, perhaps, bring a couple of ghastly boiled fowls, with long, headless necks, one leg resting peacefully on its breast, and the other pointing wildly to the sky; these are for our special delectation. Very likely there are also some yangona roots. A man now comes forward stooping, and sits down near us on his heels and presents the mangeto. Our master of ceremonies receives it with clapping of hands, and then proceeds to divide the food, keeping a certain amount for our escort, and leaving the rest for the villagers who have provided it. Our fellows get hold of immense chunks of pig and huge yams, and fill themselves as full as they can, eating on until we really think they are drunk with it, they become so stupid. What a time those prisoners had! What Fijian would not be a prisoner in like circumstances?—for the natives do not think it much of a disgrace to be prisoners. The natives of the village walked off with their share to their houses.

After the mangete there was an inspection of the school children in the native church. We suspected that several of them were children for that occasion only, as they must have been quite eighteen years old, but, of course, they helped to make a show. They sang a "meke" or sort of song, descriptive of a disease they had been suffering from, and its cure by means of sulphur. From this village we followed the course of the river Singatoka, there being a road, or, rather, a narrow footpath, all the way. This is often bordered by, or passes through, native gardens, or plantations of plantains or taro, and at other times runs through low bush or high grass, something like Pampas grass, which effectually prevents one from leaving the path or taking short cuts. In the afternoon we reached Raiwanka, a fine village with a broad "rara"— a street or open place—in the middle, and on each side two rows of houses, with, as usual, plenty of cocoanuts. I shall not again describe the mangete. Suffice it to say, we had one presented at every village we passed through, and occasionally it was brought to us on the road when we passed near a village without entering it. At Raiwanka we had a very good native house allotted to us. At first it seemed an inconvenient mode of living, but afterwards one gets used to it, and ultimately enjoys its perfect simplicity.

One enters on hands and knees into a dark interior—I say dark, because it is generally pretty late when one finishes the day's travel, and even at midday a house with no windows, and only one or two very small entrances, seems dark after the glare outside. Presently one discovers a big post in the centre, and two or three wooden pillows, or rather head-rests, generally made of a piece of bamboo. We each choose a spot to sleep upon, and put our boxes near it, and the provision boxes are placed between the roof-pole and the door. We get hold of a candle, and make it stick on a box, and then we all sprawl about on the floor and vote what we will have for dinner, and wait patiently while it is cooking, or if there be a bathing-place, as there generally is where we stop, we have a bath. When dinner comes we sit on the floor; plates, knives, forks, and spoons are strewn round us; and our cook brings in preserved soup boiled and served in its own tin, then some meat treated in the same way, with, perhaps, some yams and taro from the mangete, and we finish up with bread and jam, and drink either tea, cooked in a "billy," cocoa, or whisky. After a while we tie up our mosquito nets, and get our rugs and turn in. We rise early the next day, take soap, toothbrush, and even razor and looking-glass down to the river, and perform our toilet there. Then have a cup of tea and some biscuits, and having packed up, we are off. We stop for breakfast about ten, or later, to take our midday rest.

It was a very pretty scene, our leaving Raiwanka. We shook hands with some of the principal men, and then started ahead of our long line of attendants. All the village, of course, took care to see us start, the women keeping in the background, and peering out of the houses, the children looking wide-eyed at us, the very small ones stark naked. A laughing, merry group from the village follows us some distance. We made a short stay at Vunavuvindra, crossed the river, which was about up to the waist, and then reached Matinavato, a grand pile of rocks, with a precipitous face on one side, from underneath which a clear, cold spring came forth. The path most of the way was arched over with a sort of mulberry, a row having been planted on each side. We saw a great quantity of castor-oil plants on our way, and late in the afternoon, as we approached the village of Baimana, passed a very fine banyan tree.

On entering this village we met the magistrate from Fort Carnarvon, who had come down to meet us. The chief here was the proud owner of a rather good heifer, about half-grown. I suppose it was a fancy of his, for there were no others in the place. It was completely master of the village, but luckily it was very quiet; whenever it walked in any direction, the natives, however big and burly, cleared out, and it seemed very much surprised and hurt that we would not lodge for it, or acknowledge its rule.

Next morning there was quite a gay scene in the village, for we took a photograph or two of the place, and some of the people, including certain of the women, understood what we were about, and came out specially smart in consequence, some with green garlands thrown gracefully across their shoulders, and others with decorations of leaves over their sulus. The women, however, do not "take" very well. Being photographed is rather a solemn thing at the best of times, and when a Fijian woman is standing up before a white man with a queer instrument, and the whole village is looking on, no wonder if she feels as if she was about to be martyred, and loses her pleasant, genial, half-smiling expression.

A ten-mile ride under a hot sun brought us to Fort Carnarvon, where there is a handful of native constabulary, well drilled and armed, with between two and threescore

HEAD OF A FIJIAN (MALE).

prisoners. The fort is on the summit of a mound which slopes down to the river Singatoka, about two or three hundred yards off, with mountain ranges a few miles away in every direction. It is surrounded with a bamboo fence, overhung in many parts with mulberries, and surrounded in its turn with a ditch. There are a good many dwellings inside the fence for the native constables, the native officer, the prisoners, and the magistrate, who has five houses for his quarters, each house, however,

RIVER BATHING-PLACE.

only consisting of one room. There was a splendid bathing-place in the river below, and as Baimana had no such accommodation, we were very glad to pay it a visit. On Sunday I went to church in the morning. The native clergyman, or reader, had on a white shirt, not badly washed and ironed, and a sulu. A white shirt is the distinctive mark of a teacher or clergyman here, apparently. He read the prayers and lessons in Fijian, with great distinctness I should say, and read out a hymn, each line, after he said it, being sung very loudly to a wondrous variation of the Old Hundredth. One of the native constables led, and the others gave their ideas of the tune at the same time.

Another Sunday when I was present the magistrate's bulldog, Tiger, sat immediately opposite the reading-desk, and seemed never to take his eyes off the preacher. I never before saw a dog apparently so much impressed, or so reverent in church. The next day we had a great array of school children from the villages near. As before, several were rather advanced in years. They were put through their paces in reading and writing and some simple sums, which they did on slates in the orthodox fashion. They were spread out in two long lines inside the fort, and we sat above them on the stone front of the house; altogether there were about a hundred and seventy of them.

The next day the Administrator, Lieutenant Malan, the magistrate, and I, started on an expedition to the top of Tomainivi. I was mounted on a very old grey horse, and had to get off and scramble up all steep bits, as I was afraid of knocking him up, and I often let him help me by holding on to his tail, much to the amusement of the natives. We crossed the river, and soon reached Matuwalu, where they sent a man or two aloft for cocoanuts, which we soon finished. We had pigs, yangona, yams, and sugar-cane in the mangete here. Most of the older women have their lips, and all the space between their noses and chins, tattooed a uniform blue colour. The men are not much given to this form of decoration, though many of them are tattooed a little about the body and limbs, but it seems to be just according to the fancy of the individual. We saw here a man who had the bad reputation of having murdered a whole family on a plantation not far off.

From this place we ascended by a path, from which we got lovely views. Our way lay through parched grass, and high stuff like Pampas grass, until we reached the forest, which was at a height of about 1,300 feet. It was full of ferns, one sort having fronds twenty feet long. The wild ginger is very effective amidst the other foliage, for it has perfectly straight reddish-brown stems, and at the top great leaves pointing upwards, these leaves being between three and four feet long and a foot broad, and the stem and leaves together reaching a height of from twenty to perhaps thirty feet. Then, besides sarsaparilla and shaddocks, the latter covered with the fruit, and the ground below strewn with it in every stage, from ripeness to rottenness, there were lemons, caladiums, dracaenas, tree ferns, climbing ferns, rattans, various flowering shrubs, and a great variety of ferns. We reached a height of nearly three thousand feet, but afterwards descended some thousand feet to a stream, where we camped in the middle of the forest. We had sent some men on in front, and they had made us a capital shelter of small poles, covered entirely, sides and roof, with wild ginger leaves, tied on with creepers, and the floor strewn with grass. There were a good many men waiting to receive us with a mangete. Some of them had their faces painted: one had all his face below the eyes black, with a broad streak of black down the middle of his forehead; another appeared with his nose painted red, red spots on his forehead, and the rest of his face black. Most of the men shave; they take a great deal more trouble with their hair than any other men I ever met, and are very particular about polishing up their arm-rings of shell, which they wear just above the elbow; and there is a great deal of quiet swagger in the way some of them walk. I was told that they shave with flakes of glass, and the following petition, which I saw on a slate, was translated to me:—"Be of a good mind like unto a dove, and give me a razor to shave myself, as it hurts me to shave with glass." A Fijian's hair is a study. And one sees such varieties of ways of dressing it. Many have huge, shock heads of hair, but most carefully combed, sticking out straight away from the head all round, and beautifully trimmed at the ends. Others have the same arrangement in front, while behind a number of little corkscrew curls hang down to the neck, each tied at the end. Yet others have their hair sticking out in all directions, but in locks, like locks of wool. Then there are so many colours of hair, from red to dark brown, and sometimes, owing to the use of lime, two or three tints are to be seen on one head. Very often you notice a man or woman with hair like a well-powdered flunkey's, being plastered close to the head with lime, while others have a *poudré* appearance.

The next morning we started pretty early, and found it pleasantly cool in the forest. We had lunch at a place where we found natives waiting for us with a mangete. Opportunity was taken to photograph the chief Rawabalavu, who looks well enough pleased at the operation, and perhaps at the compliment of being included in the same picture as the Administrator. These natives had come from the town of Nabutautau, one of the last strongholds of the "rebel" mountaineers. All the way occasional glimpses of the valleys on each side below us, and also of distant mountains, were to be had. We were in the forest nearly all day, and then went down a steep decline to the Singatoka river, and came to the little town of Nandrow, a village of some score of houses. We had placed at our service a small house, which was rather difficult to get into, and still more difficult to get out of, the entrance was so narrow, and not more than two feet nine inches high. One could manage to crawl in, but in crawling out, the floor being one or two feet above the level of the ground outside, curious gymnastics had to be resorted to. This town lies right at the bottom of a gorge with an abrupt face of rock opposite, and the river makes a great noise. The buli (or chief) is a fine, tall old man, who walks about holding a staff about seven feet long.

Next day, up we had to go some seven hundred feet by an excessively steep path; the horses we had sent round by a long detour. We reached Nangatangata about ten, but did not enter the village. It was amusing to watch an incipient flirtation between a girl from the village and one of our attendants. He gave her a fine reeking chunk of pig and some yam from the mangete in a banana leaf, and as she took it she put her hand below and pressed his. The children were much amused and astonished at the horses, and were delighted when we opened their mouths and showed their teeth. Probably no horses had been in this part before. After going through the forest for some way, we descended to Na Bilia, a village consisting of thirteen houses, which, like most of the houses about here, look like small, bad haystacks, for they are thatched to the ground, and are nearly round, but with the sides slightly flattened, and generally a little raised on stones. In the mangete here were some bowls of freshwater prawns and small fish, mixed up and floating in liquid; but, dearly as we all loved prawns, the whole thing looked too nasty for us, so I contented myself with sitting under an orange-tree and drinking quantities of water. Another steep pull up a hill that looked impossible for horses, but which they managed to climb, although it consisted of a slippery rock tilted sideways, and then the forest was again reached. Here Mr. Thurston found what he believed to be a new variety of fig, some of the bunches of which are over five feet long, with a small, insipid fruit about an inch in diameter, some red and ripe, and others green. The tree grows to a height of from twenty to thirty feet.

After a rest at Na Matakula we started for the base of Tomainivi, leaving our horses, and only taking food for a day or two. We had only about three miles to do, but it was up and down a steep hill through the forest. After going about half the distance we had a beautiful view of the valley below us, with wooded hills all round, and the highest point of Tomainivi opposite and well above us, though we were up some three thousand feet. The only sign of man anywhere to be seen was the little grass hut they had prepared for us a mile or so further on. After a very steep descent, we reached a stream falling over rocks like a mountain stream in Scotland, and then crossed a level plain of grass which had been formerly cultivated for taro, and arrived at our camping place, where the men soon made shelters for themselves.

Next morning we were off by six, and after half a mile in the open entered the forest. We found a very rare climbing pineapple and a new creeper with bell-shaped flowers of a waxy white, some of them with a pink tinge. A path had been cut for us nearly to the top of the mountain, which we reached about nine o'clock. The forest was very thick all the way to the summit, which we found was about five thousand feet above the level of the sea. It was rather foggy at first; but after breakfast, which we took there, the fog cleared off, and gave us a fine view on three sides—in one direction right away to sea, where we could make out several islands, including the Yasawas and Mamanuca, while nearer we had magnificent views over the island, and saw several distant peaks, such as Mount Pickering, Mount Evans, and Mongrodo. Before descending we drank the Queen's health, and formally named the highest point of Tomainivi Mount Victoria. We got back to our camp late in the afternoon.

We were off early next day, and breakfasted at Na Matakula. A native had picked up one of our empty green cartridge cases, and put it through the hole in his ear, and it was no doubt admired as a pleasing variety in ear ornaments. The native eye perhaps tires of seeing old round tin match-boxes, and occasionally small empty medicine bottles used as ear ornaments. Na Matakula is at the head of a charming valley of park-like ground with hanging woods on the slopes on each side, and the valley itself has great stretches of grass, interspersed with trees here and there, and with forests at the northern end. As it is at a considerable elevation it would make a splendid sanatorium for Fiji. In crossing a little bridge—made of three or four poles with earth on them—over a nearly dry watercourse, my horse, which I was leading, put his foot through, and then tumbled over about six feet below on his back into mud and water, but luckily was not hurt. Passing through the forest for three or four miles, and several times crossing and recrossing a nearly dry stream edged with ferns, we emerged into the open at a dip in the top of a high range of mountains, which

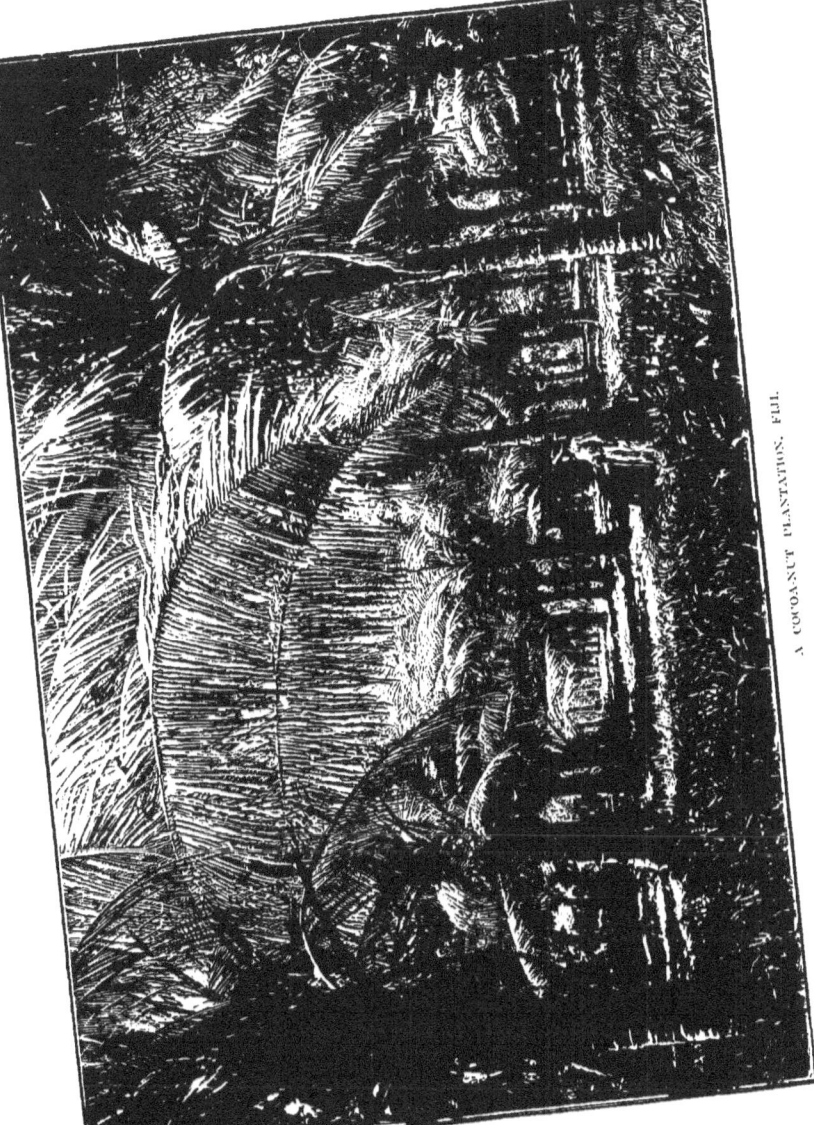

A COCOANUT PLANTATION, FIJI.

a certain position, and at others every other performer would fall into an almost sitting posture, while the intermediate ones would lift high their clubs, and hold them up as if about to brain a conquered foe, both sets staying perfectly motionless for a while, when they would change to some other graceful movement.

The next day our party separated. I could not tear myself away so easily from uncivilised life, and so, while the rest of the party went back to Suva, I turned inland once more to spend a little more time in the Tholo district, and returned to Nailanga a month later, when the manager of the New Zealand Sugar Company's plantation at this place was obliging enough to allow me to go in their S.S. *Rarawei* to Levuka. The trade wind was dead against us, but it was pleasantly cool in consequence. We anchored for the night at Ellington, close to the mainland, and to leeward of a small island, and, finding the night hot, slept on deck, sheltered with an awning. The next day we entered Viti Levu Bay, and were much interested in seeing a fish-weir which the natives had put up. There were two long fences of reeds eight feet high fastened to posts; these were about a hundred yards long, and converging to a point thus, $\Lambda$. At the apex was a circular fence, making a trap about twelve yards across, into which the fish were guided by the fences, but from which they could not easily escape.

In the afternoon we approached the island of Ovalau, and soon after saw Levuka, a much prettier town than Suva. The hills rise to a considerable height immediately behind it, leaving very little room for houses between them and the shore; and the whole is covered with trees to the water's edge, the great number of cocoa palms and breadfruit trees looking very pretty. There is a road all along the shore, and even at low water the sea comes up to it. On the land side of the road are the shops and houses and hotels, while a little to the right and left of the town are native villages, and to your right, as you look seaward from the town, the old Government House, but it is round a projecting space of mountain, so that you cannot see it from the town. Levuka seemed to me a cooler place than Suva, as at the former place the trade wind blows directly ashore, while at Suva it blows rather along the coast. They have a pleasant club here, right down by the sea. Levuka was the capital of Fiji until recently, when it was supplanted by Suva, although Levuka is much more centrally situated. After a short stay, I went on to Suva. On the voyage we saw the greater part of the hull of the *Syria* on a coral reef, with her stern reclining a few yards further off. She was a coolie ship, and when she was wrecked about fifty coolies perished; close by the sharp black fin of a big shark appeared above the water as he swam slowly along.

A FIJIAN LAGOON (MANGO).

## YASAWA-I-LAU.

The Start—Fijian Hospitality—A Beautiful Cave—A Weird Scene—More Caves—Late Dinner—"Mekes."

ONE of the most charming expeditions which the traveller in Fiji can make is to a group of islands called Yasawa-i-lau, about forty miles from Ba, in Viti Levu (the vowels are pronounced as in Italian, and the last letter, as the diphthong in the English word "loud"). We went in two cutters, one *Na Vulori* (*The Flora*), of about ten tons, the other, the *Kathleen*, somewhat larger. They were decked boats, with tiny cabins, and the crews were Fijian. Our party consisted of Mr. Alexander Eastgate (whom we called the Commodore, as he commanded the squadron), Mr. Le Hunte, Mr. Marriott, my sister, and myself. We dropped down at the mouth of the Ba river one evening, so as to be ready for an early start next morning, when we had a delicious sail across, and cruised about among the islands, passing exquisite little bays, edged with gleaming coral sand, the luxuriant vegetation growing right down to it, and the native houses peeping out from groves of bananas and cocoanut palms. We dropped anchor off one of these native towns about five o'clock, and went ashore, where we found houses ready for us, a native magistrate having landed beforehand to prepare the inhabitants for our arrival. In all our travels we found the Fijians very hospitable. They always prepared houses for us with plenty of clean mats, and would bring a present of food, *i.e.*, pigs, cooked whole, with piles of yams, besides dainties, such as boiled chicken, taro, bananas, and cocoanuts: in general, the women would bring the food in procession, crouching as they walked, in token of respect.

The next day we embarked about ten o'clock, and went to another island for the night, and on the third morning made a very early start for the one containing the caves, of which we had heard so much. Having landed, and while breakfast was being prepared, we went to see one cave that was close by, a most beautiful one, quite Gothic in structure—paving, arches, and pinnacles in the Early English style; at the bottom clear, blue-green water, of great depth. The Fijians at once jumped in, and began swimming and diving, and one could see them when quite near the bottom, so exquisitely clear was the water. The cave was a very large one, with entrances from it into others; and when the natives shrieked and groaned in these adjoining caverns, we could hear the voices dying away, and sounding very demoniacal. Altogether, the scene was quite weird, when peopled with dusky figures, either in the water, or clambering about the rocks and jumping from great heights into the water—the highest leap was over forty feet. They generally come down feet foremost, dividing the water with them, instead of with the hands, as one is accustomed to see done. The light came from an opening very high up, but we could not see it from where we stood.

A "MEKE."

After gazing our fill, we returned to breakfast, and enjoyed a native dish called loti, which our Commodore had got a party of men to come over and make for us, bringing the necessary implements and materials in their canoe. It was brewed in a huge "go-ashore," as the Maoris call it, or three-legged iron pot, is stirred with the stem of a cocoanut leaf, is poured out with a ladle made of a cocoanut shell lashed to a reed, and is served in banana leaves laid on trays of plaited cocoanut leaf. The kitchen was the seashore, so that the scene was quite picturesque. The loti is made with bananas and cocoanuts, and is very delicious. After breakfast we started to climb the hill, in quest of more caves, and a very rough and steep climb it was over scoria, making us very hot, and, therefore, most grateful for the cool shelter of the caves when we reached them, and for draughts of cocoanut milk from the nuts which the natives had thoughtfully carried up. The first cave we came to was like the interior of a splendid church, with fine arches, niches for saints, a magnificent pulpit, side chapels, tombs, places for holy water, &c. It was not difficult, even, for the fancy to discover gas-pipes in the roots of the baka-tree (a sort of banyan), which ran perfectly straight down the walls, and along the ground. There was also a long creeper, hanging clear from the roof, which did for the bell-rope. The walls and groined roof were of white, tinged in parts with blue and green. Some places looked like a bridecake, lavishly iced, with the sugar running over.

From this cavern, we made our way to another through passages in which we had to crawl, one, indeed, being so very narrow that it was a mercy none of us were stout. This second cave was a very lofty one, and the bright light shining through a rift in the roof, a great way up, gave the effect of moonlight or limelight; indeed we, some of us unintentionally, grouped ourselves quite dramatically, two of the party reclining on a bank of the lovely white marble-like formation, under the full strength of the light, whilst a group of natives lurked close by in shadow. After leaving this cave, we had a fearful scramble up steep rocks, with very insecure foothold: indeed, in one place, I was panic-struck when told to climb over a shoulder of rock overhanging a steep descent, and shrank into a cleft, feeling I must end my days there, being unable to retreat or advance, but the Fijians are ready and clever, and they soon got me over the perilous place, some hoisting me up, and one crouching down so that I could make a step of his back. After this clamber we sat to rest and cool ourselves at the entrance to another cave, out of which a blast of delicious cold air came, but the approach was too precipitous for us to enter, so we had to be satisfied with peeping down into its uncanny depths. The rest of the party afterwards went to the top of the hill; but when I heard that I should have to make my way over rocks with a sheer precipice of some hundreds of feet on one side, I thought discretion the better part, and sat down while the others completed the ascent. Where I waited, however, the view was magnificent. I could see all the Yasawas; and the sea was of the most brilliant blue. The return journey was comparatively easy, and on reaching our encampment we were regaled with pineapples and cocoanut milk. By-the-bye, on this island, which was a rugged, uninhabited one, we picked quantities of those small scarlet berries with a black speck on them that are used to ornament boxes, &c. They grow in pods, which burst open when ripe, and the clusters of these pods look very pretty with the rows of bright little berries showing from the inside.

We embarked about three o'clock, and had a sail of six hours before reaching our destination for the night—a very lonely town, the capital of the group. As the Fijians always take two hours, at least, to prepare dinner, ours that night was a very late one; fortunately, we had had a substantial afternoon tea on board, and it being a lovely moonlit night, we sat patiently on the beach till dinner was announced at eleven o'clock. Even in a small open boat the Fijians are equal to the task of making tea, for they carry their fire in a wooden box with some earth at the bottom, and soon have the kettle boiling. Not having matches, they carry fire-sticks to light the inevitable saluka, of which I have spoken in the preceding article, and without which they could not be happy. Arriving so late at this place, we had to be satisfied with one house, but across one end was a slight screen of reeds about four feet high, which made it a house of two rooms instead of the usual one large apartment. When all our beds were up it looked like a gipsy encampment. The bed consists of a mosquito net, with a square of calico for its roof, and muslin curtains hanging down all round, enclosing a mat, pillow, and shawl. One hangs the square of calico from the rafters, and spreads out the mat, tucking the curtains underneath it all round.

The next morning we said good-bye to our beautiful fairyland, and started for Ba; but to our delight the wind proved unfavourable, and after beating about for a few hours, we sailed for an island we had not before visited. It was Sunday, and we had service on board in Fijian. In Fiji houses evening prayer is customary, when every one is prayed for, from the Governor down to our humble selves. One of our party had been nicknamed "the Dormouse," and I am afraid that our feelings were not so devout as they ought to have been when on one occasion we heard him prayed for with great fervour as "Mini Dormausi."

There was a light breeze when we again made a start, and we sailed peacefully along till about four o'clock, when we cast anchor off a native town and went ashore. Next morning we were at last left our islands behind us, to our great regret. However, we were becalmed half-way across, and had to sleep on board. It was an exquisite night, and some of us preferred the deck as being cooler than the cabins, and were rewarded for our enterprise by a splendid sunrise. We did not reach Ba till one o'clock, when we had our first meal for the day. Travelling in Fiji, by the way, makes one used to waiting; a favourite word there is "malua," which has several meanings, the chief one being "by-and-by."

Some of the best "mekes" we saw were at the great meeting or "bose" at Ban, —once the native capital of Fiji, and situated on a small island of the same name in the Yasawa group—at which Sir Arthur Gordon kindly arranged that we should be present. A great number of men dance in these "mekes"—one hundred or more at a time. They dress themselves up in white tapa cloth, which hangs in festoons from waist to knee, giving them the appearance of ballet-dancers in short skirts. Then they have streamers all about them, and altogether they look very smart. On one occasion each man had a long spear and a fan, and they went through all sorts of evolutions, a combination of a ballet-dance and military manœuvres. They have wonderful figures, and their weapons are wielded with singular precision and nerve; the accompanying music is a monotonous chant from a number of people sittting on the ground and beating time on their wooden gongs.

THE CITY, FROM KANGAROO POINT.

## HOBART.

Situation—Cape Pillar and Tasman's Island—Port Arthur—Cape Raoul—Franklin Island—The Derwent—A General View—A Bird's-eye View—Main Road—Macquarie Street—The Royal Society's Museum—Franklin Square—The First Australian Brewery—The Queen's Domain—Domain Road—Government House—The Botanical Gardens—Distinguished Legislators—The High School—Liverpool and Elizabeth Streets—The Bank of Van Diemen's Land—Memorial Church—"Mr. Robinson's House"—The Roman Catholic Cathedral.

VISITORS to Tasmania are often asked whether they most admire the situation of Hobart or of Sydney. The question is not an easy one to answer, from the fact that the approaches to the two cities are of a widely different character. Few sights are so exquisite or so surprising in their beauty as that which bursts upon the visitor to Sydney when the ship which has conveyed him along the coast of New South Wales enters a passage through the lofty cliffs, and the whole of Port Jackson opens at once to view, showing the city as it stretches along the further shore, with its lovely suburbs of villas and gardens adorning the creeks and inlets, and extending for miles around the bay on either side. If the day be fine, and the approach be made soon after sunrise, before the glare of the sun begins to impair the clearness of vision, the view is one of enchantment. It is one of those sights which are remembered as an epoch in one's existence. The approach to Hobart is scarcely less lovely, but it is less striking. The beauties of the city's surroundings open gradually to the view. Hobart stands at the head of an estuary, which joins the ocean forty miles off. The coasts close in very slowly as we ascend the bay. There are no surprises such as await the traveller who enters Sydney Heads for the first time; but there is a progressively increasing beauty and grandeur in the scenery as we advance. And when at length, after four hours' journey from the Heads, we turn a slight bend in the coast, and come in full sight of the city, with its long suburb of Sandy Bay, backed by a range of lofty hills culminating in Mount Wellington, we are quite able to understand how Hobart may challenge comparison with Sydney for beauty of situation, though the beauty is of an essentially different character.

The visitor to Hobart by one of the regular lines of steamers which trade to that port must come either from Melbourne, Sydney, or New Zealand. Whichever of these be his route, he must round the south-eastern promontory of Tasmania to enter Storm Bay. The island, at this point, terminates in a grand headland, nearly 900 feet high. It is named Cape Pillar, from a tall rock, shaped somewhat like an obelisk, which

CAPE PILLAR.

rears itself from the water close by. Near this again a rocky, lofty, and barren island rises to a height nearly equal to that of Cape Pillar. This is named Tasman's Island, and as we round it we see a series of basaltic columns rising directly from the water, and looking so graceful and fragile that their endurance of wind and weather seems almost marvellous. The sight of Cape Pillar and Tasman's Island is singularly striking, and as we proceed westward the same character of rugged majesty prevails. Soon we pass the mouth of a deep bay encircled by mountains, which look blue in the distance. This is the far-famed Port Arthur, associated in the minds of men with all that was most hateful in the history of Van Diemen's Land, at the time when the island was one vast prison. Passing the mouth of the bay, we come to another headland, correspondent to Cape Pillar, and similar in character. This is Cape Raoul, 750 feet high. Here also a beautiful set of basaltic rocks extends outwards from the cape, and forms one of the noteworthy sights of the southern coast. The beauty of these rocks was somewhat impaired in the early part of the year 1884 by the wanton inconsiderateness of the captain of one of the ships of the Australian squadron, who, by way of exercising his men in gunnery practice, directed them to aim at the heads of these columns. Fortunately they had been repeatedly photographed before this stupid outrage was committed, so that we know how they used to look while they were still uninjured.

A little less than two hours' run from Cape Raoul brings us to a small wooded island rising high out of the water, and known officially as Franklin Island, but more familiarly as Betsy's Island.* It lies near the head of Storm Bay, and at the mouth of Frederick Henry Bay, close to a strangely-shaped promontory known as South Arm. This island was the private property of Lady Franklin till about twenty years ago. In those days a mania prevailed for the acclimatisation of all sorts of English birds and animals, useful and useless. An Acclimatisation Society was formed. Some of the older members of it had been in correspondence with Lady Franklin ever since her husband ceased to be Governor of Tasmania. At their suggestion she was duced to make a present of the island to the Society. Hares, partridges, pheasants, and other birds and animals dear to the sportsman were introduced, and the little island was soon overrun with their offspring. An old Scotchman was placed in charge as gamekeeper, and for a while all lovers of sport rejoiced in the existence of a preserve so well suited, apparently, for supplying live game to all parts of the colony. The affair, however, proved a failure, and the Acclimatisation Society is now remembered chiefly in connection with the names of two men, of whom one was an enthusiast in natural history, and the other no less an enthusiast in all that related to field sports. Both of these gentlemen are now dead. One of them was a son of John Woodcock Graves, the Cumberland poet, who wrote the most spirited and popular hunting-song in the English language, "D'ye ken John Peel?" Old sportsmen who have heard this song sung by their fathers more than sixty years ago will be surprised and interested to learn that the author was still alive and residing in Hobart in the year 1886. He died in the month of August of that year, and although he was not, as the newspaper obituaries stated, in his hundredth year, he had reached the ripe age of ninety-one.

A short distance to the west of Franklin Island is a lighthouse, popularly known as the Iron Pot. The Government have now given it the more euphonious name of the Derwent Lighthouse. It is erected on a smooth reef of low shelving rocks, and serves as a guard against a very serious danger to ships entering the estuary of the Derwent. Here it is that Storm Bay may be considered as ending; and from this point onwards the scenery changes its character, as we sail up the Derwent

* The correct name is Betts's Island, the first owner having been a person of the name of Betts. Popular usage has sanctioned a different spelling.

## A GENERAL VIEW.

estuary. Due west of the lighthouse lies Denne's Point, the northern headland of Bruny Island. Between Bruny and the mainland lies D'Entrecasteaux Channel. On the further side of the channel, in a line with Denne's Point, and overlooking it from the top of some commanding cliffs, are the houses of the two pilots, who act under the authority of the Marine Board. No vessel can pass the lighthouse unseen by them, and it is their duty, in turns, to board every ship entering the Derwent, with the exception of those steamers or coasting vessels which hold exemptions from pilotage.

From this part onward the Derwent is about two miles wide up to the immediate vicinity of Hobart. The town itself is not visible till we get within about a mile of it, when a bend in the beach-line brings it full in view. It is beautifully situated on the lower slopes of Mount Wellington. The visitor who approaches it by water sees on his right hand a series of bays and inlets backed by a line of high wooded hills, which terminate beyond the town in one of commanding height and beautiful contour, known as Mount Direction. Close to this is another of peculiar shape, called the Quoin, and these, with a third named Grass-tree Hill, close the view to the right, as seen in our approach by water. Then, carrying our eye to the left, we see Government House standing on a bright green promontory, which shuts off the view of the higher bends of the river. This is a remarkably fine building, constructed of the excellent freestone of the colony. It is much the handsomest of all the vice-regal residences of Australia, though not nearly so large as that of Melbourne. Immediately to the left of Government House rises the Queen's Domain, or People's Park, which, as seen from the water, presents the appearance of a hill of considerable height but gentle slope, wooded to the summit. Then in the foreground we see the wharves and shipping, and at the back of them, on the edge of the Domain, Christ's College, popularly known as the High School, standing at the head of a fine, sloping lawn of two acres, surrounded by beautiful shrubberies; and above the college the new houses of Glebe Town, piled in apparent confusion, and standing out white and bright against a dark background. In the foreground, as the eye travels to the left, we have a forest of masts, and in the background Trinity Church, with Perpendicular Gothic tower, standing on the apex of one of the numerous hills which constitute the site of Hobart. This is the only church in the island which rejoices in the possession of a peal of bells. Further to the left we see in the foreground a mass of fine public buildings, and in the background a series of hills, up which the streets of the suburbs seem to run almost into the region of cloudland. The view is closed to the left by Mount Wellington, rising more than 4,000 feet above the sea level.

Such is the aspect of Hobart as seen from the bay. A still higher appreciation of the beauty of its situation may be obtained by crossing the river to Bellerive in one of the little steamers which ply thither at half-hour intervals. From this point of view Mount Wellington forms the background, rising far above the highest parts of the city, which we now see encircling a deep and lovely bay. This is a sight on which the eye can feast for hours without satiety. But if we wish to know what the town itself is like, there is no view to be compared with that which is obtainable from the terrace of Christ's College. All the handsomest and largest public buildings are seen close at hand from this position; and for a town of its size, Hobart has a large share of handsome public edifices. The college is so situated that the view all round from its terrace forms a magnificent panorama. We here face the bay, and in consequence have Mount Wellington on the extreme right. The range already mentioned as lying at the back of Sandy Bay stretches forward on the right till it terminates in Mount Nelson. Nearer, and still on the right, is St. George's Hill, covered with houses, and surmounted by a church, with a tall tower terminating in a sort of cupola. Still somewhat to our right, and much nearer, we look down upon a mass of handsome public buildings, as already mentioned. Most of these are of the Italian style of architecture, and built of the fine freestone of the colony. In the immediate vicinity of Hobart an admirable freestone of slightly yellowish tinge is obtainable in large quantities; and at Bellerive, on the opposite side of the river, there are quarries of a perfectly white stone, which has been largely used for building purposes in the other colonies, as well as in Tasmania. The view in full front commands the bay, which here seems to be shut in by South Arm and Betsy's Island. The panorama terminates to the left in Kangaroo Point (Bellerive), on the other side of the river, and in the Domain Hill on the Hobart side. Domain Hill rises close to the left of the college grounds, and shuts off the view on that side.

While, however, the view from the college terrace is that which shows Hobart to best advantage, it is not the one which best enables us to see the plan of the town and the direction of the hills. To get a comprehensive bird's-eye view we must ascend one or other of the streets which run up the sides of Knocklofty, a hill on the west of the city, one of the lower spurs of Mount Wellington. Several of the streets of Hobart run parallel to one another, and terminate in steep ascents on the side of this hill. From the top of Liverpool Street or Goulburn Street, or, best of all, from Lansdown Crescent, which lies high up on the side of the hill, one gets a fine and extensive view, comprehending the whole of the city and the harbour. On a fine day the white buildings, the deep blue water, and the brown wooded

THE FRANKLIN MONUMENT, FRANKLIN SQUARE.

hills beyond Bellerive, add to the other beauties of the scene the charm which results from contrast in colour.

The streets in Hobart are not so wide as those of Melbourne and of other Australasian towns of later date. They cross one another in nearly parallel sets, but not absolutely at right angles. The extremely uneven character of the ground has from the first prevented the monotonous regularity which characterises so many colonial towns. The busiest thoroughfares of the city are Liverpool and Elizabeth Streets. Most of the best shops in the town are to be found in these two streets. At its eastern end Liverpool Street runs out into the Domain, while on the west it runs far up into the hills, and terminates in a series of villa residences. Elizabeth Street crosses it almost at right angles, extending to the wharves on the south and far out along the Main Road to the north. The name of Main Road is given to the very fine coach road,

THE HIGH SCHOOL.

made by convict labour, which runs from Hobart to Launceston, and passes through several of the principal townships of the island.

Of all the streets in the town, Macquarie Street is especially noticeable to the lover of the picturesque. It is a street of fine public buildings and handsome private residences. It runs from the Queen's Domain up to the foot of Mount Wellington. From the lower end of it one can see more than a mile in a straight line, until the view is shut in by a slight bend, which seems to lead into a region of gardens and cultivated woodland before it is closed by the mountain background. At the Domain end it crosses the railway and the Town Creek, between which lie the gas company's works. A little beyond the creek, and on the right side, we pass the New Market, a sort of arcade running from Macquarie Street into Collins Street. On the left, proceeding upwards, we have the Royal Society's Museum, a handsome stone building, containing good collections of all that one expects to find in a museum, together with a very valuable library of scientific works. A few yards higher up we come to the Town

Hall, another handsome stone building, containing the municipal chambers and corporation offices on the ground floor, while the first floor is occupied by a spacious assembly room, much in demand for balls, concerts, lectures, and public meetings. This room contains a large organ, of excellent tone. One wing of the building is appropriated to the public library, a most valuable institution. It contains about 9,000 volumes, and is open to the public for nearly twelve hours every day. In connection with it there is also a spacious news-room, furnished with the principal English and Australasian papers, as well as with the most popular magazines and reviews. Women as well as men avail themselves largely of the privilege afforded by the reading-rooms.

A little further up the street is Franklin Square, a public pleasure-ground, prettily laid out in walks and shrubberies, and adorned with an ornamental fishpond, stocked with gold and silver fish, and planted with water-lilies. In the very centre of the square, on a pedestal of fine Tasmanian granite, is a bronze statue of Sir John Franklin, the Arctic explorer, who was Governor of the colony from 1837 to 1843. In front of the pedestal is a large bronze cannon captured during the Crimean War, and presented to the colony by the British Government. Just beyond Franklin Square, and on the same side of the street, are the Post Office and other Government buildings, containing the offices of all heads of departments. On the opposite side of the road is the Church of England Cathedral, a massive stone building, in a somewhat incomplete condition, since it has neither chancel nor tower.

We now come to a region of banks and offices, and a little way further on to a house which has an historical interest, not only as being itself one of the oldest houses in the colony, but as immediately adjoining the spot on which stood the very first dwelling erected in Hobart. It is a tall, flat-faced house, of a style of domestic architecture common in England about the beginning of the present century. For many years it was the principal hotel in Hobart, and though it has not been used as such for fully thirty years, the name of Macquarie Hotel still clings to it by persistent tradition. It is now a private residence. Many persons who were alive within the last ten years remembered when this was the only house on its own side of the street.

There are two other objects of historical interest in this street. One is the Hutchins School, noteworthy in the history of the colony as the first grammar-school established in Tasmania; the other, nearly a mile further on, and at the extreme end of Macquarie Street, is the Cascade Brewery—important not merely in the history of Tasmania, but in that of Australia at large, as the first brewery erected in any of the Australian colonies. It is of this that Sydney Smith speaks in a clever article on Australia published in *The Edinburgh Review* in 1823. "What two ideas," he says, "are more inseparable than Beer and Britannia? What event more awfully important to an English colony than the erection of its first brewhouse? And yet it required in Van Diemen's Land the greatest solicitation to the Government and all the influence of Mr. Bigge to get it effected."

The above passage, indeed, gives but a faint notion of the hard battle which the founder of the brewery had to fight against the Government of the colony before he was enabled to take possession of a suitable site, and to obtain the water privilege essential to his operations. His life was an eventful one. A native of France, driven thence in early life by the terrors of the Revolution, Mr. Degraves took refuge in England, became a naturalised subject, then a colonist, and ultimately the founder of the most famous brewery in the Australian colonies. The original building has long given place to a handsome, massive edifice of grey stone, most picturesquely situated at the foot of a richly-wooded hill, which forms one of the lower slopes of Mount Wellington.

Mention has already been made of the Queen's Domain. This, the chief recreation-ground of the city, is situated on the eastern side of it, between the town and the Derwent, with a frontage looking out on the bay. Suppose a pear sliced lengthwise from the stalk, and one of the halves placed on its flat side—that half pear would give a tolerably correct notion of the general contour of the Domain; the smaller end being the one nearest the city, and the larger end representing the wooded height. A road runs round this hill near its base. Following the road, you come back to your starting-point, after a delightful drive of about a mile and a half through a wooded region, sufficiently open to show a charming succession of views. The part of the road along the river-side is on a lower level than the portion which overlooks the town. Going out by the lower road, and enjoying the view of the bright blue waters of the Derwent, which is here about a mile wide, we soon arrive at the entrance gates of Government House.

Thirty years ago the residence of the Governor of Tasmania was a long, low wooden building situate in Macquarie Street, running across the end of Elizabeth Street, so as to shut off the view of the bay, and, with its garden, occupying the whole space included in the sites of Franklin Square and the Town Hall. The present building was commenced during the period of exceptional prosperity which succeeded the discovery of gold in Victoria, and was completed in the year 1858, Sir Henry Fox Young being Governor at the time. Its architectural beauty deserves great praise. The ball-room, dining-room, and drawing-room will not easily be forgotten by anyone who has seen them; and the gardens, stretching down to the river, owe something of their beauty to the good taste of each successive Governor. Following the Domain Road for a short distance, we come to the Royal Society's Gardens, also called the Botanical Gardens. They immediately adjoin the gardens of Government House, and are beautifully situated on the slope of the Domain, between the road and the water. The Main Line Railway runs through the gardens near the waterside, and is crossed by an ornamental bridge. The grounds are well kept. They are planted with trees, flowers, and fruit from every part of the world, and are under the management of the Royal Society of Tasmania, a society established in 1844 for the purpose of developing and illustrating the natural history, the productions, and the physical character of the island. Great taste has been shown in laying out the grounds; and for the accommodation of the public numerous garden seats have been placed in positions which command lovely views of the broad, blue Derwent, with its brown background of wooded hills.

Following the Domain Road from the gardens, we find it rising gradually, till it has rounded the broader end of the hill. Here we get a magnificent view of the valley of the Derwent, extending many miles, till it is shut in by hills looking faintly blue in the far distance. Having rounded the end of the hill, we arrive at a gate, which leads out towards Newtown, one of the suburbs of Hobart. A little way outside this gate we see a handsome private residence, with a fine garden and grounds. This belongs to the family of the Hon. T. D. Chapman, by whom it was built, and who died here suddenly in the early part of the year 1884. For more than thirty years Mr. Chapman had been one of the most prominent and distinguished of Tasmanian legislators. Before the introduction of constitutional government he had been amongst the most active opponents of the transportation system, and from the time when the Parliamentary system was established in Tasmania, Mr. Chapman was always a leader, either on the Ministerial or the Opposition side of the House. He held office in several administrations, and no man could be named who has occupied such a conspicuous position in the political history of the colony, or who has so influenced its legislation.

TRINITY CHURCH.

Proceeding past the gate just mentioned, but not through it, we soon arrive at the highest point of the Domain Road. The slope is now downwards. On our right we catch frequent glimpses of the town through openings in the trees. Ere long we again come within sight of Government House, now lying below us on the left, and at length we arrive at the spot whence we started round the Domain by the lower road. Meanwhile we have passed the wooded hill, and have arrived at a large open space, extending to the river on the left and the harbour in front. This part of the Domain may be considered the recreation-ground of the city. Here were played all cricket and football matches for many years, and it is still used largely for practice and for matches of secondary importance in both those games; but in the early part of 1882 a new and well-appointed cricket-ground was opened on a plateau some way up the Domain. It was inaugurated by a match between the Southern Tasmanian Cricket Association and an eleven from Melbourne. A new road has recently been constructed from the old recreation-ground to the new cricket-ground, and near the junction of this with the Lower Domain Road a drinking fountain has been placed as a memorial to the Hon. Charles Meredith, who was for many years one of the most distinguished amongst the public men of Tasmania, and had been a prominent member of three different administrations.

establishment marks an era in the history of the colony. It contributed greatly to regularise the means of exchange. During the first and great part of the second decade of the present century there was little or no English money in the colony. A system of barter prevailed. Pounds and chests of tea, bottles and hogsheads of rum, sacks of corn, and other articles, had a conventional value as equivalent to so many shillings or pounds. A hogshead of rum was the upset price of certain town allotments in the Sandy Bay suburb of Hobart, and within the last twenty-five years some of the original purchasers of these allotments were still living. When Sydney Smith in one of his essays represents a New South Wales juror as excusing himself for non-attendance at the Assizes on the ground that he had sent a man fifty miles with a sack of flour to buy a pair of breeches, and that his messenger had not returned, he pretty accurately describes the system of exchange actually prevailing in the earlier days of Van Diemen's Land.

As an almost inevitable consequence of the inconvenience connected with transactions of this sort, there arose a system of payment by promissory notes, which passed from hand to hand, and which led to frequent loss and litigation where the notes were not issued by men of undoubted solvency. Some merchants of established reputation combined a sort of banking business with their other transactions, receiving deposits, and issuing notes on engraved forms, similar to those of regular banking establishments. Early in the second decade of the century the local government adopted a system of currency which, we believe, was peculiar to this colony. They imported Spanish dollars, intrinsically equal in value to five shillings of English money, and to prevent exportation they cut out a "dump" from the middle. In payments from the Treasury they issued the "dumps" at 1s. 3d. each, and the mutilated dollar—or ring-dollar, as it was called—at five shillings. About the years 1819 and 1820 there was a large influx of gentlemen colonists, and these found it their best policy to change all their money into dollars before emigrating, since they thus got 6s. 3d. currency for every five shillings expended. Even then the amount of coin in circulation was inadequate to the requirements of business. Hence, when a company of leading merchants and settlers established the Bank of Van Diemen's Land, obtaining a charter from the Governor-General, issuing their own notes, and importing specie to a considerable extent, the relief to all business transactions was immense. But the adoption of the English currency came much later. For more than twenty years after the establishment of the bank the ring-dollar, at five shillings, was the recognised standard of currency in Van Diemen's Land.

GOVERNMENT HOUSE.

After passing the Bank of Van Diemen's Land, there is little in Elizabeth Street to interest us beyond the numerous shops, which are not generally either large or showy. From the point where it crosses Liverpool Street there is a continuous rise for more than a mile. At its junction with Brisbane Street is a handsome church with a spire. The spire is not quite lofty enough to be in perfect harmony with the rest of the building, but the church is an ornament to the town in spite of this slight defect. It belongs to the Congregational body, and is named the Memorial Church, having been erected in memory of the Rev. Henry Miller, who was the first, and for some years the only, Congregational minister in the Australian colonies. Just beyond this is a large square stone house, which was for many years the residence of Mr. Henry Hopkins, the founder of the wool trade of Tasmania. When he arrived

GOVERNMENT HOUSE FROM MACQUARIE POINT.

in Hobart, about the year 1820, he found that the settlers were in the habit of burning their wool to get rid of it. He made himself known as a purchaser, and was able to buy at a very low rate, and to buy largely. Shipping the wool to England, he made enormous profits, and laid the foundation of a large fortune. Others followed his example, and it was not long before the settlers discovered that wool was the most valuable and important product of their estates.

A little way further on, on the left-hand side of the street, there is a house which is noticeable in the history of the colony as the one to which the small remnant of aborigines still surviving in the year 1834 were brought by Mr. Robinson, a man who devoted himself for years to the task of conciliating those poor savages and preserving them from total destruction. In the local publications of that date, and in narratives of visitors to the colony, it is spoken of as "Mr. Robinson's house." It stands a little below the present level of the street, and is remarkable for a peculiarly-shaped roof. A good account of the aborigines, of the so-called Black War, of Mr. Robinson's missions, and of the final extinction of the race, will be found in "Fenton's History of Tasmania."

From the point which we have now reached, Elizabeth Street is suburban in character, and for about three-quarters of a mile consists mainly of private residences. There is a gradual ascent to a point known as Swan's Hill, which marks the town boundary. Here begins the suburb of Newtown, and here a glorious prospect opens. We see Newtown itself extending more than two miles from the spot where we are standing. A mile off lies the Invalid Depôt, or Queen's Asylum, with a

ENTRANCE TO THE ROYAL SOCIETY'S GARDENS.

church tower rising from the centre of the building. On the left is the Wellington Range. To the right of the township we see the valley of the Derwent for more than twenty miles, with the river itself looking like a series of lakes, owing to the windings of its course and the frequent interceptions of the view by low hills along its nearer bank. Then, on the right, about three miles off, rises Mount Direction, imposing in its altitude, and beautiful in its contour; and far away the view is closed in by mountain ranges, looking pale and blue in the haze of distance.

Amongst the noteworthy public edifices of Hobart a prominent place must be given to the Roman Catholic Cathedral. It lies on the western side of Harrington Street, which is parallel to Elizabeth Street. It is a handsome building in the Perpendicular style. Close to it lies the Presentation Convent of St. Mary, another large and handsome building. Both the cathedral and the convent are built of white

Tasmanian freestone, and, lying high on a steep hillside, are visible from every part of the town. The view from the convent is a very extensive and lovely one. It takes in the High School and Glebe Town, with the wooded Domain as background, the bay, Bellerive, with the hills that lie beyond it, and all the left bank of the Derwent, as far as South Arm and Betsy's Island. The residence of the Roman Catholic bishop lies on the steep hillside, immediately above the convent grounds, and forms part of this handsome group of ecclesiastical buildings. The sisterhood who occupy the convent devote themselves chiefly to the work of education, and have a large number of pupils.

The only noticeable ecclesiastical buildings in Hobart, besides those to which reference has been made in other connections, is St. George's (Anglican) Church, standing out conspicuously on a hill, and distinguished by its Grecian portico and its composite tower and cupola. The architectural style is that which prevailed amongst the London churches erected about the end of the last or beginning of the present century, before the revival of Gothic architecture. The Anglican churches of St. John, Goulbourn Street, and All Saints, Macquarie Street, may, however, be cited as graceful specimens of modern Gothic.

ABORIGINES OF TASMANIA.

## THE ENVIRONS OF HOBART.

Mount Wellington—Cook's Monument—A Magnificent Prospect—The Pinnacle—"The Organ Pipes"—Lost on the Mountain—The Wellington Falls—Brown's River—Kingston—Queenborough—The Bonnet Hill—Mount Nelson—Mount Direction—The Largest Man in the World—Risdon—A "Rupert of Debate"—Kangaroo Point and Bellerive—Mount Rumney—Newtown—Elwick Racecourse—A Landslip—Austin's Ferry—Bridgewater Causeway—Newtown and Cornelian Bays.

VERY prominent amongst the surroundings of Hobart, both for beauty and for grandeur, is Mount Wellington. There are other mountains in Tasmania which rise to a greater height above the sea, but there is not one which looks so lofty. Its lower slopes extend to the water's edge, and thus its whole height of 4,166 feet is seen at a glance, and no part of its grandeur is lost by any imperceptibly-ascending approaches. It is generally the first object of interest to visitors, and no one willingly leaves the city without having made the ascent of the mountain. The distance from the Post Office to the summit is about seven miles. The toil of the ascent has been much lessened by the construction of the Huon Road, since by it one can drive nearly four miles, and save the effort of scaling a very steep hill. The old ascent was along Macquarie Street, past the Cascade brewery, and on by some wood-cutters' tracks. To a good pedestrian this is still the most interesting way of seeing the mountain, since it leads through some magnificent forest-land containing fine specimens of the giant eucalyptus, for which Mount Wellington is famous. But since the construction of the Huon Road this mode of ascent has been little used.

To enjoy the excursion thoroughly, a day should be chosen which seems likely to be fine but not very hot. The start should be made as soon as possible after breakfast. Luncheon-baskets should be provided. Then, having made all requisite preparations, we drive out to the end of Davey Street, a distance of about a mile, and emerge upon the Huon Road. This runs along the mountain side, with a gradient of one foot in fifty, is admirably constructed, and is a fine specimen of engineering skill. A drive of about three miles brings us to a wayside hostelry, known as the Fern-tree Inn. Here the vehicles may be left, and, taking our luncheon-baskets, we follow a track leading to the waterworks, whence the city receives its copious supply of fresh, clear water. Here is seen a structure popularly designated "Cook's Monument." It is not, however, a monument of the great navigator, nor, in fact, of anyone else, but a memorial structure, recording the inauguration in the year 1861 of the waterworks and reservoir constructed by the Corporation of Hobart, during the Mayoralty of Mr. Henry Cook. It is situated in a beautiful grove of fern-trees, known as the Bower. Here are benches and roughly-constructed tables, eminently convenient for picnic parties. A finger-post indicates the commencement of the "Mountain Road." It is a steep path, quite impracticable for vehicles, though not absolutely so for a well-mounted horseman. On gaining the summit of the first acclivity, we arrive at a tolerably level bit of road. Proceeding along this for about a quarter of a mile, we come to a steep much more fatiguing than the last. Several breathless halts will generally be demanded before the top of this second acclivity is reached. We are now at the part known as "The Springs"; and by this time the exertion of the walk will probably have produced a craving for a draught of the bright, tempting water which here gurgles over white pebbles in a narrow channel.

From this part of the mountain-side a wonderful panorama meets the eye. No description can do justice to it. In front and away to the left is seen the winding course of the noble Derwent—now diminished in the distance to a mere streamlet, now spreading out into a lake, and anon peeping out in azure patches among the countless hills and mountains extending tier after tier into the faint blue of the far distance. Plains green with verdure, and dotted with villages and homesteads, are to be seen at intervals, while the city itself nestles far below at the foot of the mountain; and away to the right we look over and beyond the bay, and see the open ocean sloping upward to the line of the horizon. Near "The Springs" is a hut occupied by an old couple, from whom cooking utensils, plates, and teacups can be hired if we wish to take our luncheon here on our way up, or a cup of tea on our way down. Proceeding from the hut along the watercourse, we are not long in arriving at the last of the steep ascents. A resolute effort soon brings us to the top of this, and here we find a wooden structure with a heavy sloping roof, covered with turf and brushwood. This is known as the ice-house. It contains snow gathered from the mountain-top during the winter months, and tightly packed, to be used by the confectioners in Hobart in the preparation of ice-creams. Just beyond the ice-house stretches a vast plain, consisting of enormous rounded boulders firmly wedged together. This is the far-famed "Ploughed Field." It requires some care in crossing, since it is often necessary to jump from one boulder to another: but there is no danger of serious accidents. After it is crossed, there is a long but easy ascent to the wide table-land at the summit. Nothing in the appearance of the mountain has prepared us to suspect the existence of such a plain at its top, and the sight of it always comes as a surprise to those who make the ascent for the first time.

The soil of this elevated plain is soft and spongy. It strikes cold to the feet, even in the warmest weather, though at this elevation the air is never very hot. The cold moisture of the turf is due to the melted snow. For nearly half the year snow lies unmelted on the top of the mountain, and for some distance down its sides, and it is this which keeps the springs running, and renders the supply of water continuous. Keeping near the edge of the table-land for about a mile, we come to the very highest point of the mountain. It is known as "The Pinnacle," and is marked by a square pile of logs, which can easily be climbed by men, and without much difficulty by any ladies who are anxious to feel that they have "done" the mountain thoroughly.

KANGAROO POINT, FROM HOBART.

The pile of logs was erected as a landmark by the men engaged in the first trigonometrical survey of the island. Not far from the base of the pinnacle is an abrupt and deep precipice, where, in ancient days, part of the mountain must have fallen away, laying bare a perpendicular face of rocky columns, known as "The Organ Pipes." This forms one of the most marked peculiarities of the mountain as seen from below; but we can scarcely form, even approximately, an estimate of the height of the columns till we look down and see how very far below us lie "The Ploughed Field" and other parts of the mountain at the foot of the precipice.

The view from the pinnacle is bewildering from its extent, but is scarcely equal in beauty and interest to the one which we obtain from "The Springs." Distance does not always lend enchantment to the view. It will sometimes happen that a bank of clouds lies between the top of the mountain and its lower slopes, intercepting the view beneath, while the atmosphere above is quite unclouded. It will even chance at times that showers fall from those clouds while the sun is shining brightly on the summit; and on such occasions we see the curious phenomenon of a rainbow far down beneath our feet. It is this descent of cloud which sometimes causes persons to lose their way on the mountain side. What is cloud at a distance is dense fog when one is actually in it. Even on good roads there is nothing so bewildering as fog; and in the perplexing labyrinth of forest tracks the attempt to find one's way is hopeless when the mist has descended on the mountain.

Occasionally a member of an excursion party gets left behind, and does not return at nightfall, or some schoolboys go up the mountain and have not returned home by the next morning. In such cases search parties are organised, a code of signals is arranged, and an energetic search instituted. This is generally successful; but it will happen at times that the wanderer has unconsciously passed to the back of the mountain, and emerges, to his great surprise, at New Norfolk, or on the northern side at Bridgewater, or on the southern side at the Huon. It is many years since anyone has actually perished through losing his way on the mountain. The last case of the sort was that of a Dr. Smith, who had taken a passage to Hobart as surgeon on board the ship *Derwentwater*. He went up the mountain on the 23rd of January, 1858, in company with some of his shipmates. but was missing when they returned. His companions went in search of him next day. The mountain tracks were not nearly so well defined or so well known then as they have since become, and when two days had elapsed without bringing any news of the wanderer, the whole community became alarmed. Numerous search parties were organised by persons well acquainted with the mountain. The Freemasons especially bestirred themselves in the matter, since Dr. Smith was one of the fraternity. The search was continued till the 28th of the month. On that day his dead body was found near the edge of "The Ploughed Field," where he had perished from fatigue and exposure. A small monumental structure marks the spot where he last drew breath, but his remains were brought down from the mountain and interred in St. David's churchyard. A tombstone erected by the Masonic brotherhood records the date and manner of his death.

The Wellington Falls are amongst the attractions of the mountain. They lie towards the back of it, on the southern slope, and may be reached by a walk of four miles from "The Springs." The water falls 210 feet, and the scenery around is very imposing. The view extends southward as far as the townships of Franklin and Victoria.

Among the pleasant excursions which may be made in the neighbourhood of Hobart few are more popular than that to Brown's River. This name, which belonged originally to a little stream discharging itself into a small bay, has been extended to the bay itself and to the township which has grown up about the banks of the river, and which is officially known as Kingston. The town lies about ten miles south of Hobart. The chief attraction of the place is a beautiful bit of coast and a beach of fine sand, generally displaying a large and varied accumulation of shells heaped in a curved line near the high-water mark. The beach, with its firm sand and its low, flat-topped rocks, is one of the pleasantest places imaginable for a lounge, and a few hours may always be spent there delightfully in reading, smoking, or simply enjoying the sunshine and scenery. Not far from the beach lies "The Blowhole," which is an object of unusual interest. In a field at the top of some cliffs on the southern bend of the bay is an opening of considerable width and formidable depth. Looking down, we see water below in a constant state of flux and reflux. The sea has worked a tunnel through the cliffs, and a fall of earth from above has opened out this dangerous chasm.

There are many pleasant walks in the neighbourhood of Kingston. It is a favourite honeymoon resort, and a week at Brown's River is the immediate sequence of a large proportion of the marriages contracted in Hobart. But apart from the attractions of the place itself, the mere journey to and fro well repays the time devoted to it. The road from Hobart to Kingston is one of the great works of Colonel Arthur's government. A better made road could hardly be found, even in England. Starting from the city, we pass through the pretty suburb of Sandy Bay, gradually descending till we reach a point at which the road is very little above high-water mark. On our way we pass the Queenborough cemetery, a large oblong enclosure sloping down towards the road, and conspicuous from its white headstones and monuments. Soon the lowest level of the road is reached. The water is now very close to us. On our left is the long, sandy beach, whence the district is named; on our right are highly cultivated lands, stretching back to the Nelson range of hills.

About a furlong of level road brings us to the commencement of an ascent which is continuous for nearly all the rest of the journey. We pass through the village of Queenborough, which gives its name to a large electoral district. The road then leads us by the foot of Mount Nelson and runs up the side of some hills which form part of the Nelson range, being so admirably graduated that we are scarcely conscious of ascending till we look back and see how far below us are the parts which we traversed ten minutes previously. Then, too, it winds round the head of ravines, showing gullies, watercourses, and openings extending far back into the hills, while on the other side the view of the estuary, with its islands, promontories, and inlets, increases in extent and beauty as we rise higher and higher. Within about two miles of the highest part of the road is Mr. Moir's shot-tower, the only one in the Australias, we believe. It is built of the fine white stone so plentiful in Tasmania, and standing as it does on one of the lofty cliffs which skirt the bay, it forms a grand landmark conspicuous for many miles. Close to the tower is the owner's residence, a pretty stone building in a well-kept garden extending from the road to the edge of the cliff. The tower is 176 feet high from the ground, but the fall for the molten metal within is about 200 feet.

The road continues to rise till it rounds the end of the hill that terminates the range, and which from the peculiarity of its shape is called the Bonnet Hill. Then comes a rapid and well-graduated descent to the Kingston township. At the foot of the hill is an inn, where horse and gig can be left while we go for our stroll on the beach. The excursion, by the way, may be made by means of a public conveyance which leaves the Hobart Post Office at nine every morning, and the Kingston Hotel at four in the afternoon.

Mount Nelson, which has been referred to in the previous article, is a conspicuous object from the town, and has special importance as a signal station. Ships entering Storm Bay, whether from east or west, can be seen from the top as soon as they pass Cape Raoul on the one side, or the more distant Tasman's Head on the other. Information is at once transmitted by telegraph to a nearer station on St. George's Hill, and this in its

THE SHOT-TOWER, BROWN'S RIVER ROAD.

turn hoists a flag, which indicates the character of the coming ship and the port whence it sails. The code of signals is published in the various local directories and almanacks. The height of the Mount is 1,191 feet. It lies about three-and-a-half miles south of Hobart. The walk to the top is not arduous, and may be shortened by aid of the Sandy Bay omnibus. The prospect is very fine. On the one side we have an excellent view of the city, on the other of the estuary, the lighthouse, the islands, the channel, and Storm Bay, opening out to the ocean. The station officer is generally willing to allow visitors to use a large standing telescope of long range, which shows distant objects with remarkable clearness.

On the northern side of the city, across the river, and about four miles distant, lies Mount Direction. There is no regular conveyance to it, but a cab will take the visitor

MOUNT WELLINGTON, FROM THE HUON ROAD.

as far as Risdon Ferry. The ferry-boat is worked by a wheel and rope. It has a wide platform, and is sufficiently strong and large to take a heavily loaded waggon and horses across the river. It was worked for many years by Mr. Jennings, now landlord of the Harvest Home Inn, on the Newtown Road, and supposed to be the largest man in the world. Mr. Jennings had not then acquired the excessive corpulence which has made him one of the memorable sights of Tasmania. The visitor to Mount Direction can either take his cab across the river or leave it at the ferry-house. The ferry lands him on the Richmond Road. Following this for about half-a-mile he comes to a gate leading to a causeway across a narrow inlet of the river. Turning to the left at the end of the causeway, and following a road winding along the beach, he comes to another gate opening on a private road, which leads to the residence of the lady who owns the lower slope of the mountain, and from whom leave ought to be obtained before commencing the ascent. The height of the hill is 1,212 feet; it is much steeper than Mount Nelson, and the ascent is rather toilsome, but the view from the top amply repays the exertion. A more lovely combination of landscape, mountain, and river scenery could hardly be found in any part of the world. It may be mentioned incidentally that in the veranda of a house near the foot of the mountain is suspended a series of copperplate engravings of remarkable historical interest. They represent the military exploits of Louis the Fourteenth of France in his great campaign of 1672. It is a striking instance of the persistence of family likeness that the face of the *Grand Monarque*, as delineated in this very interesting series, bears a strong resemblance to that of Louis Philippe, the last Bourbon ruler of France.

Near the foot of Mount Direction lies the scattered hamlet of Risdon. This has importance in the annals of the colony as being the spot on which the first encampment was made, when the Government of New South Wales, in the year 1803, decided on occupying Van Diemen's Land as a settlement for doubly convicted prisoners. It was here also that the first hostilities with the natives took place. A large hunting party of the blacks had driven a herd of kangaroo before them, and were emerging towards the camp. There was nothing to indicate hostile intention, but the officer in command of the soldiers was unfortunately absent, the men took alarm, and fired into the approaching line of natives, killing women and children as well as men, and thus commencing that lamentable war of extermination which every successive Government endeavoured to prevent, but which none was able to control.

It is commonly but erroneously supposed that the name Risdon is an abridged form of Rest-down, as indicating the spot where the first set of immigrants rested. As a fact, the name, in its present form, was given by a Captain Hayes, who explored the shores of Storm Bay as early as 1794, and went a considerable distance up the Derwent. In a chart of the coast which he prepared, the Risdon Creek is somewhat exaggerated in size, and is marked as Risdon River.

Later on Risdon had celebrity of another sort, as the residence of Mr. Thomas George Gregson, who for nearly fifty years was one of the foremost public characters of the colony. He was one of an important class of gentlemen colonists who were attracted to Van Diemen's Land about the years 1819 and 1820 by a system, which

Governor Sorell inaugurated, of giving grants of land, varying in extent according to the amount of capital brought by the individual settlers. Mr. Gregson was an eager politician, a man of great natural eloquence, and of an impetuosity which made him quite a "Rupert of debate." When responsible government was conceded to the colonies he became Premier of the second administration framed under the new system. The pretty cottage which he inhabited stands on a small hill facing the causeway which leads to Mount Direction. It is said to have been the residence of the first Lieutenant-Governor, when Van Diemen's Land was still a dependency of New South Wales, and there is a tradition that an old ivy-covered chimney standing in the garden of the cottage was the first piece of brickwork ever erected in Tasmania. For many years Mr. Gregson's cottage was the scene of the most genial hospitality. In his later years health and spirits broke down under the pressure of overwhelming calamities, but to the last he retained the warm attachment of not a few devoted friends.

Mention has already been made of Kangaroo Point, or Bellerive. The latter is the name of the pretty little township which has arisen on the Point; the former name dates from an early period of the colony. At the first settlement of Van Diemen's Land the new colony had to rely almost wholly for its food on supplies from New South Wales. But in the year 1806 a disastrous overflow of the Hawkesbury River destroyed the crops in New South Wales, and thus the elder colony was too straitened in its own means to send any supplies to its offshoot. At this period of distress the younger colony was almost entirely dependent on kangaroo hunting. The forests on the left bank of the Derwent furnished a large supply of kangaroo and wallaby. The carcases used to be brought down to the Point, and borne across in boats to Hobart Town. Hence the little promontory derived its name. It lies across the river, opposite to the south-eastern edge of the Domain. Steamers start from each side every half-hour, and as the crossing occupies little more than ten minutes, a visit to Bellerive may be paid at any hour, and without any special preparation. The convenience of easy access renders it a favourite place of residence to persons having business establishments in town. It is also a favourite resort for parents with young children. On that side of the promontory which is not visible from the town there is a fine beach of firm white sand more than a mile long, where a family of young children will find amusement for hours together, digging with their wooden spades, or dabbling with bare feet in the gentle surf. It has already been remarked that the view of the town and mountain from Bellerive is the grandest and most comprehensive that can be obtained anywhere.

Within easy distance of Bellerive is Mount Rumney, 1,236 feet in height. Of late years it has come greatly into vogue as a favourite resort of lovers of the picturesque. Following the road which leads from Kangaroo Point to Sorell, a walk of four miles brings us to a red gate. Passing through this, three roads are seen branching off in different directions. The middle one leads to Mount Rumney. It is a bush track, with a good many deviations; but as the trees along the direct route have been "blazed," there is little danger of losing one's way. The view from the top

NEWTOWN.

is magnificent. It includes the Wellington range and Hobart on one side, while in other directions the eye ranges over the fine coast scenery of Pittwater, Storm Bay, Norfolk Bay, Tasman's Peninsula, Forestier's Peninsula, and Bruny Island. It is estimated that more than 300 miles of varied coast line are seen from this point at one view, so deep are the indentations of the coast, so numerous the smaller islands and peninsulas, and so vast the extent of sea and land visible from the top of Mount Rumney.

Newtown is a very favourite residential suburb of Hobart. On the hillside stand handsome villa residences, with fine gardens. A well-known authoress, describing it forty years ago, wrote thus:—"The scenery around Newtown (where many of the wealthier merchants, Government officers, and professional men have tasteful residences), is the most beautiful I have seen on this side of the world, very much resembling that of the Cumberland Lakes. The broad and winding estuary of the Derwent flows amid lofty and picturesque hills and mountains clothed with forests, whilst at their feet lie level lawn-like slopes, green to the water's edge. But the most English, and therefore the most beautiful, things I saw there were the hawthorn hedges. It seemed like being on the right side of the world again to see rosy children with boughs of flowery 'May,' and to feel its full, luscious perfume wafted across me." Such did Newtown appear in the eyes of a new arrival forty years ago, and such might stand as its description in the present day. More houses have been built since then, more orchards and gardens planted, more "bush" cleared, but in all salient points it is the same—as English, and as beautiful.

A stretch of level road leads us to the Elwick racecourse. All is lovely here, and

# A GREAT LANDSLIP.

the Elwick course is probably the most beautiful for situation of any in the world. On one side is the broad river, dominated by Mount Direction, on the other, the glorious range which culminates in Mount Wellington. It lies on a promontory, washed on two sides by the waters of the Derwent, and fringed with trees on the land side. The ground has just the amount of undulation desirable in a racecourse. The grand stand is a handsome and solid structure, and adjoining it are saddling paddocks, and every other requirement of a well-appointed racing-ground. The principal meeting of the year is generally fixed early in February, a time when Hobart is full of visitors from the other colonies. There are two days' races, and on the afternoons of those days shops, banks, and Government offices are closed, and the whole community devote themselves to holiday-making. A short branch from the Main Line Railway leads to the entrance-gates of the race-ground, and crowded trains run to and fro during all the racing hours. With all this, the Cup day is not so popular a holiday as the Regatta day. The latter may be considered as the national holiday, and the one which brings the most unmixed enjoyment to all classes of the community, including those by whom horse-racing is regarded with disfavour. Nevertheless, the bright summer day, the pleasing excitement of a crowded field, and the beauty of the ground, with its surroundings, attract to Elwick on racing days many persons who have no particular interest in the horses.

If, as we pass the racecourse, we glance towards the Wellington range on our left, we notice a long, yellow-looking strip of bare rock down the side of one of the mountains. This is the famous landslip of 1872. On that portion of the range two mountain rills unite and form a stream, known as Humphrey's Rivulet. The township of Glenorchy derives its water supply from this rivulet. In the first days of June, 1872, heavy and continuous rains swelled Humphrey's Rivulet and its affluents, and saturated a considerable extent of the upper side of the mountain, where the almost impenetrable scrub was interspersed with enormous gum-

THE GRAND STAND, ELWICK RACECOURSE.

trees, and the gravelly soil easily absorbed the water till it reached the underlying rock. Then, owing to the steepness of the hillside, a strip of land one hundred acres in extent, thus loosened by the rain, slid down into the narrow bed of the rivulet, taking with it a perfect forest of trees, some of them forty or fifty tons in weight, and with them a mass of undergrowth and boulders, thus completely damming up the rivulet and keeping back its swelling waters. This dam increased until it was sixty feet high, forming a lake three hundred yards wide and nearly sixty feet deep, and so completely choking off the flow of water that the rivulet almost ceased flowing, in spite of the heavy rain. At ten o'clock on the night of the 4th of June an appalling sound, like the explosion of a powder magazine, was heard for many miles. So terrific was the crash, that persons residing at Risdon, six miles off across the river, sprang out of bed, thinking that the roofs of their houses had fallen in. The dam had given way, and this immense mass, urged by the weight of a million tons of water, was borne down the mountain side like an avalanche, sweeping everything before it. Only one life was lost, but buildings, gardens, and orchards were hopelessly destroyed. It is estimated that the amount of earth, rock, and timber brought down by the landslip would have been sufficient to construct a causeway across the Derwent at the part where the rivulet discharges itself into the larger river.

Beyond this lies a cultivated district, with just sufficient woodland to add charm and variety to the landscape. Several fine country houses are passed; and one range of farm-buildings standing near the road may be considered a model of its kind. It has also a further interest, as indicating the position of what was once known as Austin's Ferry—the connecting-link between the northern and southern portions of the main road before the Bridgewater Causeway was constructed. The road rises gradually for some miles, until at a certain point we find ourselves at the brow of the acclivity, and look down upon a stretch of road extending two miles, parallel to and near the river, which has widened out very considerably at this part. The Bridgewater Causeway is seen nearly at the end of our view, for the river bends a little distance above the Causeway, and a high mountain, named the Dromedary, cuts off the view in that direction. As we descend the hill, we see on our left a little chapel peeping out amidst trees on a private estate. We learn that this estate is called Hestercombe—a name which will excite warm interest in the mind of anyone who has lived in West Somersetshire, since it is the name of one of the loveliest spots in the beautiful valley of Taunton Dean. It appears also that the original owner of the estate was a Mr. Govett, and this is a peculiarly Somersetshire name. At the end of the descent there is a stretch of straight road as far as the Causeway. The railway at this part runs parallel with the main road, between it and the river. A sharp bend brings coach or train on to the Causeway, which lies across the river at right angles with the direction of the road.

The Bridgewater Causeway is one of the most remarkable of that fine series of public works which was commenced during the rule of Colonel Arthur, and carried out by his successors, at a time when the Government had an unlimited supply of prison labour at its disposal. The construction of the Causeway is said to have been suggested by a prisoner of inventive talent, who was working on the road near Bridgewater. At this point the river is nearly a mile wide, but it is very shallow for a considerable distance from the right bank, deepening progressively towards the left bank, along which there is a deep channel, available for navigation. In the shallow portion of the river a roadway was constructed by means of many thousand cartloads of earth and rubbish, emptied into the water until the mound rose to a suitable height above the surface. Then a few yards were flanked with stonework, and a secure road formed for carrying the work a little further. Thus, bit by bit, a strong and permanent roadway was constructed for about three-quarters of the whole distance. The deeper portion was spanned by a bridge on piles, as far as the deep channel; here the communication is completed by a drawbridge, which is opened when steamers or other vessels require to pass through. The main road from Hobart to Launceston crosses the Derwent by means of the Causeway. It was opened for traffic by Sir William Denison in 1849, and contributed greatly to the progress of the colony, by increasing the facilities of communication between Hobart and the midland and northern districts of the island. The Main Line Railway also uses the Causeway up to the deep water, but has its own set of piles and drawbridge.

The story of the manner in which the idea of the Causeway originated seems rather a tradition than an ascertained historical fact. It is certain, however, that the Hobart Town Mechanics' Institute used to possess a very pretty model of this Causeway, and this was said to be the work of the prisoner who suggested the notion of it. The story further states that he obtained a conditional pardon as a reward for his ingenuity.

At Newtown the Risdon road branches off to the right from the lowest point of the suburb. If we take this turn we pass for about a quarter of a mile through a succession of pretty villas and gardens to an inlet of the Derwent, known as Newtown Bay; and if, instead of proceeding along the Risdon road, we round the head of the bay, we arrive at a large cemetery situated on a promontory formed by the Newtown Bay, and by another, named Cornelian Bay. The latter, as the nearer to Hobart, has given its name to this burial-ground, which is generally spoken of as the Cornelian Bay Cemetery. The first interments took place here in 1872, an Act of the Legislature having previously closed all graveyards within the town boundaries, and prohibited what it rather inaccurately designated *intramural interments*. The cemetery has been neatly laid out with walks and shrubberies, and some parts of it are thickly studded with monuments and headstones, but it is so spacious that it will hardly be overcrowded a hundred years hence

## GOLD.

The First Rush—Victoria Deserted—The Reflux—Life at the Diggings—A Primitive Post Office—Ingenuous Advertisements—Law and Order—The Composition of the Police—The Force of Nature—"Big Finds and Petty Squabbles"—Open Rebellion—"From the East and the West, and from the North and the South"—Murder and Rapine—The Murder at Indigo Creek—The Gold Escort Attacked and Defeated—A Raid on a Ship—Sailors' Luck—The Mongol and his Tribulations—Boisterous Extravagance—Pegging out a Claim—Mining Processes, Past and Present—Alluvial Mining—The "Jewellers' Shops"—"Shepherding"—Big Nuggets—Quartz Mining—A Novice's Impression of a Gold Mine—Mount Brown—Kimberley.

THE WHIM.

FOR years before Hargreaves' discovery of gold in Australia there had been reports and rumours of the fabulous wealth that lay hidden beneath the surface of the earth. The aborigines had found gold; the lonely shepherd, whose lot in life lay far from the busy haunts of men, had found it; the convicts had found it. Still, these stories were few and far between, and but little credence was given to them. Men were not seeking gold; the hopes of the majority were centred in pastoral pursuits. They had no desire to see their peaceful pastures invaded by a throng of eager gold-seekers, and many, doubtless, shared the freely-expressed opinion of one of the first Governors —that the finding of gold and the consequent rush of free immigrants would be the ruin of colonies intended solely for convicts and their keepers.

It was hardly likely, however, that so much wealth would remain hidden for long before the advancing tide of civilisation. The gold discoveries in America took the world by storm, and Australia sent her quota of emigrants—some 300—to seek their fortunes among the rocky sierras and deep cañons of California. So it happened that Edward Hammond Hargreaves, an Englishman of thirty-three, who had spent more than half his life in Australia, while prospecting among the hills of California, was struck by their similarity in contour, outline, and geological characteristics to those about his home at Bathurst, and on his return to New South Wales he informed the Government that for a consideration he would show them where to find gold. The times were changed, his offer was accepted, and in February, 1851, the business of gold-mining in Australia may be said to have fairly begun.

As soon as it was known that gold had been found a rush took place, and nearly half the male population of Sydney were to be found washing for gold at Summer Hill Creek, Bathurst, or on the way thither. The quiet little gully became the scene of busy life, and men of all ages and all ranks might be seen crowding along the banks of the creek anxiously searching for the precious metal. The news soon spread far and wide, and thither came eager gold-seekers from all parts of Australia, but more particularly from the neighbouring colony of Victoria.

Victoria, it will be remembered, had just succeeded in procuring separation from New South Wales, and now the sudden exodus of her population threatened her very existence. Clearly the only way to check this wholesale emigration was to find gold

A GOLD RUSH.

within her own boundaries, and accordingly a reward was offered for the discovery of a paying gold-field near Melbourne. Rumours of the presence of gold in Victoria had not been wanting. A convict shepherd had found it in the Pyrenees; someone else had found it at Clunes, afterwards a paying gold-field; in fact, it had been found all over the colony, but nowhere in sufficient quantities to attract attention. Now, however, that a reward was offered, the whole country was overrun with anxious prospectors (the ordinary term for men who go out expressly to look for gold in new ground), many of whom had the vaguest notions of what they had come out to seek. Soon gold was discovered in the valley of the Plenty, near Melbourne, and an eager rush took place. It was not, however, very rich, and when, in August, 1851, came news of the discovery of gold by a man named Hiscocks, near the little township of Buninyong, the fickle crowd deserted the Plenty, and before long over 10,000 men were turning up the earth at what is now the prosperous and rising town of Ballarat. Afterwards gold was discovered in large quantities on the Bendigo Creek, now Sandhurst, at Mount Alexander, afterwards called Castlemaine, and also in the Ovens district. In New South Wales, too, mining at Bathurst continued to pay, and fresh fields were discovered, but in the matter of gold the glory of New South Wales pales before that of her younger sister, and in an article on gold-mining it is chiefly of Victoria that we must speak.

Victoria at first, like the rest of the colonies, was a purely pastoral country. Men counted their wealth, like the patriarchs of old, by their cattle, and lived a peaceful, uneventful life, settled quietly in what they hoped were to be their homes for years to come. In Melbourne, too, life flowed on calmly as in a well-to-do country town. Among these quiet people the knowledge of the wealth hidden away in their midst, to be had, perhaps, for the mere scraping of the earth, by one whose only stock-in-trade was a pick and spade and tin dish, came like a bombshell. Straightway the desire for gold took hold upon every member of the community. The clerk left his desk and the merchant his office, the doctor his patients and the lawyer his clients, the tradesman deserted his shop and the carpenter his bench; all ranks of society were seized with the same thirst for gold, and all alike were to be found on the now well-beaten tracks that led to the newly-discovered gold-fields.

Property in Melbourne went down, till, according to the expression, it could be bought for a mere song. Those who were wise in their generation bought up all they could, and waited for the turn of the tide that came only too quickly, but the majority were eager to be off. It was well-nigh impossible to get any work whatsoever done; the streets in the earliest gold-mining days were empty and deserted—the very policemen had gone to the diggings.

Meanwhile, in the gold-fields all was busy life. At every rush the course of events was much the same. In those days they never dreamt of quartz batteries, deep sinking diamond drills, and all the wonderful and expensive machinery that is now used to get at the precious metal. A man, having come to the conclusion that his particular claim was played out, or arriving late on the scene, and perhaps finding all the likely spots taken up, shouldered his "swag" and set out in search of "pastures new." Sometimes he had a mate or mates, sometimes he went alone, but as a rule a party of prospectors was composed of half-a-dozen old miners who knew what they were going out to look for. Meanwhile the "green hands" and "new chums" stayed with the crowd. Generally the prospectors possessed a dray, in which were packed their tools and a few stores, and then, heavily armed, they went out into the wilderness to seek their fortunes.

The greater part of Victoria was a wilderness in those days, but of danger there was little, save that every-day danger of the Australian bush, want of water. An occasional wandering tribe of aborigines, too, might prove troublesome, but that hazard was lessening daily. They had never been very numerous, and the squatters had from the first been waging continual war against the dark-skinned denizens of the bush, who, now reduced to half their original numbers, entertained a wholesome fear of the white man's firearms. Into the virgin forest, then, went these prospectors, among the hills and into the gullies, where the foot of civilised man had never yet trod. What if they did disturb the ferns and the trailing creepers, and turn the pretty silver creeks rushing down the rocky hillsides into dirty, yellow-tinged streams, and the fern-clad gully into a desolate waste? No one ever saw the beauty they spoiled, no one very likely ever would have seen it, and these men, selfish as they no doubt were, have helped to build up a mighty colony.

It was along the banks of the creeks and water-worn gullies that these prospectors first sought gold. For of the two sorts of gold-mining, viz., alluvial and quartz, alluvial was the one first in vogue, being the easiest, and requiring little or no technical knowledge. The newest "chum" could trace the bed of a dry creek above ground. Equally easily recognised was the bed rock, though it might be a hundred feet below the surface; and the water-worn gravel and sand, which the diggers washed for gold, and consequently termed wash-dirt, was nothing, in point of fact, but the bed of an ancient creek, which in olden days had carried down the gold from its home in the quartz hills. Having found what they sought, their natural desire was to keep it to themselves. But this was well-nigh impossible. It began to be whispered in the nearest township that So-and-So's party had struck gold in paying quantities at such-and-such a place, and within a week thousands of men had "rushed" the creek, which a few days before the little party of prospectors had called their own.

A "rush" on the early gold-fields was like nothing else in the world. One day the lovely gully, the wild, dense bush-land, untouched by the hand of man, and in less than a week a place thronged with busy life. Rushes varied in size, sometimes consisting only of a few hundred men, while at others there were thousands in the field. The new-comers on their arrival hastened to "peg out" their "claims" in what appeared to them the most desirable spots, or took gratefully what the first comers had left for them. The ring of the axe was heard, the great forest trees fell before strong and sinewy arms that had learned to wield the axe in the forests of California. For miles around the land was denuded of timber, tent-poles, firewood, and timber for the new claim being an absolute necessity.

The climate of Victoria is mild compared with that of England, and the summer is very hot—hotter, perhaps, thirty years ago than it is now—but, south of the dividing range, at least, there are certainly three months of bitterly cold weather, when some shelter is necessary from the cutting wind and the driving rain. Consequently, as by magic, in less than a week a large canvas-and-bark town had sprung into existence. A somewhat ramshackle and tumble-down town it was, certainly, for each man was in haste to be rich, and gave little thought to his personal comfort meanwhile. The great aim of all was to have the dwelling close to the claim. This, of course, was not possible where the ground was rich and the claims lay close together, and, accordingly, there sprang up a long, irregular line of huts and tents. Tents were most in favour, as being the simplest and easiest shelter to provide; but bark and slab huts were by no means uncommon. Uniformity there was none: each man built his house according to his own taste. Here was a frail bark hut, through the holes and crannies of which the cold wind must have whistled full often; there a neat white tent, the property of some new "chum" who had been fortunate enough to get it safe up country. In marked contrast would be the tent next door—a piece of tattered canvas, so old and ragged and brown that it is surprising it held together at all. Farther down the embryo street might be seen a neat hut built of slabs, with a weather-proof bark roof; the property of an old bushman, this. He and his mate understand how to make themselves comfortable, and the axe, which the new "chum" next door—residing in a tumble-down mia-mia, a mere shelter of boughs or bark, of which a black fellow would be ashamed—finds an unconquerable difficulty in using, is in his deft hands a powerful and useful tool.

PROSPECTING.

Inside these huts and tents very little furniture was to be seen. The floor, of course, was the bare earth, and a standing bed-place or bunk was generally considered a necessity, but there was very little else. Some luxurious soul might make himself a rough wooden table, or rig up a few convenient shelves, but this was rare. Boxes and the flour-barrel, as a rule, did duty as seats, and the early digger's sole possessions were his mining implements, his blankets, a tin billy, and a frying-pan. All else was considered

A POST-OFFICE AT THE DIGGINGS.

superfluous, and looked upon as luxurious. The digger himself was usually attired in a blue or red shirt, moleskin trousers tucked into high boots, and a slouch hat, while at his waist were pistols and knife, without which weapons of defence and offence no man was seen. In the middle of the camp was the inevitable grog shanty and general store, a place where anything was to be bought, from a needle to a sheet anchor, from the digger's tent to the chamois leather bag in which he carried his gold. The owner had found, in the sale of bad liquor at exorbitant prices, a surer road to wealth than any gold-mine in the colony. "Man must drink," might have been written of the early digger; and if he can't drink good liquor, he will drink bad, and if even that fails him, he will console himself with Worcester Sauce or Friar's Balsam.

The practice of "shouting," or treating, was then common, far commoner even than it is at the present time, and it was not unusual for a lucky digger to spend £100, or even £200, in "shouting," not only for his friends, but for any strangers who happened to be hanging about the bar. It is only fair to add, so extraordinary were the prices, that he received for this outlay perhaps £10 worth of liquor. Thus it happened that the grog shanty—usually a large tent with a counter down the middle, the stock-in-trade on one side and the customers on the other—was generally, especially in the evening, crowded with men drinking, fighting, quarrelling, playing cards, exchanging their hard-won gold for the necessaries of life—one and all aiding the publican to pile up for himself a snug fortune. If the "rush" were large there were often three or four of these stores, but, as a rule, the impassable state of the roads and the high price paid both for stores and cartage required a large capital, and practically forbade competition.

As soon as the "rush" became an undoubted fact a post-office was established, and, though it was primitive in the extreme, and letter-carriers were, of course, unknown, it was an undoubted boon to the inhabitants. Kelly, the author of "Life in Victoria," gives the following description of the first Ballarat post-office, which bears a strong family resemblance to those on all the diggings in the colonies in the old days:—

"The St. Martin's-le-Grand of Ballarat was a very primitive establishment, contained within a moderate-sized log-cabin, the greater portion of which, even after subtracting the household corner, was devoted to general business, and the person who wanted an ounce of tobacco was attended to before the man in quest of letters. The whole exterior of the edifice was papered over with quaintly-worded and ingeniously-spelled advertisements in writing. If you could find a vacant space you were at liberty to occupy it, but woe betide you if caught either in pulling off or over-riding a previously posted notice, which, under pick and shovel law, were allowed to remain till they fell off. I annex a few as a general specimen:—

"'If this should meet the eye of John Tims he will hear of his shipmate at Pennyweight Flat, next tent to the tub and cradle.'

"The sign of a store, I presume; but if not so understood, rather a vague direction in a district like Pennyweight Flat, where some thousands were at work, each party with a tub and cradle.

"'James dakin notyces the publik agin thrustin his wife.'

"'Pat Flynn calls on biddy to return to the tint forninst the cross roads.'

"'Ten pounds reward for my black mare. No questions asked nor ideas insinuated.'

"But no indication where the reward was payable.

"'For sale several houseboldt an kulenary articles as also a numerous frackshun of odds & ends at the Tent opposite the Frenchman's store at the Ureka.'"

Soon after the "breaking out of the gold" the Government had seen the absolute necessity of putting someone in authority to check the lawlessness of the nondescript crowd gathered together on a gold-fields' "rush," and accordingly on every diggers' camp was a Gold Commissioner, and if it were large, there were three, and sometimes four. The Commissioner's camp was invariably set on a little eminence overlooking the diggers', and presented a marked contrast to it. Down there every man was as good as his neighbour, were he peer of the realm or foul-mouthed convict from the reeking gaols of New South Wales or Van Diemen's Land; but up in the police camp the old order prevailed: each man had his well-defined rank, and the Commissioner was lord of all. In front of the camp, so as to be plainly visible to all, was the flagstaff, from which floated the emblem of British rule, the Union Jack, and facing that were the Commissioner's tents, usually four in number—a mess tent, an office tent, a bed tent, and another for his clerk. These, in contrast with the diggers', were all floored with hard wood, carefully lined with green baize, and furnished with every luxury—as luxuries were then understood. At the back were the tents of the twenty or thirty troopers in form of a square, and behind them again were the stables for the horses.

Close behind the Commissioner's quarters was the all-important gold tent, guarded day and night by two armed sentries. In it were strong cedar boxes, and here was deposited the surplus wealth of the diggers' camp. Every man brought his gold, were the quantity great or small, in a leather or canvas bag, and handed it over to be placed in the strong box. A ticket with his name on it was attached to the parcel, and he received a receipt signed by the Commissioner, who was thenceforward responsible for the safety of the gold. When sufficient quantity was collected, usually from 60 to 90 lbs. weight, the escort started with it for Melbourne. In the early days, when the roads were well-nigh impassable, all the gold had to be carried on the backs of pack-horses, and the precious metal being dead weight, and apt to give the horses sore backs, from 20 to 25 lbs. weight was considered a fair load for each horse. The gold was packed in leather bags made something after the manner of old-fashioned purses; these were carefully locked in the middle by the Commissioner himself, and then slung across the pack-saddle. The day on which the escort started was a great day in the camp, and crowds turned out to see them set off. Usually the escort consisted of from ten to twelve men. Four pack-horses—about the usual number—required a man apiece to lead them, and as these men were necessarily much hampered, six heavily-armed troopers formed a guard. The Commissioner or an officer of police commanded the escort, and was responsible for the safety of the gold, and generally there was the sergeant, twelve men in all.

A fine body of men were the police of those days. They were all young, or at least men in the very prime of life, and though their uniform was much the same as that of the present trooper, their orderliness, their natty get-up, their well-kept horses and shining accoutrements, contrasted forcibly with the careless and ofttimes frowsy attire of the diggers in the camp below. The Gold Commissioner wore as uniform a cavalry officer's undress, namely, a dark braided frock-coat, with a cap bound with gold lace, and, of course, the usual boots and breeches. He and his clerk were gentlemen by birth and breeding, but most of the policemen were drawn from the working classes. In the early days, however, many young men, the sons of gentlemen, came out to the colonies with the very laudable object of making their fortunes. The only question was "how?" That question was at first easily answered, "By gold digging, of course." But gold getting in theory and gold getting in practice were two very different things, and many of these young men, unaccustomed to manual labour, and with no practical knowledge to guide them, not merely found gold digging unprofitable, but in very many cases starvation absolutely stared them in the face. Glad enough, then, were they to secure a "billet" in the police force, where they were well paid and the work was not hard, or beyond their powers. These young fellows were formed into a separate body, called "cadets," the only difference between them and the regular police being that they were supposed to be eligible for promotion. Some few, indeed, did rise to the rank of superintendent or inspector, but the majority, as the country became more settled, drifted away into other paths of life more suited to their status and education, while the few who remained were merged in the ordinary police force, never rose beyond the rank of senior constable or sergeant, and were fain to confess that their emigration to the "new and happy land" had in all probability ruined their lives.

Another class of peace preserver to be seen in the Commissioner's camp was the black trooper. These men were recruited from the aborigines of the Murray District, and, strange to say, although coming from the midst of savagery of the very lowest type, they made most excellent policemen. Among men where discipline was most strict, where accoutrements, horses, clothes had to be kept in the very highest state of perfection, the black fellow was no whit behind his white comrade. Tall and slight, often good looking, a splendid horseman, managing his horse with grace and ease, this son of that race which is truly counted one of the most degraded in the world was the beau ideal of a trooper. Unfortunately there was a reverse side to the medal. It was utterly impossible to civilise the black man. After three months or so of civilised life he would beg a holiday, and return for a little to his own people. Then, should anyone pay a visit to the blacks' camp, a mile or so down the creek, there might be seen prone on the ground, or crouching beneath a wretched mia-mia, that hardly served to keep out the weather, a dirty, unkempt savage, stark-naked, save for an opossum rug or a filthy blanket, surrounded by gnawed bones, fighting dogs, and all the conglomerate filth of a blacks' camp. And this, alas! was the manner in which the smart black trooper spent his leave. Over and over again the experiment has been made, only to prove that it is

BREAKFAST ON THE GOLD-FIELDS.

utterly impossible to civilise the Australian black fellow. The smartest man in the troop would have pined and died if he had not occasionally gone back to his original savagery, whence he returned to his duties with a fresh stock of energy and life. About 1855, however, recruiting from the blacks was discontinued, chiefly because, although they made good troopers, they were hardly to be relied upon, and in any case the dignity of a white man was always terribly outraged if he was run in by a black fellow. One or two, however, were for many years kept attached to each camp, where their services as trackers were invaluable; and when we think how often, even at the present time, when law and order rule supreme, and the country is rapidly becoming settled and civilised, the services of the black tracker are put in requisition, it will be seen how trebly necessary they were in the early days of which we speak.

For the first two or three years the history of the goldfields may be summed up briefly as a record of big finds and of petty squabbles between the diggers and those who were supposed to be their guardians. On whose side the fault lay it is perhaps difficult to say after this lapse of time, but it is very evident that the law of the land was a good deal to blame. The licence-fee and its collection were a standing grievance. No man might dig until he had taken out a licence, for which he paid at first 30s. a month, afterwards £3, and then again 30s. Even this lower amount was a most exorbitant sum for a poor man to pay, though, doubtless, many could have paid it quite easily. This licence the digger was required to produce whenever and wherever a trooper might ask for it, or he ran the risk of being arrested there and then, and spending the night in the "logs," as the lock-up was termed. Faults there were on both sides, of course, and if the police were arbitrary, the diggers were most certainly lawless. "Joe, Joe! traps, traps!" shouted the populace in scorn and derision whenever they were beyond the reach of the arms of the law. "Traps, boys, traps! yah! Joe, Joe!" cried even the children, with hatred at their hearts, as the trooper trotted past them. It is little wonder that matters came to a crisis towards the end of 1854, when the diggers of Ballarat, who certainly had more to complain of than those on the neighbouring fields, rose in open rebellion, and were utterly defeated at the Eureka Stockade. After this lamentable event, of which an account is given in a later article (p. 263),

A BLACK TROOPER.

the licence-fee was done away with, an export tax on gold levied, and the Miner's Right substituted, so that for £1 a year a man had the right to dig for gold, and, what was still more valued, this Miner's Right carried the franchise along with it. Gold Commissioners were done away with, at least in name, and an officer, called a warden, substituted, whose duties, however, were practically exactly the same as those of the obnoxious Commissioner—the administration of justice on the gold-fields, and the hearing and settling of all cases that might arise between partners, also cases of encroachment, trespass, and disputed boundaries. For many years there were no courts, and cases were heard by the warden, generally on the very spot where the dispute arose; it is only of late that these cases on the gold-fields have been determined in the ordinary court-houses.

Gold is the magnet that attracts all, old and young, rich and poor, good and bad alike, and by the end of 1851 the fame of the Victorian gold-fields had spread to the uttermost parts of the earth; the tide of immigration had commenced, and from all parts of the world came emigrants for Victoria. They came by hundreds and thousands, men from every nation under the sun. First came those from the neighbouring colonies, and South Australia was nearly emptied of her male population; they poured across the border from New South Wales; they crossed Bass's Strait from Tasmania; they came, not only white men, but Maoris, across the stormy seas from New Zealand. Then from England arrived ship-load after ship-load of emigrants who, as they passed through the Heads, cheered lustily for "the new and happy land." The news spread farther afield, and all sorts and conditions of men came from Europe and America; even the dark races of India and the East were moved by the impulse, and from China came the yellow-faced Mongolians, not by tens or hundreds, but by thousands. So great was the rush that in one year the population of Victoria was doubled, and yet the cry was "Still they come!" Amongst so many it was hardly likely that all the immigrants would be desirable colonists. Ribbonmen from Ireland, Chartists from England, Socialists from Germany, Communists from France, Carbonari from Italy, the disaffected from all lands, met on the gold-fields. But the worst evil lay close at home. From the neighbouring colonies of New South Wales and Tasmania came the offscourings of their reeking gaols—ticket-of-leave men, men whose time had expired, men who had escaped, conditional-pardon men, all well versed in crime, past masters in every iniquity under the sun. The natural result followed: murder and rapine were rife on the gold-fields. Bushranging was common; every man went heavily armed, and no man's life was safe; while the prevalence of such names in Victoria as Murderer's Gully and Deadman's Flat tells its own miserable tale. In the grog-shanties many a cruel scheme was hatched which the lonely gullies and desolate bush tracks saw put into execution. "Bail up, throw up your hands!"—the Australian equivalent for "Stand and deliver!"—was a common cry, and since dead men tell no tales, murder was often added to robbery, or, with a cold-blooded cruelty such as was to be met with only among the "old hands," the victim would be beaten badly, rendered incapable of moving, and then left to take his chance of life, or, perhaps, still worse, would be bound to a tree and left to die by inches. One who has written of Victoria's early

## A TYPICAL CRIME.

days, tells how he, with a companion, was lost on the ranges near Ballan. His mate knocked up entirely, and earnestly praying not to be left to die alone in the bush, he, as a forlorn hope, climbed a tree and "coooyed" at the top of his voice. Much to the surprise of both men, there came across the tree-tops an answer so faint that at first they feared it might be an echo. Another cooey and another answer set all doubt at rest, and so raised the hopes of the well-nigh dying man that he made another effort, and accompanied his friend in the direction whence the sound proceeded. After proceeding some little distance, to their intense astonishment they came upon two men bound back to back to a tree. Hastily loosening their bonds, they asked how they came there, and were told they were two diggers who, on leaving Ballan the day before, had been "stuck up" and relieved of their little store of gold-dust. Naturally they had offered some resistance, but had been overpowered, and one was badly shot in the leg. Not content with appropriating their hard-earned gains, the cold-blooded thieves had tied them so firmly to a tree that their death would have been certain had no one passed by, of which there was little chance. Almost certain, too, but for this opportune meeting, would have been the death of the two travellers, for though the little township was scarcely a mile away, the chances were a hundred to one against their hitting the track.

Even close to the camps, too, murder might be done with but little fear of detection. It was so easy—so very easy. Shouts and cries were but little heeded on a rowdy diggers' camp; and as for pistol shots, every man carried a revolver, and made a regular practice of firing it off every evening, in order to clean it; so that the report of a pistol attracted no attention at all.

The murder of the German on the Indigo Creek is a case in point. The land round the creek, though rich in gold, was barren and sterile; the gully lay low, and by October the ground was baked hard and dry, so that the diggers on the camp were even more dependent than usual on the neighbouring townships for their supplies. Upon the ranges at Wooragee, near Beechworth, dwelt a German, who, having found the land about his new home rich and fertile, had made for himself a large market-garden, disposing of his surplus vegetables among the diggers' camps around; and, since cabbages in those days were worth from two to three shillings apiece, laying up for himself, we have little doubt, a comfortable independence. Periodically he, with his bullock-team and dray laden with fresh green vegetables, visited the camp at the Indigo, where he found a ready sale for his wares. One hot, still evening, just at dusk, the German, having disposed of his vegetables, stopped his empty dray at the grog-shanty known as "Forty's," because the Forty Thieves were popularly supposed to congregate there. Little he cared for the bad reputation of the place. He did not propose to stay there, but tossed off his "nobbler," paid for it out of the little store of gold-dust he had that day received, called out in his broken English a cheery good-night to the men standing at the open door, and, shouting to his team, moved off slowly along the track into the darkening night. No one but his murderer ever saw the poor fellow alive again. A man named Ryan, an "old hand" from Van Diemen's Land, noticing the empty dray, and inferring, consequently, the full pockets, slipped unnoticed from the shanty, followed the team, stole softly up behind the vegetable hawker, and, almost within sight, certainly within hearing, of the Commissioner's camp, shot him through the head, robbed the dead body, and was back at Forty's, smoking and drinking with the rest, before his short absence had been noticed. By-and-by some belated traveller—or digger whose claim was farther out—noticed a team of bullocks with an empty dray straying from the track, and, recognising them for the property of the German vegetable hawker, began to search for their owner, who, according to the manner of the time, he concluded, was drunk. Soon he found the body, still warm, and raised the alarm at the police camp. Promptly the search began; but there would have been little chance of the

A STORE AT THE DIGGINGS.

murderer's being discovered had it not been for the anxiety of the culprit himself. Day after day he haunted the police camp, wanting to know if anything had been discovered, questioning the troopers, endeavouring to throw suspicion first on one man, then on another, till, finally, the suspicions of the Commissioner were aroused, and he ordered Ryan into custody. One way and another evidence of his guilt came pouring in, and in the end he confessed to the murder, and was hanged for it.

A case of gold robbery on a much larger scale was the "sticking up" of the gold escort between McIvor, or Heathcote, as it is now called, and Melbourne. The escort, though private, and not that of the Government, was strong and well armed, and had under its care several thousand pounds' worth of gold. The bushrangers, taking advantage of a turn in the rough bush track at a place called the "Mia-Mia," felled trees, and erected for themselves a sort of barricade along the side of the road, in such fashion though, that the advance guard passed without taking any particular notice of the fallen timber, and certainly never suspecting that men were concealed there. Then, as the pack-horses bearing the gold came up, the bushrangers shot them down, and the fight raged furiously round the fallen horses. Taken by surprise as they were, the troopers gallantly defended their charge; but it was an unequal fight. The bushrangers were hidden, and could aim at their ease, without fear, while the troopers, standing mounted in the open, made capital targets, without being able to retaliate. Finally they abandoned the gold and fled, and the bushrangers made off with the booty. Though a vigorous search was at once instituted, the lost gold was never recovered, nor were the bushrangers ever taken. The popular and prevailing belief has never been contradicted; they are supposed to be the same men who made away with the *Madagascar*. Not that it was ever proved that the *Madagascar* had been made away with; but some time in 1857 this vessel, one of Messrs. Green's line of clippers, sailed away from Hobson's Bay, with a rich cargo of specie, and was never afterwards heard of. By-and-by her name appeared on that saddest list of all, "Missing," and then the rumour spread—whence it arose no man could tell—that the miscreants who had "stuck up" the escort at the "Mia-Mia" had either secreted themselves on board the ship, or else, in the dearth of men, had been hired as part of the crew. Then, when the vessel was fairly at sea, they came out in their true colours, overpowered, and very probably, if the story be true, drowned the rest of the crew and passengers, scuttled the ship off the coast of America, and, with the stores of gold they thus made their own, began life afresh in California, or perhaps in some of the Republics of South America.

Another gold robbery which occasioned a great stir at the time was that of the ship *Nelson* as she lay in Hobson's Bay, close to the shore. Her crew had deserted her, no uncommon thing during the first few years after the "breaking out" of the gold, and though she lay ready for sea, no men could be found willing to work her. The captain, in despair, had gone off to seek recruits, and the ship was left in charge of two men. At midnight there stole

THE WHIP. "HAUL UP!"

a boat from the shore, which made softly and silently for the *Nelson*. Quietly her crew stole aboard, and before the sleepy watchman could give the alarm, both he and his mate were overpowered and bound; the gold was quickly taken out of the hold, and before the pair had recovered from their astonishment, the boat and its crew were ashore again. The gold was hidden in the sand, and next day was taken to Melbourne in an open buggy. Very little was afterwards recovered, and the daring robbery was never brought home to anybody, only, as was but natural, the outcry against the old hands from Tasmania and New South Wales became louder than ever. Decidedly these were not a desirable class of immigrants, and it was little wonder that the Government had done its best to check their incoming. This was by the Convicts' Prevention Act, which Victoria, in despair, and in defiance of all precedent, passed, compelling all persons coming from the neighbouring colonies of New South Wales, Tasmania, and the more distant Western Australia, to prove, not only that they were free, but also that they had never been convicts.

As we have said, it was no uncommon thing for ships to lie idle in the bay for lack of hands to work them home again. Their crews deserted wholesale, coming out, in fact, for that very purpose, for the gold-fields seem to have had an irresistible charm for the sailor, and the number of "Sailors' Gullies" that are even now in existence bears witness to the large number of this class there must have been at one time on the diggings. So great did the evil become, and so hopeless was it to think of preventing the men from rushing for a share in the gold harvest, that at last it became a regular practice for ship-masters to divide their men, one-half going up to the diggings under his charge to try their luck for a month or six weeks, and then returning to give the mate and the rest a turn. As a rule, at the end of the appointed time, the crew returned to their duties cheerfully, even gladly foregoing any further chance of a fortune, for digging was work to which they were unaccustomed; it was toilsome in the extreme, whilst they, with no technical knowledge to guide them, were exceedingly likely to be taken in by the designing men who swarmed at that time on the gold-fields. Yet sailors' luck is proverbial. Kelly tells a story of a party of sailors he met at Ballarat with their captain in charge, in whose case the proverb was certainly exemplified. These men, thinking it hardly worth while to sink a hole on their own account, bought for £15 one which its former owner, having sunk to 45 feet without finding gold, was anxious to be rid of. Accordingly he had carefully salted it, and the sailors, seeing gold glittering in the dirt, gleefully concluded the bargain, rigged a windlass, and unsuspectingly set to work. In a few days they were down 80 feet, and had struck a fresh gutter of rich wash-dirt, which yielded them an average of an ounce to a tub, or an aggregate of over £3,300.

Another class of immigrants came in such numbers that special laws were enacted for their benefit, not only to govern them, but to keep them out of the colony. These were the Chinese, who, as has been previously said, once the news of the discovery of gold had been bruited abroad poured into the colony in one never-ceasing stream. They were thrifty, they were sober, they were industrious, they could live where a European would starve, and, for the most part, they did live upon what

ATTACK ON THE GOLD ESCORT BETWEEN M'IVOR AND MELBOURNE.

the white men abandoned as useless; and yet there went a cry over the colony that Ishmael was taking the portion intended for Isaac—a cry for protection from these strangers. Accordingly a poll-tax of £10 was set on every Chinaman who landed in the colony, and rigidly enforced, although many came from Hong Kong, and were, therefore, to all intents and purposes British subjects. But the patient new-comers from the Flowery Land were not so easily "done." If they did not choose, or had not sufficient money, to pay the heavy tax, they disembarked at Sydney, and painfully made their way from the Braidwood and Kiandra gold-fields, high among the snowy Alps, down to the Murray, and thence into Victoria, or else they went round to South Australia, and by toilsome marches crossed the dreary desert that lay between them and the land of promise.

Loud protestations arose from the white men. These strangers settled among them were not of them, they were mere birds of passage; they brought nothing into the country, while they lived on the merest pittance, saving all they could to return to their own land: not even, could they help it, were their very bones allowed to rest in an alien soil.

It is true these immigrants were drawn from the very lowest ranks of society— for the most part from the river-folk of Canton. They were not very cleanly, nor, perhaps, very honest if temptation were put in their way. They were addicted to opium-smoking, and they brought with them leprosy and other diseases common to Eastern nations. Still, the white men were hardly so immaculate themselves that they might venture to sit in judgment. The Chinaman had no friends. Wherever he was met he was beaten and ill-treated, and at one period riots against the Chinese were common all over the colony. On the slightest pretext, or on no pretext at all, the Chinese camp would be rushed, and the unfortunate occupants driven from their tents and huts. On one occasion the diggers, among whom was a large sprinkling of the Yankee element, at a rush on the Buckland River, celebrated the glorious Fourth by an unprovoked attack on the unoffending Chinese camp. There were about 800 Chinamen and not a quarter as many white men; but the Celestials made little or no attempt to defend their household gods, and fled out into the bush, pursued for some distance by the valorous diggers. Word of the state of affairs at the Buckland was soon brought to the nearest Gold Commissioner, about ninety miles away. He at once came down with twenty troopers at his back. He was too late, however, for many of the Celestials. As the little band of troopers rode through the bush on that bitter July night, they came across unfortunate Chinamen lying alone, dead and dying, wantonly murdered by the drunken rioters. Some were hidden away in the scrub, shivering with cold and fright, too terrified almost to move, while others, in little parties, crouching round a handful of fire, endeavoured to shelter themselves from the keen winter's wind. Short and sharp was the Commissioner's justice. He and his troopers promptly reinstated the Chinamen, and if it was whispered that, in the redistribution of claims, the lion's share, or, more properly speaking, the best holes, fell to the foreigners, few will be found to blame the Commissioner now, and none dared do so then.

The Buckland men, however, in those days found many who sympathised with them and would gladly have followed their example. But in spite of all opposition, the Chinamen, patient, long-suffering, and industrious, made their way. Their camps were little towns, often containing 4,000 or 5,000 inhabitants. They had their own theatres, their own shops, their joss-houses, or temples, and then, as now, they were governed by their own laws among themselves, though outwardly they were amenable to the laws of the land in which they sojourned. Their secret societies or guilds were then, as they are at the present time, powerful and widespread. A Chinese interpreter soon became a necessary addition to the Government staff on every diggers' camp; and the Chinese were a recognised evil throughout the land.

"FOSSICKING."

Those were the days of sudden and unexpected fortunes, and consequently of lavish expenditure and reckless extravagance. The lucky digger, who, in England, had hoped for nothing better than 15s. or £1 a week, once such easily won wealth was his, spent it right royally. "Lightly come, lightly go," runs the proverb, and it was more than exemplified during the first few years of the gold rushes. Did any actress take the popular fancy, she was nightly showered with nuggets instead of bouquets, and the very sweepings of the theatre were worth a small fortune to the caretaker. Did the digger fancy a game at skittles, he set up bottles of champagne as ninepins, when champagne was £1 a bottle, and bowled against them till every one was smashed. Was he hungry, then it struck his fancy that he would have a sandwich, in which a £1 or even a £5 note took the place of the more ordinary and much more digestible and nutritious beef or ham; and it is related that when the diggers first elected a member for the Ovens, so overjoyed were they that they actually shod his horse with gold, and, forming a procession, escorted him from the Woolshed to Beechworth in noisy triumph.

In the early days a claim was twelve feet by twelve for each man, and this space, accordingly, the digger on his arrival on the gold-field proceeded to peg out. Of course, there were other ways by which a man might become possessed of a claim; he

CRADLING AND PANNING.

might buy one already in working order, or he might take one abandoned by someone else, but the most usual way was to peg out a new claim for himself. Then he and his mate—as a rule the early diggers worked in pairs—if they were not "shepherds," a slang term for men who waited to discover the lay of the gutter—began sinking their shaft. If they came on the wash-dirt within a few feet of the surface, well and good; this simplified matters exceedingly. The wash-dirt was taken out and put in a tub, water was poured on it, and the stiff clay puddled with a spade until it was thoroughly well mixed with the water, when all the more liquid portions were poured away. More water was poured on, and the process repeated, not once, but again and again, till at the bottom of the tub remained only the heavier sand and gravel containing the gold, which was, in fact, the heaviest of all. The residue was then put into a dish remarkably like the domestic milk-pan, water was poured on it, and a few twists and turns sufficed to separate the gold from the dirt, and to show the anxious digger whether he had in his pan a small fortune, or not even "the colour," that is, not the minutest particles, of gold. This last operation, called panning off or out, required some niceness and dexterity in turning the wrist, as an awkward twist might succeed in upsetting the pan. The first day or so on a "rush," tubs and pans, or even pans alone, would be the only means used for washing the gold, as it was utterly impossible that a digger should burden himself with much impedimenta on his way to the diggings, but as soon as the "field" became an established fact "cradles" made their appearance on the scene, and rows of them might be seen lining the banks of the creek. The cradle was used midway between the tub and the pan, and was a wooden box shaped like a cradle set on rockers, and having an upright handle fixed at one end with which it was rocked, while inside were shelves and obstructions to catch the gold, the water and mud making their way out through an opening at the bottom. It will be seen that a cradle was by no means a perfect machine, as the shelves, unless very carefully looked after and frequently cleaned, were apt to become covered with a smooth coating of sand and mud, and much of the gold was then carried away with the mud and water. It has now been almost entirely given up, and for the thousands that once were rocked along the banks of the creeks on every gold-field, hardly one is to be seen. Sluices, or "long toms," as they are called, or else the puddling machine, have entirely taken their place. The long tom, which bears a family resemblance to a cradle, is a long narrow box, with an iron bottom, and a grating, or "hopper," as it is called, at one end. The stuff is put in the long tom and washed down it by a strong stream of water, the force of which separates the gold from the dirt, while any lighter particles that are carried off with the escaping mud and water are caught by a "ripple," that is, a small wooden bar fixed across the end of the box, and should any escape that, it is caught on the "blanket," usually a piece of green baize fixed on an inclined plane outside the long tom. The long tom cannot, however, invariably be used in alluvial mining, for in some soils the water, instead of separating the gold and dirt, cakes it all together in one hard ball, which succeeding washing only serves to make more compact, and then it becomes necessary to substitute the puddling machine for the long tom.

The puddling machine is a circular contrivance, the bottom and sides consisting either of iron or of hard wood, while fixed in the centre of the circle is a horizontal beam, to which are attached two harrows. This beam is moved usually by horse-power, but not infrequently, in these later days, by steam, and dragging round with it the harrows, it thoroughly mixes the clay and water. The water is brought in at one side, and the mud, or "sludge," as it is called, is carried off by a gutter or pipe at the other. The gold remaining at the bottom of the machine is finally cleared by panning off.

In the present day, when gold getting has been brought to the highest state of perfection, it is a matter of course that not a particle of the precious metal is allowed to be wasted, but in the old days it was not so, and both through ignorance and from carelessness much was cast away that is now counted valuable. Many men, both Chinese and Europeans, make comfortable livings picking over abandoned claims, or washing once more the sludge from old puddling machines and the refuse from quartz batteries, usually called "tailings." These men are always known as "fossickers," and are said to be "fossicking."

As we have said, when the ancient river-bed was within a few feet of the surface, gold-digging was neither toilsome nor expensive, but when sinking to 30, 60, 200, or 300 feet became necessary, matters assumed a different aspect. The dirt had to be got out of the drives somehow, and various devices were used for the purpose. The commonest was the ordinary windlass and bucket, or if the shaft were a large one there might be two buckets, one at each end of the rope, one being drawn up as the other was let down. The "whip," too, was a good deal used in the early digging days, and was made by fixing a stake about twenty feet long firmly in the ground, so that it started at an angle of about forty-five degrees, the end projecting over the mouth of the shaft. In this end was fixed a grooved wheel, round which ran a rope with a bucket attached to it, this bucket being raised and lowered by a horse travelling backwards and forwards. Hand whips were also used, but it is obvious that whips are at the best both clumsy and awkward contrivances.

Far more useful, and, at the same time, more complicated, is the "whim," also worked by a horse. This is a structure of strong timber, keeping in position a horizontally-working drum, round which the ropes attached to the bucket are wound. Underneath the drum is a long beam with shafts, to which the horse is harnessed. In these days of big companies, of quartz reefs and deep-sinking, huge poppet-heads are erected over the mouth of the shaft, and the heavy cages are raised and lowered by steam, much in the same manner as in the coal mines in England. In some few mines ladders are used for the purposes of ascent and descent, a practice brought into vogue by the Cornish miners, but never in very high favour with Australians.

In the early gold-field days, as has before been said, only alluvial mining was pursued, and probably the richest alluvial claims in any part of Australia, or, for that matter, in any part of the world, were to be found on Ballarat. Along the Buninyong Road, especially, were some of such extraordinary richness that they were known as the "Jewellers' Shops." The history of one of these, called the Blacksmith's Claim, because its first owner belonged to that craft, reads like a page of romance. The blacksmith, with a party of eight, all novices, sank the shaft in so irregular and unworkman-like a manner that it was absolutely at the risk of his life that a man made the descent to the bottom. Without opening out a regular drive, they washed all the stuff within reach, and, after realising £12,800, offered it for sale; but so wet and rotten was the ground, so badly sunk the shaft, that at first no purchaser could be found. At last a party of ten plucked up courage, and bought all right and title to the claim and tools for £77. They entered into possession at noon one Saturday, and long before the sun set had in their possession £2,000 worth of gold. By working day and night in spells till the following Monday, they raised this to £10,000. Then, after the usual reckless manner of lucky diggers, they let this mine of wealth, and went on the spree for a week. Their tenants made good use of the time at their disposal; they opened up two drives, and, before the week was out, were the happy possessors of £14,400—all taken out of the claim. The other party then returned, and after a week's work, during which they realised £9,000, they sold out to a storekeeper for £100, who put in a gang to work in shares, and these, labouring in desultory fashion for a fortnight, took out £5,000. At the end of that time one of the party, an old hand from Van Diemen's Land, undermined the props, and next morning, on returning to work, the men found the whole of the workings had fallen in. The rest of the party appear to have taken this misfortune very calmly, and to have completely abandoned the claim, for no mention is made of

QUARTZ CRUSHING.

their further proceedings; but it is related how the author of the mischief coolly marked out a claim twenty-four feet square on top of the ruin, and, working with a hired party, sunk a shaft straight as a die for the gutter. The first tubful of wash-dirt they raised turned out 40 lbs.' weight of gold, and the next two averaged 10 lbs. each; and, as Ballarat gold was, and is, superior to any other at all times, fetching at least £4 an ounce, those three bucketfuls of earth were worth £2,880 to their fortunate possessor. Altogether, out of that small area, hardly larger than a good-sized room, was taken in a few weeks gold worth nearly £60,000—"an amount," says Kelly, "unequalled in the annals of gold-digging, and which may never again be paralleled." There were other claims among the "shops"—all, it was said, equally rich; but lucky diggers seldom kept account of their

## "SHEPHERDING."

gains, and even if they had, it would be monotonous to recount them one by one. This much is certain, that after these claims were considered worked out, a party got a lease of the five acres on which they stood, and realised a large fortune by washing up what the first diggers had left behind them. Even at this time fossickers, both European and Chinamen, may be seen picking over the old "Jewellers' Shops," and in spite of byelaws, the sweepings of the Buninyong Road are regularly washed for gold.

As the alluvial gold was found in the ancient river-beds, it was the aim and object of every man to discover,

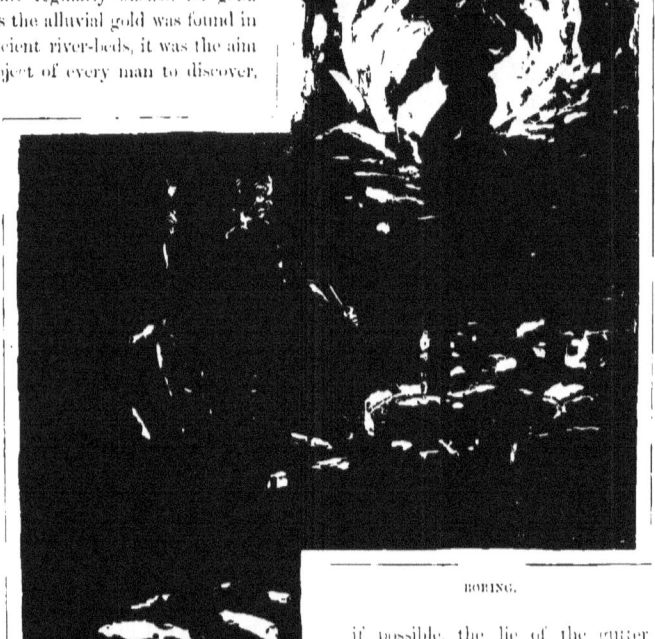

BORING.

if possible, the lie of the gutter before sinking a shaft, as it was little use sinking if there were no probability of striking the wash-dirt. This then gave rise to the curious practice called "shepherding." It was impossible to fix by law how much work a man should do in order not to forfeit his claim; therefore the shepherd would take out a few spadefuls, and then contentedly sit and watch to see if his neighbour succeeded in finding the gutter.

Of course, as soon as the latter had struck wash-dirt, the gentle shepherd at once began sinking, while should the first man find no bottom, the shepherd had been spared a great deal of unnecessary labour. It not unfrequently happened, however, that the shepherd lost by his waiting, for, having reached the gutter, he would find that his neighbour had driven underground and taken away the valuable wash-dirt—a thing easily enough done, for permission to go down a shaft was seldom accorded in the early days, and a refusal would have excited no surprise. Of course, gold-fields' law in such a case would punish the dishonest digger, if it could catch him, but he had in all probability cleared out by that time. In later days shepherding was done away with by the law known as the frontage system, which enacted that when a gutter was discovered the miner should take up a frontage of undetermined width on the course of the lead, so that if a shaft were sunk and the gutter not found, his labour was not lost, for he still had a right to work to the right or to the left, as the course of the gutter might lie.

It is in alluvial mining only that nuggets are found, although pieces so rich in gold that they are called by this term are frequently broken off the parent rock. The "Welcome Nugget" was discovered by a party of twenty-four at Bakery Hill, Ballarat, at a depth of 180 feet, on the 15th June, 1858, and weighed over 180 lbs., or in avoirdupois weight, 1 cwt. 1 qr. 12 lbs., of which about 10 lbs. consisted of quartz and clay. It was sold by its fortunate owners for £10,500, which proved a little above its value, for, on being resold in Melbourne, it only brought £9,325, at £4 4s. 11d. an ounce. The "Blanche Barkly" was found by a party of four, quite by itself, at Kingower, Victoria, at a depth of thirteen feet, and within five or six feet of holes that had been dug three years before. It was twenty-eight inches in length, and ten inches in its widest part, weighed 145 lbs. 3 oz. 13 dwt., and was worth £6,905 12s. 9d. Its peculiar brightness and beauty (only 2 lbs. out of the 145 being quartz) made it exceedingly valuable, for it was taken to England, and its fortunate owners were at one time drawing £30 a week by showing it at the Crystal Palace.

Four seems to have been a fortunate number. That was the number of the party of men who found at Canadian Gully, Ballarat, either in 1852 or 1853, the nugget which takes the third place on the list. It weighed 134 lbs. 11 oz., and was worth £5,532 7s. 4d., but, unlike the "Blanche Barkly," was not attractive-looking, both gold and quartz being dark-coloured, and we presume the gold was not so pure, or else the precious metal was cheaper at Ballarat in these days, for its value is calculated at £3 17s. 9d. per ounce.

An aboriginal boy found a prize he little expected, and perhaps hardly valued, when, in July, 1851, among a heap of quartz on the surface of the ground, about fifty miles from Bathurst, New South Wales, he unearthed a nugget weighing 106 lbs. troy weight. It was in three separate pieces, but has always been considered as one nugget. It could, however, hardly have been so beautiful as later specimens, for it contained a large proportion of quartz.

But the nugget before which all others pale was the "Welcome Stranger," found at Dunolly, Victoria, by two men on the 5th February, 1869. It was close to the surface, being barely covered with earth, and was within two feet of the bed rock. Its weight was never correctly ascertained, as before bringing it to the bank its finders appear to have endeavoured to melt it down, in order to get rid of the quartz with which it was partially mixed. The mixture, however, was very slight, and it looked at the first glance like one solid mass of gold. When first it was weighed it was found to turn the scale at 2,280 oz., of which 2,248 oz. were pure gold, its value in coin of the realm being £9,534.

These, then, are some of the larger nuggets which have been discovered in Australia, but since anything in the shape of a lump of gold, whether it weigh 2,000 oz. or only a few dwts., is known as a nugget, the number found is by this time innumerable. Mr. Brough Smith in his book upon gold-mining has given a list of no less than 150 that have attained some celebrity. Of these twenty-eight were found in other parts of the world between the years 1502 and 1869, while the Australian record only covers a period of eighteen years.

SECTION OF "STOPE."

It may be interesting to note that the largest non-Australian nugget he gives us an account of was found at Miask, Ural Mountains, Russia, and weighed 96 lbs. 16 oz. 2 dwt. It has never been melted down, but is preserved in the Museum of Mining Engineers, St. Petersburg. Its exact value cannot, of course, be ascertained, but is supposed to be £4,508 19s. 3d.

Quartz mining entirely differs from alluvial, is more expensive, and requires greater labour, more complicated machinery, and consequently greater returns to make it pay. The first attempts at quartz crushing were rude in the extreme, and a humble machine, called a "dolly," was used. A large tree-stump was chosen, and the centre slightly hollowed; in the hollow was placed the quartz, and a heavy stake shod with iron was fastened to a sapling and used for crushing the quartz, the crushed quartz being afterwards cleared by panning off. This, as may be seen, was an exceedingly laborious and unsatisfactory way of getting out the gold, and before long quartz-crushing batteries were introduced. A battery consists of a number of cast-iron stampers worked by steam power, and crushing the quartz to a powder in a long iron box known as the stamper-box. Each stamper now weighs 8 cwt., though in the early days they were content with much lighter ones, and many batteries were to be found with stampers weighing not more than 3 cwt. Any number of stampers can be used, from five upwards; as a general rule, however, twenty are found amply sufficient to crush the quartz raised from one claim. At the Black Hill Company, Ballarat, they have the largest battery in the colonies, which consists of forty stampers. The quartz is placed in hoppers, and carried down to the stamper-box by shoots, and there crushed to a powder so fine that it is washed by the constantly-running water through a grating or sieve containing 190

"TIMBERING."

holes to the square inch. Every five heads will crush five tons in eight hours, and to do that properly they require eight gallons of water per minute. Every eight hours a thimbleful of quicksilver is put in the stamper-box, and this amalgamates all the gold, save a little so fine that it escapes through the grating along with the crushed quartz. It is not, however, wasted, for the quartz is washed over copper plates carefully prepared with quicksilver, which catches all the gold that has escaped from the battery. The gold is afterwards cleared from the quicksilver by retorting. The battery works day and night, from one o'clock on Monday morning till twelve on Saturday night,

## A RICH YIELD.

and the noise, as might be expected, is deafening. So accustomed to it, however, do the dwellers around become that the unexpected stoppage of a battery will waken a whole township from its peaceful slumbers.

Gold can, of course, be extracted from the quartz by the very rudest contrivances if only time is of no consequence and the stone is rich enough. Two small boys at Bendigo once, so the story goes, came to the owner of a battery with about 20 lbs.' weight of quartz on their backs and asked leave to use the pestle and mortar he kept for testing samples. Leave being readily given, they set to work, and, by dint of patient labour crushing the whole of their load, they were rewarded, to the intense

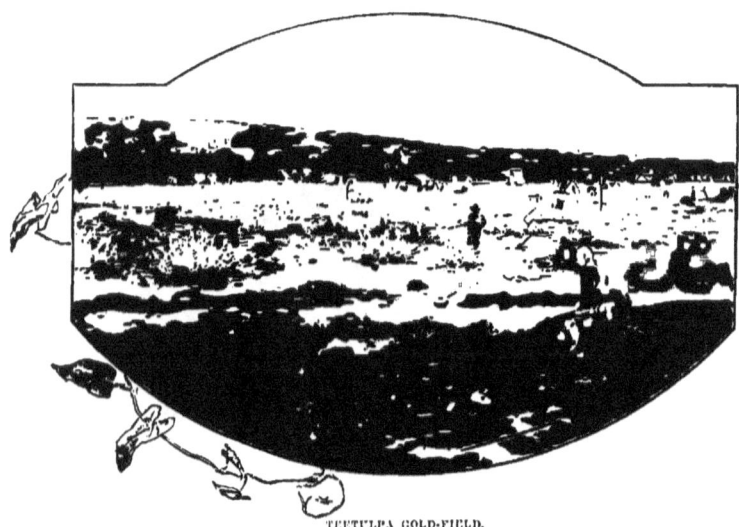

TEETULPA GOLD-FIELD.

astonishment of the bystanders, by very nearly 13 lbs.' weight of pure gold. The locality where they found this treasure-trove these fortunate urchins, with a shrewdness not uncommon to young Australia, kept a profound secret, and ten days after came again with a barrow-load, which must certainly have yielded them over £1,200. The eldest of these young "millionaires of the future" could not, says the narrator of the story, have been over twelve years of age.

Gold-mining at the present time is a very different thing from what it was thirty years ago. All the large mines are owned by great companies, and mining is recognised as an important industry. The great "rushes" of former years are either utterly deserted, lonelier, perhaps, than ever before, for the slight tokens that man has left of his presence, or else they have become thriving towns, differing after all but little from

English towns of the same size. Mounds of earth, indeed, red, white, and yellow, are seen everywhere, and towering above them are the poppet-heads of the claims in work, while the clay-daubed miner with his tin billy is as common a sight as a collier in Northumberland.

Globe trotters and strangers from all parts of the world come to the great gold-centres and desire above all things to inspect the mines, but, after all, there is not much to see. In some mines the visitor, in order to save his garments, puts upon him others that are kept for the purpose. In many, however, this kind attention is forgotten, and not long ago a visitor, described as an "awful swell," had to roll down a "jump-up" in the only ordinary suit of clothes he has with him. History records that he finished his visit in his dress suit. The stranger is placed on the cage, an old miner is put in charge of him, and he descends 100, 200, 1,000, or even 2,000 feet, as a rule in pitch darkness, for the candles, after guttering a great deal, go out in consequence of the draught. Arrived at the bottom, he has his candle relighted, and finds himself standing at the bottom of a shaft, with drives branching out to all points of the compass, along one of which he is taken. It is always dirty, generally muddy, and he is lucky indeed if it be not in some places ankle-deep in water. He goes down "jump-ups" and up "winzes." He sees men at work in all kinds of uncomfortable attitudes, their candles stuck by mud against the walls. He squeezes close up against the wall as a truck laden with quartz or "mullock" comes rushing past; and he is shown, of course, some of the richest stone in the colony, which, to his inexperienced eye, presents not a trace of the precious metal, while he is constantly stopping, to the no small amusement of his guide, to inspect more closely the mica or mundik which glitters in the candle-light. At the end of the drive he will come upon the "stope," which is a boring following the descent of one of the veins of quartz, with small shafts at intervals, through which the quartz is lowered to the level below. The air, even though the mine be well ventilated, is hot and close, and the miners look pale and ghastly in the artificial light. Still, he is told that the miner's is not an unhealthy life, and is well paid, for the mere pitmen earn £3 a week for eight hours' labour per day, while men in responsible positions, engine-drivers and others, get more. The stranger breathes more freely when he regains the light of day, politely tells everyone he has been charmed, delighted, and deeply interested, and goes away feeling firmly convinced that the interior of a gold-mine is not a place a man need see more than once.

There is plenty of gold in Australia yet, though the old days when every man sought for himself have almost passed away. Diamond drills have of late years come into use, and fresh leads are by their agency being discovered every day. We have said nothing of the gold-fields in Queensland, Tasmania, and New Zealand, though they are by no means to be despised. Still, gold-mining goes through much the same phases all the world over, and mining in Victoria remarkably resembles mining in any other colony.

Some of the gold-fields of New South Wales deserve special mention, because at Mount Brown, north of the Darling, at which place there was a great rush in 1880, quite a new process—new, at least, to Australasians—of separating the gold from the surrounding alluvial, prevailed—one, however, not much in vogue, nor ever likely to be wherever water is fairly plentiful. At Libbaborough—one of the fields at Mount Brown—however, and in all that district, water is conspicuous, as a rule, by its absence. Men had little enough for their own use—none whatever for washing gold. It is necessary, then, under these circumstances, to break up the wash-dirt as fine as possible, and on some day when the wind is high to pour it rapidly backwards and forwards from one tin dish to another. By degrees, the greater part of the dirt blows away in the form of dust—red dust it was at Mount Brown—and is thus got rid of. The heavier portions which contain the gold are then again crushed, and the same process gone through again and again, till at last so little remains that the digger is able to clear his pan by blowing the dust away, and what gold there is can be clearly seen in the bottom of the dish.

At Mount Brown, on a windy day—and such days are the rule, not the exception, since the country for miles towards the north, including Sturt's Desert, is one vast arid plain, over which the scorching hot winds blow for weeks together in the summer season—with five or six hundred men at work "dry-blowing" dirt, the whole plain for miles was enveloped in one vast cloud of dust. Worse still, even after the gold was secured few men could indulge in the expensive luxury of a bath, but remained, perforce, with all the signs of their toil thick upon them. Mount Brown in 1880 was hardly a desirable, or even an ordinarily-pleasant place in which to reside. In the latitude of, and barely forty miles distant from, Sturt's Depôt Glen, the heat in summer is always very great, and with water at three shillings a bucket, as it was in those days, it must have been something appalling. Flour, too, rose till it reached two shillings and sixpence a pound; and when an ordinary loaf cost ten shillings, it will easily be seen that only extraordinarily rich yields could make the field pay. Soon, however, the rush there melted away, and the place assumed the ordinary aspect of a small and unimportant mining township.

In Kimberley alone, in the north of Western Australia, the old order still prevails. There, where the gold-fields are nearly three hundred miles in the interior, men crowded from all parts of Australasia, bringing with them, since it is a bare and desolate land, all the necessaries of life, even as they did thirty years ago in Victoria. On the road, or, rather, rough track, were seen all manner of conveyances, from the rich man's bullock-dray to the modest hand-cart or still more humble wheelbarrow. But, in spite of the promise of great things, there are signs that the glory of Kimberley has already departed. The drawbacks are numerous, and the field must be rich, indeed, that could stand against them, for the water is scarce, the blacks are troublesome, the climate is tropical and unsuited to the white man, and, above all, the gold first found in the gullies and flats is already worked out, and there are not appliances for further search, for Kimberley itself is beyond the very outskirts of civilisation, and it soon promises to become that abomination of desolation, a deserted gold-field. Teetulpa, in South Australia, it may be added, is the newest of the gold-fields, having only come into being in November, 1886.

A NEW GUINEA TEMPLE.

## NEW GUINEA: PORT MORESBY TO KEREPUNA.

An Island with a Future—Missionaries and Traders—Port Moresby—Elevara—Native Occupations—The Sources of Fever—Funeral Customs—An Unexecuted Sentence—The Ascent of Mount Pullen—The Laloki and Goldie Rivers—The Guilelessness of the Natives—Their Treatment of Women—Court-hip and Marriage—Betel Chewing—Native Hunting—Kapa-Kapa—Hula—The Bau-bau—A Clever Trickster—Kerepuna—Nature and Civilisation—Work Days and Rest Days—Festivities—Spirit-seers—Canoe Makers—Fond Farewells—Rejoicings.

IN New Guinea, a mighty island, generously productive, basking under the rays of a fiery sun, yet fanned by the balmy monsoon, with all the conditions of health and happiness within its range, waits with its many attendant isles, as the best portions of Upper Queensland also wait, upon the coming of civilisation. A mighty island it truly is, and it is surrounded by others ever varying, and bewildering in their loveliness, while beyond these are yet others, protected in most parts by gigantic barrier walls of coral-reef from the boisterous ocean, which perpetually lashes and roars outside—barrier walls with splendid gateways every few miles opening from the turbulent ocean—for the Papuan Gulf and Coral Sea are ever more or less tumultuous—to the mirror-like lagoons inside, where ships of all sizes may venture, and ride out the wildest storm in safe and quiet anchorage. Then there are wide bays and peaceful harbours, with smooth, shell-strewn shores of golden sand, fringed with fruit-weighted banana, palm, and mammy-apple trees; and beyond these, indented mountains, reaching far above the rain-clouds which they gather about their steep sides.

Without wishing to understate any of the real difficulties which must attend either a visit to, or a stay in this country, it must be said that, in comparison with what it has been, New Guinea is safe and open to the foot of the European, and that this comparative safety is due to the heroic and unselfish labours of the missionaries and the no less heroic, if more interested, exertions of the dauntless traders who have from time to time settled upon these coasts.

The first point of attraction to which all travellers tend is the English headquarters—Port Moresby. Yet this is by no means the most interesting portion of British New Guinea, although interesting enough to the new arrival, who sees for the first time the naked, copper-tinted savages paddling about the ships in their catamarans and canoes. A feeling as of cold water running down the back is apt to take possession of one when the first half-dozen stalwart, mop-headed young natives leap aboard, for they are treacherous and remorseless in avenging wrongs, real or fancied; but this sensation quickly passes away as we look upon their mild, intelligent faces and shapely limbs while they come up and stand gazing about them wonderingly.

PORT MORESBY.

A long line of native houses, built upon piles, stretches in front of us, partly in the water, and with the entrances facing the shore; at the other side, and above them, wave the feathery fronds of palm-trees, and dotting the hillside are the few wooden houses belonging to the white residents. At present these houses can be easily counted. Here is the Bungalow, or Government Residence, a small cottage with a veranda in front, raised on piles, with a fence round it; and here is the hut built for the surveying party who are planning out the site of the new city. Grenville it is to be called, although why so, with such a lovely native name as "Elevara" to hand, is more than I can imagine. The Messrs. Hunter, twin brothers, who might well take the part of the two Dromios, from the exact resemblance each bears to the other, act as interpreters and mediators between the Government and the natives. The white portion of Port Moresby consists of their house, of Mr. Goldie's store and residence, and of the mission and native school-houses, these last occupying the hill above the little sea village of Elevara. To these, perhaps, should be added the new gaol, which is being built on the new city site on the other side of the bay.

The village of Elevara lies directly under the hill upon which the mission-house is built, and is separated by an open space of about 400 yards from the other village of Hannabada. The natives of these villages appear to live in amity with one another, although they belong to distinct races, called the Motu and Koitapu tribes.

The principal occupation of the natives at Moresby is the making of earthenware vessels and pots for cooking purposes. This manufacture of "hodu," as it is called, is chiefly in the hands of the women. The men fish, and go out to friendly tribes and villages along the coast as well as inland with the crockeryware, exchanging it for commodities which they themselves require. The women are also the gardeners; and although they merely scratch the surface of the ground, and insert the seeds or shoots which they wish to grow, the generous nature of the soil is such that the result is all that could be desired. Outside the villages, and behind the mangrove and croton bush, gardens and orchards are found in a state of picturesque confusion, the ground strewn with a litter of dead banana and palm-leaves, whilst out of this chaos of decayed vegetable matter rise flourishing groves of palm and other fruit trees. Here the women—that is, the old women and matrons—labour during the day, trimming, planting, and gathering, while the maids and boys bask in the sun, or work about the houses, preparing the cocoanuts, yams, and taros for the home-coming of their fathers and mothers. Each garden is protected by fences of twig palisades from five to seven feet in height.

The neglected and decaying *débris* of orchards, mingling with the dead vegetable accumulation of ages, is partly the cause of the malaria and fever that sap the energy of natives and Europeans alike. The breeze which night and morning comes without fail from the valleys and inland mountains, bears upon what ought to be health-giving wings these blood-poisoning exhalations. Another, and, I think, the most dangerous, source of the fever is to be found in the filthy habits of the natives, and their very abominable burial customs and superstitions. They are an intelligent, hardworking race, open to conviction and quick at imitation, but as yet they have not been taught the necessity of altering these old customs, and so one or two deaths in a village are quite sufficient as a start to spread a general plague. The natives observe the rites of burial and pay respect to the dead to such purpose that one dead ancestor is almost enough to slay not only all his or her descendants, but all their friends, and, indeed, all their enemies to boot, for miles around. While the remains last, the departed themselves cannot possibly be overlooked or forgotten. Every breath of that fatal land-breeze wafts them potently, not only before the remembrance, but right down the throat. To enter a village even months after the death of a villager is an experience which can be neither imagined nor described; and to meet a full-fledged mourner is about the most awful trial the olfactory senses can possibly experience. Amongst the New Guinea natives in their present stage of social development one might deem it a blessing to be deprived altogether of the sense of smell.

There had lately been an increase of the death-rate at Kerepuna and Moresby, and in consequence, Elevara and Hanuabada were filled with sable-coated mourners, and the air was laden with fever germs. To call New Guinea essentially unhealthy, when the causes are so vividly apparent, is to write an unwarranted libel on the country. It is, in fact, too mountainous to be in itself insanitary; while the winds by day sweep through the gullies, laden with ozone from the surrounding ocean, and by night return to the sea from the mountain-crested clouds. The conditions seem to be all on the side of health, and ready to the hand of man whenever he likes to work out the problem of sanitation in the tropics.

The main, or, rather, only, street in the native village at Moresby runs along the sands of the bay for about half-a-mile, the native huts being built upon the seaside in such fashion that, when the tide is high, they are nearly surrounded with water. These huts, well thatched with palm-leaves, and firmly secured by ropework fastenings, have only one outlet at either end. In front of each doorway broad platforms, made up raft-fashion, and joined together with cross pieces of timber, are raised on the piles, the whole being, on the land side, five or six feet from the ground. As the shore slopes upward between eight and ten feet above the level of the flood, each house is separate from the others, yet all are so closely adjoining that it is quite easy for one neighbour to pass from his platform to the one next door, and so on along the whole village. Each house has its own rustic ladder placed against the platform and doorway. They are all substantially built, the piles being very closely placed together, some straight, some twisted and forked, all being rough, undressed limbs and branches of gum and cotton trees. The effect of the whole is decidedly picturesque. The small canoes float upon the water, or lie grounded between the piles when the tide is out. These canoes are made from trunks of trees, and are ten to twenty feet in length, with the inside chipped and hollowed out; and there is no attempt at ornamentation, except the outriggers, which balance them when sailing. They never upset, no matter how crowded, and go along remarkably fast, whether propelled by the paddles or under sail.

Here and there, as you walk along the village, you will come upon an old man chipping away with his stone or iron adze at a rough trunk, making a new canoe. It is a labour of time, but these sons of Nature are gifted with great patience. I have heard it said that it takes them twelve months to sharpen their green-stone axes, and yet they will part with one for eight or ten sticks of trading tobacco.

In front of the houses sit the old women making their earthenware jars and pots, with wood fires near at hand to dry and harden them when wrought into shape. Very deft they are at this work; and they generally cut rough ornamental borders round the edges. The pots are black, and when completed look like ironware. It is a pretty sight to see the women at work, with the thin vapour from the burning wood curling up amongst the tree shadows and mingling with the purple fumes of the setting sun.

Inside the houses it is always twilight, for there are no windows, and as you look in at the doors—a thing the inmates do not like strangers to do—you see, as soon as the eye gets accustomed to the dim obscurity, that everything is clean and neat. Mothers and children are sitting or reclining on the bamboo floors, with spears and shields, &c., ranged along the walls, making delightful Rembrandtesque pictures.

On the other side of the street are planted thick groves of palm and banana trees. In these groves—or, rather, by the side of the street, sometimes in the very centre of it—you may stumble upon little bamboo-protected mounds with planks laid across, and palm-leaves covering them. These mounds are graves, placed opposite the

NATIVE DWELLINGS AT PORT MORESBY.

houses which the deceased occupied when alive. It is from these mounds that the odours issue that so constantly remind the stranger of the family bereavement. Long-snouted pigs, assisted in their investigations by hundreds of mongrel-looking native dogs, snort and burrow about the graves until they are driven from their pastime by the ash-blackened widow, husband, son, or daughter, left behind to mourn.

When a death occurs in the family the friends assemble and lament. Then they dig a hole, either under the house or in front of it. If near the water, the grave is dug about two feet deep. The bottom of it is spread over with palm-leaves, upon which the body is placed; more leaves are added, and over these twigs and planks are laid. This is the custom of the Motu tribes, and along the coast. Inland the survivors hang dead bodies upon trees, and observe practices which are too horrible to be related.

From Mr. Andrew Goldie's journal, of which he kindly permitted me to make use, I take the following extract regarding the funeral ceremonies:—" About three hundred

## FUNERAL CEREMONIES.

natives were assembled. Two men and two women carried the body, which was that of a woman, out of the house to the grave, which was a few feet in front of the house, and only eighteen inches deep. There was a mat laid in the grave, upon which the corpse was placed. The husband was then dragged out of the house in great grief, and, throwing himself down upon his dead wife, wept piteously. Her daughters and near relatives stood over the grave crying with great violence, and tearing their hair and faces with their hands. The other natives stood quietly looking on—that is, with the exception of about twenty young men, who were ranged in a straight line, with drums in their hands, beating time to a very solemn chant which they sang. After about an hour of this ceremony, the relatives were removed, and the body covered over with matting, two heavy boards of old canoes being laid on the top, so that the pigs might not get at it, and so the dead was for the time left alone. The near relatives went into mourning by blackening their bodies all over with ashes. As soon as anyone dies in the village a large drum is beaten at regular intervals, something like our village bells at home." Mr. Goldie, I may add, is a safe authority on New Guinea, having lived long and travelled extensively in the country in which he has vowed to spend the remainder of his life.

It may here be mentioned that at Yule Island, to the west of Port Moresby, I met a boy going into the woods at sundown. His body was smeared over with ashes, and in his hand was a firebrand, which he was blowing to keep alight

ELEVARA.

ANOTHER NATIVE HOUSE

as he walked along. He looked miserable in the extreme, and upon my stopping him to ask what was the matter (Father Verjuice, a French priest, acting as interpreter), he informed me that his father had lately died, and, being the eldest son, he was compelled to go and sleep in the woods alone every night for six months. The firebrand was to light a fire with when he got there, to keep away the wild beasts and the ghosts. He confessed that he was horribly frightened at the idea of ghosts, and he looked it.

At Kerepuna I passed a tomb where three widows of a chief were imprisoned. An enclosure had been built over the grave about the size of a large rabbit-hutch. It could not have been more than three feet high and four or five feet square, and this space was completely covered, except that there were spaces between the planks for ventilation. As we passed the bereaved ones, each stretched out a skinny, blackened arm and hand through the cracks for "koko" (tobacco). The husband had been dead nine months, and during those dreary months these poor widows had not been permitted to go outside their prison. The relatives fed them by pushing yams through the crevices, and thus they were forced to stay, willing or otherwise, over the decomposing remains of their late lord and master for a period of three years.

At Aroma a ghastly widower made great friends with me, and wanted to embrace me, which honour I energetically declined. Feeling lonely, no doubt, and longing for company, he was good enough to choose me as his friend, but there was too strong a savour of the cemetery about him to excite my complete sympathy.

For utility in the way of harbourage, Port Moresby is nearly all that could be desired. The Government authorities have made a wise choice in the site of the new township, to windward of the native villages, and protected by the hill behind it, with deep water close up to the beach, and a considerable area of flat ground. I went with the Government surveyor over his new site—through native gardens, with the road cut in a straight line, and fruit trees cast down where they interfered with the line of direction. The natives made a great outcry over the destruction of their gardens, and demanded a life or two as compensation. However, they were fain at last to be content with payment in the current coin of the land—"koko." The surveyor, who with others of his party had been condemned to death, worked on, perfectly indifferent to threats and dark glances. It was hard work to clear these roads, the ants constantly tormenting the men, and the under-bush being very dense. The plan has, however, been carried out successfully; and as we passed through the clear-cut roadways, fenced with the dead timber, amid avenues of crotons, mangroves, castor-oil trees, sago, betel palm, and stunted gum-trees, hearing the surveyor explain his designs, we felt that although the gaol was early on the ground, more agreeable consequences of civilisation would quickly follow.

From Mount Pullen, the highest point in Moresby, a splendid view of the port and harbour, as well as of some of the country inland, can be obtained. Like all the mountains, Mount Pullen is exceedingly steep, and to climb to its top is to achieve quite a feat. Getting a little Motu boy as my guide, I started off one morning a little after sunrise. When we were past the garden fences, my guide struck out at a rate which I could hardly keep up, and with an ease and utter unconsciousness

SUNRISE AT YORK ISLAND, TORRES STRAITS (p. 200).

of fatigue that astonished me. He never paused, except when I was breathlessly forced to ask him, and then he looked with wonder at the tired white fellow.

Our route lay up a pathway made by the natives, the highway, so far, to the interior. At the point where the track left the path, just as I had emerged from a thick copse, I came suddenly upon a party of mountain natives, armed with shields, spears, bows and arrows, decorated with feathers, and painted with designs in white, red, and black, looking altogether very formidable. Having heard much of native treachery, and not knowing whether these were enemies or friends, I felt somewhat uneasy, and looked at my revolver. However, I became reassured on seeing my young friend walk on towards them calmly and address some words to them, upon which they drew to one side and permitted me to pass. My boy told me that these men had come down with birds and plants, orchids and crotons, &c., to trade with the white people in the village on the coast, and that they always travelled ready for fighting, as they never knew the moment when they might be attacked.

At length, after many rests, and much panting on my part, we reached the top. Beside me grew a large cotton-tree with tortuous limbs and snaky branches, devoid of leaves, and twisted and gleaming like dried, bleached bones, but with the scarlet blossom festooning the bare limbs here and there, like bits of red rag tied round a dead tree. Behind the cotton-tree lay a dense scrub, with interlacing bush, and tendrils crossing backward and forward, and up and down, like trellis-work. Where the trees were not, tall grass between six and eight feet in height, was growing—silvery, shining grass, which, where the sunshine fell, looked almost like snow. From these bowers, as I tried to force my way through them, myriads of amber-coloured ants fell upon me, getting down my neck, and covering me with vicious bites. Through a parting on the thin side of this lovely natural trellis-work I looked towards the far-away mountains and valleys of the interior. Tier behind tier they rose, some beneath me where I stood, like sugar-loaves or pyramids, with straight, steep sides, mostly grass-covered, although here and there dense forests of trees were spread out; the valleys were so deep that the purple shadows hid their details; between the cones were vistas of plains, with miles of forests yet to be cleared away when the European takes possession and transforms these vast tracts into rice and sugar plantations. Amid the lofty rugged ranges of which I have spoken flow the Laloki and Goldie Rivers, the junction of which was discovered by the gentleman after whom the latter stream is named. He speaks of it as very treacherous, with shifting bottom, and swarming with alligators. The banks in some parts are very precipitous, in others flat and densely wooded, the jungle being so dense that to get through means a very free use of the axe. Supple-jacks and tendrils, ant-infested, mesh about the traveller like a close network, prickles and thorns tearing the skin and clothes at every step; these, with palm-trees in many varieties, and clumps of fern-trees, over twenty feet in height, make up a truly tropical scene of untrammelled nature, with butterflies of every shade and size on the wing, carrying patches of the glowing sunshine into deep recesses of shadow.

The Laloki lies about four hours' hard walking past the village of Mourmin, and about thirteen or fourteen miles from Port Moresby. At the junction of the two rivers the scenery is very pretty and open, the Goldie winding along by the foot of the mountain, with trees drooping over the banks. About here a little gold has been found, and it is believed to lie in great quantities in the heart of these volcanic ridges.

The Laloki is a fine river, fed by numerous streams rising in the Astrolabe ranges. It has very precipitous cliffs and banks, and at some points it is a hard

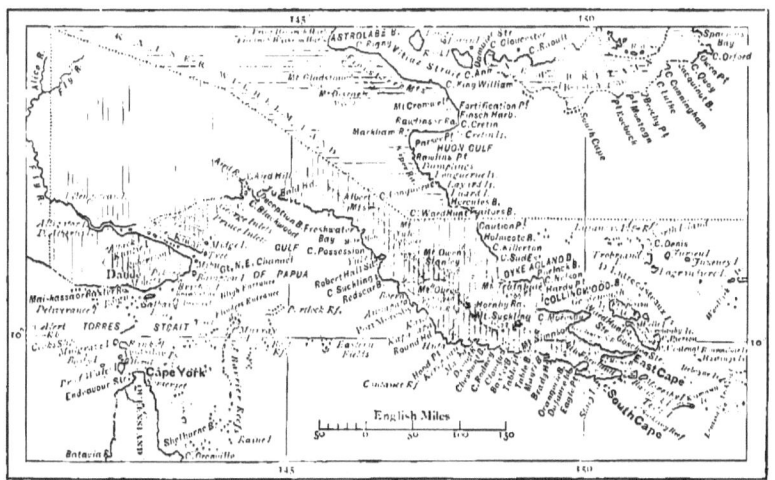

SECTION OF NEW GUINEA.

matter to follow the stream up, rapids occurring here and there both above and below the great falls, which Mr. Goldie and Mr. Chalmers agree in considering indescribably grand. The mountains run at a sharp angle on both sides, and in some places have cliffs, one to two thousand feet high, tower above the mighty trees in the gloomy depth of the gorges below.

For many miles a full body of clear water leaps down deep shelves and over huge rocks, between time-worn precipices. Then there is a clear space, where it surges round a wooded island in the centre of the stream, smooth with the velocity of its deadly race. Next it takes a mighty leap of about a thousand feet clear, only broken in its course by a huge block of rugged boulder in about the middle of its fall, and then into the tree-hidden, boiling cauldron it flings its vast strength with a thunderous din; anon breaking over cliffs and rocks in foamy masses, far below where the eye or the ear can follow, while up in the air, above the cedar tops,

## THE FAR VIEW.

the mist-clouds float, sun-pierced, with the rainbow hovering perpetually within the gauze-like fumes.

From where I stand, on Mount Pullen, I turn to the wide expanse of ocean which lies in its amethyst repose. I can look through the fathoms of water that cover the snowy beds of coral, and see the pale green and the intense violet of the deep passages between. Away near the horizon-line are the gleaming fangs that ever gnaw at the hidden reefs. Nearer, jut out the dark brown and grey rock promontories, which spread round like a crescent moon, forming the almost land-locked bay. Two or three small craft are rocking in the deeper waters. Bêche-de-mer and copra boats come into the port for provisions. The *Governor Cairns* is waiting upon his Excellency, the Hon. John Douglas, and the tiny mail steamtug, *The Victory*, upon us, a shoal of canoes with water-tanks on board surrounding the latter, and crowds of natives filling her barrels. The tide is far out, and the shallow waters are swarming with little black dots wading—native

A TREE HOUSE.

boys and girls basking in the sun, or fishing with their nets and many-pointed fishing-spears. There lies Elevara, with the picturesque, Gibraltar-like rock-mound behind it which I saw last evening purple under the setting sun. And there is Hannabada, fringing the sands, the white settlers' huts and cottages overtopping both villages. The shining sides of the hills opposite me are white in the forenoon rays, strongly in contrast with the violet shadows of the distant ranges; and

A HEATHEN TEMPLE.

altogether it is a bewitching scene of rest and beauty, the gardens breaking the monotony with their lovely bewilderment of tangle. Before long all this natural confusion, and these picturesque if fever-infested huts, will be done away with, and that grassy and tree-covered lair, where the kangaroo and wallaby now hide, will be covered with square-built streets and trim wooden erections, while white helmets and duck pants will replace the dusky skins of the natives.

The danger of the fevers of which I have spoken lies along the sea-shores, and in the valley swamps; but on the mountain ridges it is impossible to catch malaria, while the tribes to be met there, like all mountaineers, are free from some of the vices of the lowland natives—more honest, although dishonesty is a vice which I, for my part, never encountered, even on the coast; they are also truthful, and generous in their intercourse with strangers. Hunters who have gone up in search of game have told me that they felt no insecurity when amongst these hill tribes; they were tenderly looked after, and all their goods guarded jealously during their absence, and restored to them intact upon their return. Furthermore, the presence of a white man with firearms is regarded as a boon to be appreciated and taken great care of. Constantly in danger as they are of surprises from hostile tribes, they look upon the visitor as a protection, since he is dreaded by their foes. Apart, therefore, from the unavoidable risks which attend the ignorance of language and customs, a man who trusts the natives implicitly, and sets aside fear of treachery, will find that the further inland he travels the greater is his safety. I would advise all future visitors to this country to boldly strike out for the interior.

Whatever may be said against the burial customs of the natives, enough cannot be told in praise of their treatment of their women, or of the high standard of morality between the sexes. Before marriage woman is treated as a queen; her will is paramount, and often she abuses her privileges, and behaves very harshly to the humble aspirant to her hand. Young men have to stand back and wait till she shows her preference, and after the happy youth is so far favoured, and has then shown, to the satisfaction of the family, that he is rich enough to pay what they demand for the bride, he must go through a month of probation, obeying all the lady's whims and caprices while she is examining his points critically, and studying his character. Doubtless, at times Love sits in the scales and favours him during his period of probation; but the ladies seem as a rule to go into the contract with the sedateness and method of a French courtship, except that the woman has the principal "say" in the matter, and appears to calculate with a coolness and acumen which seem almost incompatible with partiality or passion.

Here is an amusing incident which occurred while I was at Moresby, and which illustrates this very methodical system of courtship. A youth, whom we called the "Larrikin," because he was always in mischief, fell in love with one of the belles of Hannabada; and, selecting him from amongst all her other hibiscus-adorned suitors—for the village dandies decorate their dyed and frizzled "mops" with hibiscus blossoms—she graciously permitted herself to be engaged to him, that is, she took him on approval. According to custom, "Larrikin" became a guest in the house of the maiden, ate with its inmates, went out fishing with her, and made himself generally useful and agreeable to the intended father-in-law. In fact, he became both a slave and a prisoner in the house of his lady love; the father going about with the lovers constantly, never leaving them for an instant alone together, and devoting his whole time to the task of watching over his daughter. For three weeks all went fairly well, Larrikin much subdued and snubbed during that interval. A splendid fellow he was, worthy of the love of any maid, and as a specimen of humanity worth twenty of the girl he was fawning upon, for she was undersized, and as nearly ugly as a New Guinea girl of sixteen could be; and I daresay he was just congratulating himself that his troubles were nearly over, when the maiden suddenly discovered a wart on his little toe, and ignominiously dismissed him from her presence, taking straightway the next best favoured rival on the same terms.

Poor Larrikin, for this slight and only blemish, became an outcast, without the chance of getting a wife in that village, for no other girl would have him after his rejection. Jeered and scoffed at by everyone wherever he appeared, he was forced to take up with us whites for company; and he retaliated by playing pranks all round. He was a good-tempered young Adonis, and was only humorously cynical towards the scornful fair one, pretending that he did not care much about his rejection, and wearing more hibiscus flowers than ever in his hair, out of bravado, I suppose; but I noticed that he smoked a great deal at the bau-bau, and chewed, nearly constantly, the betel-nut.

A LIME CALABASH.

When all has gone well, and in a manner satisfactory to the lady, the final ceremony takes place; that is, the young man brings his pig, and what else has been demanded from him as purchase-money for his wife, and a feast is held, after the ceremony of blessing the two made one has been performed. But the troubles of the poor bridegroom are not nearly over yet. He has got the daughter, but the father has now to be conciliated. He is the master of the husband, who must reverence him and bend before him each time he passes, and obey all his orders, until he receives permission to take home his wife and fall into the ordinary routine of life, but even after that, a quarrel will send his wife home to her parents, and more presents have to be rendered up before he can have her home again, so that the husband who would not be ruined must be affable, and stand always on his good behaviour.

The women all work, and do not consider this a hardship, for industry is one of the virtues they practise, and idleness would be regarded as a vice. After the little period of petty tyranny which has been described, husband and wife settle down to the duties of life, rearing children, accumulating property, and raising pigs. The natives are very fond of their pigs and dogs, and sleep with them, attending to them with quite as much tenderness as they show towards their own offspring.

Young girls tattoo one another by degrees until they are completely covered to the waist with scroll-work; they also, when in a genial mood, frizzle the locks of their young men and brothers. Only the women are tattooed or dressed, the men and boys being perfectly nude, with the exception of a cord round the loins.

To strangers, the habit of betel chewing is very obnoxious. You will meet old and young, male and female, with the lime calabash hung about the neck, and with lips blood-red and teeth jet-black, where not entirely worn down to ugly stumps through this indulgence. Probably, if you are in favour with some native, he will present you with a nut and a bite at his pepper-stick, and then as naturally as an old Scotchman may hand you his snuff-box, he will pass over his little calabash, with spoon attached, this spoon most likely cut from some small human bone, in order that you may help yourself to a lick or two of the lime powder. They will tell you that it is good for the fever. Perhaps it is; but that it is not good for the teeth, a look at the mumbling, toothless old men and women will at once convince you. Yet it is astonishing how quickly the European gets accustomed to betel chewing and bau-bau smoking, many of the traders presenting the same appearance about the lips and teeth as the natives. Fortunately the latter have not yet taken to the fire-water, all the spirits which come into the country being entirely consumed by the white residents.

Some of the calabashes are very beautiful in design, made from cocoa-nut gourds, and the ornament cut through the fibre and then burnt in with a fine-pointed firebrand, the lines being symmetrical and in parts very delicate, as are those upon the musical instruments, war implements, and pipes, or as they call them, "bau-baus."

Leaving Moresby while yet the silvery morning vapours hung over the villages and softened the outlines of the lofty mountains behind, we take our course along the coast-line inside the reefs, for outside the sea is very rough; and although the steering is difficult and dangerous, since we are surrounded on all sides by coral hummocks and sandbanks, yet here the water is pleasant and calm, while the coast is so close at hand that we can see the villages and natives distinctly as we steam slowly along.

Our pilot has climbed to the mast-head, and clings with bare feet to the rope-work as he looks keenly ahead, guiding the man at the wheel with his hand, zigzag, as if we were in a cab winding about a narrow, crowded street; while the sun shines down on the mottled-coloured waves and palm-fringed shores. We first pass Pyramid Point, bold and tawny tinted, with ranges lost in the white lustre of the clouds, and villages peeping from the bottom of deep gullies, half concealed in the large-leafed bowers, and next, Bootless Inlet, threading our way very gingerly, and lost in admiration of the ever-changing beauty of the scene.

As we sail along we can see our channel winding about the hummocks, and seeming to be closed up a few yards ahead. We do not make great progress, as we have often to back out and find another passage. Round us the sea is clothed with delicate shades of green, varied by sapphire threads of deep water. As we look shorewards, we see natives wading about with their nets and many-pronged spears, or marching along the shores with their burdens on their backs; while at some points volumes of blue smoke wreathe up above the tree-tops, and show us where they are burning out the wallabies and kangaroos.

When the natives set out upon a hunt, they do it on a large scale, going to the

THE OWEN-STANLEY RANGES FROM THE SEA.

ground, fasting, in single file, and in dead silence—for it is a sign of bad luck if a single word be spoken. They fix upon a hollow, surrounded by steep ridges; they then attach a chain of nets to stakes round this amphitheatre, leaving three open spaces, at which some of the hunters wait, hidden by the long grass, which also conceals the kangaroo. After this arrangement is complete, they set fire to the grass, which, being dry in hunting seasons, burns quickly. This is the cause of the clouds of smoke that we see. As the grass flames up, the hunters yell wildly, and utter strange sounds, the effect seemingly being to stupefy their victims, who try in vain to escape from the snare. Those that make towards the open parts are instantly speared by the hunters waiting for them there.

Daylight is nearly over; we are still winding about, and at last decide to anchor on a reef near Kapa-Kapa, where we have a view of the Owen-Stanley ranges, with Round Head, a most glorious sun gilding sea and sky. After some dodging about to find a safe hold for the anchor, we brought to just as the sun was dipping behind the distant reefs, the dark blue tumble of waters beyond the white surf-line cutting it in half. Sunsets are always beautiful, if short-lived, in the tropics, but we had lately been having a storm, which was still raging outside; and with the haze which a storm brings with it, this sunset was doubly beautiful. The sun floated in a violet veil, orange lustred, with a scarlet glow above the haze; only a few feather-shaped wreaths broke upon the graduating tints, mellowing from purple at the horizon through the changes of orange, scarlet, gold, green, to an indescribable opal, which covered the upper space with translucent beauty. Through this we seem to feel the dawning of the coming stars, as we take our eyes away from the burnish upon the wavelets close at hand and glance overhead. Then comes the hush of the evanescent twilight, and with the eyes of heaven looking down upon us, we turn our gaze shorewards, to where Mount Owen-Stanley would be visible, had we light enough to perceive it, and were there an upper space sufficiently free from mist. To-night the mountain is completely shrouded behind the grey wall, and only portions of the nearer ranges can be caught, with the village fires of Kapa-Kapa dotting the shores. The only chance we have of viewing these stupendous ranges, rearing themselves nearly 14,000 feet above the level of the sea, and as yet unexplored by the feet of civilised man, is during the few minutes immediately before sunrise. We watched our chance, and fortune favoured us next morning by giving us a clear sky, and for a brief space we had an unimpeded glimpse, such as is not often obtained from this point.

Completing another stage of our journey, we land at the village of Hula, and are well treated by Kema, a native trader, who acts as interpreter between us and the natives. Kema has been educated by the missionaries, and sings us hymns in the South Sea language, while he sees that we are not overreached by the men and women who bring their spears, nets, and ornaments to traffic with us. He is the only man among them who is dressed, and he is very loudly costumed in a coat of bright yellow, with red and black spots. To his house the girls and old women came in great crowds, without the reserve which the women show in other parts, and here we had to taste the betel-nut and smoke the ban-ban, an attempt over which we nearly choked.

The bau-bau is a long and thick bamboo cane, with one end stopped up and the other left open. A little hole is made near the closed end, into which the tobacco is inserted, wrapped in a leaf, cigarette fashion. A man lights the tobacco, while one of the girls sucks at the large open end until the hollow tube is filled with smoke, after which the plug is withdrawn, and the pipe passes round, each one sucking a mouthful of smoke and swallowing it!

It is a lovely walk along the smooth white sands, scattered over with pieces of branch coral, and shells of all shapes and colours. I can hardly move forward for stooping to pick up specimens — spider shells, cowries, large and small, exquisitely shaped and delicately tinted. But the natives laugh at me for wasting time over such rubbish, even while they are good-natured enough to ease me of the labour of carrying it. The sea is on one side, and the jungle a few yards on the other, a jungle formed of a variety of trees—the erythrina, or coral-tree, covered with scarlet blossoms, the umbrella-tree, with its great leaves, crotons of all colours, palms and bananas. There is also a most luxuriant undergrowth of creepers, grasses, and shrubs. The houses are like the Motu buildings, square, with sloping roofs and high

THE BAU-BAU OR PIPE.

piles. The women are taller and finer-looking than those of the Motu tribe. Some we see blackened over, showing us that Death has been busy, but those who are not soot-coated are very fair, and all are lively and merry.

The women here are said to be less shy in their intercourse with strangers than those of any other part. This is only true of the unmarried; after marriage they become very reserved. Mr. Goldie tells a story of one girl at Hula who played him a smart trick while he was buying fish from her. She came to him with a basket-load, and he bought one after a long bargaining, and gave it to his man, who placed it in a bag behind him. The girl disappeared for a moment, and brought out another, and then others. The purchaser, who appears to have been looking more at her than at her fish, had bought about half-a-dozen, when, struck by the very remarkable resemblance of the seventh fish in size and shape to the other six, he watched her as she disappeared, and caught her in the very act of abstracting it from his bag. She had sold him the same fish seven times over, and laughed heartily when caught in her trick, making good the bargain by giving him the contents of her basket.

The natives enjoy practical joking, and nothing delights them so much as the thought of over-reaching you in a bargain. A whole crowd will laugh uproariously if they see you offering more than they expect for an article which they bring to sell. They will pat you on the back, and cry out "Oh! Oh! Koi-koi!" which means that they have gammoned you, and are writing you down an ass.

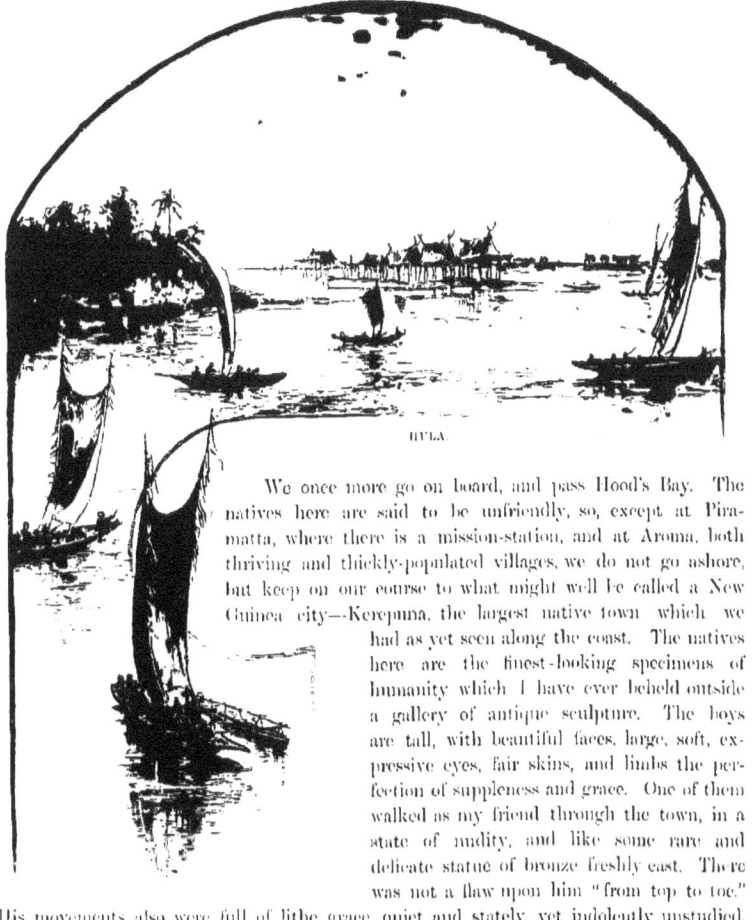

HULA.

We once more go on board, and pass Hood's Bay. The natives here are said to be unfriendly, so, except at Piramatta, where there is a mission-station, and at Aroma, both thriving and thickly-populated villages, we do not go ashore, but keep on our course to what might well be called a New Guinea city—Kerepuna, the largest native town which we had as yet seen along the coast. The natives here are the finest-looking specimens of humanity which I have ever beheld outside a gallery of antique sculpture. The boys are tall, with beautiful faces, large, soft, expressive eyes, fair skins, and limbs the perfection of suppleness and grace. One of them walked as my friend through the town, in a state of nudity, and like some rare and delicate statue of bronze freshly cast. There was not a flaw upon him "from top to toe." His movements also were full of lithe grace, quiet and stately, yet indolently unstudied. When he leaned against a tree, waiting upon me as I sketched, I could hardly keep my eyes off him, and yet he was only one of many equally noble examples of the most perfect work of creation—man.

As we landed, three natives came forward to greet us, the tallest nearly seven feet, and handsomely proportioned. He good-naturedly offered me his broad shoulders as a seat. There was room for two men as big as I to sit upon those brawny shoulders,

## A STATE OF NATURE.

while he had strength enough to carry a dozen. He lazily leaned upon a huge branch of gum-tree, which he carried about with him as a staff. His two companions were each over six feet, but not quite so good-looking as he, and both much darker in colour. They were all perfectly nude, as the males always are, except for their waist-belt of twine, and they were without a single trace of self-consciousness. So Adam might have stood in the garden before the angels when Eve rose up from her first

TUPUSELEI.

sleep and saw that she was not alone. Only by paying a visit to Kerepuna can members of civilised races tell how much we must have degenerated.

At Kerepuna there are steeple-like structures that appear to be used as places for keeping watch. Inside all was dark and empty, while on the platforms, raised high in front of them, by which you enter, we found large stains of blood, as if they were used for slaughterhouses. High into the air these spires rise, sixty, eighty, a hundred, and in some cases over two hundred feet, with poles projecting outwards, and extending upwards far above the thatched portion. These poles have streamers flying from them —woven grass and palm-leaves, and in their slender tracery and confusion of lines appear very light and graceful. The houses are built facing one another, as at Tupuselei, with a narrow street of sand between. The streets as in a village of olden times, offer vistas down which the delighted eye wanders. Deep shadows lie under the piles and broad eaves, while the full glare of a tropical sun bleaches the hot sands and the grey silver bark of the beams. The thatch of palm-fronds is of a grey stone colour. Thus in this picture of light and shade, except when a gay-coloured parrot flits across the scene, or a gorgeously-tinted butterfly lights it up, there is little positive colour, until the glance of your eye reaches the bright green and russet leaves of the banana, in all its various stages of whole and tattered flutterings, or alights upon the deeper tones of the Papuan apple-tree, its top weighted down by its generous load of fruit. Of these you catch glimpses over the roofs of brown-grey thatch in the distance, for Kerepunu is placed in the centre of gardens. Occasionally there passes a brown male figure or a tattooed female, the one with his fishing gear or hunting spears, the other, it may be, with two water-jars, going to or coming from the wells; or it may be that as you turn a corner you will come upon a group of women preparing the taro and yams for dinner, or young mothers playing with their brown babies, while on verandas tame parrots and cockatoos are nibbling away in sleepy contentment.

Two rest-days are observed in every six, the people dividing their time by working two days and resting on the third. On working-days you will find the township quiet, and open to inspection, but on play-days it presents quite a different appearance. Then the streets are crowded with workmen, hunters, warriors, women, and children—the young girls decked out with gaily-striped grass petticoats, or "ramuas," stained red, yellow, and black, while the men are decorated with their hornbills, shark-teeth necklaces, and twisted cane or hair armlets. The feathers of the cassowary hang over their breasts, and scarlet tufts of the bird of paradise are stuck in their hair. They are also adorned with breastplates of mother-of-pearl (very precious to them), with love-tokens consisting of boars' tusks, spun cloth, beads, and fine feathers, and with pink coral nose-sticks, their frizzed hair standing out all round their heads, while their ears are hung with strings of fine shells. The warriors will parade armed with their carved battle-axes and spears, their bows and arrows, their war-clubs, their richly-cut wooden swords, large and small, and their tall wooden shields, some quaintly carved, others mat-covered and embroidered with feather and shell. The fishermen play with their fish-prongs, while the young boys practise the throwing of the spear, their sires looking on and encouraging them in their exercises.

All day long, on these Sabbaths, it is a festive scene of life and movement, big feasts being prepared by the women, while the men lounge about or hold their games. Even on festive occasions the latter are temperate. In their general behaviour they are grave and silent, only giving a guttural grunt of satisfaction when a point has been scored, or, it may be, a loud laugh of derision over some mistake perpetrated or jest achieved. It is a most ordinary sight to see two or three brother-dandies or braves walking along with heads erect, their arms flung lovingly about one another's necks. During the day they will hardly speak to the girls, the men keeping much to themselves, and leaving the women to congregate and gossip together.

In the same affectionate manner do the men treat a stranger when he has been

## THE MAN-TRAP.

approved of. It is a case of David and Jonathan. Your friend will put his arms round your neck, and draw yours round his, and will proudly take you amongst his relatives. They lay aside suspicion very quickly, and give full trust and confidence when once they have become friends.

Of course, betel-nut and lime chewing and bau-bau smoking are the order of the day during these festivals. It is only at such times that I ever saw the men speak to the women. Generally a man will hold out his bamboo pipe to some girl whom he is passing, and she, taking hold of it, helps him to light it, sucking it for him, and then handing it back when full of smoke, and quietly resuming her seat and her task of peeling the yam or spinning the matting. When they are tired out with their spear-throwing, wrestling, man-trap practice, and other amusements, they gather to their own family circles, and begin to feast. The man-trap, by the way, is a very formidable weapon, composed of a long, sharp-pointed stick, with a hoop attached to the end. The sharp point projects into about a third of the hoop, leaving plenty of room for the pursuing hunter to fling it over the head of the running victim. The hoop catches him under the chin, and jerks back his head against the sharp point at the nape of the neck, pithing him as oxen are pithed in the shambles.

A BATTLE-AXE

When night comes on fires are lighted in the streets, and songs are sung, dances danced, and merriment made within the ruddy glow, or under the pale lustre of the moon. And what glorious nights they are in this tropic land, when the moon is full and streaming down over the roof-tops, making ebony and silver of the platforms and the posts! In the warmth of the wood fires lie the old men and women, the fathers and mothers, while the young men and maidens dance to the sound of the drum and rattle, or of the reed pipes, shaped after the pattern of Pan's. I saw some of these pipes, and wondered to find that they were not a whit different from the reed pipes which we used to see in England at fairs, tied to the breast of the drum-beating showman, or which we see in the hands of Greek fauns.

WOODEN SWORDS AND DRUM.

Of course there will be love-making on these gala-nights, in spite of all rules and regulations. Young girls will steal out from the shadow of their homes, and find their way through the trellised lanes into the dewy gardens and woods to meet those whom they are beginning to like well enough to put into purgatory. In these gardens and woods, in the pale light of the great moon, the dusky nymphs and fauns are

gliding about through the dead banana-leaves and dew-drenched grass. The reed "raumas" of the nymphs will not be any the worse for the dew-drenching, and the fauns wear nothing to spoil. The fireflies flash in the black shadows, and drips of lustre filter between palm-fronds and mammy-leaves, making patches of tarnished silver on the corrugated trunks, or gleaming in diamond sparkles upon the gauze-like spider webs which float from branch to branch in the soft night gale.

At times the spirit-seërs come into the village, and then wild expectation is raised. They are melancholy men, these wizards, and hold a faith somewhat akin to that of the spiritualists of England and

KEREPUNA.

America. They say that they are possessed by the souls of the departed, who speak through them, and tell what is going to happen. The people have great faith in these spirit-men, and evidently hold some kind of religious ceremonies, and believe in a future existence. Their ghostly visitors do not depend alone upon verbal demonstrations, but have masks and other disguises with which to terrify the credulous villagers, who, however, seem to know that it is all humbug, since they are ready to sell the spectre-masks to strangers for "koko," although while the performance lasts they believe in the spirit which boo-boos behind the mask, and seem to be horribly frightened.

We saw some very fine canoe-making at Kerepuna. All round the coast, latakois are to be seen, double-decked, with single, double, or triple sails, with handsome outriggers and carved prows, fringed round the gunwale with cowrie shells and birds' plumage, with ornaments at the mastheads, and streamers flying from all points—vessels which can be handled with great dexterity, and which fly and tack before the wind like sea-birds. They are sometimes from a hundred to two hundred feet in length, although they mostly range from fifty to sixty feet. They are

CHIEFS' HOUSES, KEREPUNA.

usually the common property of a village, all helping to build and work them, so that the loss of a latakoi is a calamity to the whole community. Towards the end of the dry season the men make an annual trip round the coast for trading purposes; and when they are ready to go, the wizards are called in to predict the future. First, there is solemn music, while the Fates are being propitiated, after which, if the predictions are favourable, a universal farewell feast is held, when all make merry. While the women dance and sing, the young men show off by tacking and manoeuvring their vessels in front of the dancers by the sea-shore, accompanied by their sweethearts, gaily dressed, their breasts and heads covered with rare orchids and scarlet hibiscus-blossoms. The ladies beat upon their drums which are covered with iguana and alligator skins—shake their bone and shell rattles, and laugh at the jests of the young men.

Each trader is a warrior, and goes all prepared to fight for his rights, for there are pirates to be encountered, and enemies who may kill and eat him. Wherefore he and his comrades carry the full complement of palm-wood spears and war-bows, with stacks of poisoned wood arrows. The wind is boisterous in some parts, and may blow them ashore on a land where only death or torture awaits them. They depart on their voyages with the same anticipations with which a soldier goes forth to a foreign campaign, and when the canoes part from the latakois the tears are plentiful. But when the south-east monsoon has ceased to blow, and the north-west monsoon comes with its drenching rainfall, the women know that their husbands will soon be home, if they are coming at all, and they prepare accordingly. If disease has broken the ranks, or disaster overtaken the cargo, then there are heard wild weepings and wailings, for they know that the next months must be full of privation; but if the cruise has been successful, then out with the drums and on with the hibiscus-blossoms. The sun has no need to shine to make them merry; they can dance in the pouring rain.

They will know well enough when they see the first speck of sail rounding the far-off headland. Ships can crawl when dejected, as they can fly when successful, and an empty vessel does not grip the water like a full one. Here they come, and not a streamer wanting. With a slanting swing they heave round the promontory, jaunty and with the sails low, sweeping the roughened waves. They know full well that they are watched by that anxious crowd of women and old men on the shore, and it is not in human nature for them not to show off, so they tack till they nearly run the carved nose against the bluff, and then again to seaward, with a jerking of ropes and a reckless swinging of sails.

"Aha! they have got the sago!" and each woman darts indoors to put on her best "rauma," while the old men haul out the canoes through the white surf and shallow waters: then out come the women adorned with their best, carrying their carved paddles, and leaping about. They dash over the curling waves towards the daring sailors—away under that rain-bulging sky, with the white-crested waves breaking over their faces. The lithe arms are active with the carved paddles and with the cocoa-nut scoop that clears out the water as it washes in: and the lagoon is covered with those tiny, women-worked craft, all heading towards the flying crescent-shaped double sails, while the moist air is filled with glad shouts of welcome.

NATIVE WAR SHIELD.

## NEW GUINEA: KEREPUNA TO CAUTION POINT.

Cloudy Bay—South Cape—East Cape—Heath, Palm, and Dinner Islands—A High Sense of Honour—Milne Bay—Cliffy and Teste Islands—A Nocturne—Caution Point—German New Guinea—An Expedition up the Aird River.

TO describe the houses of Kerepuna is to describe nearly all the houses along the coast from this point to East Cape and Teste Island. No two villages, however, are exactly alike in design; and there is hardly a single tribe that has not quite a different language. This circumstance, by the way, makes it difficult to travel among the natives of New Guinea, although none of the languages are in themselves difficult to learn.

Leaving Hood's Bay, in which stand Piramatta, Aroma, Kerepuna, and many other native towns and villages, we sail along towards Cloudy Bay, past Cape Rodney, Baxter Bay, Table Point and Bay. As we pass the lofty ranges on our left, they take upon them the varied lights and shadows of the day as it advances from morning to midday, and on to the golden greys of afternoon and the royal purple of evening. We gained glimpses of Mounts Suckling and Obree, with numerous unnamed ranges towering between us and them, all grand and all abruptly rising up one from the other; of dense forests and bare cliffs, and chasms down which we could look till sight was lost in the purple obscurity; of hill-sides, seamed with stream-courses and broken by waterfalls; of gullies where the alligator was lurking with her young, and the wild boars were wandering in droves. We passed long cane-grass, tall enough to hide a man on horseback, and patches of jungle where the rifle bird and the laughing jackass roosted. Across Cloudy Bay we sailed, with the sky piled up with rain-clouds, and the mountains dark and blurred. The savages here are very ferocious, and slay and eat all whom they can catch. As we pass Amazon and other bays, including Orangerie Bay, the scenery grows hourly more rugged, and, at the same time, more sylvan; then come more islands, and points, and bays, until, leaving behind Mounts Suckling and Simpson, we got round South Cape and the North Foreland.

Next morning the sun rose over South Cape with the tints and some of the weird and fantastic outlines of that picture of Turner's, "Ulysses." The mountains looked like giants waking up from sleep and flinging up violet arms out of rose-tinted into saffron-coloured hazes. There were vast rocks standing up clear from the mountain sides like spires and battlements—pinnacles from a thousand to four thousand feet in air. Great cones rose from the water's edge at sharp angles, but covered to the very summit with native gardens and zigzag paths, along which women blithely bore their laden baskets. No mountains can be compared to these for diversity of shape and stupendous grandeur, or for the fearsome hollows where the morning shadow sleeps. It looked like Dante's land, only that it was too fertile and too highly cultivated.

At South Cape there are many villages, not far from the mission station, and as it was a Sunday morning, we saw the gaily-attired procession of converted natives go

CLOUDY BAY.

filing into church. Gowns of all shades passed along the silent beach, and gleamed fitfully between the fruit trees—white, cream-tinted, yellow, rose-hued, scarlet, crushed strawberry, browns, and varied depths of blue and green. The rainbow was fully represented this quiet Sunday morning while the stalwart South Sea Island teacher was beating upon an empty tin can which did duty for bell or gong. It is true that the natives might have supplied him with a better instrument to call to prayer, but the tin can represented civilisation, as did those many-tinted gowns, while the iguana-skin drum and cassowary fringes would have looked heathen.

Going ashore, and to church also, we were honoured with a place beside the teacher and his wife, one of the most lovely South Sea Island women I ever beheld. We could follow the airs sung, although we could not keep up with the words. Beyond the teacher's house is a beautiful water-pool, with a fall coming from a high rock, the whole densely hung with tropical foliage. On the beach many canoes were drawn up, with matting over them to keep them from the sun; there were also crowds of natives, who sat beside the canoes and huts, minus gown or dress. I have no doubt the entire drapery of the Cape was then being steamed in church, while the nude portion of the community patiently waited their turn.

Returning to our boat, we go on through China Straits, passing close to many islands, with great walls of solid rock in some places sheer from the sea, guarding bright coves and inlets. As we left East Cape behind, the sun was fully up, and vouchsafed to us rare treats of light and shade. Of course it was very hot, even with a head-wind, under such rays. Our costume consisted of very thin pyjamas, and light canvas shoes to keep our feet from contact with the hot deck or the burning sands. A few moments in the sun burns blisters on our arms and feet, and when we pass from under the awning it is like standing upon a heated oven. Yet it is astonishing how quickly the human frame becomes accustomed to tropical skies. Already I like the heat, and prefer the sunshine to the shade; and after being blistered over once or twice, the skin gets tanned, and the sun no longer burns, but only warms. A night which would be midsummer at home makes one shiver with cold. Even the mosquitoes seem to be less troublesome, and to stab one with more leniency than they did before.

Heath Island now bursts upon us as we round a promontory of rock and beautiful vegetation—Heath Island, with a deep translucent bay and snowy sands, with overhanging branches, and trees shooting up into the azure space and half covering the hill-sides, with masses of rock peering out from banks of rich tropical flowers—altogether the perfection of an island. From beetling cliffs, reflecting themselves in the deep, clear, smooth waters, trail parasites and creepers, covered with blossoms of all hues.

DINNER ISLAND.

At the extremity of the cone a hut appears, empty and going to pieces. It was raised here by an unfortunate trader who not long ago was attacked and slaughtered by the natives.

Another turn, and Palm Island lies on our left, with Dinner Island in front of us, where we drop anchor and go ashore. Here we met Tom, a South Sea teacher, coal-black and massive, who is to go with us up Milne Bay to settle a dispute, and conciliate the natives of Gile-Gile, who have been ill-treated in some way, and want a life. He explains the cause of the discontent as we steam up Milne Bay, or rather Gulf, as it ought to be called. It appears that a man who was in charge of the

Copra station had stolen some hens, which had been left there by the missionary. The natives regarded them as a sacred trust. The man, hearing that they were going to murder him, had decamped, and was now staying at Dinner Island. Tom was going up to claim the hens, and inform the natives that he was satisfied, and so ought they to be. But they were not easily brought to reason, their honour as protectors having been wounded. One of our party told them, through Tom, that the hens were their own property, not Tom's, because after they had been left behind they were the property of those who lived on the land. He also offered to settle the question once for all by paying the full price of the poultry in tobacco, but neither Tom nor the simple-minded savages could grasp the subtleties of this legal quirk. The original hens belonged to Tom, so he and the chief agreed that all the progeny must still belong to him, and doggedly stuck to these simple lines of possession. At last the gentleman who represented the intricate honesty of refined civilisation was fain to leave the savage chief and the half-savage teacher to settle the matter according to their own simple code of morality. Tom, as a truthful man, translated the remarks of the representative, but did it sulkily—remarks which the chief received with lowering brows. Tom then stated his own case, in his own way, of which the chief saw the force, and at last consented to leave vengeance alone, finishing up by saying, "Hens belong to you, not to me; and I will not kill white thief unless he comes to Gile-Gile!"

Milne Bay has not yet been much traversed by vessels, and the shores have been little visited, the natives here being cannibals — cannibals, indeed, of a peculiarly desperate kind. As I walked about sketching, with these facts in my mind, I did not feel over comfortable, nor was I very sorry when we turned our backs upon these specimens of savage life. Somewhere about this part, I am given to understand, there is an inland tribe who go about in bands to trap unwary travellers. They do not attack parties, but lie in wait for single victims, whom, when caught, they kill and cut up, carrying the pieces about for trade purposes amongst the native villages, much as butchers do with sheep and cattle at home. They are the professional butchers of New Guinea.

Gile-Gile lies at the head of Milne Gulf, with houses on both sides of the Bay. A large river runs into the Gulf at this point, and the native houses on the other side are built upon the neck of land between the Bay and the river. Ahead of us the water narrows in winding passages towards a chain of high mountains, with overhanging banks of foliage. The effect of these mountains, through this leafy framework, is very soft, and as rain falls nearly every day throughout the year, the cloud effects from Gile-Gile, looking up and down that broad sheet of water, which spreads out like a lake, surrounded by lofty and rugged mountains with silvery-grey distances and cool shadows, are beautiful and ever-changing.

From China Straits, as we return, we get a fine view of Mount Cloudy in the distance—a single cone, abruptly rising to an immense height from pyramidal-shaped sides. A quick run past headlands and smooth bays, and for a short time we get clear of land, to bring up before long at Teste Island, which lies off the coast of East

Cape—a large, fertile, and beautifully situated isle, forming the centre of a cluster. Here we find Cliffy, Bell, West, Boat, and other islands, all extending seaward and shoreward, dotting the bosom of the open ocean with most marvellous formations. It is night before we reach Teste Island, an hour or so before moonrise, but our pilot knows the way well, and so, through the shoals and treacherous reefs, he drives straight along, like a London cabman who knows how to handle his horse. He does not fear to skirt the extreme limits of safety, almost grazing those deadly, wave-covered walls of coral. Once on these, there could be no getting off again. The delicate coral branches, fan-shaped and rose-shaped, so slight and tender that the least pressure breaks them off in flakes, appear harmless enough, as we lift them gingerly in our hands for fear we should break off a petal of that snowy, or amber-tinted, or rosy sea-flower. But they will tear in an instant through the strong sheets of copper which line the bottom of the ship, crunching through beams and planks like the sharp teeth of rats, and leaving ghastly holes for the water to rush through. A heave of a high wave, or the white surf that is always lashing over the outside barrier, will land a vessel on their tops, and the next return may heave her off again; but between that wave and wave the deed has been done, and almost before a boat can be lowered the ship has sunk to limitless depths.

Fortunately for our peace of mind, our pilot knows the passage, although there are no charts yet made which can be relied upon. A phosphorescent rush of fire-sparks is furrowed up as we plough along, and a pale, dull whiteness, with a narrow thread of blue-black close alongside, at times shows us the proximity of a reef. The round dome of heaven, like a punctured canvas roof, with denser patches of darkness where the smoke rolls from the funnel, meets our eyes as we glance up from the star-reflecting ocean to the star-filled sky. The gentle breezes humming through the cordage and through the grass dresses which we have hung over the rail to air, lull us into reposeful inattention to all things material. But we duck our heads, and wake up quickly, as a thick blackness seems to fall suddenly upon us, and while we look up, startled, great cliffs and rocks, with intense black shadows, seem to be sliding down upon us. We are so close that it seems as if we could touch them with our hands, while they overhang so much as to give the impression that they must fall and crush us to pieces.

We are now grazing the sides of Cliffy Island, an immense rock, perforated with vast caves, where myriads of sea-birds make their homes, and with a water-worn line cut clean all round it at its base. Trees and luxuriant herbage deck the top, but in the lower part all is steep, or rather projecting, precipice. From the side we are rounding, the island shelves inwards very abruptly, giving a decided top-heavy appearance. Beyond it, and about two miles distant, looms the dusky outline of the Bell Rock, rising bell-shaped out of the sea, and over four hundred feet in air. But to-night all its lines are indistinct, and only visible where they intercept the stars.

Ten minutes longer, and we bring ourselves to anchor as near Teste Island as we dare approach, and as soon as may be we are over the side, into the dingey, and pulling for the shore, with canoes and natives alongside showing the way. As we strike the beach, the moon rises over the eastern edge of the island, just where the palms and houses of the natives are placed. A promontory shelters these houses from the sea-gales, and forms a secluded cove fringed by layers of coral reefs, so that the pool within lies almost without a ripple even while the waters are tossing outside or moaning at the bar. It is a pretty, irregularly-built village, with palm-trees growing by the sides of the houses and lining the sands. As we waded over the shallow places, and walked towards the trader's house, we watched the moon lift itself above that dark promontory—the broad golden disc fringed and zigzagged by the tops of bushes and trees. Softly it rose and paled its fires, the sands growing whiter as the light strengthened and objects became more sharply defined—thatched houses on piles, with palms, breaking the straight lines and casting dark shadows along the beach—a canoe rocking with upright mast in the bay, the waters of which, as they catch the gleaming moon-shafts, appear to become more ripply. The solemnity of a great silence was over all, for this was one of the working days, and now in the evening everyone seemed to be asleep. Even the natives who were with us when we landed had glided away silently and gone to bed, leaving their curiosity, now that they were satisfied we were not enemies, to be indulged on the morrow. We went to one of the houses, and peered into the darkness within. Deep breathing, and a grunt or so, told us that all were asleep except the watchers, who had grunted their disapproval at our impertinence; then we went back to the trader's bungalow, and were shown a spare room into which our guides had gone. It was a large apartment, something like a barn, with a cane floor raised, as usual, from the ground, about forty young men and boys being huddled together, and asleep; there they lay at sixes and sevens, their limbs in all sorts of positions. The wonder is that some of the lesser fry were not squeezed out of existence beneath the weight of the elders; yet they

1. TRADING VESSELS.
2. SOUTH CAPE.
3. PALM ISLAND.
4. NATIVE HOUSE WITH PALMS.

all seemed comfortable, and not even the light, held over their faces, disturbed their slumbers. These young Spartans have worked hard all day, and are tired out, but to-morrow they will be up at dawn to begin again; they want neither couch nor covering to make them sleep, nor will they grumble if awakened suddenly, as they were at our arrival. They are accustomed to surprises; and he who sleeps after the first warning to wake up does not live long.

We slept that night much in the manner of the country, and, albeit troubled a good deal by hosts of mosquitoes, found our quarters on the whole comfortable. Next

TESTE ISLAND.

morning we took our bath in the crystal lagoon. No danger of sharks here, for it is well protected by the reefs. It is a dazzling morning; the natives are plunging about beside us, and the islands seems afloat on the sapphire sea. Bell Rock, with its fissures and rosy lights, or amber where the grass grows on its shelves and tops, turns out to be a vast upheaval of basalt, over four hundred feet to its pinnacle; Cliffy Island, looking as if it had once received a buffet on this side which had sent it all agee, has a perfect cloud of birds soaring about its dark purple sides; West Island, with its grassy slopes slanting from us, is bathed in the gilding of the rising sun; and Boat Island resembles some huge hippopotamus fallen asleep. Over the reefs, flying fish, dolphins, and other ocean denizens, are sporting in the cooling fluid; there are also crescent-shaped fins floating quietly about, as near as they dare come to our bathing-place; while the white foam breaks merrily against the fretted underledges of the rocky cliffs.

Ashore, the parrots and cockatoos are chattering noisily amongst the branches. Near the copra traders' sheds a great tamarind-tree grows, with corrugated trunk and half-exposed roots, its gnarled branches twisted round each other, or flung far apart, and dense with leafage, under the shelter of which crowds of men, women, and children sit, with their mats, calabashes, baskets, and other curiosities, waiting until we come to buy from them. Behind them are groves of deliciously green fruit-trees, cool shadow-spots, where the grasses, long and fresh, are all misty with the sheen of heavy dewdrops. It is a golden idyll of tropic life, from which we must tear ourselves before we are nearly satisfied, to hurry away on the swift wings of the monsoon.

Our easterly limit was Caution Point, which we reached by way of Cape Moresby, Collingwood and Dyke-Acland Bays. This brings us to the German division of New Guinea. Of this I may say, from inquiries made, that it is a very large slice of the island. One of the most recent explorers, who was with me on the voyage down to Brisbane, tells me that the cases of fever are very mild in this part of the country, and quickly cured, and that already they have begun to colonise. He explored most of the level country, and found the Augusta River navigable for large vessels for a distance of 310 miles—a broad, smooth river, ten to fifteen fathoms deep all the way, and over 1,000 feet broad. The land on both sides was open country from thirty to fifty miles deep, and would make splendid sugar and coffee plantations. The natives were numerous and fairly friendly, open to conviction, and not at all difficult to manage. These details were kindly imparted to me by Dr. Knappe, German Consul at Samoa, who had been exploring New Guinea for his Government.

Since the above was written, I have had intelligence of a most successful expedition up the Aird River, which will go far to open the hitherto almost unknown interior of this land, and which proves that it may be penetrated with impunity. This expedition was organised entirely at the expense of the enterprising firm of Messrs. Burns, Phelp, and Co., for the purpose of discovering an easy way into the interior, with a view to future trading enterprise, and was placed under the leadership of Mr. Theodore F. Beven, an able New Guinea explorer. He writes:—" We steamed in the *Victory*, seventy miles from Cape Blackwood as the crow flies, in a northerly direction into the mountainous ranges, finding a broad channel which carried three to seven fathoms of water right into the Aird River. After following it up, we found it was only one of the many mouths of a great fresh-water river coming from the ranges inland, a magnificent stream which we followed to the head, eighty miles in direct line from the coast, carrying good water all the way to the mountains. On returning down the river we struck a fresh branch and came out in Deception Bay; going hence to Motu-Motu, and returning, searching the coast, we found a magnificent new river, with an entrance over three miles wide, close to Bald Head. We proceeded up this river one hundred and ten miles, passing through ranges and gorges, in places 1,500 feet high. The country is splendid scrub country, with very rich agricultural land on both rivers."

## NEW GUINEA: YULE ISLAND AND THE TORRES STRAITS.

Yule Island—Motu-Motu- Across the Papuan Gulf—Darnley Island—The Murray Group—Yorke Island—Lotus-eaters.

AFTER returning to Port Moresby from the east, which we did in a day or so, we bore towards Yule Island and the west of British New Guinea. Yule Island lies about sixty miles from Port Moresby, and is separated from the mainland by a narrow strip of sea. I should say, from what I saw, that it is one of the healthiest places along the coast for Europeans. Here we walked through fields of cane-grass twelve to fifteen feet high, so that we had to keep hard on the heels of our guide, or we should soon have been hopelessly lost. On the hills it does not grow so tall, and as we ascend walking becomes easier, except for dense patches of jungle here and there, the lair of the wild boar and of other game. From the hillside we had a fine view of the sea and the mainland, with Mount Yule and other hills, and dense forests—jungles of sago, cedar, cotton, eucalyptus, and umbrella trees. Crotons and castor-oil plants meet us at every turn, and orchids exquisitely shaped and tinted cling wherever they can find a dead branch to beautify.

Hospitably received by the three French priests who have here taken up their abode, also by the Protestant native teachers, who are living in unity with them, we explored the island, and saw two native villages, beautifully built in the centre of palm-groves, with the grey sand swept carefully every day, and the roads kept like garden walks. There is here a lovely smooth shore, with rugged promontories jutting out; and as we turn corners we find ever fresh treats for the eye—dark openings in the mangrove jungle, caves, and arches, shells jingling against one another as the white surf-line laps amongst them.

Our last stoppage on the mainland is the important township of Motu-Motu, the best point on the highway inland towards Mount Yule. Here Mr. Eidelfelt has taken up his post, with his plucky young wife, and means to prosecute his botanical and other studies on this scientifically fertile mountain. During his former stay he was strictly vegetarian, and had perfect health, although taking no precautions against fever, his immunity from which, however, may be due to his living as much as possible on the ranges and as little as possible on the coast. The town of Motu-Motu lies in Freshwater Bay, but the coast is difficult of approach. The surf was too heavy for the dingey to be brought out, and through our glasses we saw three canoes swamped as the natives tried to launch them. At last we anchored in the lagoon at the mouth of the river, and got ashore by a circuitous route.

It was night when, bidding farewell to New Guinea, we lifted our anchor and steamed across the tempestuous Papuan Gulf—a night of clouds and gloom, with waves running wickedly past us, and curling up into white crests, like snarling black dogs showing their teeth. The "Gulf" is like the Bay of Biscay always, or nearly always, rough. We had steam, so we passed over it in comparative ease, although in one part we stuck fast on a sand-bank, and had to wait for high tide to got off again. We also had many miles' dodging about to find our right route before we sighted Bramble Cay. From this point all went smoothly. We soon sighted the magnificent Island of Darnley. As Mr. Norton, now curator of the Hobart Museum, an old explorer in these parts, says, it is "one of the largest and most fertile of this fruitful archipelago; an undulating sea of tropical verdure clothes lofty

MURRAY ISLAND.

DARNLEY ISLAND.

hills and tranquil valleys, broken only by rugged cliffs and crags of sombre-tinted rock, and here and there a scanty patch of bright-foliaged bananas, papopaws, and sugar-cane, flourishing freely among the yams and taro in the rudely-cultivated plantations of the miserable remnant of a once-powerful race, whose silent and deserted villages may still be seen nestling under the evergreen canopy of the cocoa-nut groves, fringing the small snow-white beaches dotted at frequent intervals along the reef-encircled foreshore of this island."

From Darnley to the Murray group of islands the sea is filled with shoals and reefs, so that it must be traversed by day. One of the natives acted as pilot—a tall, handsome, brown fellow, who glanced with wounded pride when the captain doubted his directions, the captain being one of the old school, and strongly objecting to receiving orders in his own ship from a "nigger." However, the native knew his way, and by sundown we were anchored safely before the mission-station, and were welcomed on shore. The native king of the island came out to meet us with his boat's crew

MOTU-MOTU.

dressed in full naval uniform, his cutter carrying the Union Jack, and his crew like a Custom House crew on State service.

This island is one of the principal stations of the Mission Society, and is very finely situated in the centre of Meer and Dower Islands. Fertile, as all the islands are, Murray is composed of a large volcanic hill, with the crater visible from the sea. The mission-houses are built upon terraces, and provided with gardens, along the sheltered side of the hill. We walked through the plantations and gardens, and up a winding pathway, very beautiful, to the mission-house. Here we were most kindly treated by the missionaries, one of whom acted as our guide, and showed us over the island. It appears to be healthy, although the missionary's wife has suffered much from fever, while their two pretty children are rather fragile-looking, but, like the native children with whom they play, they seem to live half their lives in the sea, and swim like ducks, talking the native language even better than their mother-tongue. The description of Darnley applies equally to Murray, which we left with a profound feeling of respect for the solitary and delicate lady who lives and works with her husband and children amongst these only half-tamed savages. Another ten hours' steaming, and we anchor at Yorke Island. The stars are rising, and the effect is peculiarly beautiful, though not more so than that of the sunrise which greeted us next morning. Here we find the bêche-de-mer being prepared for the Japan and China markets, with the iron sheds where it is smoked, and the natives who work and prepare it for the trader. They permit him to stay with them, and they help him with his work, in return for which he keeps them all. Life is easy on these islands, the natives working only when inclined, and this style suits the present trader, who finds it best for his own interests, and not opposed to his inclinations, to let them have their own way. The native king is the best dressed man on the island; he comes out, when strangers arrive, with an old red soldier's jacket and cap. The trader himself possesses one pair of trousers, much patched, and portions of a red flannel shirt, the patches artistically, if not scientifically, put on by the king's sister, whom the trader has married—a coal-black, stalwart Torres Strait queen. The island is almost flat, but richly wooded, and well guarded by reefs—the ideal pirates' isle; and when we turned westward we felt as if it would not be very difficult to become reconciled to this aimless but happy lotus-eating life.

PROW OF A NEW GUINEA CANOE.

## ADELAIDE.

"A Model City"—The Plan of the City—South Adelaide—Victoria Square—King William Street—The Post Office—The Town Hall—The Town Clerk—The Terraces—Hindley Street—North Adelaide—The Anglican Cathedral—A City of Churches—Religion and Morals—The River Torrens and its Bridges—Old Parliament House and New Parliament House—The Public Library, Museum, and Art Gallery—The University—The Park-lands—The Suburbs—The Mails—Port Adelaide—Semaphore—Largs Bay—Glenelg—Proclamation Tree—The First Government House—Brighton.

ADELAIDE, besides possessing the nicknames of the "farinaceous village" and the "city of churches," has been described in the columns of a well-known London paper as "a model city"—and in many respects it deserves the compliment. Many Australian cities have been carefully planned and laid out, but it may be doubted whether in any other case such skill has been shown. The good people of Adelaide have reason to be proud of Colonel Light, the officer of the Royal Engineers credited with the design of the city, and to treasure his portrait and his statue. Like all large cities, Adelaide has a great many suburbs, and with them covers a great space of ground; but there is no modern city in which the distinction between city and suburbs is so clearly marked. It is as clear as in the case of cities of old time, which were walled about. The Adelaide walls are park-lands, which are highly valued, and which will be more and more valued as time goes on. According to the familiar illustration, they are the lungs of the city. One accustomed to the crowding of English towns might think that, if anything, Adelaide was over-provided with lungs; but he would also hold that this is a fault, if fault it be, on the right side. The park-lands are in most part still waste lands. Their extent has been too great for them to be laid out as yet, but they cannot be built over.

Adelaide proper consists of two main divisions, North and South Adelaide, separated by the river Torrens and the uneven ground on its banks. Each division has a separate and independent plan, and the park-lands, which surround the whole, also intervene in rich profusion between the two. This intervening space has been used for large public institutions, many of them standing in their own grounds—the railway station, Parliament House, Government House, the Public Library, the University, the Hospital. These, however, may be said to belong to South Adelaide, because they are on the south side of the Torrens, though they lie outside its plan. South Adelaide is an oblong—one mile on the shorter side, and one-third of a mile more on the longer, but any appearance of stiffness in this arrangement is avoided by a prolongation of the southern side and a kind of bulge in the south-eastern corner; yet of this corner it is true, as Mr. Trollope observes, that there is "a regularity even in the irregularity. This terrace, on the map of the town, takes the form of a flight of steps, for nothing so irregular as a sloping or diagonal line has been permitted in the arrangement of the streets." The streets, as in so many colonial cities, are laid out regularly, on the Philadelphia model, parallel and rectangular, and the meridian line has been strictly preserved. The streets run strict north and south, strict east and west. But streets of a mile long, crossed by streets more than a mile long, without any variety, would be intolerably stiff, and an attempt has been made to avoid such stiffness by the introduction of certain squares, which are public gardens—not like London squares, the preserves of families that enjoy a private key. Of these, Victoria Square—at the corner of which stand the Government Offices—is in the very centre of South Adelaide, and the four other squares, with their outward corners rounded, divide the space between the central square and the corners of the town. The five squares are arranged like a card with five pips.

The central street of Adelaide is King William Street, and it is quite appropriate that the main street should be called after William IV., seeing that the city took its

KING WILLIAM STREET.

name from his consort. It is written that the original designer meant King William Street to be rather a residential than a business street, but designers cannot always have their way, and business has gravitated towards King William Street, and now all the chief banks and insurance offices, as well as the Post Office and the Town Hall, are to be found there. As elsewhere, the banks vie with one another in the splendour of their buildings. For a long time, some of them were content to be housed in very poor quarters, but the force of competition has compelled all, one after another, to spend large sums of money upon architecture, to the very great advantage of the appearance of the city.

The two most conspicuous buildings in this part of the town—the Post Office and the Town Hall—demand some description. The foundation-stone of the Victoria Tower of the former was laid by the Duke of Edinburgh on the 5th of November, 1867, upon

ADELAIDE
Supreme Court.
Botanical Gardens.
Museum & Art Gallery.

the occasion of his first visit to Australia. The Post Office is very handsome, as it ought to be, for it cost a great deal of money. There is a large central hall for the use of the public, round which the offices are grouped to which those who have dealings with officials need access. On its suitability to its purpose let us hearken to the opinion of a business man, Mr. H. G. Turner, of Melbourne:—" The central hall, which is ninety feet by thirty-five feet, and sixty-five feet high, is abundantly lighted from the dome, and paved with Minton's tiles. Cool in summer, and protected in wet weather, it presents the beau ideal of a place for the public to do business in; and all requisite information, meteorological, postal, and nautical, is displayed with lavish abundance and electrical promptitude. There are probably not half-a-dozen buildings in all the colonies that can surpass it for architectural merit, and not one for adaptability to its objects." The building is of the Palladian order of architecture, with a tower, to the top of which visitors are taken by zealous residents to see the view. As the lantern for signalling the arrival of the mails at night stands over 150 feet from the ground, there are a good many steps to ascend in order to reach it, but the exertion is amply rewarded, especially if the visitor should desire to understand the geography of his surroundings. The whole plain is visible, from the sea to the Mount Lofty Range, whilst Adelaide, with its suburbs, lies at the feet like a map. The Adelaide Post Office, it should be mentioned, is enriched with a pleasant chime of bells. Both the Post Office and the Town Hall are built of a beautiful white freestone, which is brought from quarries about fifteen miles from the city.

The second tower that is at once seen in Adelaide belongs to the Town Hall, on the other side of King William Street. Here there is a large room used for public meetings and entertainments, and there are the municipal offices. In the Council Chamber there are portraits of some of the early explorers, governors, and city magnates; and the Town Clerk has, with some trouble, made a record of the persons, without a single exception, after whom the streets and squares of the city are named. It has been well said that this functionary, Mr. Thomas Worsnop, is, in a literary sense, the true Recorder of the City. He has published an excellent "History of the City of Adelaide," to which all who desire to write adequately about Adelaide must acknowledge obligations.

In many cases Adelaide is the first Australian city visited by tourists from Europe. Visitors will be interested to notice the importance attached to municipal institutions in the colonies. Stately town-halls and spacious municipal offices are the outward tokens of this importance. These will be found, not only in the capital cities, such as Adelaide, Melbourne, and Sydney, but in much smaller places. The visitor will soon remark the buildings in the numerous suburban cities that cluster round each capital. In this matter Australia may be compared in her newness with the old cities of the Low Countries, though it has not fallen to her lot to have such rare architects as those who built the Hôtel de Ville at Louvain, or that at Ghent. It is in the zeal to exalt city government, and to house it handsomely, that the point of the comparison lies. It is of interest to dwell on this further, for Adelaide was not only the first city in Australia to have a municipality, but, in the proud language of Mr. Worsnop, it is "the birthplace of municipal government in the whole British Colonial Empire."

## THE TERRACES.

King William Street is probably the broadest street in any large town in Australia with the single exception of Sturt Street, Ballarat, and, at its northern end, one of the handsomest streets that can be seen anywhere. In former days it was divided into two parts by Victoria Square, though the square was always bisected by the street that runs from east to west. Traffic was diverted to the right hand and to the left in a manner that was more picturesque than convenient. In a struggle, however, between the picturesque and the convenient the latter always prevails, and now the great central square of the city has been cut up into four small squares, and the broad King William Street passes through its midst. No little regret was felt at the destruction of trees, for trees take long to grow. It certainly seems a pity that all the trees were cut down, and that no compromise was effected by preserving at least some of them in belts. Even now, for the sake of the future, the road crossing the square should be replanted with all convenient speed. Australians, accustomed to the freedom and space of the bush, take an especial pride in broad streets, which are often much wider than is at all necessary. Due care is, no doubt, being taken for the future needs of traffic; but it should be remembered that broad streets, in order to bring out their full beauty, must be planted. Otherwise, the broader the street, the more the dust.

The boundaries of South Adelaide, on each of its four sides, are called Terraces, though the houses are not in a continuous row as in a London terrace. In Adelaide a "terrace" means that there are houses on one side of the road but not on the other. On this account the terraces are popular, and land along them commands a high price. Here we will borrow a description from an account by the literary Melbourne banker before quoted, Mr. H. G. Turner:—

"From the West Terrace there is a fine expansive view over the breezy plains stretching to the ocean beach, and which takes in the shore from Glenelg to Larg's Bay, with the shimmering waters of the gulf beyond. The only encroachments on the park-lands facing this terrace are a reserve for cemetery purposes, which is not maintained in as good order as it should be, and the buildings connected with the Observatory. On the reserves facing South Terrace there are no buildings, while on those fronting the East a very excellent racecourse has been laid out, with a commodious grand stand and the other appurtenances of this popular sport.

"The view from the East Terrace is probably the finest in the city, and many of the houses upon it are indicative of the wealth and taste of their owners. The ever-varying light and shade which animates the picturesque outlines of the Mount Lofty Ranges, facing this terrace, is a continuous delight to the eye. The dark foliage of the olive plantations, contrasting with the brighter green of the orange groves; the sombre eucalyptus and the verdant clump of English deciduous trees, the brightness of the freshly growing crop, shaded off into the darkness of the adjacent gully, and the park-like aspect of the intervening lands, make up a picture of simple Arcadian beauty. In no other city in Australia is the *rus in urbe* so accessible, and to those accustomed to the Yankee-like stir and bustle of Melbourne, it seems incredible that such a peaceful panorama can be enjoyed within almost a stone's-throw of streets that rival some of the shopkeeping centres of trade in the capital of Victoria."

The most fashionable of the terraces, however, is North Terrace. Indeed, by a bull which is perhaps permissible, it has been said that the "West End" of Adelaide is the north. North Terrace is the chief place for professional men, especially doctors. What a number of doctors there seems to be in Adelaide, and how well they appear to

THE ROSARY, BOTANICAL GARDENS.

flourish! On the North Terrace also is situated the Adelaide Club. To the hospitality there so kindly shown many a visitor feels himself indebted.

The streets that run parallel to North Terrace, and nearest to it, are important from a business point of view—Hindley and Rundle for shops and retail trade, Grenfell and Currie for warehouses and wholesale places of business. It may be noted that each of these pairs makes really a single street, for, except King William, no name for a street is carried right through this part of Adelaide. As compared with the breadth of King William Street, these streets are scarcely wide enough for the business done in them; whilst the pavement is certainly too narrow. Some of the shops are large and excellent. Hindley and Rundle Streets have the glory of being the first streets in Adelaide in the order of formation. In Hindley Street is situated the Adelaide Theatre, which was described only three years ago as "undoubtedly the prettiest and best in Australia." Even if it cannot now be rated quite so high, it will hold a forward place, for it is excellently planned and elegantly decorated.

## THE ANGLICAN CATHEDRAL.

Whilst South Adelaide has more and more a tendency to become nothing but a place of business, like the City in London, North Adelaide is, and will most likely continue, a place for residence. It stands higher than the other part of the city, and rises somewhat abruptly from the valley of the Torrens. The eminence is not great in itself, but as in the city of the blind the one-eyed man was king, so in a flat city advantage is naturally taken of rising ground, and the southern edge of North Adelaide is very valuable. Pleasant views can be obtained thence, and from a sanitary point of view the rise in the ground is treasured. The greater part of North Adelaide is laid out in an irregular parallelogram, with a square in the centre, called after the Duke of Wellington. At its south-east corner are two excrescences, two other parallelograms, the lines of which bear no relation to the lines of the main parallels. There are thus produced a few curves pleasant to the eye. As a rule, the parallels in North Adelaide are not too regular, but yet preserve their characteristic.

The Anglican Cathedral (St. Peter's) stands near the entrance to North Adelaide. It is very lofty, and, when completed, will be a fine Gothic church, especially as seen from the inside. The outside is spoilt by the deplorable meanness of the tower, and will remain spoilt unless some sudden accession to the church funds should enable the authorities to build a worthier tower. There is often a difference in the way of regarding a cathedral church; that of the worshippers is different from that

FOUNTAIN IN THE BOTANICAL GARDENS.

of some who are willing to help, but might be described in the words Lord Eldon is said to have used of himself, when he explained that he was "not a pillar of the church, but a buttress—a supporter, but one that never went inside." The former want a church, good for hearing, good for music, suitable for crowded services and majestic functions; the latter want an ornament for the city. If the two objects cannot be combined, it may reasonably be conceded that the former view has the better claim to exclusive consideration.

Adelaide is especially strong in the matter of churches. There is, as we have seen, an Anglican Cathedral—St. Peter's; there is a Roman Catholic Cathedral, of stately proportions, dedicated to St. Francis Xavier; and both the Anglicans and Roman Catholics have plenty of other churches. Moreover, all the denominations are well represented. Perhaps the Presbyterians are not so strong as in some other colonies, for Adelaide is by no means a Scotch colony. There are Scotchmen there, as everywhere else in the world, and, of course, prosperous Scotchmen, but not in any preponderance. Indeed, Adelaide is a well-mixed community, and there is no disproportion either of nationality or of religion.

One of the cardinal ideas of those who founded the colony of South Australia was that it should enjoy the most perfect religious freedom. This idea has been fully carried out. There are those in England who fancy that the absence of an Establishment would produce an absence of religion. A visit to Australia would convince such of their error. To no place can they be recommended to pay their visit sooner than to Adelaide, for in none could they learn the lesson quicker. A glance at the streets of Adelaide shows at once that there has been a rivalry of churches, which, desiring an outward and visible sign of progress and prosperity, have built spacious edifices that are in many cases ornaments to the town, and, where they are not handsome, are very useful. Most of the colonists belonged to the great English middle class, and the denominations specially recruited from that class—the Wesleyans, the Congregationalists, and the Baptists—have numerous adherents, adequate funds, and vigorous life. If one denomination be stronger than another, it is probably the Wesleyan. But it is not only in buildings that religion shows its strength in Adelaide. An Adelaide Sunday is a Puritan Sunday—probably it is more Puritan than in any other Australasian city, except those that are distinctively Scotch. In other matters also, such as having a vigilance committee to look after the morality of young men, Adelaide inclines, not without protests, to this Puritan side in religion. The city, like the colony generally, is quite satisfied with religious equality, and has no hankering after the principle of an Establishment. Even the Anglicans, who hold the same doctrines as the Established Church in England, do not wish it, though they have at times difficulties as to funds that may make them desire endowment.

The intervening space between North and South Adelaide is the part of the city which can lay most claim to beauty. The river Torrens is not in itself a fine river. It has the weakness of many Australian rivers, and seems unable to make a channel for itself all the way to the sea. If reproached upon the score of deficiency of beauty, the river Torrens might well urge in its defence that it has always been very useful to the people of Adelaide. Not thirty years ago the citizens used to rely upon the river for their supply of water, which was retailed by water-cask at a charge of a florin or half-a-crown a load. This very primitive water-supply was superseded by a regular system, the river Torrens being tapped higher up; and this diversion of a stream never very strong naturally diminished its volume. The constant growth in the size of the city has made it necessary that a fresh and larger reservoir should be built. The original dam is about eight miles off; the new reservoir is in the park-lands. It may, however, be conceded that formerly the Torrens, at the part between North and South Adelaide, was not beautiful, and that Mr. Trollope was right in repudiating a laudatory expression which he had heard employed—that it was a pretty stream. But a few years since Adelaide was blessed with a remarkably energetic mayor, who summoned art to the assistance of nature. Just below the town the river has been dammed in such a way as to give the appearance of a broad river, or almost of a lake, to that which used to be an Australian creek. The main road that unites the heart of South to the heart of North Adelaide, itself in a line with King William Street, crosses the Torrens by a fine bridge, with a very broad span. Boating-clubs have been established, and rowing is very popular. Just beyond the river is an oval, used as a cricket and football-ground. On a Saturday great crowds gather there, though the interest taken in athletic sports is hardly so keen as in Melbourne. Besides this central Adelaide Bridge, the river is also crossed by two other bridges, at convenient distances above and below. The lower is called after the Queen—Adelaide is nothing if not loyal—and the higher after the Prince Consort. The latter is not far from the Zoological Gardens; the Victoria Bridge occupies the site of the Ford where, in former days—i.e., before 1861, when the waterworks were completed—the watermen filled their carts. It is described as having been a specially busy spot on the occasion of a fire, when the sum of £5 was awarded to the man who first brought his full water-cart to the scene of the fire.

South of the river, opposite North Terrace, there is a series of institutions, standing in grounds of considerable size. Let us begin at the west end, and take them in turn. The railway-station is not beautiful—few are; it has, however, the great advantage of being central, and is conveniently arranged. Old Parliament House and New Parliament House stand side by side, and form a great contrast. Simplicity marks the old, and splendour will mark the new, when it is finished. Some hold that the expense of the new building is a burden on the shoulders of the colony greater than it is fairly able to bear, for the cost is estimated at over £100,000. This expenditure will certainly give a magnificent building, worthy of any legislative body. The outside is to be of Kapunda marble. Surely, if we take pride in our Parliamentary system of government, the Parliament of a country ought to be well housed. On the other side of the road stands Government House, surrounded by pleasant gardens.

According to law, the "Public Library, Museum, and Art Gallery of South Australia" only came into existence on July 1st, 1884. That was the date fixed by the Act of Parliament for its commencement, but the institutions with the conglomerate title had really existed much earlier under the title of the South Australian Institute. In the final report of the Board of Governors of the Institute, mention is made of the twenty-eight years of its existence, and a claim put forward which no one will refuse to acknowledge—"that the South Australian Institute had done good work in its day, and had been instrumental in scattering the seeds of intellectual cultivation and development far and wide over the colony. The Board hands over the trust to its successors with the earnest hope and full confidence that in the future, with a higher prestige and larger means, they will realise to the utmost the ends for which the South Australian Institute was established in 1856." The South Australian Institute was the product of a society founded in London only a few days after the establishment of the colony. This society, under the title of "the South Australian Literary and Scientific Association," chose eighty-two books in London, and sent this handsome library to the colony. Though books were dearer in 1834 than fifty years later, probably many an individual settler had a larger collection; and having performed this difficult task, the London society seems to have disappeared. These eighty-two books went to a Mechanics' Institute founded to receive them, and the Mechanics' Institute underwent various chances. First it flourished, then it succumbed to a rival subscription library; then there was an amalgamation, and at length, in 1856, by Act of Parliament, the Institute was established. Its first local habitation was in a building in King William Street. As time went on, a better building was erected on North Terrace. As time went on further, newer buildings were required. The very handsome Museum was erected, part of which is now used for the Public Library. A portion of the work of the Institute is continued in the old building by the Adelaide Circulating Library, the books in the Public Library never being allowed to circulate. In the Art Gallery there is already the nucleus of a good collection of pictures.

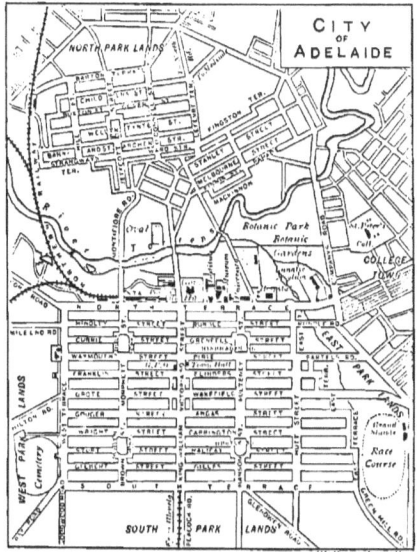

The next building is the University of Adelaide, a description of which will be given under the head of Australian Education. Beyond the University, and in a close proximity to it, which must be very convenient for the medical student, stands the hospital.

In every direction, as the visitor walks about Adelaide, he will in a short time reach the park-lands. This article began with park-lands, and to them must now return. These park-lands are indeed the distinctive feature of Adelaide. There is a total of about 2,000 acres. Those that go round the two parts of the city average about half-a-mile in width. Those that intervene between the two parts are much wider, but also much more irregular in shape. The park-lands are reserved in perpetuity for the use of the people. No private house can ever be built within their bounds, but portions of them are used for public purposes. In the intervening park-

## THE EXHIBITION.

lands, various public buildings are established, and parts are marked off for the use and advantage of clubs and other sections of the people. The last of these institutions is the Exhibition. The Great Exhibition of 1851 in London was only permitted to be built in Hyde Park on condition that at the close of the Exhibition the building should be entirely removed. No such condition has been made in the present case, but the land round Adelaide is not yet quite so valuable as that in London. For all that, the park-lands are zealously watched. More than once there has been a political crisis in South Australia, with a singularly empty exchequer, but no politician has been found to propose the sale of a portion of the people's city domain in order to replenish it. The lands bring in a small revenue, for citizens are allowed to depasture cattle on payment of a small fee. But the glory of the park-lands, if not of all Adelaide, is the Botanical Gardens.

All modern cities have many suburbs, and Adelaide does not prove the rule by exception. People like living away from their business, and enjoying country air, as modern conveniences of locomotion readily permit. Adelaide has the proud pre-eminence of being the first Australian city to really adopt the tram; but, always modest, she has kept herself to the horse-tram, whilst Sydney has steam motors, and Melbourne, much later in the field, uses the continuous cable system. Some of the Adelaide suburbs are commonplace—some are exceedingly pretty. It is unfortunate that, as a rule, the native names have not been preserved. Medindie stands almost alone as keeping such a name. Most of the names of suburbs are Cockney reminiscences, and often of quite middle-class parts of London, such as Islington and Hackney; Norwood, Brompton,

TORRENS LAKE.

PORT ADELAIDE LIGHTHOUSE.

From a commercial and business point of view, the suburbs that serve Adelaide as seaports claim most attention. Adelaide is the Brindisi of the Australian Continent; that is to say, it is the place at which the mails arrive, and are thence distributed by railway through the colonies. By landing the mails at Adelaide, at least a day is saved to Sydney and Melbourne correspondents. Of course, it is easy to imagine places which would give quicker mails—for instance, Port Darwin; but, in spite of the remarkable enterprise of South Australia, it must be many years before the northern territory can be connected by rail with the southern parts of Australia. No doubt a day will come when all Australian letters from Europe will be landed on the northern shore, and that will probably be before the time, which also is surely coming, when the Indian and Australian mails will be conveyed from Calais overland to India, but it need hardly be said that that day has not yet dawned.

In Port Adelaide the city has a splendid harbour. It is perfectly land-locked, and therefore very safe, but unfortunately it is by no means easy of access. Sailing ships which are not in a hurry use the services of a tug and go round to Port Adelaide, but steamers, in connection with which time seems always an object, avoid the Port. With respect to the best place for steamers there is a bitter dispute. One of the great lines that run to Australia uses Glenelg, and the other Semaphore. Not a little jealousy exists between the Orient and the P. and O. lines, and a similar jealousy has been established between their two ports of call. It may be said at once that both seem very pleasant places, rich in seaside villas and baths, just the spots for heat-oppressed citizens to seek ozone—and in the summer season Adelaide can be very hot—but it must be added that neither is a satisfactory port of call. Each is an open roadstead, sometimes acquainted with very rough weather, when passengers, especially ladies, have to be hoisted on board. Each has a long jetty, but in neither case can ocean-going steamers come alongside. In the contest it is generally believed that ultimately Semaphore will win. Glenelg stands by itself. Semaphore has Port Adelaide behind it, and the influence of the Port in all matters maritime is exceedingly strong. A semaphore is properly a signal-post, and, in the days before telegraphs, the arrival of ships used to be signalled across to Port Adelaide by means of flags hoisted at the semaphore, but although this particular method of signalling is now unnecessary and almost obsolete, the whole place has retained the peculiar name. The name, by the way, had once a very good chance of wide fame, as the authors of the well-known operetta *H.M.S. Pinafore* have said that their play was originally christened Semaphore. Semaphore is now a quiet seaside place, stirred once a fortnight into activity by the arrival of a steamer from England; once a fortnight by a departure. Glenelg is a very similar though a rather larger place, with some handsome villas standing in pleasant gardens. In both the train is allowed to run through the streets in American fashion, though a hand-bell, suggestive of muffins, is rung all the time that the train is moving in a street. The railway to Semaphore is a continuation of the line to Port Adelaide. A little above the Port the line, by means of a swing bridge, crosses the broad creek—the word is here used in an English, not an Australian sense—upon which the Port is situated. If it were not for the Port there would have been no Semaphore, and Glenelg, being a little further south, would then have remained in undisputed possession of the steamer traffic. The narrow, sandy tongue of land between the estuary and the Gulf is known as Lefevre's Peninsula, and is about two miles across. A little north of Semaphore is Largs Bay, named probably by some patriotic Ayrshireman, after the place where the Danes were defeated by King Alexander of Scotland nearly 600 years before.

> "Of Largs he saw the glorious plain,
> Where still gigantic bones remain,
> Memorial of the Danish war."*

* Scott: *Marmion*, iii., 24.

Largs, in Ayrshire, is now a fashionable watering-place, with fine houses in front, and dirty, tortuous streets behind. The Largs of South Australia is struggling into existence as a watering-place and a port. It enjoys a long pier and a dock. Probably the importance of the two places, Largs Bay and Semaphore, will increase because of the difficulty that ships experience in reaching Port Adelaide.

Port Adelaide is nearly as old as Adelaide, and it has always tried to keep abreast of the times in the matter of harbour improvements—the deepening of the channel, the removal of rocks, and the construction of wharfs. It has now over 13,000 feet of wharf frontage, adequately provided with steam cranes and all the needful paraphernalia.

Glenelg has an especial claim for consideration, in that it was the place where, more than fifty years ago, the colony of South Australia was proclaimed. The old gum-tree under which Captain Hindmarsh issued the proclamation and took possession of the country is still preserved, under the name of Proclamation Tree, though it is in a very advanced stage of decrepitude. The following is the inscription that it bears:—

> ON THIS SPOT,
> ON THE 28TH DECEMBER, 1836,
> THE COLONY OF
> SOUTH AUSTRALIA
> WAS PROCLAIMED AND ESTABLISHED
> AS A PROVINCE BY
> CAPTN. JOHN HINDMARSH, R.N.,
> THE GOVERNOR THEREOF,
> ACTING IN THE NAME AND ON
> BEHALF OF
> HIS MAJESTY KING WILLIAM IV.,
> IN THE PRESENCE OF THE
> CHIEF OFFICERS
> OF THE GOVERNMENT, AND
> OTHER COLONISTS.
>
> ———
>
> ON THE 28TH DECEMBER, 1857,
> THE RECORD OF THE ABOVE FACT
> WAS HERE PUBLICLY AFFIXED BY
> SIR R. G. MACDONALD, KNT., C.B.,
> GOVERNOR-IN-CHIEF OF THE PROVINCE,
> IN THE
> PRESENCE OF THE ASSEMBLED COLONISTS
> TO COMMEMORATE THE EVENT
> OF THE
> COLONY ATTAINING ITS 21ST YEAR
> AND TO TESTIFY THEIR FEELINGS BY A
> DAY OF PUBLIC REJOICING.
> GOD SAVE THE QUEEN.

This inscription, on a metal plate, was fixed to the tree, it will be observed, on the day that the colony came of age. Grand preparations were made to celebrate the occasion by an enormous picnic in the neighbourhood of the old gum-tree.

When some 20,000 persons had gathered together, some from distant parts of the colony, and all in gay holiday attire, a pitiless storm of rain came on and broke up the entertainment in great confusion.

Perhaps because of this example, the fiftieth anniversary of the foundation of the colony was celebrated in a much more quiet fashion, though in a South Australian December most people would gladly take the ducking in payment for the pleasure of knowing that rain was falling on a dry and thirsty land. On the twenty-first anniversary

PROCLAMATION TREE, GLENELG.

thousands had to wait in the rain for the return of a few omnibuses; on the occasion of the fiftieth, two railways were carrying passengers between Glenelg and the city.

Everything was in a very primitive state when Captain Hindmarsh, the founder of colony, landed. It is recorded that the pianoforte of his wife was floated ashore, but there is no record of its tunefulness after the operation. The first Government House was built by the sailors of H.M.S. *Buffalo*, the ship that had brought him to South Australia. The following is the description given of their handiwork:—" Mud walls, about five feet high; two rooms, of six feet each, without flooring [it is to be presumed six feet square: there certainly was no room for the piano!]; a thatched roof [apparently of reeds]; two doorways, for egress and ingress [to serve as windows as well as doors];

but both fireplace and chimney were lost sight of till the place was built." Luckily, the climate is dry, and cooking operations could be carried on out of doors. It need hardly be said that Glenelg has long ago passed out of its primitive stage, that its houses are admirably built, or that all the comforts of civilisation can be procured there.

Further down the coast than Glenelg is a quiet little seaside place called Brighton, to which, especially in hot weather, those citizens resort who find Glenelg too fashionable or noisy. It has the reputation of being exceedingly quiet; there are people who would say it is dull. Like many other colonial places, it has made a mistake in taking the name of the English seaside town, but it is not so ill-advised as to challenge comparison with the most famous of British watering-places.

## BALLARAT.

Virgin Forest—The Gold Fever—Mounts Buninyong and Warrenheip—Black Hill—The City, the Town, and the Borough—Sturt Street—The Public Buildings—The "Corner"—The Town Hall—The Miner's City—"Our Lake"—The Botanical Gardens—Ballarat East—Bridge Street—The Chinese Quarter—"Hunting the Devil"—The Suburbs—Lal-Lal - Bakery Hill—Bungaree—An Irish Settlement—Bits of Old England.

THE CATHEDRAL.

UP among the hills to the north-west of Melbourne, one hundred miles from the capital by rail, though not seventy as the crow flies, lies Ballarat, the metropolis of the gold-fields, and the second town in order of importance in Victoria. The last census gave the population as nearly forty thousand, and a stranger may see at a glance that the majority of these forty thousand souls are well to do, and that poverty, the bitter, grinding poverty of the Old World, is unknown here. In 1851 the ground on which Ballarat now stands was virgin forest and park-like lands, untouched by the hand of man, barely even visited by him. It is true, it was part of a sheep-run, owned by some brothers named Yuille, but a solitary shepherd, or an occasional tribe of wandering black fellows, were the only human beings who visited the site of what is now a bustling town and an important mining centre.

The Presbyterian minister, Mr. Hastie, was then, and is still, settled at the older town of Buninyong, seven miles away. He gives the following description of the place:—"I often passed the spot on which Ballarat is built, and there could not be a prettier spot imaginable. It was the very picture of repose. There was, in general, plenty of grass and water, and often I have seen the cattle, in considerable numbers, lying in quiet enjoyment after being satisfied with the pasture. There was a beautiful clump of wattles where Lydiard Street now stands, and on one occasion, when Mrs. Hastie was with me, she remarked, 'What a nice place for a house, with the flat in front and the wattles behind.' Mr. Waldie had at that time a shepherd's hut, about where the Dead Horse Gully is, on the Creswick Road, and one day when I was calling on the hut-keeper, he said that the solitude was so painful that he could not endure it; for he saw no one from the time the shepherds went out in the morning till they returned at night. I was the only person he had ever seen there who was not connected with the station."

The aborigines, though not numerous, were treacherous and cunning, and very troublesome, and not only stole anything they could lay their hands on, but murdered, in cold blood, any solitary hut-keeper or lonely shepherd they happened to come across.

In 1851 gold was discovered by a man named Hiscocks, in the little gully near Buninyong which still bears his name, and, as by magic, the low lands round the Yarrowee Creek were crowded by adventurers eager to find the precious metal. They came by thousands and tens of thousands, from all parts of the colonies, and from the uttermost parts of the earth, until soon the whole of the valley was white with their tents. Their watchfires by night lit up the lonely forest, and their presence scared away for ever the dingo and the kangaroo from their wonted haunts. Ballarat, or more

MOUNT BUNINYONG, FROM LAL-LAL.

properly Ballaarat, in aboriginal speech, means a resting-place, but it was a resting-place no longer. He who came in the old diggings days came not to rest, but to work, to work untiringly, from break of day to sunset, sometimes, perhaps, to be rewarded with wealth beyond the wildest dreams of the avaricious, oftener to slave for the merest pittance, still hoping on, if not for a fortune, at least for enough to enable him to go back and live in comfort in his own land. No one came to settle at Ballarat, every man was but a bird of passage, and, at first, no man dreamt of making a home here. Slowly, but surely, this transitory character of the population passed away. The surface diggings were worked out, and men could no longer start on their own account. The claims were sunk deeper and deeper, more capital was required, and more special knowledge. Companies were formed, and gold-mining became a recognised industry, carried on as regularly as cloth-making or coal-mining. Moreover, the land around proved fertile, and suitable for agriculture, and soon every acre was settled, mostly by men of the farmer class. Ballarat became not only a mining centre, but also the market of a large and prosperous agricultural district.

It is a pretty town—a very pretty town—strangers declare. Standing in Sturt Street, and looking east, one sees it is set in an amphitheatre of low eucalyptus-clad ranges, with two larger hills, that serve to break the monotony. Mounts Buninyong and Warrenheip are about two thousand feet above the sea-level, and

THE "CORNER."

some seven miles apart, rising from the ranges —square, solid-looking hills, covered with forest. They are remarkably alike in contour, and hardly to be distinguished one from the other. The inhabitants of Ballarat and the surrounding districts for a long time fondly cherished the idea that these mountains were extinct volcanoes, and proudly showed to visitors the outlines of the old craters. When a popular science lecturer pointed out their error, he was hardly thanked for tearing away the halo of romance which they had contrived to throw around their hills; and forthwith other authorities were consulted, who confirmed the first views upon the subject.

BALLARAT AT TWILIGHT.

"It is not true that second thoughts are best,
But first and third, which are a riper first."

From the top of either Warrenheip or Buninyong, a splendid bird's-eye view is to be had of Ballarat, and a capital idea is to be gained of the straggling way in which the town is built. The ranges which surround the town are for some reason, best known to the early settlers, not called by the quaint, and often pretty, native names, but rejoice respectively in such appellations as the Dead Horse, White Horse, Black Horse, and Magpie Ranges. A spur of the Dead Horse runs right up into the town itself, less than a mile, in fact, from its very centre. Forty years ago Black Hill, as it is called, reared its dark crest, clothed in dense forest, over the lonely gully where now stands Ballarat East, and its steep sides were untouched by the foot of civilised man. But those steep slopes proved rich in gold. The forest has long since disappeared, and the hillside has been tunnelled through and through, burrowed into, cut away, and turned over, till half of it has disappeared. Its former shape has been entirely lost, and Black Hill presents to the town a scarred white face, precipitous in some parts, with mounds of earth, old mining machinery, and heaps of quartz and "mullock,"* which gleam white and look not unpicturesque in the sunshine.

Ballarat is divided into three parts—Ballarat West, Ballarat East, and Sebastopol—the city, the town, and the borough. The West is the aristocratic and business portion of the town. Here are all the best shops, and the best hotels, the lawyers' offices, and the mining exchange. Here, too, are the principal churches—the Anglican and the Roman Catholic Cathedrals, the Presbyterian Kirk, and the new Wesleyan Chapel; and here, too, are all the handsomest houses. A visitor is struck with the neatness of the broad, straight, well-kept streets, running at right angles to one another, and carefully planted with trees—oaks, elms, Oriental plane-trees, Californian pines, and, of course, the blue gum. Sturt Street, the principal street, and one of the three chain roads of the colony, bears off the palm for beauty. It has kept its original width of two hundred feet nearly throughout, and is broader than most of the famous streets of the world. As with the "Unter den Linden," at Berlin, a handsome avenue runs straight up the middle of the street for fully a mile. It strikes one at first as being all of gum-trees, tall and straight, with thick, close foliage, for they have been carefully pollarded in their youth, and not allowed to straggle and grow ragged and untidy, as is the wont of trees of their kind when left to their own devices; but on a second glance it is seen that each gum alternates with a deciduous tree—an oak or an elm, or an Oriental plane-tree. Very pretty and cool this avenue looks in the early summer, before the hot winds have withered and shrivelled the leaves of the foreign trees; and their delicate green makes a lovely contrast to the darker hue of the eucalyptus. These, too, are covered with white blossoms, which fill the air with their aromatic perfume, and which bring into the town great flocks of parrots, rosellas, in all the glory of their gorgeous plumage, blue and green, red and yellow, and parroquets, all clothed in vivid green. These birds whirl in screaming flocks round the gum-trees, feeding on the white blossoms, and, in their turn, proving a sore temptation to the young colonial, who, satchel on back, is wending his way slowly to school, unwilling to leave the bright sunshine. Parrots are easily brought down by "shanghais"—the name in this part of the world for a catapult: but a wise Town Council, having a due regard for the windows, not to say for the persons, of the citizens, has for-

---

* "Mullock," the heaps of waste earth at the mouth of a shaft.

bidden the use of all shanghais within the town, and many a small boy, in the first flush of joy and pride at a successful shot, is compelled to flee from Nemesis in the shape of a stalwart Irish policeman, who, armed with all the terrors of the law, swoops down upon him. In the summer evenings, too, this avenue is much frequented by another set of people. It appears to be the favoured place of the lads and lasses of Ballarat for courting, and the old, old story must have been told again and again under those gum-trees in Sturt Street.

In this street are most of the shops and principal buildings. At the intersection of Lydiard Street, right in the centre of the town, is a monument to the ill-fated explorers, Burke and Wills, a nondescript erection, originally a fountain, but now a lamp-post; and a little farther down, opposite the Post Office, has recently been placed a handsome statue, in white marble, of the poet Burns. What Burns had to do with Ballarat no one seems exactly to know; but since he is there, and much admired, there seems every probability that Tom Moore, also in white marble, will soon join him. The Post Office, on the north side of the street, close to the Burke and Wills monument, is a square white building, to which extensive additions are being made. On the south side is the Mining Exchange—the "Corner," as it is popularly called. Here the sharebrokers may be seen transacting their business in the open street, and on busy days stretching right across to the gardens that adorn the middle, buying and selling, shouting and gesticulating as if their lives depended on it, as their livelihood most undoubtedly do. Unluckily, it is not always busy times on the Corner, and on a day when shares are down and stocks are dull, the Corner men are hard put to it to employ their time. A Chinaman trudging along, under the heavy weight of his baskets full of vegetables, is eagerly seized upon, and his cauliflowers and cabbages put up to auction, while John himself squats down on the pavement, a smile on his stolid, yellow countenance, for he knows that whatever the result he will be a gainer by the transaction. The dark Indian trader from Cashmere, plodding patiently along with his great white bundle on his back, can now do a brisk business, while a load of wood—be it the humble one-horse load, or a great waggon that requires at least six horses to bring it down from the ranges—is a perfect godsend, offering as it does excellent opportunities for a raffle, the driver meanwhile, leaning carelessly against the wheel, cracking his long whip in a most artistic manner to wile away the time pending the completion of the bargain. The honey merchant and the bird hawker, too, find for their wares a ready sale among the good-humoured Corner men.

Higher up is the Town Hall, a fine building with a lofty tower, from which a splendid view of the surrounding country can be obtained; and higher up still are the Roman Catholic Cathedral and the principal Presbyterian Church. Both of these are substantial buildings of bluestone, whose dinginess is relieved in the case of the latter by a spire and facings of white freestone, while round St. Patrick's Cathedral are handsome, well-grown English trees. The Hospital, still farther up Sturt Street, is a large white building, set in a pretty, well-kept garden, and is very old, as buildings go in Ballarat, having been begun just after the Eureka riots in 1855. The need of some place for the sick and wounded was then sorely felt, and this led to steps being taken for the erection of a hospital. The site chosen, though only three-quarters of a mile from the present Post Office, in the very heart of the town, was then in such thick bush that, strange as it may seem to a modern traveller on the well-kept highway, it is recorded that many persons lost their way between it and the little township on the banks of the creek. All up Sturt Street are shops and houses and buildings; and improvements are going on everywhere. The streets are full of busy life, though not the life of a metropolis; rather it is the ordinary traffic of a well-to-do, up-country town—loads of hay and straw from the agricultural districts of Learmonth and Windermere, carts laden with potatoes from Buninyong and Warrenheip, and great loads of wood on creaking waggons that require at least six or eight horses to move them. An occasional bullock-dray, laden with wool bales or wattlebark, drawn by its patient team, reminds one of the outlying stations, whilst a great locomotive moving from the foundry where it was manufactured, to be delivered at the railway station in Lydiard Street, connects the old life with the new.

Everywhere are evidences of the chief industry of the town, and a stranger cannot help feeling that Ballarat was made by the miner, and is still, to a certain extent, the miner's city. Here and there, in all directions, even in Sturt Street itself, are mounds of upturned earth, red and white, and not unpicturesque in themselves, but often grass-grown and deserted. Sometimes the remnants of the old wooden buildings that protected the mouth of the shaft are still left standing, utterly dilapidated and moss-grown, but yet oftener even that has disappeared, and all that remains is an old iron truck, or a chain or two, eaten away by rust, and the tall mound, twenty, thirty, or even fifty feet high. Sometimes, particularly in Ballarat East, these wrought-out workings are just those of the surface diggings, and there the ground—acres of it—has been turned over and over. No shafts have been sunk very deep, so there are no tall mounds of gravel and quartz to glisten in the sunshine, but the whole surface presents the appearance of some desolate graveyard, where no kindly hand has planted gardens, or raised monuments to the dead.

Many of the workings, both old and new, are of great extent, and many parts of Ballarat are tunnelled under by drives, where, far below the surface, the miner earns his daily bread. Many of these drives are deserted, but others are in full swing. Generally they are far enough below the surface for the safety of those above, but not always, and it is no uncommon thing to see houses out of the perpendicular, and going to rack and ruin, because the earth has given way beneath them. Sites may be observed where no attempt has been made to build, because the ground is rotten and unsafe. In Ballarat East, St. Paul's Anglican Church has twice come to grief. Once the whole body of the church went, and left the tower standing alone. It was rebuilt on the other side of the tower, and, then, to the astonishment and disgust of the congregation, the earth opened, and if it did not exactly swallow up the chancel, it at least dropped it down too many feet below the rest of the church to allow of a comfortable celebration of Divine Service. And at the present moment the destruction of St. Paul's is again threatened by mining operations. The old Supreme Court, in Lydiard Street, was another place that suffered, and had to be abandoned, as it was impossible to add to it, on account

LAKE WENDOUREE.

of its foundations being undermined. Appropriately enough, it is now used as the School of Mines. Those wrought-out workings, which are near the centre of the town, are fast being levelled and carted away, as the demand for building sites becomes greater, and pretty cottages and blooming gardens take their place. Ballarat is sometimes called the Garden City, and seeing that its chief industry is gold-mining, this might seem strange, were it not that nowhere do shrubs, flowers, and trees flourish so well as on the levelled workings of the wrought-out claims, where the ground has been trenched and dug over and over again. Mining is now generally carried on by large companies, which employ hundreds of men, and machinery in itself worth a small fortune. Digging by one man, or by small parties, is not often seen within the precincts of the town. And yet this mining on a small scale has not been quite abandoned in Ballarat. In the Main Road, Ballarat East, there may yet be seen small parties of men working in co-operation, and leading that independent life which appears to possess a vast charm for the old gold-miner.

Going west, up Sturt Street, the shops gradually grow fewer and fewer, till when the avenue comes to an end, even the smallest of them have disappeared altogether, and villa residences take their place. Here the character of the street changes. In the town the City Council have laid it out with an avenue in the centre, and two roads, one on each side. Here, beyond the shops, are two avenues, one on each side, with a road in the middle, which runs for another mile—quite, in fact, into the open country. These avenues are of Canadian elms and silver poplars, and as yet are young, but they promise to be in time as handsome as their well-grown sisters in the centre of the town.

To the west of Ballarat, within the bounds of the city, lies what in the eyes of its inhabitants is its greatest attraction. On arrival, the first question asked of a stranger is not "Have you seen the mines?" but "Have you seen our lake?" And yet, after all, "our lake" is but a small sheet of water. Lake Wendouree (accent on first and third syllables), known in the old days as Yuille's Swamp, is about four miles round, and not more than a mile across; but, though not a large lake, it is certainly a very pretty one. It is enclosed in a reserve well planted with a variety of trees, while all round the margin of the lake itself are rows of weeping willows, which thrive wonderfully. On the eastern or town side of the lake are most of the boathouses, the number of which shows how much this sheet of water is appreciated. Twenty or thirty small yachts are there, miniature steamboats ply for hire, and on a public holiday the little lake is crowded with every imaginable kind of craft, from the tiny canoe with its solitary occupant, to the steamer crowded with men, women, and children, of a more sociable disposition. Strange to say, the lake lies higher than a great part of Ballarat, so that from the deck of one of the steamers there is on a fine day a glorious view. The town itself, save for the houses that surround the lake, is barely visible, but the hills beyond stand out clearly, and bound the horizon. To the north is Mount Rowan, a conical, treeless hill, whose softly rounded outlines and vivid green form a pleasing contrast to the stern squareness of Buninyong and Warrenheip, and the darker eucalyptus-clad ranges which bound the picture on the east. In the foreground the white cliffs of Black Hill gleam in the sunlight, and nearer still are the weeping willows at the water's edge. On the western side are the Botanical Gardens, where foliage of every shade and hue meets the eye. Great care has been exercised in laying out these gardens, and though the oldest oak there has barely reached his majority, trees grow more quickly in Victoria than in their native England, and oaks and elms, poplars and ash-trees, begin to make a good show. Much of the grounds is, strictly speaking, not garden at all, but park-like land, carefully planted with trees. Here on Sundays and other holidays the good people of Ballarat come to hold high festival, to picnic, and to thoroughly enjoy themselves. Every variety of deciduous tree is found, and numbers of the fir tribe of all descriptions, and from every part of the world. Here and there, too, remain, by way of contrast, an old gum-tree, or a she-oak, the latter in its ragged greyness looking strangely out of place among the brighter-hued trees from other lands. Right at the back of the gardens is an avenue of golden wattles, which, in the springtime, make the air heavy with their delicious perfume.

As we look round on the pretty scene, it is hardly possible for us to conceive that thirty years ago these gardens were thick bush land, the haunt of the dingo and the kangaroo, and that the bright little lake was a dismal swamp overgrown with reeds and rushes, looked on askance by the blacks as the reputed home of the mysterious "bunyip," and a place where the digger from the canvas township down by the creek might be sure of bagging a black swan or a wild duck for his evening's meal. The wild duck and the black swan still visit Wendouree periodically, and are carefully protected by the City Council, which makes every endeavour not only to preserve the native birds and animals that already make the lake their home, but to add fresh specimens to the list, and in every way to increase the attractiveness of the lake. There is a story told that one of the City Fathers, who, having been to Europe, had seen the wonders of the Old World, was desirous of introducing Venetian gondolas, which he thought would pay well, and prove a great attraction. At a meeting of the City Council, without describing a gondola, except by name, he proposed that they should import at least a dozen. Then arose another Councillor. He also was in favour of progress, and highly approved of the idea, being as anxious as anyone to add to the attractions of the lake; but, like John Gilpin's wife, he "had a frugal mind," and thought a dozen far too many to import at once—the climate might not agree with them—let the City Council import a couple to begin with, and then they might breed! This novel description of breeding has not yet been attempted at Ballarat, and the lake has no gondolas.

Beyond the Corner, Sturt Street slopes steeply down, and at the bottom of the hill Ballarat West comes to an end and Ballarat East begins. The change from the new to the old town is most striking. Bridge Street, the principal street of Ballarat East, is a continuation of Sturt Street, but is only a third of its width, and is consequently far too narrow to admit of any ornamentation in the shape of trees or gardens, such as adorn its younger rival. It consists almost solely of shops, where a great deal of business is done. On Saturday night—market-day—so dense is the crowd from end to end, that vehicles are not permitted to pass down the street. Near the middle it is cut in half by the Yarrowee Creek, once a limpid mountain stream, known as the river Leigh, rushing down from the hills amidst rocks and ferns, creepers and mosses, but now a huge gutter, well boarded over, into which the drainage of city and town is emptied. Bridge Street lies very low—is, in fact, the lowest part of Ballarat, and in the

THE LAL-LAL FALLS.

olden days was visited periodically by floods, which swept out the shops, and drove the inhabitants into their upper storeys. At first, beyond an abundant use of profane language, not by the way an uncommon thing on a gold-field even without a flood, nothing seems to have been done, but of late years the Water Commission has built a large dam across a gully about four miles from Ballarat, and so created at the Gong-Gong a pretty reservoir for the storage of water and relieved the people of Ballarat of their annual flood. Ballarat East being the site of the old mining camp, the streets do not preserve the same regularity as in the city, for having followed the lines of the diggers' tents, they twist and turn, and bisect one another without respect to order or convenience. Bridge Street branches off into two streets, Victoria Street—or the Melbourne Road, as it is generally called—and the Main Road. Going up the latter, which is a copy of Bridge Street, only dingier, we come to the Chinese quarter. There are about two thousand Chinamen " on " Ballarat—let the reader notice the use of the preposition; on a gold-field, therefore on Ballarat—and they are, of course, common enough in all parts of the town, for the yellow-faced, blue-bloused vegetable hawker, with his neatly-coiled pigtail and his eternal smile, is an everyday visitant in most households, where he is hailed with delight by the children, and trusted implicitly by the house-mistress, who vaunts the superiority of her John over everybody else's John. Here, down in Ballarat East, is John's abiding-place. The Chinese camp itself is simply a collection of tumble-down bark huts, built without the slightest attempt at regularity, and sadly in need of repair.

From the ridge-poles of most of the huts are to be seen long strips of meat and fish drying in the sun, while the family utensils, scanty in the extreme, are ranged outside the doors. There are plenty of children playing about, for though there are no Chinese women, a certain class of Europeans seem to have no objection to John Chinaman as a spouse, and the little half-caste children are, as a rule, very good looking. The Chinese are not confined to the camp, but all along the Main Road

THE POST OFFICE.

their shops are to be seen full of china, common English ornaments, and unsavoury-looking eatables; outside swings the sign, a long coloured board, on which, in quaint Chinese characters, are painted the owner's name and occupation. John Chinaman makes, but he does not mend. Many of these shops have their shutters up, and the whole place has a generally tumble-down, uncared-for appearance. You may, and often do, see spruce, clean, neat Chinamen, but their houses are invariably out of repair, and sadly in need of the coat of paint which they are never likely to get.

In former days there was at Ballarat a Joss-house, and the Joss was sumptuously lodged among gold and scarlet banners, and much tinsel-coloured paper, and sweet-scented sandal-woods, but the whole, being very combustible, one day caught fire and was burned to the ground, the Joss himself being consumed in the flames. Since then the new Joss has been much more humbly lodged, the Chinese being of opinion that as he could not take care of his finery, it was hardly worth while supplying him with more of it.

A quaint Chinese custom, called " Hunting the Devil," is thus described in one of the local papers:—" The Chinese residing in the district had a high time of it at midnight on Sunday, the occasion being the annual ceremony known as 'hunting the devil.' A huge fire was lit in the yard of the Joss-house at Golden Point, and two or three cooks were in an adjoining shed engaged in fashioning the many mysterious dishes of which the Orientals are so fond, one, it is said, being a pie of roasted tom-cat, which is believed to confer on those partaking of it many virtues. The priest chanted some Chinese poetry in a weird sort of way, and several others accompanied him on the tom-tom and other musical (?) instruments. The scene was such an extraordinary one as might well have been calculated to frighten his Satanic Majesty away did he happen to be in the neighbourhood. The festivities were taken part in by about one hundred Celestials, who frequently adjourned to the Joss-house and bowed to Joss; then adjourning to a couple of adjoining rooms for a smoke of opium. After all was over, about £30 worth of poultry, pastry, &c., subscribed for by the richer Chinese, was distributed amongst their poorer countrymen, who came from far and near to receive the luxuries."

In Ballarat East are many worked-out diggings, notably along the Buninyong Road, In the old days, so rich were these diggings that they were known as the Jewellers' Shops, and it is related, as a proof of their wealth, that two men working for six weeks in one of these claims made, *as wages*, eight pounds weight of gold apiece. Now they are absolutely deserted, save for an occasional "hatter,"* Chinaman, or European, who finds it worth his while to wash "tailings." That it *is* worth while, especially for a Chinaman, who can live on less than a white man, is very evident.

In the old days men were more careless, and left behind them much that is counted valuable nowadays. Many of the roads in Ballarat are made with the refuse quartz left as valueless by the miners, and as the quartz is gradually ground down to powder by the constant traffic, men find it pays them to wash the sweepings of the roads for the specks of gold it is sure to contain. As soon as this became generally known, the roads were in danger of being swept bodily away, and the Town Council found it necessary to frame a bye-law forbidding the sweeping of the roads by anyone but the authorised town scavengers. Nevertheless, on the Buninyong Road, almost any evening, may be seen men, Chinamen generally, shovelling up the dust and mud, in order to wash it for gold. This is, perhaps, the foundation of the belief that in Ballarat the streets are paved with gold.

Beyond Ballarat East lie many little townships, or rather hamlets, which owe their origin to the early gold-seekers. Canadian and Magpie, Napoleon and Durham—so varied are the names—all lie within a short distance of Ballarat towards Buninyong, itself a pretty little town, at the foot of the hill of the same name. It is fully ten years older than Ballarat, and, unlike it, does not owe its origin to the gold. The place was situated on the old bullock-dray road to Melbourne, and about 1841 a public-house was put up there as a resting-place for the drivers of stock. Round this a little hamlet gradually sprang up; for many men, both bullock-drivers and others, found it convenient to leave their wives and children in some place where they were safe from the prowling aboriginal, and the other dangers of the bush. But the discovery of gold killed Buninyong.

* "Hatter," a man working alone on wrought-out and deserted claims—hence any man working and living alone. A man working alone on a new gold-field is, however, called a prospector.

It is still a pretty little town, nestling up against the hillside, but no business is done there. Its streets are empty, and no house has been built for years. As it was in 1850, so it is now; progress has passed it by, and the inhabitants of its prosperous neighbour call it in derision the "ancient village." Buninyong is an aboriginal word, meaning "knee hills," and the mountain was so called by the black fellows, because it was supposed by them to resemble the raised knees of a man lying on his back.

Leaving the little town, and skirting the eastern side of the hill, the road passes through some very pretty country, mostly agricultural, till about twenty miles from Ballarat it comes to another little township, that of Lal Lal, the aboriginal term for falling water. Lal Lal is on a creek of the same name, and the Falls there are a favourite place for picnic parties from Ballarat. In fact, this is the furthest limit for them. No one on a day's pleasuring bent goes further, by road at least, than Lal Lal. Once a year, on New Year's Day, a race meeting takes place, and thousands of people visit the Falls. Unfortunately, like most of Australia's rivers, the creek is nearly dry at that season of the year. It is possible, by a judicious use of stepping-stones, to cross dryshod, while it is always easy, by taking off shoes and socks, to wade, so that the Falls on the 1st of January are not at their best. Still, the water falls over rocks at least one hundred feet high, and makes a cheery babble among the stones beneath. It is pleasant on a hot summer's day to lie down among the ferns and scrub at the bottom of the gully, and with the cloudless blue sky above to listen to the murmur of the waters and the drowsy hum of the insects, and watch the sunlight making delicate tracery with the fern fronds on the stones and rocks that guard the creek. Far away, down the gully, you can see waving corn-fields, and range after range of wooded hills, which fade away in the blue distance. To the left, too, is Buninyong, the hill to whose side it clings, hardly to be recognised as the one which overlooks Ballarat.

If, instead of leaving Ballarat by the Main Road, you choose the other branch of Bridge Street, the Melbourne Road, you ascend the steep slopes of the hill, Bakery Hill, of diggings days' notoriety, and find yourself in a broad street, as wide, indeed, as Sturt Street, bounded on each side by an avenue of gum-trees. The street is not otherwise remarkable. The houses are for the most part one-storeyed brick cottages, set in nice little gardens, just the kind that are described in auctioneers' advertisements as "eligible villa residences." About a mile from Bridge Street is the Orphan Asylum, a large brick building, on the very outskirts of the town; around it are the wrought-out workings of the old Eureka lead, and just behind it, not half a mile away, is the Eureka monument, erected on the very site of the Eureka Stockade.

Leaving the Orphan Asylum, and passing under the arch of the Geelong and Melbourne Railway, you find that the town has been left behind, and that you are in the open country. Warrenheip, which means in the aboriginal tongue "emu-feathers," as the trees upon it were supposed by the blacks to resemble the plumage of that bird, is close at hand, and the road takes you fairly into the district of Bungaree and the Bullarook Forest. Here is some of the finest land in the colony—rich chocolate soil—in which potatoes and corn grow to perfection, and which, in some parts, is worth £60 an acre. Most of the first settlers in Bungaree were, for some unknown reason, Irish, and

Irish they have remained to the back-bone. Mostly Roman Catholics, and hanging together as they do, they have become quite a power in the land, and as they belong to the electorate of Ballarat East, their vote is enough to turn an election, and is consequently eagerly sought by would-be M.P.'s. They generally contrive to make things "warm" for the unfortunate candidate for Parliamentary honours who has earned their displeasure. Never an election passes but the unpopular candidate has received some marks of their favour in the shape of rotten eggs, dead cats, or stale cabbages, while lucky is he whose buggy has not been smashed, nor his scrutineers beaten. It is related of one unfortunate man, whom they had put out, that after the declaration of the poll, rising to address the electors, with wrath and bitterness in his heart, he began—"Gentlemen of Ballarat,

CHINAMEN'S HUTS AT GOLDEN POINT.

and savages of Bungaree!" But spite of their addiction to whisky at election times and on market-days, the men of Bungaree are to be applauded for the industry and vigour with which they have converted the heavily-timbered forest lands into fertile farms and rich pasture; and it is hardly necessary to add that these sturdy Irish farmers have brought to their new home under the Southern Cross the hospitality and warm-heartedness that have ever distinguished their countrymen in all lands.

Ballarat is surrounded on all sides by small townships, which, like Ballarat itself, owe their origin to the miners, and are mainly dependent on the gold for their existence. Creswick, about eleven miles to the north, connected with Ballarat by railway, has about four thousand inhabitants, and several paying claims; and twelve miles beyond it, on the same line of railway, is Clunes, a town of about the same size, and greatly resembling it. Kingston and Smeaton are small hamlets among the hills that surround Creswick, and not only is gold found there, and paying claims worked, but the land is rich.

Still smaller are Smythesdale and Scarsdale, hamlets to the south of Ballarat, which, set among scrubby ranges, where the land is poor, depend entirely on the yield of gold for their existence. To the west of Ballarat the character of the country completely changes, and at Learmonth and Burrumbeet, instead of thickly-wooded ranges, we see softly-rounded, conical hills isolated one from another, and for the most part

THE CITY, FROM BLACK HILL.

treeless. This formation begins at Mount Rowan, about four miles from Ballarat, and behind it is Dowling Forest, which is not, and never was, a forest at all, but rolling, park-like lands, entirely free from undergrowth, and with pretty trees dotted here and there. Here, in Dowling Forest, at the foot of another hill, Mount Pisgah, is the racecourse; and the people of Ballarat claim for it that, if it is not the most important, it is at least the prettiest course in the colony. Learmonth and Burrumbeet are little agricultural townships on the shores of lakes five miles apart, the one thirteen and the other fourteen miles from Ballarat. Lake Learmonth is a pretty little lake about the same size as Lake Wendouree, and though no Town Council has made it the object of its care, its beauties are far greater, for it is embosomed among hills whose gently swelling slopes come down to the water's edge, and are mirrored in its shallow depths. The country is purely agricultural, the earth has never been turned up in the greedy search for gold, and the little township on the margin of the lake, surrounded by farms, with their neat hedges of gorse, privet, or thorn, and their well-grown English trees, reminds Englishmen, they say, more of home than any other place about Ballarat. At Burrumbeet the scene is more desolate: the hamlet is on the borders of a lake thirty miles round, and the farms appear larger and more scattered. Few persons ever venture on the lake, for it is deep and treacherous, subject to sudden squalls, which are dangerous in the extreme, and more than one victim lies beneath its brackish waters. Both Learmonth and Burrumbeet send rich stores of grain and farm produce to Ballarat, and much of the business of all these little towns finds its way to the Golden City in their midst.

Mining is, of course, a very fluctuating source of wealth, but more leads are being discovered and opened up, and the gold-fields of Ballarat are far from being exhausted. The districts round are fertile, and every day sees land increase in value; and thus, rich in mines, and girdled with farms, and its situation high among the hills giving it a much more bracing air than that of Melbourne, so that it is becoming quite a sanatorium for all parts of Victoria, the place has before it, its people hope, a future of great prosperity.

GOLD MINERS' TOOLS.

## THE EUREKA STOCKADE.

Bakery Hill—Desolation—Mutterings before the Storm—A Miscarriage of Justice—The Fate of the Eureka Hotel—The Reform League—The Meeting on Bakery Hill—Declaration of War—The Stockade—The Night Attack—An Awful Scene—The Sequel.

THE greater part of Ballarat East is built on the low-lying flats of the Yarrowee Creek, which are bounded on the west by the plateau on which stands Ballarat West, while on the east it is overlooked by Bakery Hill. Bakery Hill is now much built over, but behind the houses the red turned-up earth and the deserted workings still bear witness to the industry of the early miners. Here among the worked-out and abandoned claims, about half a mile behind the Orphan Asylum, is situated the Eureka Stockade reserve—a reserve set apart by the Town Council as a memorial of the historic fight between the diggers and the authorities on the morning of Sunday, 3rd of December, 1854. Uncared for, and enclosed only by a white picket-fence, sadly in need of a coat of paint, there is nothing to mark the reserve from the surrounding diggings, but close to the street—Eureka Street—which in the old days was the track followed by the bullock-drays from Melbourne, stands a blue stone monument, whose only beauty consists in its severe simplicity and solid strength. Seemingly the Town Council have already more than half repented the building of that monument, for it is unfinished and neglected, and the guns which are to stand at the four corners have never even been placed on their carriages, but lie rusting and half buried in the grass-grown earth. There is no beauty about the place; the native trees have long since disappeared, no kindly hand has planted others, and even the grass finds but scanty nourishment among the stones and rubble thrown up by the miners. No one lives there, few people go there, and only the old residents remember the early days when gold first "broke out" at Ballarat. A stranger may show a passing interest in the place, and then for his benefit is told once again the half-forgotten story of the Eureka Stockade.

Long before the fight at Ballarat there had been murmurings and discontent on the gold-fields. The license fee was high at first, 30s. a month, then double that, and afterwards 30s. again, besides which the digger was required to produce his license whenever it was demanded by the Commissioner, or by any of the troopers. Thirty shillings a month was an exorbitant sum; many a man could not make so much at such uncertain and untrustworthy work as gold-digging, and have enough for his necessary expenses, though doubtless many could have paid it easily. Then arose the difficulty of collecting this unpopular poll-tax. Men would not pay willingly, and the troopers therefore had to collect it by force. It is laid to their charge that they used more violence than was absolutely necessary. Certain it is that the difficulty of collecting the license fees became greater and greater as time went on. Armed troopers, in small parties, swooped down on the diggers at unexpected times, and a cry of "Traps! traps!" was sufficient to send every man flying for refuge to his claim, with intent to there remain hidden by friendly mother earth till the coast was clear. Matters were in this strained state not only at Ballarat, but on every gold-field throughout the colony, when a new police magistrate for

Ballarat, or rather, as it was then called, the "district of Buninyong," was appointed. He was a tall, good-looking man, with the manners and address of a gentleman, but was utterly unscrupulous, and in fact was, as the diggers declared, a "thorough bad lot."

On Specimen Hill, a little ascent over against Bakery Hill, was a small hotel, or rather shanty, half wood and half calico, kept by a man named Bentley. This place was in no good repute, but offering as it did the attractions of bowling-alley, skittles, billiards, and unlimited liquor so long as there was money to pay for it, it was much patronised by the diggers, and was open, as a rule, and generally crowded, both day and night. Much, of course, of the diggers' hard-won gains found its way into Bentley's pocket, but beyond bestowing a few hearty curses on the money-grubbing publican, they would not have grumbled at that. Bentley, however, was generally believed—and the popular impression has never been contradicted—to be the creature of the gentlemanly Police Magistrate, who received most of his profits, or at the very least shared them. To this shanty, then dignified by the name of the Eureka Hotel, there came one night a young man named Scobie, who to his surprise found it shut up. As this was contrary to custom, he beat at the doors, shouted, and created such a disturbance as finally had the effect of bringing out not only the landlord, but two or three other men. A scuffle ensued, Scobie was assaulted, and died soon afterwards of his wounds. Then Bentley and the others who had taken part in the disturbance were brought before the police magistrate and the two resident Commissioners, and, in spite of the remonstrance of the junior Commissioner, and to the astonishment and disgust of the diggers, were acquitted.

So high ran the popular indignation at this miscarriage of justice, that on the 12th October, 1854, a public meeting was called to consider the best method of bringing the culprits to justice. The meeting was held just outside the Eureka Hotel, and on the very spot where Scobie had met his death. A large crowd collected, and the camp officials, not unnaturally fearing some act of violence, sent a guard of police to protect the hotel, with its obnoxious landlord. Several men rose up and addressed the diggers. At first it seemed as if things might pass off quietly, but the speeches grew more and more inflammatory, the crowd increased rapidly, and at last Bentley, who evidently considered discretion was the better part of valour, was seen to leave the back of the building, mount his horse, and set off at full gallop for the police camp, with the intention both of saving his life, which he evidently considered in danger, and of sending more help to the police stationed at his hotel. His flying figure and terror-stricken face as he raced down the gully which separated Specimen Hill and Bakery Hill from the camp on the opposite plateau attracted the attention of those diggers who had not attended the meeting, and leaving their holes and their tents, they joined the crowd in front of the Eureka Hotel, which must by that time have numbered nearly ten thousand men. For a moment the issue seemed doubtful. But the slightest thing sways a crowd. A boy, thoughtlessly, more in sport than in earnest, took up a stone, and flung it at the glass lamp which hung in front of the hotel, smashing it to atoms. The fate of the Eureka Hotel was decided. As the glass fell jingling down on the stones beneath, from a hundred throats burst the cry, "Down with the place! down with it! Burn the whole place!" And the excited mob rushed on the house. It was carried in a moment; such a multitude was irresistible. The police gave way at once, and the place swarmed with men whose blood was up, and who in their indignation wrecked the house in less than five minutes. Then one man, to finish the work, gathered an armful of paper and other combustibles, and set light to them in the windward corner of the bowling-alley. In one moment the place, built as it was of canvas and wood, dry as tinder now with the suns of early summer, was one mass of flames, and in less than a quarter of an hour not a vestige

THE EUREKA STOCKADE MONUMENT (FROM THE DESIGNS)

remained. Then the diggers, hearing the tramp of the soldiers and police coming to the rescue, quietly dispersed, fully satisfied with the vengeance they had taken.

But the Government could hardly let this flagrant act of disorder pass unnoticed. It was impossible to punish eight thousand men, yet the difficulty was to find the ringleaders. It was no easy task to pick them out from among so many, and yet some there must have been who were more to blame than the rest.

Finally, three men were pitched upon. It was urged by the rioters that this was an unfair choice, for though one of them had been present at Bentley's Hotel, yet, far from assisting, he had used his best endeavours to dissuade the people from taking the law into their own hands; and that, as for the other two, they had never been there at all. What was the truth upon this subject it is impossible to say after this space of time, but the magistrates disagreed with popular opinion, and the three men were committed for trial. Bail was speedily found, and a large crowd, awaiting the prisoners opposite the police camp, escorted them back to the township in the gully with many shouts of defiance, and much firing of pistols into the air.

Meanwhile the authorities in Melbourne, seeing that something was seriously wrong on the Ballarat gold-fields, sent a special Board of Commissioners to inquire into the affray by which Scobie lost his life, the result being that the police magistrate was dismissed, whilst Bentley and his associates were sentenced to three years on the roads. The diggers, however, were not satisfied with this tardy justice. They wanted manhood suffrage; they wanted short Parliaments; and, above all, they wanted the abolition of the license fee, and the liberation or acquittal of the three prisoners. These three men were—wisely, perhaps, considering the state of popular feeling—brought to trial in Melbourne, and as the jury recommended them to mercy, were sentenced to terms of imprisonment varying from three to six months.

At this, indignation in Ballarat knew no bounds. A Reform League had been formed to air the grievances of the diggers, of which League the Secretary, Mr. Humffray, was a man of moderate views, sincerely desirous of attaining reasonable ends by moderate means. But there were wilder spirits than his in the League, disaffected Irishmen and foreigners—Italians, Frenchmen, and Germans—who would stick at nothing, and by them the Secretary was regarded with dislike and suspicion. As soon as the conviction of the prisoners was known in Ballarat, Humffray went to Melbourne and procured an interview with Governor Hotham, who intimated that if a proper memorial were sent to the Government the prisoners might be released. But the turbulent spirits in the League, distrusting Humffray, sent delegates of their own, and on the 25th of November two men, an Irishman and an Englishman, arrived in Melbourne to *demand* the release of the prisoners. Such a demand was, of course, refused by Governor Hotham and his Ministers. Anxiously the diggers at Ballarat awaited the return of their delegates, and a monster meeting was called for the 29th of November, on Bakery Hill, so that the members of the League, and all others interested, might hear their reports.

Bakery Hill on the 29th presented a scene of the wildest excitement. The sky was cloudless, and the sun shone warm and brilliant. To the east was Warrenheip, its virgin forest still untouched, while to the west, on the opposite plateau, could be seen the white tents of the Government camp peeping between the trees. All the trees were gone by this time from Bakery Hill. Here and there might be seen a stump burnt and blackened, but the surface of the hill itself was covered with upturned earth thrown out from the claims, while here and there was a digger's tent, with his simple household possessions ranged outside. Down in the gully beneath were the soldiers and police, drawn up in order, ready, in case of any outbreak, to at once quell it. On top of the hill a platform had been erected, and over this, for the first time, floated the insurgent flag, the stars of the Southern Cross on a blue ground. On this platform the chief members of the League took their stand with the delegates, who were to deliver their reports, and around it surged a crowd of over twelve thousand people, men from every nation under the sun, whom lust of gold had brought to this out-of-the-way corner of the earth. Fair-haired Swedes and dark-eyed Italians, fiery Frenchmen and phlegmatic Germans, canny Scotchmen and reckless Irishmen, miners from the tin mines of Cornwall, and pickpockets from the slums of London, together with "old hands" from Van Diemen's Land and New South Wales. The majority were young, or men in the prime of life, and almost all were diggers, clad alike in the ordinary garb of a digger, the flannel shirt, trousers tucked into their long boots, and slouch hat, while all, or almost all, carried arms—revolvers and long knives. The meeting was a turbulent one; the diggers were wild with a sense of injustice and injury, and the speeches from the platform were not calculated to calm them. Peter Lalor addressed the meeting, and so did the returned delegates from Melbourne. Speeches were also made by Frederic Vern, a Hanoverian by birth, and a little red-haired Italian named Carboni Raffaello, to whose being conspiracy was essential, and whom, on account of his gift of tongues, Peter Lalor, the undoubted leader, made his *aide-de-camp*, as he (Lalor) knew no language but his own, whilst many of his followers were foreigners in like predicament. Humffray, who was a Welshman, brought down the wrath of the meeting on his head by still counselling moral force, and was stigmatised as a trimmer. One man in the crowd, having raised his voice in favour of constitutional action, was hardly saved from the infuriated diggers by the influence of the chairman and his associates. Several resolutions were proposed, and carried unanimously. Another meeting was called for Sunday, the 3rd of December, to choose a committee for the Reform League, and before dispersing the crowd made bonfires of their licenses, and all the arms and ammunition were distributed that the rebels could lay their hands on. Such was the declaration of war, and it was much to the surprise of the troops in the gully that the meeting of the 29th of November passed off without any open violence.

Acting under the orders of Governor Hotham, who, stout old sailor as he was, thought he could manage these turbulent diggers as in the old days he had done his ship's crew, the authorities on the 30th made another effort to collect the license fees. The whole force, both soldiers and police, turned out, and the diggers fled before them. Once or twice they made a slight attempt at resistance, and shots were fired, and stones thrown at the advancing troops. Some few prisoners were made, and then the force returned to camp. But now the most desperate among the diggers, with Lalor as their leader, and Vern and Raffaello as his coadjutors, hoisted the insurgent flag once more on Bakery Hill, and, kneeling around it, swore, with right hands uplifted, mutual defence. When the rebels were about a thousand strong they marched in procession, bearing the flag before them, to the site of the present Eureka monument, close to the old Melbourne road, and established themselves in an entrenched camp, or rather stockade. It is a fact to be noted that although twelve thousand people had been present at the meeting the day before, had applauded the most seditious speeches, and had openly burned their licenses, yet now that war was actually declared, and Lalor and his friends were in arms against the Government, the number of their followers had dwindled to a thousand, while later on, on Sunday morning, when the soldiers attacked the Stockade, their strength from one cause and another had actually decreased to about three hundred. All work on Ballarat ceased, and the people were in a state of the wildest excitement, all waiting, as it seemed, the issue of this daring rebellion.

Though many would not join the insurgents, still the majority sympathised with them to a certain extent, and none were found willing to help the soldiers or the police. It seems incredible that any man in his senses could for one moment have seriously contemplated the overthrow of a Government, and the establishment of a republic, with a handful of men, not a thousand strong, the half of whom were armed with picks and shovels, and pikes made of pieces of steel fixed on to long poles. That Lalor and his associates did contemplate this is evident, and Lalor's "minister of war" drew up a Declaration of Independence, in which this is distinctly stated. The insurgent camp, the Eureka Stockade, as it was called, was situated on the top of Bakery Hill, and was surrounded by a rude fence of slabs, strengthened wherever they thought necessary by overturned carts, boxes, barrels, and anything, in fact, they could lay their hands on. The rebels were no engineers, and the ground enclosed was over an acre in extent —far too large for their purpose.

Drilling went on with vigour, and small armed parties were sent out to forage, for the rebels were not only short of arms, ammunition, and supplies, but of money as well. This difficulty was surmounted by giving the storekeepers written receipts, certifying that the goods had been received, payment to be expected when the new republic was firmly established. These pioneers—the would-be founders of another nation—were not clever, apparently, with the pen. Here is one of the precious receipts which have come down to us:—"Received from the Ballarat store 1 Pistol for the Comtee X. Hugh M'Carty. Hurras for the people." Another.—"The Reform Lege Comete—4 drenks, fower chillings, 4 pie for fower of the neight watch patriots.—X. P." Whether the proprietor of the Ballarat store ever realised on that transaction is extremely doubtful, but at the rate charged, his losses on the "neight watch patriots'" supper must soon have been made up.

Meanwhile, at the Government camp, Captain Thomas, the commanding officer, had not been unmindful of the treasonable proceedings that were going on around. There were two companies of the 12th and 40th Regiments stationed at Ballarat, together with nearly a hundred policemen. Reinforcements were hourly expected from Melbourne under the command of the Major-General, Sir Robert Nickle; and Captain Thomas, while waiting, put his camp into a state of defence. The women and children were placed in a building supposed to be shot-proof, and the men were kept under arms night and day. These precautions were very necessary, as the Government officials had no means of arriving at any clear idea of the exact number of the rebels. That they, if only unanimous, must far outnumber the soldiers and police seemed certain. The suspense grew very wearing, and the men waited impatiently the moment when they should either attack or be attacked. On Saturday, the 2nd of December, although the troops from Melbourne had not yet arrived, Captain Thomas decided to wait no longer, but to endeavour to crush the insurrection at one blow. To do this he knew he must carry the Stockade by storm. He dared not attack in the daytime, because he had no force to leave behind to protect his own camp, but a night surprise, and especially a Saturday night surprise, would, he felt sure, be effective. On Saturday night, as he knew, many of the diggers would be away, some at their own homes, and more in the drinking and gambling saloons, of which there were enough and to spare in the little township down in the

DISTANT VIEW OF BALLARAT, FROM MOUNT WARRENHEIP.

gully between the two camps. And of those who remained in the Stockade, many, he knew, would not be so modest in their libations as the "lower height watch patriots" who shared "4 drinks" among them. There was little sleep in the Government camp that night, and long before the first faint streaks of the early summer dawn appeared in the sky Captain Thomas had his little army—in all nearly three hundred police and soldiers—fairly on the march.

The Eureka was not above two miles away, but to reach it the little force were obliged to steal down the gully, and through the sleeping town. Silently they marched, one hundred and seventy-six foot and one hundred mounted men, through the spectral white tents, past the claims, deserted now, and up the steep incline of the opposite hillside. So well was the project carried out, that they had encircled the Stockade on all save the southern side before the rebels discovered their proximity. As soon as the alarm was given in the Stockade, a volley was fired in the direction of the advancing troops. It checked them not a moment, and they came on little the worse for it. "For," says one of his historians. "Captain Thomas knew that undisciplined men firing upon a body of men advancing up a steep incline were sure to fire over their heads." The event proved the correctness of his theory, and, with a shout and a cheer, the Government men reached the Stockade, and in spite of the stout resistance of a body of pikemen, and the sharp but desultory fire of the other rebels, carried it. The foot police entered first, and were met by a body of pikemen who stood their ground sturdily, but the soldiers ably supported their allies, and the fight was continued hand to hand within the palings. For a few minutes the insurgents held their own bravely, then their ammunition began to fail, and they fell back before the steady advance of Captain Thomas's men. The flagstaff in the centre was soon reached, and the soldiers tore down the Southern Cross and trampled it under foot. Then it was each man for himself; the rebels turned and fled, dashing down the hillside, taking refuge in the holes, fleeing away to the ranges, for the Republic of Victoria was utterly crushed at its very birth, and its supporters were in no wise anxious to answer for its deeds. In less than five-and-twenty minutes, before the rising sun had dispersed the shadows and mists of the early morning, Captain Thomas found himself master of the Stockade on the top of Bakery Hill.

This result had not been gained without bloodshed. Captain Wise, the second in command, lay mortally wounded. Lieutenant Paull was also hurt. Four of the soldiers were dead, and about a dozen more wounded, while no less than fifteen of the rebels lay dead, and as many more were wounded, many of whom afterwards died. About a dozen of the rebels, seeing no chance of escape, surrendered—among them Raffaello, Lalor's aide-de-camp—and were marched by their captors down the gully to the Government camp, and then put in the lock-up, the soldiers sparing neither jeers nor taunts by the way. All the tents and the barricades, everything, in fact, that would burn, was fired by the attacking party, and soon the site of the Eureka Stockade, the stronghold of the Republic of Victoria, was covered with smoking ruins. The soldiers, having taken away their dead and wounded, left the camp, which was immediately "rushed" by the friends and relatives of the diggers. An eye-witness thus describes what followed:—

"The scene was awful—twos and threes gathered together, and all felt stupefied. I went with R—— to the barricade. The tents all around were in a blaze. I was about to go inside, when the cry was raised that the troopers were coming again. They did come, with carts to take away the bodies. I counted fifteen dead, one G——, a fine, well-educated man, and a great favourite. I counted fifteen others, but the spectacle was so ghastly that I feel loathing at the remembrance. They all lay in a small space with their faces upwards, looking like lead. Several of them were still heaving, and at every rise of their breasts the blood spouted out of their wounds, or just bubbled out and trickled away. One man, a stout-chested, fine fellow, apparently about forty years old, lay with a pike beside him. . . . I counted fifteen wounds in that single carcase. Some were bringing handkerchiefs, others bed-furniture and matting, to cover up the faces of the dead. Oh, God! sir, it was a sight for a Sabbath morn that I humbly implore heaven may never be seen again. Poor women, crying for absent husbands, and children frightened into quietness. . . . A little terrier sat on the breast of the man I spoke of, and kept up a continuous howl. It was removed, but always returned to the same spot, and when his master's body was huddled, with the other corpses, into the cart, the little dog jumped in after him, and lying on his dead master's breast, began howling again."

The leaders of the rebellion escaped, and the authorities, though they had a great many prisoners, found they were ignorant men, for the most part of no account, who had been led away, and were more sinned against than sinning. Peter Lalor, the leader, had been shot down early in the fight, and, as he lay on the ground, some friendly hand covered him from sight with slabs. After the fight was over he was taken away to the ranges, and afterwards smuggled into Ballarat, to the house of a certain Father Smythe, a Roman Catholic priest, who had more than sympathised with the rioters. Here Lalor's arm was amputated, and though a reward of £200 was on his head, and the secret of his hiding-place was known to many people, he was never caught. For Vern's apprehension a reward of £500 was offered, the authorities erroneously supposing him to be the leader of the riot, and £200 was also offered for that of another of the leaders. Great black and white placards containing full descriptions of the three men were printed, and fastened on trees in and about Ballarat, but, although the whereabouts of the men was widely known, none betrayed them.

Ballarat was like a great swarm of bees which has been rudely disturbed, and Captain Thomas kept his little force close within the precincts of the camp, anxiously awaiting the arrival of Sir Robert Nickle, the Major-General, who was hourly expected. But the diggers were utterly crushed. Those who were coming from Creswick to join the rebels returned quietly to their work, and the men at Ballarat, though they buried their dead with all the pomp and ceremony they could command, gave up all idea of openly opposing the Government.

All Sunday and Monday the men in the camp remained under arms, and on the Monday some shots were exchanged between them and the diggers. So strained were their relations, that probably it was a relief to both sides when early on the morning of the 5th the advance guards of Sir Robert Nickle's force were seen defiling from the ranges, and long before nightfall eight hundred men, with four field-pieces, and a large body of blue-jackets from H.M.S. *Electra*, were in camp. Next day martial law was proclaimed, and in obedience to a general order many of the inhabitants brought in arms and ammunition, but it was very evident that Captain Thomas had utterly crushed the insurrection, and in less than a month, all further apprehension of an outbreak having ceased, the Major-General, with the guns and the sailors, marched back to Melbourne, leaving about eight hundred men as a guard at Ballarat.

MONUMENT TO DIGGERS WHO WERE KILLED IN THE RISING.

Not till the 1st April, 1855, were the State prisoners brought to trial on a charge of high treason, and acquitted, amidst the cheers of the people. After this the rewards for the capture of Lalor and the other leaders were withdrawn, and the three were once more free men. And so ended the Ballarat riot—a foolish, wanton waste of life, by which nothing was gained, for the amendment of the mining laws and abolition of the license fee would most certainly have been attained quite as easily without bloodshed. That the diggers were wronged — bitterly wronged—there is no doubt, and a number of disaffected Irishmen and foreigners, the sweepings of Germany, France, and Italy, to whom all rule was obnoxious, seized the opportunity to stir them up to strife. Governor Hotham was not far out when he stigmatised the leaders of the rioters "as designing men who had ulterior views, and who hoped to profit by anarchy and confusion," and as "men who were not suffered to remain in their own countries in consequence of the violence of their characters, and the deeds they had done."

It is an old story in Ballarat now. The town has extended its arms right round the lonely bush cemetery, where soldiers and insurgents alike sleep their last, long sleep, and where monuments, of which we give illustrations, have been raised to their memory. The gully, where nestled the tents of the diggers, the steep hillside up which the soldiers charged, and the plateau on which was the Government camp, are now thick with houses. A peaceful and prosperous city has taken the place of the old turbulent gold-fields township, and the Eureka Stockade is all but forgotten.

## A STRANGE CHANGE.

"The whirligig of time brings in his revenges," and Mr. Peter Lalor is now the Speaker of the Victorian Lower House. Curiously enough, the leader of the Eureka rioters is in these days the strictest advocate of law and order, and is acknowledged by all to be the best Speaker who has ever presided over the deliberations of the Legislative Assembly.

MONUMENT TO SOLDIERS WHO FELL AT THE STOCKADE.

## THE DAILY LIFE OF THE BUSH.

Stations and Stations—Sheep or Cattle—General View of a Good Station—"Running In"—Bush Hospitality—An Ardent Dancer—Loafers—"Mustering"—Stock Whips—Catholicism—"Sprees"—A Thriving Drunkard—"You see."

"DID you not find it terribly dull in the bush?" is a query that very frequently greets the country visitor on his arrival in town. Like most other questions, this admits of more than one answer. As Addison's shrewd old knight observed, there is much to be said on both sides. Much, of course, depends upon the tastes and mental resources of the individual; much on the society, surroundings, and thousand and one other circumstances which go to make any place pleasant, or the reverse, residentially. Speaking broadly, however, and supposing the individual to be a person of average mental and bodily activity, a life in the wild bush, or in "the back blocks," as it is called, is not by any means so dull as might at first be supposed, even to one who has been bred and educated in a town. By a "bush life" is meant chiefly life on a sheep or cattle-station, or on a remote selection; the life of the Australian bush township is in many respects different, and to most people far less agreeable, but of this a more detailed account will be given later on.

The term "station" or "run" is a pretty comprehensive one, and may include nearly anything, from the large country house and estate in the neighbourhood of Melbourne or Sydney, almost English in its comfort and even luxury, to the "slab" or "wattle and dab" hut far away in the back country, where the pioneer squatter who has just taken up fresh land, with perhaps two or three white assistants and a few blacks, leads a life of unceasing toil and watchfulness, and carefully tends his few sheep in the wilderness. Then, again, it may be either a sheep or a cattle station, or a combination of the two, and the life on each of these differs considerably from that on the others. As a rule, the country when first occupied is used to run cattle, and as things are gradually got into order sheep are either wholly or in part substituted, being at first shepherded, and afterwards allowed to roam at large in enclosed paddocks, from a few acres to many square miles in extent. Accordingly a greater degree of comfort is usually found on a sheep than on a cattle station.

The homestead, or "station" *par excellence*, is generally a wooden building, large and straggling, and, in parts where the heat is extreme, supported on piles driven into the ground. It is usually built in the shape of a hollow square, with the fourth side open, or closed only with a low fence. It is almost invariably surrounded, on two or three sides at least, with a broad veranda, beneath which the greater part of the "indoor" life is spent, especially during the summer months. Besides this, there are generally numerous detached buildings, the kitchen, bachelors' quarters, billiard, play, or lumber-rooms, stables, a store, offices, men's hut, and a wool-shed, at distances from the main building varying from a few yards to a mile or more. All these are almost invariably of a single storey. A two-storeyed house in the bush is a veritable *rara avis*, and is evidence of a high stage of civilisation.

At a little distance is the stockyard, where the horses or cattle are "run in," and also the slaughter-yards, fowl-houses, and piggeries, with the miscellaneous sheds inseparable from a country house in all parts of the world. Although there are almost always stables of some sort, the reader must not imagine that the horses on a station are usually kept in them, as they are in England. Commonly, one or two are kept either in the stable or in a small paddock, where they can be easily caught in case of emergency, and for the purpose of "running in" the rest. This "running in" is effected in the following way: A man mounts the stabled horse and rides after the others, which are scattered over the horse-paddock, feeding. The horse-paddock is often four or five square miles in extent, and is frequently intersected with gullies, clumps of ti-tree, and other timber. As soon as the rider sees the horses that he wants, he gets in front of them, rounds them up, and drives them before him towards the yards. Any recalcitrant animal that endeavours to break away is soon brought to reason with the terrible stockwhip. Arrived at the yard, in which a gap has been left by taking down slip panels, the horses rush in pell-mell. The panels are then replaced, the horses required are caught and bridled, and then the rest are turned out again to graze once more. It is not always an easy thing to catch your horse even in the yards; but, though here and there an ill-conditioned brute will always remain troublesome, after a little practice you can catch most horses easily enough. Only it is well to watch, lest, as you are making for your own horse, some other animal's heels come into unpleasant neighbourhood with your head.

The squatter's house, built where possible on the banks of a river, lagoon, or creek, stands in a large garden well stocked with vegetable and fruit-trees, and a lady's hand is often visible in the profusion of flowers. Frequently, too, vines, honeysuckle, and creepers are trained over verandas and walls; a lawn, more or less level, suggests tennis; and there is a boat, or punt, upon the water in the distance. There are generally at least two "living" rooms, besides the "office," where the squatter makes up his accounts, pays his men, writes his letters, and keeps his guns. The rest of the house is occupied by his wife and family, governess, servants, and visitors from town or from neighbouring stations, who are sure of a hearty welcome; for the hospitality of the bush is proverbial. Indeed, it is often remarked that a house there is never so full but that it will hold half-a-dozen more. When all the beds in all the bedrooms are occupied, "shake downs" are made up on sofas, billiard-tables, and camp bedsteads, on and under tables, and on the floor. When there is no more room inside, the residue of the guests sleep on the veranda, whilst the late arrival, who can find no vacant space to spread his blanket even there, will find a comfortable "camping-ground" in the harness-room. A place is found for everyone, even if everyone is not always in his place. As may be imagined, some of these places of rest are not quite so luxurious as the proverbial bed of down; but the fatigue induced by exercise in the pure, strong air of the bush makes the visitor ready to sleep soundly even on the bare ground.

The elasticity of a bush house is pretty thoroughly tested on the occasion of any social gathering, such as a wedding, kangaroo battue, or ball. Indeed, the zest with which Australian country people enter into amusements of all sorts, and the enormous distances they will travel to attend them, are notorious. There is a story extant of a young squatter who was anxious to attend a ball at a neighbouring station, but was unable to get away from his work until nine o'clock on the morning of the dance. The place was seventy miles away. But that was a trifle. Mounting his best horse, with the valise containing his dress-clothes strapped in front of him, he started on

1. A HORSE AND CATTLE STATION.   2. MILKING.

his long ride. Rain had fallen, and the going was heavy, but by dark he had almost reached his destination, only to find that, in Antipodean phrase, the river was "down," a broad sheet of water lying between him and the "haven where he would be." Nothing daunted, however, he first unsaddled his horse, and, hobbling him by the fore feet in the usual manner, turned him loose to graze. He then disencumbered himself of his boots and superfluous garments, and, having firmly strapped his valise upon his head, entered the water, swam across, and presented himself at the house *en déshabillé*—like the character in *The Stranger*, "not, indeed, dead, but very wet." It is added that, having danced all night, he re-swam the river in the morning, and was back in time to start shearing on the following day. Some people hint, however, that in this exploit he was actuated by another fair and goodly reason, over and above a passion for the waltz. It is pleasing to be able to add that the young gentleman's dancing days are not by any means over, and that the fair loadstone who exercised such a magnetic attraction upon him became in due time his wife.

Dancing, however, is by no means the only amusement, though a "hop" is almost invariably the culminating point of riding-parties, kangaroo hunts, and other festivities, for dwellers in the bush will organise a carpet-dance on the smallest provocation and at ten minutes' notice.

But the reader must not imagine that station life is nothing but one round of enjoyment. There is work—and hard work too—to be done, and even visitors find

A STOCKYARD.

themselves, after a few days, joining in the daily routine of the station. In the bush there is no sympathy for the "loafer." Indeed, the word there carries with it a meaning far more odious than to the ears of a townsman. And yet the breed does unfortunately exist even away in the "Never Never Country," the wilds of Queensland. The affable traveller is by no means unknown who will ride up and, introducing himself in the blandest of tones as Mr. De Courcy Montmorency (his real name being Muggins), ask for a "shake-down" for the night, his horse, as he explains, having "knocked up." On the following day he makes no proposal to move from his comfortable quarters, and will hang on sometimes for months—sitting at the squatter's table, drinking his wine, smoking his tobacco, and boring his friends, disregarding the broadest hints, until at last the master of the house, grown desperate, informs him that his horse will be at the door at a certain hour the next morning. Even then it is ten to one if he does not, on some excuse, hang on a few days longer, and if finally he has not to be almost pushed out of the door. It is men of this class that are the pests of society in the bush, abusing, as they do, that spirit of free and open-handed hospitality which is one of its chief charms. The bushman's hospitality transcends that of the Arab. The writer has known a squatter sit for several evenings in his bedroom, smoking in gloomy solitude, rather than have to endure the odious society of one of these loafers in his sitting-room; and yet he would not tell the man in plain words to go. "I can't turn the fellow out," he said; "it seems so inhospitable." The man had come without an invitation, and had already been staying there five weeks without moving so much as a finger to make himself useful.

In the morning, immediately after breakfast, the horses are run in from the horse-paddock into the yard—for no one in the bush will walk if he can help it; he will rather spend half a day trying to catch a horse in the paddock, under a broiling sun, than walk a couple of miles. Once in the yard, each man catches his horse, and, having bridled and saddled him, sets out on his day's work, often remaining out from daylight till eight or nine at night. Only the ladies, and perhaps a man or two who have work about the place, remain at home. The rest will, in an hour's time, be scattered in all directions—some riding along fences, to see that they are sheep or cattle-proof; some off to distant paddocks, to draft sheep, or to run in fresh horses for the work of the station; some to clear out water-holes, or to distribute the rock-salt for the stock. Occasionally, when "mustering" has to be done, you will see ten or a dozen mounted men start off at daybreak, and see them return at nightfall with jaded horses, driving before them, with "a running fire of stock-whips," a mob of perhaps five or six hundred cattle. These stock-whips, by-the-bye, are very formidable weapons in the hands of a man who knows how to use them, though a "new chum" is more likely than not to cut out his own eye if he attempts to crack one. With about a foot and a half of handle, and a lash from ten to sixteen feet long, they can be made to resound with a crack considerably louder than the report of a pistol, so that the noise can be heard under some circumstances at a distance of a mile or more, whilst on occasion the stockman can literally "cut a piece" out of a refractory beast. The reader can imagine the noise that is made when a dozen of these whips are all being cracked at once. For it is the sound, and not the lash, that is chiefly relied on, the cattle flying from the crack of the whip far more than from its sting.

The social life of the bush, in all its freedom and simplicity, is well illustrated by the character of its religious observances, which are eminently suited to the circumstances of the case. The bushman, as a rule, has the greatest respect for religion in the abstract, and the very haziest notion of the dogmas peculiar to any particular creed, though, as a rule, he professes adherence to one of the leading sects; for there is no Established Church in any of the Australian colonies. He considers it a point of honour to attend the service, or, as he calls it, the "preaching" of any clergyman who comes round to the station where he happens to be working. The writer, when staying at a small station, was present at a service conducted by an itinerant minister of the Bible Christians. It was held in the dining-room. There were present the master and mistress of the house, who were Presbyterians; the governess, an Irvingite; the overseer, a member of the Church of England; two Roman Catholic women servants; a Chinese gardener, and five men from the "hut," not one of whom was of the same creed as the parson. They all, including the Chinaman, took part in the service with the greatest decorum, and would have regarded it as a gross breach of bush etiquette if they had not done so. The effect was singular. After service the minister smoked a pipe with the squatter, and they discussed whisky-and-water and the Land Act until the small hours.

Even the bush, however, is not entirely free from religious bickerings and intolerance, and this is more especially the case in the small towns, or, as they are usually called, "bush townships." There the different denominations quarrel and cavil to their hearts' content. There is more joy over one not particularly clean "cross-breed" enticed from the opposition fold, than over ninety and nine snow-white merinos that have never belonged to the heretical flock. The quarrelling, however, does not usually set in until the township has become thoroughly established and fairly prosperous; for in the first days of settlement everybody has too much on his hands to find time for it; and Presbyterian, Anglican, Wesleyan, and Jew will all unite in furtherance of the Fancy Fair to build the Catholic Church, which, a few years afterwards, some of them would be almost ready to pull down. Nor is it only in religious matters that these petty bickerings are aroused: municipal and social differences excite the wildest animosity, and politics lend a helping hand, until in some places one half of the township is not on speaking terms with the other half. It is only fair to add that a case of real distress will unite for the nonce all denominations, cliques, and political parties in the cause of charity.

The bush parson, of whatever denomination, makes his head-quarters at some country town, and from this centre makes pastoral excursions into the surrounding district, visiting remote selections and splitters' camps away back, riding immense distances and undergoing great hardships often for a mere pittance. Especially is this the case in very sparsely-populated country, such as the district of Queensland known as the "Never Never Country"—presumably because a person who has once been there invariably asseverates, with more or less solemnity, that he will "never, never," on any consideration, go back. The creed chiefly represented in the grazing districts is the Presbyterian, a large percentage of the squatters being North Britons; but other denominations also have their ministers. The standard of education among bush parsons is not as a rule high—a fact that can hardly be wondered at, considering the small opportunities afforded them for study; but brilliant exceptions are occasionally met with, and the writer has overtaken on a bush track a traveller in shirt-sleeves and a cabbage-tree hat, mounted upon the sorriest of weeds, who has proved to be a cultivated scholar and polished gentleman, and whose conversation has beguiled many a weary mile. Amusing stories are told of the adventures of "new chum" parsons, and hoaxes and practical jokes upon them are not unknown, but these are generally considered unfair. For the most part they are treated with consideration and respect.

The great vice of the bush is drinking. Not that as a rule bushmen drink when at work, but it only too often happens that at periods varying from two months to a year they obtain a cheque for the full amount of their earnings, ride into the nearest township, hand their cheque to the publican, and remain in a state of intoxication until that worthy declares that their money is exhausted and pushes them out into the street, or, as an exceptional favour, allows them to sleep off the effects of the poison upon the tap-room floor. This is called, in bush vernacular, "a spree." As soon as his "spree" is over, the bushman will return to his work, and for the next

A TWO-STOREYED HOUSE IN THE BUSH.

six months touch nothing stronger than tea. What makes these orgies the more injurious is the poison supplied to the unfortunate men. Provided that it burns the palate and intoxicates the brain, the bushman is not very particular as to the taste of his drink, and no stuff is too vile to use for the laudable purpose of emptying his pockets. In the absence of other liquor he has been known to "spree" on "Painkiller." The intelligent reader may perhaps infer from these remarks that the bush publican is not, as a rule, a model member of the commonwealth, and in this surmise he would be tolerably correct. Yet the rule is not without its exception, and many bush hotels are conducted as decently and honestly as need be. Bush publicans sometimes make large fortunes, turn squatters, and become eminently respectable members of society; but more often they themselves succumb to the vice upon which they have thriven, and die in poverty.

Hard drinking is by no means confined to the labouring men; most neighbourhoods can point to shocking examples in the way of drinking squatters and settlers. These, having larger opportunities, drink more persistently and continually than the station "hands." It is hardly necessary to say that their affairs usually go from bad

A STOCKRIDER.

to worse, until they end by losing stock, station, and all. Sometimes, however, nature is too bountiful for them, and they thrive in spite of themselves. A story is told of a Queensland squatter which well illustrates this. Some years ago he and his brother, members of a good English family, had taken up a run a long distance "back," *i.e.*, far in the interior. Their drays had been down to Rockhampton with wool, and were returning with stores for the station. Amongst other things ordered was a five-hundred-gallon tank, and Mr. Bibulus, thinking it a pity that this should come up empty, gave orders that it should be filled with rum. On its arrival, a general orgie of all hands took place, until the liquor was exhausted. A friend of the writer chanced to call at the station the day after its arrival, and was greeted by the proprietor—" Oh, come in, Mr. Blank—come in. Delighted to see you! I'm drunk, my brother's drunk, the overseer's drunk, and all the men are drunk; and still the station pays!" Generally, however, the squatter, at all events when at home and at work, is a most sober and temperate man, rising early, and generally eating the bread of carefulness; for in spite of the boast of the hero of the above story, backed by the popular idea of the enormous profits of squatting, it is only by the greatest energy, care, and economy, that station properties nowadays can be got to pay, and even then the risk from drought and other causes is considerable.

To the student of character, a residence in the Australian bush is by no means uninteresting, the solitary life and want of society producing the most eccentric specimens of the genus man. There may be met with, fossilised, as it were, and encrusted with a coating of bush habits and ideas, characters that almost seem to have stepped from the pages of Fielding or Smollett. More especially is this seen in the old pioneer colonists from the north of the Tweed, many of whom retain almost unimpaired the ideas and prejudices of forty years ago; and you may occasionally hear, in George Street, Sydney, or in Collins Street, Melbourne, language almost identical with that which Scott puts into the mouth of the Bailie Nicol Jarvie. The newspapers literally teem with good stories anent these old "identities," and some, which the reader would suspect were inventions, or at least gross exaggerations, are literally true. For the most part, they illustrate precisely the same traits of character as their subjects would have shown in their own "land of the leal," as an eminent statesman called North Britain in one of his bursts of oratory. There is one, illustrative at once of the shrewd mother-wit of the average Scot, and of the personal peculiarity of its subject, which is perhaps worth setting down. Mr. McPanel (may he live a thousand years!) is in the habit of adding the words "you see" to every remark he makes, a custom which is well known, and is the subject of no little amusement in the neighbourhood of his station. One day his wood-shed was burned to the ground, by an incendiary fire, as was supposed, lighted by a "swagsman," or tramp, who had been refused a supper. A few weeks after Mr. McP. discovered, carved upon a gum-tree, the following:—" Mr. McPanel, you see, if you had assisted the poor traveller, you see, you wouldn't have had your shed burnt, you see!" The old gentleman carefully took out his pocket-knife, adjusted his spectacles, and for some time was observed to be very busy, when it was ascertained that he had carved underneath the following words:—" You're a (forcible but unparliamentary adjective) fool, you see; the place was insured, you see; and we're going to build a better one with the money, you see!" And he did.

## DUNEDIN.

New Zealand Towns—First Appearances—View of Dunedin from the Bay—The Surveyor r. Nature—The People—Two Banks—The Public Buildings—The Town Hall—The Athenæum—The High Schools—The University—The Churches—First Church—Knox Church—The Lunatic Asylum—The Hotels—Business in Dunedin—The Harbour—The Town Belt—The Suburbs—"Ocean Beach"—The Refrigerating Company—Dairy Farming—General Prosperity.

THE CARGILL FOUNTAIN.

THE long, narrow shape of the islands of New Zealand naturally breaks up the colony into a series or chain of districts, each link of which has its own outlet-port or focus. Hence population is more evenly distributed than is usual in colonies. Wellington, with some 30,000 inhabitants, is the political capital, but Auckland is almost twice its size, with Dunedin and Christchurch, in the order in which the names appear, separating them. For a quarter of a century Dunedin was the largest city, and though Auckland has recently overhauled it in the number of inhabitants, it still retains many claims to the premiership. So far as buildings go it is most advanced, and its commercial interests are still more important. Its educational institutions are on a larger scale, and its churches look more substantial than those of Auckland. For the last five years things have been almost stationary in Dunedin, and this gives it a more settled aspect than Auckland, where the large buildings are mostly of recent erection, and seem scarcely to have shaken down into their places. Going further back, Dunedin, which is Gaelic for Edinburgh, was founded by Scotch Presbyterians with malice aforethought, and derived "grand" ideas from the gold-fields which built up its prosperity, whilst Auckland, like Topsy, has "growed" somehow, deriving scant advantage from having been the seat of Government in early days. If one may be allowed yet other odious comparisons, I would add that Auckland has been largely affected by Sydney, and Dunedin by Melbourne, ideas, whilst semi-ecclesiastical Christchurch bears a distinct resemblance to Adelaide. For Wellington we cannot find a parallel nearer than Washington.

Auckland and Dunedin are essentially commercial cities, though the churches of Dunedin hint at the origin of the settlement. Christchurch is rather the country town where business plays second fiddle, and the squatter and farmer support the cathedral, which forms the central point. Government House, Parliament Buildings, and the Government Offices, give the key to the character of Wellington, though the rapidly extending wharves also point to its growing importance as a distributing centre.

Even the Victorian, who is popularly supposed by other colonists to look upon London as representing quantity without quality in comparison with Melbourne, always recognises that Dunedin is a city, and a fine city. The first appearance of the town is much in its favour. Whether you land at the wharf from the Australian steamer, or have come by rail from Port Chalmers, where the ocean steamers stop, you at once face the heart of Otago, as the district of which Dunedin is the capital is called. A vacant space, soon to be made a thing of beauty, gives an open view to a row of fine warehouses forming the right side of a triangle, with the railway station for its base, and the wharf, or rather the street containing the wharf, for its left side. At the apex is a fountain, erected to the memory of Captain Cargill, the founder of the province, which marks the centre of the city. Right and left runs Princes Street. At the corners are two palatial banks, and in front is the Grand Hotel, the largest and most imposing in Australasia.

PRINCES STREET.
(From a Photograph by Burton Bros.)

And the sights that precede the business-like scene round the Cargill Fountain put the visitor in a humour to be pleased. Unless he has made the journey overland from Invercargill, in which case he traverses a fertile but not very interesting district, he must come up the Otago harbour, the meanderings of which are pretty enough to delight everybody except the Sydneian, for whom there is but one harbour, and all those who live around it are its prophets. The view of Dunedin from the bay is attractive. It is a long narrow town, winding along the base and slopes of a range of hills, the lower portion of which is known as the "Flat," having been reclaimed from the bay. A belt of grass and bush land, on which building is prohibited, forms a dark background, which throws up the town as viewed from the bay, and divides it from suburbs extending along the top of the hills. Behind these rise higher hills, forming a branch of the Southern Alps, and separated from these on which the town is laid out by a narrow valley which cannot be seen from the bay. In front of the town, the bay stretches for about a mile across to the opposite peninsula, a high-lying plateau, which rises almost precipitously from the water. In the distance one catches a glimpse of the open ocean across a narrow neck of low land.

A more picturesque situation it would be difficult to conceive; it is much more picturesque, indeed, than convenient, for enormous have been the sums spent in levelling a tract of ground sufficient to lay out a main street at the foot of the hills, in cutting out tracks up the hillside, and, as the town grew more populous, in reclaiming land from the water to provide room for expansion. One feature that strikes attention as you approach, is that several of the streets ascend the hills in a direct line, and are crossed by terraces laid out horizontally. It is said, with what truth I am not prepared to vouch, that the useless expense and inconvenience of these steep streets arose from the town having been laid out on the rectangular plan in Edinburgh before the pioneers started, under the supposition that the site would be level, or nearly so. When no level site was obtainable, it came to a choice between altering the plan, or making out a new one with the usual zigzag ascents of a town built on the side of the hill. But the surveyor was not prepared to depart from his instructions on his own responsibility, and thus nature was made to bend to the Edinburgh plan. In latter days these hills have proved admirably fitted for cable tramways, of which Dunedin constructed the first in Australasia. Indeed, Dunedin is generally considered to be as enterprising a place as could well be found. The first settlement was established in 1848 under the auspices of members of the Free Kirk of Scotland, who did not welcome other creeds and nationalities, and took life hardly, without making much material progress. But in 1861, the discovery of gold-fields at Gabriel's Gully—now the pretty township of Lawrence—about seventy-two miles from the town, flooded the province with an adventurous population principally hailing from the Victorian gold-fields—the yields from which were then slackening. These "new iniquities," as they were called by the "old identities," soon made a little Melbourne of Dunedin, but without

KNOX CHURCH.
(From a Photograph by Burton Bros.)

altogether destroying its fundamentally serious character. The graft of the adventurous Victorian upon the stout and canny Scotch stock has been very successful. The moral fibre of Otago will stand comparison with that of most communities; and if Dunedin has led the way in commercial enterprise, its long-headed pioneers introduced a good system of education at the first, and established a university directly the gold flowed in, which university still maintains its pride of place.

The traveller who comes from Australia, or has been to other parts of New Zealand, will notice that the Otago type of humanity is distinct. What sailors call the "cut of the jib" bespeaks the origin of the settlement at once. Probably scarcely half the present population are Scotch by birth or descent, yet you could not mistake them for any other nationality, the Scotch having given the lead to the rest. The superior stamp of the working classes is specially remarkable. A more intelligent-looking population it would be hard to find. There is a general sharpness of feature and angularity of body as compared with the average English crowd; not much animation, but an occupied air. Country visitors are few. This is essentially a town, and the passers-by townsmen. The buildings around, and the style of the shops, are certainly superior to what would be found in an English town of the same size. It is obvious, too, that the enormous, well-built warehouses supply a much larger population than that of the province, although you will learn later that direct steam communication with England has rendered it inexpedient to keep large stocks in hand nowadays, and many of the warehouses are larger than is now necessary. Nice fresh faces the people have, not so fresh as at home, but delightful after the sallow Australian complexions, and not so different from the English as to strike attention. The proportion of young people, however, is noticeable, and also the general healthy appearance. Everybody is well, though rather carelessly, dressed, much after the Scottish fashion. Beards are much worn. The business man is in a black frock-coat and tall hat; clerks and the generality in more modest tweeds and round hats. Few have gloves with them, and of these not half wear them. After all, it is very much like Glasgow, only rather "more so."

The banks by which the Cargill Monument is flanked on either side are the Bank of New Zealand and the Colonial Bank of New Zealand. And here one must own that strangers will at first find some difficulty in discriminating between banks and insurance companies which rejoice in similar names. The want of inventive power in this direction presents a striking contrast to the American fertility of nomenclature. In the States the value of a distinctive name for advertising purposes is too well appreciated for similar names to be adopted; in Australasia one might think that new companies were trying how near they could get to the name of some old establishment without infringing the law. But to return to the banks in question. The Colonial Bank, with its clock tower and handsome arcade, looks far more like a town-hall than a bank. It was built in the days when Otago enjoyed Home Rule, and was to be the seat of the provincial authority, but when the Provincial Governments were abolished, the Provincial Buildings, as they were called, were sold to the Colonial Bank of New Zealand, an institution born in Dunedin and managed there. The Bank of New Zealand (without the "Colonial") has its head-quarters in Auckland. It is the principal financial house in the colony, and keeps the Government account. The Dunedin establishment is only a branch office, but this does not prevent it from being the handsomest building in the town, admirably suited to its purpose, and constructed with excellent taste in every detail.

A remarkable structure is the head office of the Union Steamship Company—the company which enjoys the monopoly of the inter-colonial and coast traffic. The architect has succeeded in giving the building a maritime air, by means of a number of little turrets surmounted by weathercocks. There are many more fine commercial buildings: insurance offices on a much larger scale than a prudent shareholder can approve; warehouses than which there are none larger in Melbourne and Sydney. But buildings of this type are all very much like each other, and a description of the petty differences which distinguish them could only weary the reader. Somewhat out of the ordinary, however, is the interior of Messrs. Sievwright, Stout, and Co.'s office. These gentlemen are lawyers, but they have cast aside the old-world traditions as to legal offices, and built theirs after the model of a bank, there being a large central hall, into which the light is let through a stained glass roof, with a large counter at the end of the ground floor, and offices round.

But we ought to see the public buildings first. Walking up Princes Street, we come to the Octagon, an eight-sided "square," which might be made very pretty if it were entrusted to the care of a good gardener. On the upper side of the Octagon is the Town Hall, or rather its façade, for the hall itself is not likely to be built for many a year to come. Nevertheless, the front is very imposing, and the chances are that you do not notice the posterior deficiencies of the building unless some apologetic cicerone calls attention to them. This Town Hall is no bad emblem of the history of the province, with its "grand" ideas and love of putting its best foot foremost. In the sixties and seventies everyone thought that Dunedin was going to be a little London, but the eighties have changed all that, and many are the citizens who have begun their private town-halls in the sanguine belief of indefinite progress, and were stopped short in the building by subsequent "bad times." On the lower side of the Octagon is the Athenaeum, of which no Dunedin citizen cares to have more notice taken than he can help. It is the only approach to a public library that this fine town can boast, but it is an approach carefully guarded from those who most need it by a guinea subscription, whilst both the quality and the condition of the books leave something to be desired. There is, however, a reading-room with newspapers and magazines, to which visitors to the town can have free access by giving their names to the librarian. At the University there is a library containing some good books, but it has been starved ever since the depression set in. In the Supreme Court, again, there is a legal library, to which one can get access without much difficulty. But it remains the darkest blot upon the fair fame of Dunedin that it has no public library.

Although laid out on level ground, the public gardens are pretty, but unfortunately they are situated at the northern extremity of the town, practically beyond the reach of two-thirds of the population. The Museum also is too far north to be conveniently accessible. But it is well arranged, and quite worth a visit, though neither so large nor so popular in character as the famous museum at Christchurch. The building in which it is located is remarkable for simple good taste.

Probably the largest public building is the High School, a pretentious structure, unpleasantly heavy but decidedly striking, standing out well on the brow of the hill. It is a building which conveys the just impression that the community values higher education. Nor have the school endowments been expended merely on outward show, for school inspectors declare the interior arrangements to be a model of convenience. "The boys are drafted and yarded easier than sheep," was the expression in which this intelligence was conveyed to the writer; and ample sums have been provided to secure efficient teaching. The school is attended by over three hundred pupils, whose blue cricket caps with white facings are to be seen out of school hours in every quarter of the town.

Not far from the Boys' High School is the modest building which they previously inhabited, now turned over to the girls. Such is our degenerate chivalry! But the girls are as well taught as the boys, which was scarcely the case in the days of "*Place aux dames*." One of the most

THE HIGH SCHOOL, FROM ROSLYN.
(*From a Photograph by Burton Bros.*)

interesting sights in the town is that of the High School girls going through the gymnastic exercises which form part of the school course.

It would be a weary task to count the number of primary schools in this land of free, secular, and compulsory education. Over half a million sterling a year is spent upon education by a population of just half a million. Wherever, out of the business streets, you see a good-sized building, it is safe to put it down to be a State school; and one must add that as a rule these school buildings are respectable in architecture, and admirable in their interior arrangements. They form a fitting antidote to the overpowering materialism of the business quarters of the town, which are calculated to give the impression that colonists think of nothing but money-making, and devote much more care to the glorification of their places of business than they are worth.

THE TOWN HALL, AS DESIGNED.
(From a Photograph by Burton Bros.)

In a fine open space on the banks of the Water of Leith, a stream which runs into the harbour at the north-eastern end of the town, stands the University, a fine but not exactly handsome stone building, attended by two scholastic-looking red-brick double houses, the residences of four of the professors. This is the oldest University in the colony, and, although affiliated to the New Zealand University—which, like that of London, is a purely examining body—it has been allowed to retain the designation of the Otago University, whereas its neighbours in Canterbury and Auckland have to content themselves with the title of University College. The University may reasonably be considered well equipped in the matter of professors, and on the average about a hundred students attend the lectures. The medical school has been specially successful and attractive. Besides the University, the High School, and the primary schools, there is a normal school in Dunedin which serves for the whole district.

The hospital is an ugly building, with nice gardens round it; it was originally constructed to hold an International Exhibition, and therefore is perhaps not very suitable for its present purpose. But the large empty central hall has at least the advantage of affording ample ventilation. The dormitories contain nearly 200 beds, and are lofty and admirably kept, though in the male wards male nurses are employed. Amongst other charitable institutions in and about the town are the Industrial School for Destitute Children, the Benevolent Institution, and the Church Orphanage. Nor amongst public buildings ought one to omit mention of the Supreme Court, the Post Office, the Custom House, all unpretending, useful buildings, massed round the Cargill Monument, or of the Garrison Hall, the largest building of the kind in Australasia.

Churches, as previously noted, form a striking feature in the panorama of the town. There is one on the eminence opposite the railway station, which every stranger takes for the Cathedral, owing to the prominence of its site and the pretentiousness of its architecture, which one can only describe as "wedding-cake" Gothic. It is the Presbyterian "First Church," so called, not because it was the first church built in the town, for it was not, but from its being the leading church. Another large Presbyterian place of worship in the Gothic style is the Knox Church, at the northern end of the town. A little way up the Roslyn cable tramway is the Roman Catholic Cathedral, certainly the prettiest of Dunedin churches. Both this and Knox Church, like the University and the High School, are built of a gloomy dark blue stone found near Port Chalmers, faced with a handsome white freestone which abounds in the Oamaru district. When fresh, this white stone can be carved with the greatest ease, and thus lends itself readily to ornamentation; but, unfortunately, it speedily loses its colour. St. Matthew's, southward, is a large edifice belonging to the Church of England, larger than can easily be filled by the Churchmen of the neighbourhood, and unattractive both without and within.

The inevitable Lunatic Asylum, generally the handsomest building of colonial cities, may be sought in vain. You will see it from the railway, about fifteen or twenty miles out of Dunedin on the way north, at Seacliff, where it makes up for its distance from town by the magnificence of its proportions and the luxury of its architectural embellishments. In the old world palaces are built for kings: in the new, for idiots.

The town is well paved, well lighted with gas, and well kept. Many of the streets are named after those of Edinburgh. They are mostly of good width, and recently a splendid boulevard, Cumberland Avenue, has been laid out after the most approved French fashion. The water supply is ample, but occasionally of questionable quality in summer, and never so good as a water-drinker would wish. Of the footpaths one cannot speak too highly; throughout the town they are asphalted, and even in the most out-of-the-way suburban lane comfortable provision is made for "Shanks's" mare. The ocean breezes keep Dunedin amongst the healthiest towns in the world; but this is more than its citizens deserve, for the system of drainage extends over a very limited area, and the sanitary arrangements generally are deplorable.

Cabs and hotels are practically the stranger's first want on arrival, and should perhaps, therefore, have been dealt with earlier. Waggonettes are the kind of cab most used—primitive ramshackle boxes on wheels, with leather coverings; but excellent hansoms and livery carriages are easily obtainable. The fares are about twenty-five per cent. higher than London prices. Of the hotels, the largest and best arranged is the "Grand," but "Wain's," the front of which is pretty, is also comfortable, and old-fashioned folk still keep to the "Criterion." There is likewise an excellent club, situated in charming grounds on Fern Hill. The best means of getting about are the horse tramways, which run the whole length of the town at the foot of the hills. There are also cable tramways to Roslyn and Mornington up the two hills nearest the centre. These lines ascend the most formidably steep places, sending nervous strangers' hearts into their mouths.

The business part of the town is on the flat, close to the Cargill Monument; the manufactories lie mostly northwards. It is the proud boast of Dunedin to be the most advanced of all New Zealand towns in her industries, which include woollen and clothing factories, iron-works, tanneries, breweries, oil-mills, soap and candle-making, the manufacture of coffee and spices, furniture-making, brass and iron-work, coach-building, confectionery and jam manufacture, chemical works, paper-mills, and meat refrigeration. A visit to the New Zealand clothing manufactory is specially to be recommended. It astonishes everybody by the excellence of its arrangements for the convenience and health of the hands employed, presenting, unfortunately, a great contrast in this respect to the majority of Australasian factories. In shops, too, Dunedin can claim the pre-eminence, and her connection with Melbourne has taught her tradesmen the art of dressing their windows to advantage. Among other characteristics of the town is the excellence of its medical practitioners, which is probably due to the circumstance that the medical school in connection with the University attracts good men. The extent to which the telephone is used may be quoted as another illustration of the enterprise of the citizens. The number of houses connected with the wire is far larger than in any other New Zealand town. May one also without treason hint that in the important department of ladies' dress Dunedin claims the first place? In the matter of theatres and public amusements, however, Auckland has of late surpassed her, though she has two theatres and half-a-dozen fair-sized public halls.

Before going out to the suburbs, a word must be said with fear and trembling about the harbour. If you were to believe what you hear in every other port in the colony, it is a hole, or at least a ditch, scooped out by lavish expenditure, which will soon be filled up again by sand, and is not yet fit to admit any decent-sized ship. Nevertheless, steamers of over two thousand tons burthen come up every day to Dunedin, and two ships drawing nineteen feet of water are at the time of writing at the wharf, whilst the large ocean steamers of 5,000 tons come deeply laden as far as Port Chalmers. One must admit the existence of a bar, but its surface has been dredged off, and by means of a mole, constructed by the advice of Sir John Coode, it has already been shifted a considerable way out to sea, and may be expected shortly to disappear altogether. As regards the upper harbour, it also is improving, and we need not despair of seeing the ocean steamers lying along the Dunedin wharves before many years are over. There has been a large and not invariably economical expenditure in dredging, reclamation, and other works for the improvement of the harbour, but it is improving almost daily, and the principal work which remains is to improve its reputation, for it is only two years since the inter-colonial steamers have been able to come up to Dunedin, and in 1883 the colony stood aghast at the daring of the captain who brought the first ocean steamer over the dreaded bar to Port Chalmers, the little town about eight miles from Dunedin, where, until recently, all but the small coasting vessels used to lie.

So much from the practical point of view. From the æsthetic, it would be hard to praise the Otago harbour too highly. Auckland claims superiority by reason of the richer colour of a semi-tropical climate, and the superb dominant feature of Rangitoto, the island volcano; but there is a greater variety of scenery to be obtained in the Otago harbour, though no one of the views is so impressive.

The squares, reserves, and parks, like the streets, are kept in excellent condition. To balance the botanic garden at the north-east end of the town, there are several cricket-grounds to the south-west, and also the town-belt, which divides the suburbs on the hills from the town. Some of the original "bush," which once covered the whole hillside, is to be found on this belt, giving one the idea that the scene has been shorn of much of its beauty by the clearance that has been effected. No visitor should miss the view of the city and harbour from the Queen's Drive, which runs along the middle of this belt, or fail to ascend by cable tramway to Mornington and Roslyn, the pretty suburbs on the top of the hill, where he will soon learn that the wind is given to blowing very strongly in New Zealand. It is only a fair price to pay for such glorious views as the residents of Roslyn and Mornington enjoy, and the wind is fresh and healthy.

THE BOTANICAL GARDENS.
(From a Photograph by Burton Bros.)

Going southwards from the Cargill Monument, the hills soon recede, and one comes to the genuine flat, where the town broadens into the suburbs of South Dunedin, St. Kilda, and Caversham, mainly inhabited by artizans, who may, with a little exaggeration, be said to live with one foot in the water and the other in the grave. At present constant strong winds keep these suburbs fairly healthy, but they are almost on a

NICHOL'S CREEK FALL.
(From a Photograph by Burton Bros.)

level with the sea, subject to frequent floods, and without any system of drainage. It is not rash to prophesy that some day these parts will be visited with a calamity.

At the southernmost end of the hills lies the township of St. Clair, which promises to become a fashionable watering-place. It is built partly on the flat, which is a little higher in this direction, and partly on the "rise." A pretty bit of rock gives character to the place, and there are a primitive esplanade, and a bathing-place scooped out of the rock. Thence eastward the sandy beach stretches, some three miles in length, past the Forbury Race-course, where meetings are held four or five times a year, and the "Ocean Beach," about half-way between St. Clair and Lawyer's Head. The ocean is only divided from the upper end of the harbour by some five or six hundred yards of low-lying sandy country, the neck of the peninsula. The harbour side of this peninsula is the most pleasant part of the district to live in, everywhere facing more or less to the north, and mostly sheltered from the southern winds. This is the place for beautiful gardens; there is plenty of sun, and the town commands a lovely view over the bay of Dunedin, which should be seen by night as well as by day. The season on this side of the harbour is three weeks earlier than in town.

The drive round the peninsula, as well as that up the North East Valley, across the hill to Blueskin, is not to be missed. It is a hilly country for driving and riding, but for variety of charming walks the neighbourhood of Dunedin is not easily surpassed. In every direction the scenery is different. Prettiest of all the walks is that up Nichol's Creek to the Waterfall Gully, the last part of which is through an arcade of ferns and foliage, with a torrent rushing through the rocks, over which rocks you pick your way to the waterfall. Of the harbour scenery, the finest view is obtained from the hills which divide the town from Port Chalmers, close to what is known as the Junction Hotel, because the Port Chalmers and Blueskin roads meet there. A ramble through the bush on the town-belt is no bad way of spending an afternoon. In short, Dunedin has many attractions as a summer resort, and it is strange that it is not more used as such. From Christmas to Easter the weather is generally beautiful, and the air always bright and clear. Certainly no other town in Australasia presents so many advantages of climate, scenery, and situation during the summer months.

At Burnside, about four miles out of town, are the Refrigerating Company's works, where about three hundred sheep can be killed and frozen in a day. Some six miles further west lies the township of Mosgiel, the seat of the largest and most successful woollen factory in Australasia. Mosgiel tweeds are sold in Australia in spite of the terrible duty upon them, and the chief fault that can be found with them is that they never wear out. The blankets fetch about twenty-five per cent. more than the best English blankets in the shops, and the difference in warmth is most remarkable. The reason of course is that it would not pay to mix cotton with the wool, which is obtainable on the spot, of the best quality and at prices considerably lower than in Australia. The factory is well worth a visit, being solidly built, admirably arranged, and lighted throughout by electricity. What is more, this is one of the few industries which continued to flourish through the worst of the bad times, extending its operations yearly.

Mosgiel is easily accessible by rail or road. The district around, known as the Taieri, is admirably adapted for dairy farms, and supplies Dunedin with butter which cannot be excelled. Hitherto each farm has made its own butter, and the market has been restricted to the neighbouring towns, but during the last two years, since wheat farming has proved less profitable than of yore, dairy-farming has received a great impetus, and factories are now springing up on every side, to which the milk

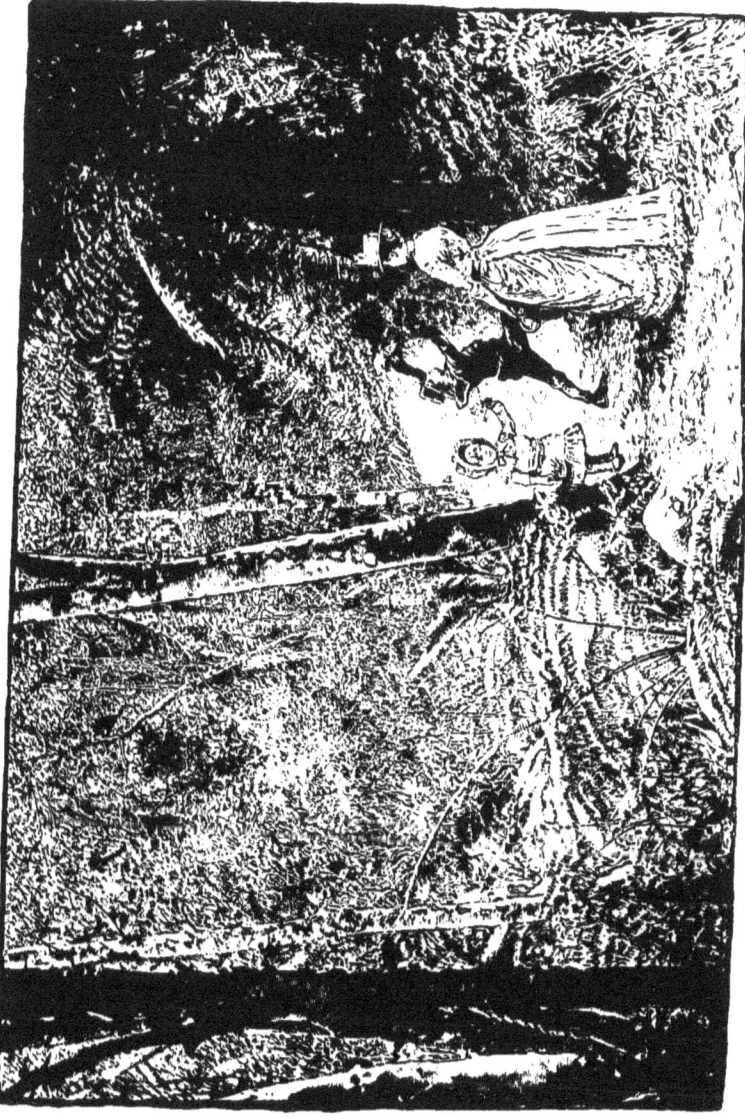

THE TOWN BELT, DUNEDIN.

from the farms is sent to be made into butter and cheese, principally exported to Australia. As soon as the Australian demand is satisfied, it is intended to send the butter to England in refrigerating chambers, so that there is practically no limit to the extension of this industry.

At Green Island, just beyond Burnside, on the road to Mosgiel, a sort of lignite coal is worked, and at Kaitangita, some fifty miles to the south-west, a little off the Invercargill route, there is abundance of excellent coal of the same kind. Its peculiarity is that it burns to a white ash, which smoulders for two or three days, occasioning many a fire in wooden houses. These lignite coals do not burn well in the ordinary English fireplaces and ranges, so that special kinds of stoves are made locally, which can only burn such coals.

And now we have seen most of what is worth seeing in Dunedin and its immediate neighbourhood. In a walk or drive round, it will be noticed that the residences of the citizens are well built, often with some architectural pretension, some of the smaller houses being perched on precipitous rocks, seemingly inaccessible. Everywhere there is an air of comfort, and an absence of all appearance of poverty, somewhat in contradiction to the grumblings about "the depression" which fill the hotels and streets. No doubt there are fewer carriages kept here than formerly, and the richer classes have suffered considerable loss by the fall of prices, which has told also upon the middle class; but the working-man still commands as good a wage as in any other part of Australasia, and no one seriously doubts that good times will return ere long, and the city once more begin to progress.

LOOKING ACROSS THE HARBOUR, FROM THE SOUTH-WEST.
(From a Photograph by Burton Bros.)

COLLIERS LEAVING NEWCASTLE HARBOUR.

## THE VALLEY OF THE HUNTER.

"Nobby's"—Newcastle Harbour—Newcastle—The Business End—The Coal Centre—The Cathedral—The Reserve—Lake Macquarie—The Shipping—The River—Raymond Terrace—Strond—Miller's Forest—Morpeth—The Paterson—East and West Maitland—Wollombi—Singleton—Muswellbrook—Scone—Murrurundi.

ENTRANCE to the region it is now our purpose to describe is gained, from the sea, at Newcastle. The voyager sees standing out conspicuously, as a gate-post, the promontory which in early maps is marked Nobby's Island. On the northern side the doorway has no such feature. There lies a low, sandy beach, curving far away into a distance which leads the eye to the blue projections on the horizon that are known as Port Stephen's Heads. "Nobby's," no longer an island, is a rugged, storm-beaten, rust-stained mass of rock, wherein strata of coal may be traced. The influences which reduced it to its present proportions still operate; time's effacing fingers will one day banish it from among the things that are. One may suppose that it was once the extreme point of the sea cliff, from which, by the action of the waves, it was separated, and entitled to the designation island. By artificial means the beach has been once more closed. Between Flagstaff or Signal Hill and Nobby's, when the Hunter River was discovered in 1797, by Lieutenant Shortland, the waves of the Pacific had free course. And even now, under the stress of a southerly gale, they dash wildly against the barrier, and throw over it masses of spume. The preliminary essential to making the estuary of the Hunter a harbour was, therefore, the closing of the gap. Convict labour was employed to quarry huge blocks of stone, and cast them into the waters that raged over the sunken foundation of the cliff which had been fretted away. A somewhat lengthened conflict with an ocean not easily quelled, in spite of its name, ended in the erection of a small sea-wall, firm and faithful. In later days advanced engineering skill, free labour, and improved appliances were brought to the work. On the structure thus raised, wind and wave beat ceaselessly; films of the stone disappear constantly under their action, so that the barrier is confessed to be but temporary. Yet there are the railway and the quarry, and necessity and man's determination, and the Pacific must own itself beaten.

The work of filling in the gap between Nobby's and the mainland did not, however, make the harbour secure, and it was not until a breakwater extending into the sea beyond Nobby's had been constructed that the mouth of the harbour was rendered impregnable to southerly and south-easterly gales. On the northern shore, also, a breakwater of less formidable dimensions has been constructed, which has had the effect of increasing the scour in the harbour mouth.

Observed from Nobby's, Newcastle presents the appearance of a city built on irregular terraces. Extending along the harbour front is a level space, but behind it the houses rise up the sides to the top of a ridge, so steep in parts that some of the streets are inaccessible save to foot traffic. On the left side, in the foreground, is Flagstaff Hill, where a fortification has recently been completed. The fort has been excavated, so that the heavier guns are below the surface of the soil, and are raised by machinery to the embrasures, discharged, and lowered for reloading. In a deeper excavation is placed the magazine. About the fort there is nothing frowning. It presents small token of the grimness of its purposes; it is, indeed, surmounted by antiquated pieces of obsolete artillery for show, but beneath these engines of war stretch slopes of green turf, which conceal the place where lurk the real weapons of defence.

"NOBBY'S," NEWCASTLE.

The business part of Newcastle is circumscribed. It is situated on the level which begins below Fortification Hill, and spreads along to where Lake Macquarie road in one direction, and the road to Wickham in another, branch off; it includes the harbour front of the city, the terminus of the Great Northern Railway, and Hunter

Street. Within it are placed the Custom House and the Colliery and Shipping Offices; in Hunter Street all the principal shops and hotels will be found, also the city market. From the point at which deep water begins, at the southern end of the harbour, all along the frontage extends a continuous line of wharf, whereon are erected the steam cranes used in loading coal. Branches from the railway run beside the wharf, as the means whereby the laden trucks are brought beneath the cranes. The steamers' wharf is in the same line further inland; next to it is a small harbour made specially for boats. This is a scene of activity in the sale of farm produce, fish, and the like. Besides the cranes other modes of loading coal are employed. Development of the coal trade in late years has called into existence a second series of cranes up the harbour, on what was called Bullock Island. The place has been re-named Carrington, in compliment to the popular Governor of New South Wales.

Newcastle is the centre of the coal-mining activity of the north. All about it are settlements depending solely on that industry. Planted originally in the wilderness, they are gradually passing from a condition of rugged slovenliness to a state of order and some beauty. For the most part they are under the local government of a mayor and councillors, and improve under it. They contribute to the city its chief support; it is, indeed, becoming a part of the nearest of them, by the progress of building over the intervening space; and Hunter Street, its main thoroughfare, always lively on pay Saturday night—the fortnightly occasion on which all workmen in the district receive their wages—is then the channel of a many-coloured stream of human existence, flowing from seven o'clock till eleven without ceasing. The mines, the ships, the factories, the houses of the city, all send tribute to the stream.

Above this busy thoroughfare are the parts of Newcastle wherein it leads its quieter life. Watt Street, which crosses the head of Hunter Street at right angles, leads thither. All the churches are on the side of the ridge, or on its summit. Newcastle is the seat of an Anglican bishop, who could boast of possessing the very ugliest cathedral in the world, a brick structure, erected in 1817 by the building Governor, Macquarie, as an inscription on its front testified. The foundations of a nobler edifice are, however, laid, and the site is one to which the finest building will but add a charm. It commands on one side the Pacific, stretching away till sky meets sea, whereon, on most days, may be descried the white wings of ocean-going ships; on another, the city, sloping to the harbour, which bears on its bosom numberless craft of varied rig and character; to the north and south the coast-line is distinguished, till the most remote headland fades away in a blue mist; while inland, in every direction, are displayed the daughter settlements of Newcastle, with railways winding in and out among them. Beyond lies an expanse of forest, whose surface varies with every change of cloud; and, lastly, there is outlined against the sky a mountain range, with which we shall make a closer acquaintance hereafter.

The city is growing fast on this hill. The Obelisk, set up to serve as a waymark to mariners, is surrounded by private residences, and house is monthly added to house. Newcastle is not rich in public grounds, but the forethought of early rulers of the colony has here supplied it with a recreation enclosure, the value of which cannot be easily over-estimated. The Reserve is a section of the sea-cliff, where it dips to form a great gulch, at the bottom of which a stream of fresh water constantly trickles. From one end of the bank of the gully to the other, and rounding its head, a semicircular walk has been formed, while beneath it, on the slope, is a continuous plantation of ornamental trees. The Reserve—variously called the Horseshoe, from the shape of the path, and the Lovers' Walk, from the opportunities it supplies for that seclusion in which two are company—intervenes between Shepherd's Hill, a higher elevation, looking seaward, of the plateau on which the domestic portion of the city is built, and that portion of the cliff which ends at the fortifications. Landward, the ground from the top of Shepherd's Hill descends in a long slope to Lake Macquarie Road; coastwards the hill overlooks a series of rocky shelves stretching into the sea, but opening here and there to small sandy beaches. On one of these the fair of Newcastle and the district take their sea-baths, while the bathing-place for men is below Shepherd's Hill.

THE BATHING-PLACE, NEWCASTLE.

With holiday-makers from inland the beaches and rocks are a favourite resort. Newcastle folk who desire change, on the other hand, repair to the green fields in the upper part of the Hunter Valley, or betake themselves to a noble inlet of the sea, about twelve miles distant along the southern coast—Lake Macquarie. To pass a few days in fern-embroidered dells, or in sailing in and out of the hundred lovely bays that diversify the coast-line, or in fishing, is the Newcastle man's ideal of bliss. Many of the more wealthy citizens have acquired land and built houses on the shores of this fine sheet of water. Here they retire to banish care. The region is traversed by the railway line in construction between the northern district and Sydney, and will thus become generally accessible. It will be a sanatorium. Abundant supplies of coal underlie its whole surface, it has immense agricultural capabilities, its stores of valuable timber are vast; and eventually a large population must here find occupation and livelihood.

Newcastle Harbour is at all seasons of the year full of vessels. The chief commodity that they seek makes it a place of necessary resort. It is true that latterly

1. NEWCASTLE HARBOUR.
2. THE RESERVE, NEWCASTLE.

a direct trade in merchandise with England, and the export at Newcastle of much of the wool grown in the northern part of New South Wales, have increased the shipping. Still, coal is the principal merchandise of the port. The dust of the city is black, so much do particles of coal pervade it, and at evening bands of men are met with grimy faces set homewards, whose occupation has been "lumping" coal—adjusting it in the holds of ships. From all quarters of the compass come vessels for coal, but the great development of the trade has occurred within the lifetime of many persons yet in their prime. Old denizens of Newcastle can remember when small vessels, coming at long intervals, were laden by barrow-loads taken across planks by convict workmen. The contrast is great between such an export and appliances, on the one hand, and the 2,113,372 tons sent away from Newcastle in 1885, and the perfection of the various modern means of loading, on the other.

Above Newcastle the Hunter is for many miles a broad stream, embracing numerous small islands. The larger of these are under cultivation; the largest, named Ash Island, is situate about ten miles from the city. The river flows between banks for the most part low, muddy, and shaded with mangrove trees, but here and there bits

NEWCASTLE, FROM "NOBBY'S."

of charming woodland scenery relieve the eyes of the voyager. Hexham, a settlement on the bank above Ash Island, is fast going to decay. From this point to Raymond Terrace the banks of the river rise; well-cultivated farms appear, principally on the left-hand bank, and the character of the country has visibly changed. Usually, the farmhouse is close to the river, which is the principal highway. A boat is always an adjunct, and a rude jetty, in most cases, juts out into the stream. At these primitive wharves small river steamers stop to deliver or receive cargo. Here, too, farmers load their boats with produce, to be taken to Newcastle for sale. The oars are plied sometimes by the sturdy arms of men, but not infrequently by those of farmer lasses, strong by dint of life in open air, and much exercise of muscle and lung.

Raymond Terrace is an old and thriving settlement on the right bank of the river. In this neighbourhood Kinross vineyard is situate, famed for its white wine, of the character of a hock. About the designation Raymond Terrace a story is told. In the olden days a surveyor, named Raymond, was despatched to the Hunter on professional work. He did the work, and sent the results to head-quarters. But being allured by the situation of this locality, he stopped there till his death—hence the site was called Raymond Terrace. The story is bald, but that is all there is of it.

The road from Maitland to the eastern coast territory passes through Raymond Terrace, where a steam ferry crosses the river. The first settlement is Stroud, twenty-eight miles away, the entrance to the estate of the Australian Agricultural Company. The village of Stroud is distinguished as the only "fenced" city in New South Wales. A mile square was set apart and enclosed by the Company, and within the boundary its servants were permitted to occupy building lots. At each entrance to the enclosure gates were erected, and the government of the settlement was rigorous. Each villager was, for instance, obliged to cultivate a flower-garden about his cottage. This was long ago. The Company failed in this attempt to acclimatise English habits, as well as in many other efforts. The modern Stroud is the property of settlers who have bought their freeholds of the Company, and are emancipated from its rule.

At Raymond Terrace the traveller first sees the fertile region which justly entitles the Lower Hunter Valley to be called the garden of New South Wales. Over against the village, across the river, lies Miller's Forest, a spacious alluvial plain, once clothed with a dense wood, but now wholly cleared, traversed by roads, dotted with farmhouses, and smiling with lucerne and maize crops. The Hunter embraces this plain in an immense bend, separating it from another expanse of agricultural land, called Nelson's Plains. This latter area is drained by the first great affluent of the Hunter, the Williams, which discharges its waters a short distance above Raymond Terrace. The Williams is navigable by large ocean steamers as far as Clarence Town, and is the medium of a great export trade in hardwood timber, brought from forests inland.

Morpeth is situate on the left bank of the Hunter, about eight or nine miles above Raymond Terrace, and at the head of the more important navigation. At Morpeth the Sydney steamers receive the greater part of their burdens of wool, hay, and other produce. Here the second great tributary of the Hunter, the Paterson, joins the larger stream at Hinton, just where the river is crossed by a steam ferry. The Paterson has its rise in mountains to the east of Scone, and drains an extensive area. Its course is everywhere distinguished by rare beauty. In its upper parts the river flows with sungilt ripples over pebbly strands; in places it laves the feet of shaggy mountains, and nourishes gay green trees and gorgeous flowers, which contrast with the sombre clothing of the hillside; ever and anon bands of rock extending from bank to bank make foamy cascades, which day and night sing a sweet entrancing lullaby. When the stream nears the haunts of men, wild loveliness is exchanged for softer charms. The channel broadens, its course winds, willows and water-oaks, the cedar, the native hibiscus, and the wild grape-vine grow in unchecked vigour on each bank, and mirror themselves in the placid waters. That is the aspect of the river for mile after mile, while the landscape on its borders varies. Open forest above well-grassed slopes, broad level tracts under cultivation, meadows with undulating surface, orange groves, vineyards, and orchards, are the elements. Paterson town is built on a hilly site where the surroundings of the stream begin to change their look. An elevation immediately opposite, rising almost directly from the water's edge, is called Hungry Hill. This ominous name is derived from a legend that, in the old convict times, an adventurous prisoner who had escaped was starved to death on this inhospitable eminence.

Morpeth, to which it is time for us to return, would probably have become one of the chief inland towns on the Hunter had the early rulers of New South Wales enjoyed any distinct foresight. As it was, they effectually handicapped the settlement. The site, called then the Green Hills, with a considerable portion of the valley river frontage, was granted to a worthy gentleman who had served his country with distinction in the Peninsula War. The Anglican church at Morpeth owes its existence to the gratitude of this gentleman. During an engagement in Spain he was in extreme peril, and was saved from death in circumstances which he viewed as providential. He vowed that, if ever he were able, he would build a church as a memorial of his rescue. The opportunity came at length. Lieutenant Close was the grantee of Morpeth in New South Wales. He performed his vow, and the church is the monument of his thankfulness. For many years prior to its erection he weekly read the service of the Church of England in a house in Morpeth. After the church was completed, he provided the stipend of the clergyman for a lengthened season, and likewise made permanent provision for paying the incumbent.

The site of East Maitland, which is the next place we come to, is admirably fitted for the position of a great town. It is elevated, so that the sea-breezes play over it; it commands a prospect of the valley of the Hunter, where that valley is broadest and most fertile. A large part of the site overlooks the plain, which at morning and evening is obscured in river mists. The facilities for drainage are great, and the eucalyptus forest grows around it, which breathes balmy influences. In the early days of the place, although land was open for sale, red tape restrictions, Government regulations bordering on the absurd, slowness of survey, and a general state of muddle, made the acquisition of allotments no easy matter. Unhappily, in the near vicinity land was obtainable at a cheap rate, and with little formality. The site of Maitland many of the older denizens of the town repudiate the distinctive title East; there is only one Maitland, they say—is divided from a portion of the valley by a water-course, called Wallis's Creek, or Brook, the term creek being used in Australia for any small stream or rivulet.* A huge slice of the area lying in an angle, this creek and the river forming the sides, had been granted to an old soldier, who is remembered only as Joe the Marine, and to his paramour, one Molly Morgan. The grant made a fair estate of immense

* See *ante*, p. 11.

prospective value. But Joe and Molly, being well-stricken in years, childless, and fond of rum, chose to enjoy the present. They were eager to sell, and stories run that many a fine allotment changed hands, a bottle of rum being the equivalent for "lawful British money." As land could be easily got, West Maitland grew with comparative rapidity on both sides of the Great Northern Road, and has at the present date a population of over six thousand inhabitants. East Maitland, favoured by State patronage, by the residence of Government officials, by the distinction, for many years enjoyed, of being the only assize town in the northern district, and by an incomparably superior site was, for a time, by dint of these circumstances, the chief town, but lost ground as the district became more populous, and has never been able to outstrip its very much better half on the other side of Wallis's Creek. East Maitland has a population now exceeding two thousand souls. In West Maitland are found the great business establishments, whose trade vies with that of the metropolis. The larger churches are in West Maitland; it is also the home of a convent of Dominican nuns, and of the chief State schools. Within its precincts all gatherings representative of the district take place. Here are found the head-quarters of the parent agricultural society of New South Wales—the Hunter River Agricultural and Horticultural Association. West Maitland is the chief cattle and horse market of the north of New South Wales; it is the seat of many mills and manufactories; and works are being constructed to supply its inhabitants, and those of all the settlements down to the sea, including Newcastle, with water drawn from the Hunter.

WATT STREET, NEWCASTLE.

The spectator standing on the Stockade hill sees East Maitland clustering immediately below him on the right hand, and rising and spreading on the gaol-crowned height opposite. Beyond stretches the river valley, wherein the winding course of the stream may be discerned. At one bend we get a gleam of its surface. In mid-distance appears the village of Largs, built on a point of high land bounding the valley on the northern side, and further still to the right a distant view is gained of the hills facing Morpeth. The landscape is pleasantly diversified—cultivation, woodland, pasture, vary it. The hill-slopes are scantily clothed with trees, and farmhouses and barns here, as

A BUSH TRACK, MURRURUNDI.

everywhere in the valley, indicate the presence of human life and activity. To the left lies West Maitland, from this point of view a compact town, apparently filling up the whole breadth of the valley. In reality it occupies only one bank of the river. Above the housetops gleam the church spires; in what seems a suburb the dwellings are shaded by trees, among which the tall poplar is conspicuous. Almost at the feet of the spectator, and just seen over the curve of the hill, runs the brook, Wallis's Creek, which divides Maitland into West and East. Its course is defined by willows and other trees, and its boundary to the south of West Maitland is an alluvial plain. Here we have the typical Lower Hunter scenery. Squares and oblongs of freshly-ploughed soil alternate with squares and oblongs of land under lucerne crop—patches of green and patches of dark brown, to which in due season are added fields of Indian corn and potato rows, thin threads of green across the dark texture. Lucerne grows so luxuriantly in this deep mould—the deposit of ages, enriched from time to time by inundation—that it may be cut from four to six times a year. The aspect of the whole expanse is that of a huge, well-tilled garden. Here and there an orchard rises above the level of cultivation, but the staple products are lucerne and maize. The farmer is always engaged either in gathering these crops, or in preparing his land for them. This Australian soil is truly well-nigh rich enough to justify Douglas Jerrold in saying that you need but tickle it with a hoe to make it laugh with a harvest.

The farther boundary of the scene we are describing is a region of hilly and broken country which comes into view at the right hand, and extends round till it dips above West Maitland. Range rises behind range in gradual elevation, the sight distinguishes each by noting how, as the distance increases, the trees on the hillsides cease to be definable, and how the blue tint deepens, till at last against the sky a solid outline may be traced, but no details. In this hilly territory many hundreds of miles are embraced. It is among these elevations that the Paterson pursues its lovely way, and on clear days, in the extreme distance, through a gap in a nearer range may be descried the mountain top where the infant Hunter rises. A stretch of comparatively low woodland lies beyond West Maitland to the north-west, but over the trees can be seen the blue crown of part of the Wollombi range, which to the south-west rises boldly against the sky, and continues round to the rear of the spectator. This range divides the water-sheds of the coast; on its sea side vegetation is luxuriant, thanks to a moisture never absent. Ferns abound, vines embrace giant trees in wild tangles, the rock lily in its season burdens the air with its powerful odour, in springtime gorgeous blooms adorn and spangle the hillside, and in profusion grows a giant red flower, made up of a cluster of chalice-shaped blossoms, wherein lurks a sweet compound to which bush-bees repair with eagerness. On the land side the range presents the ordinary aridity of bush vegetation, but in deep gorges, shaded from the sun, threaded by brooks trickling and brattling over water-worn rocks, are treasured rare beauties of tree and flower. Commonly, the Australian bush is silent. But here, from morn till eve, the air thrills with the note of the bell-bird, varied now and then by one resembling the sharp crack of a stock whip. The perpetual joyous tingling in the traveller's ears on a bright day gives him the impression that the sunshine has taken voice, an impression

## A SCENE OF DESOLATION.

deepened by the fact that though you may hear the bird's note quivering in the air close to you, the nimble songster eludes the quickest eye. The haunt of the bell-bird is a green shade; trees make an embroidered roof, through which the sun's rays are filtered; the ground is always damp, and in these favouring circumstances ferns of all kinds flourish. They carpet yards of ground; staghorns drape grey-lichened and moss-grown rocks with their tender green; on trees and boulders the bird's-nest fern with its long palm-like fronds attains splendid proportions; on the slopes which the sun reaches, the clematis bloom displays its fleece-like beauty; and timber-trees, fed by soils enriched by centuries of vegetable decay, tower majestically above a troubled sea of verdure. In such a haunt as this Wallis's Creek has its source. The spring is on the range. The young stream passes in a slender thread over mighty stones, and scoops out for itself many a hollow where the water lies in still pools, darkened by the shade of forest-oak and myrtle, and at last, gaining in size, it flows deviously through a valley ever widening, till at West Maitland its waters are poured into the Hunter.

The expanse, with its varied beauty, which we have been surveying from Stockade Hill, has at times presented another and sadder appearance. When the Hunter comes down in flood, the environs of Maitland are a spectacle of desolation. The yellow tide spreads over miles of fertile land, defeats the farmer's hopes, destroys the fruit of his labour, and ousts him for the time from his habitation. Fatal incidents have not usually accompanied Hunter floods; and since the telegraph has been available, residents in places liable to inundation may receive warning in time to avert inconvenience. In Maitland there are two flood-boat services, means of rescue in times of necessity, and of food supply to such persons as may be islanded in their houses, but are not driven from home. West Maitland is in flood seasons partially under water, and boats ply in the principal thoroughfare. In one direction, in the valley drained by Wallis's Creek, it is possible to take a boat with perfect safety some thirteen miles in a straight line. Cattle and other stock may be transported to high land, but, of course, growing crops are lost wholly, and garnered crops also, unless the farmer be prudent enough to be active in early removal. Floods are a calamity under which the region about Maitland suffered almost yearly in the interval

MAITLAND.

between 1856 and 1876, but since the latter year the visitations have been infrequent, and not alarming. In their evil there is a soul of goodness. To their recurrence in past ages the soil owes its unrivalled richness, which their modern visits serve undoubtedly to renew. The value of agricultural land ranges between £50 and £100 per acre—it has been purchased at such prices by the industrious farmers who till it—and it has attained that value because it is built up, as it were, of flood deposits.

Wollombi is a village on the Wollombi Brook, situate about forty miles from Maitland, on the road to Sydney. The thoroughfare to the Wollombi passes through Cessnock, a half-way settlement which forms an outlet to an immense vine-growing district. Vineyards clothe the slopes of the ranges, for the soil is a vegetable mould on a basis of limestone, and eminently adapted for the production of light and wholesome wines. Wollombi, a small collection of houses spread over low hills, depends for existence on the through traffic of stock, and on a limited agricultural industry.

The stream above Maitland soon shrinks; fords are numerous, alternating with long, deep pools. The borders, though not so fertile as those lower down, enriched by long-retained flood waters, are prolific; farm, vineyard, orchard, and pasture lands are the constituents of the landscape, while the uplands and hills which hem in the valley on each side are the haunts of valuable herds. Seven miles from Maitland is Lochinvar, and five miles further is situate Greta, and between the two places the road crosses Harper's Hill half-way up the steep slope of the eminence, into the side of which it is cut. The thoroughfare overlooks a scene of agricultural loveliness. Thousands of feet below, seen over the tops of the trees, are green fields, among which the winding course of the river may be traced. Kaloudah vineyard, famed among those of the Hunter, lies close to Lochinvar; and near Branxton, seven miles farther on, is a still more noted vineyard—Dalwood.

Thirty miles from Maitland stands the town of Singleton, the centre of a progressive and thriving district. Herein are carried on with vigour and enterprise the industries of cattle and horse breeding, wine making, and tobacco and wheat growing. Some of the most famed racehorse studs in New South Wales are found in this locality. Here, too, Durham and Hereford cattle of the highest strains charm the eye of the stock connoisseur; and the viticulturist who stood next to the winner of the German Emperor's prize for wine at the Victorian International Exhibition carries on his operations close to Singleton. The town is situate on the bank of the Hunter, in Patrick's Plains. That name was bestowed by the discoverer, one Howe, an Irishman, who emerged from the bush on this wide extension of the river valley on St. Patrick's Day in 1818, or thereabouts. Before leaving Singleton, we may say that its population is about 2,000, and that of the police district, 7,022.

From Singleton to its source the Hunter drains a district mainly pastoral, and possessing the same general characteristics throughout. West by north from Singleton lies Denman, where the largest inland tributary of the river, the Goulburn, joins it.

Muswellbrook is the next considerable settlement above Singleton. This is a picturesque town of nearly 2,000 inhabitants. It lies at the junction of the north-western road from the Goulburn with the great northern road, and is also a station of the

Great Northern Railway. The town is built upon the high south bank of the Hunter, and overlooks a fertile plain on the opposite shore. Its main feature is the Anglican church, St. Alban's, built of white stone after designs by the late Sir Gilbert Scott, and noted as one of the most attractive specimens of church architecture in the northern part of New South Wales. About nine miles above Muswellbrook the river takes the waters of an affluent, the Page, which has its source in the Liverpool Range above Murrurundi. Above the railway bridge the river is a shallow stream, which frequent obstructions in its bed break into rapids and even into cascades. The country it drains is wild, broken, and mountainous; but among the hills are valleys of rare verdure, and tree-shaded dells of infinite charm. One of the marvels of the

MURRURUNDI.

region is a brook, which flows on the top of a hill, and disappears in the soil; and another is a lakelet which gems a mountain's breast, and never in the driest season fails or even materially shrinks. On the margin of the river the land is invariably rich.

Scone, a town of some six hundred souls, is situate on Kingdon Ponds, a stream feeding the Page. The traveller by rail at this place traverses Turanville, a grazing estate which skill and taste have transferred into a model of what can be done in the Australian bush, by cultivation, to increase production and create beauty. Beyond Scone, the railway re-enters a region of mountains which embrace valleys—"peace reposing in the bosom of strength." Near Wingen, a wayside village, the traveller is told of a burning mountain, whose top may be descried. This mountain long enjoyed the reputation of a volcano, but is now known to be the seat of a perpetually-burning coal seam. A coal mine is in fact worked in this locality. When the country opens again it is the valley of the Upper Page, much of which is under cultivation. At the head of the valley stands Murrurundi, beneath, and in the embrace of, the Liverpool Range, which dominates the landscape everywhere. Many picturesque knolls at the foot are crowned with trim cottages, and brightened by orchards, flower gardens, or green crops. Over miles of its surface the valley is dotted with farmhouses, for agriculturists have for long years established themselves here, and share fairly with the grazier the industry of the locality. Here the Page river is a stream which has cut its way through the shallow alluvium resting on a bed of gravel. Being close to its mountain source, and subject to receipt of the immediate drainage of the surrounding hills, it is sudden and quick in flood, but the overflow runs off as rapidly as it rises. The stream has no grandeur as a river, but some of its clear, deep pools, shaded by swamp oak, are pleasant to see. Unquestionably the finest view of Murrurundi and of the valley beyond it is gained from the railway line, a few hundred yards from the mouth of a tunnel which pierces the mountain. Far below is seen the town, compactly ranked between the towering range on one side and some lower hills on the other. Beyond it extends the plain, fair and green, with river and road winding through it; and the eye follows the expanse till in the distance hills rise in terraces on the horizon, and fade away until the distinction between earth and sky is lost.

Near Murrurundi the wayfarer will notice huge mounds of stone, weather-worn, and still fretting away under the influence of wind and wet. Some are unmistakably natural, and bear trees on their summits, although no soil is apparent which may yield nutriment to vegetation. But others bear a strong resemblance to antique castles of the old world, and the imagination has no difficulty in investing them with the attributes of buildings which owe their existence to human labour.

The territory between Singleton and Murrurundi is mainly in pastoral occupation. It is the region of some of the great estates of New South Wales, rich in flocks and herds, but seldom cultivated by the plough. The most wealthy men of the colony reside in this area.

We have thus passed from the mouth of the Hunter at Newcastle to the northern extremity of the valley of which it is the principal drain, and have endeavoured to indicate its varied characteristics. The territory under notice comprises a portion of New South Wales which ranks high for beauty, fertility, enterprise, and progress, and it is no exaggeration to say that this fruitful tract, under wise and energetic labour, could be made to feed the whole of New South Wales bounteously—to satisfy, indeed, the wants both of man and of beast.

END OF VOL. I.

PRINTED BY CASSELL & COMPANY, LIMITED, LA BELLE SAUVAGE, LONDON, E.C.

UNIVERSITY of CALIFORNIA
AT
LOS ANGELES
LIBRARY

www.ingramcontent.com/pod-product-compliance
Lightning Source LLC
Chambersburg PA
CBHW030745230426
43667CB00007B/848